Understanding Media Culture

Understanding Media Culture

Jostein Gripsrud

Professor of Media Studies, University of Bergen,
Norway

HODDER
EDUCATION
www.hoddereducation.co.uk

First published in Norwegian as *Mediekultur, Mediesamfunn* by Scandinavian University Press, © Universitetsforlaget 1999.

The English language version first published in Great Britain in 2002 by Hodder Education, part of Hachette Livre UK
338 Euston Road, London NW1 3BH

http://www.hoddereducation.co.uk

Translation © 2002 Jostein Gripsrud

British Library Cataloguing in Publication Data
A catalogue record for this book is available from the British Library

Library of Congress Cataloging-in-Publication Data
A catalog record for this book is available from the Library of Congress

ISBN 978 0 340 72035 6

6 7 8 9 10

Production Editor: Rada Radojicic
Production Controller: Iain McWilliams
Cover Design: Terry Griffiths

Typeset in 11/13 pt Minion by Phoenix Photosetting, Chatham, Kent
Printed and bound in India by Replika Press Pvt. Ltd.

Contents

Acknowledgements

Thanks are due to copyright holders for permission to reproduce copyright material. Individual credits and sources are acknowledged under the relevant illustration. Every effort has been made to trace copyright holders of material reproduced in this book. Any rights not acknowledged here will be acknowledged in subsequent editions if notice is given to the copyright holder.

PART 1

The audience and the media

1 Identity: the media and our understanding of ourselves

The media and the world around us

I knew a woman of almost 90 who had a problem. Every evening she had total strangers visiting; they filled her living room and made her feel angry and afraid. Some younger relatives solved her problem, at least temporarily. They explained to her that the strangers were only appearing on TV and did not really invade her home in any other way.

Most people do not feel the media to be quite as intrusive as television was for this old lady. However, when radio was first introduced, in the 1920s, broadcasters thought of themselves precisely as uninvited guests in people's homes, and this had consequences for how programmes were made (Scannell, 1996: 19). Now we are so used to the media as intruders in our homes and everyday lives that we have stopped worrying: people are awoken by clock radios; the radio in the kitchen is switched on as the morning tea or coffee is prepared; the morning paper is skimmed while the radio or TV, or both, churn out news, chat or music in the background; driving to work or school, the car radio or stereo will be on; and both cyclists and pedestrians use personal stereos; those who travel by bus or rail may take a newspaper or book too; the streets are lined with advertising boards; at work or school there are computers linked to the Internet; and, in the evening there's the cinema, novels, radio, TV, CDs and so on. The media are simply everywhere.

It is hard to read the newspaper while shaving or searching for something in the fridge. Radio, on the other hand, may follow us everywhere in our more or less complicated morning rituals. It is a perfect *secondary medium*. That is, it is – contrary to what has been called a *primary medium* – a medium that we can use while doing something else. Radio is thus possibly the medium that best illustrates how our everyday lives are pervaded by mass media. We can hardly live in modern society without using mass media for a large proportion of each day. It is possible that more and more media are a sort of secondary media – at least part of the time. We often use them in a pretty distracted way, only half engaged in what they present.

This may be the media's fault or our own, or no fault at all. It is still true that the media connect us to the world outside of our home, our neighbourhood and workplace. They remind us that we are members of a society and a world with as many planes or levels as there are in the addresses children sometimes construct for themselves: 221 Maple Street, Birch Hill, Oxbridge 2XR 5PL England, United Kingdom, Europe, Planet Earth, The Milky Way, The Universe. Since so many people use radio, newspapers and television, not least as a ritual part of the start of a new day, there are reasons to believe that most of us feel a need to be (re)connected to this extensive, multidimensional social reality that is outside of our immediate surroundings, every day. Why? Because we are, or have become, social beings; we are part of the world and want to feel as such. This chapter is to be about how we have become as we are, and the roles the media play in our development, not least the development of our understanding of ourselves.

Socialization

Most of us scream when we are born, but it takes a while before we start talking. We sip our mother's milk, fill our nappies, are washed, cuddled and cared for. While we just cry, babble and dribble, mummy, daddy and passers-by talk and sing to us. There is quite a bit of coochie-coo, twiddly-dee and twiddly-doo, possibly also boo-boo-bee-doo, in what they say, but there are also more ordinary words and they may, in addition, sing some sweet or slightly melancholy songs. This is to say that the process of *socialization* begins before we have even uttered a word, through all the forms of communication just mentioned, through body contact, looks, humming and so on.

The acquisition of *language* is still a fundamental and decisive step in our development. As we start using and understanding language we simultaneously become both members of the cultural *community* among human beings, and aware of the *difference* between others and ourselves. We emerge as *individuals* through interaction with others, and language plays an increasing role in this interaction after the nappy stage.

The aspect of socialization that takes place among those closest to oneself, in some version of 'the family', is referred to as *primary socialization* by sociologists and social psychologists. *Secondary socialization* is the common term for processes of socialization that take place within and in relation to a series of social institutions outside of the family: kindergarten, school, sports club, church, workplace or whatever. We are told something about who we are in all such contexts, and about what is expected from us. Such information is also provided, to a high degree, from what may now form the most important institution of secondary socialization: the mass media.

We get to know them from a very early age – the radio and the TV set, the first simple books, the CD player and our parents' newspapers. They provide pleasure, information, anxiety, and opportunities or inspiration for play. They are partly incomprehensible, partly addressing us directly: '… and now, I'll tell you a story!' They address us in our homes, and so they are different from all other forms of secondary socialization. The media are in a sense the long arm of society, leading in to what we can call the *sphere of intimacy* (we will focus on the public sphere and democracy in Chapter 8); they compete for our attention with mum and dad, boyfriends or girlfriends, the dog, and whomsoever else is more or less part of the household; they interfere in conversations or interactions in a number of ways.

The media contribute significantly to the definition of the world around us, and thereby also to the definition of ourselves. They present ways to understand the world, to represent the world, in images, sounds and writing. They suggest ideas of what is important and what isn't, what is good and bad, what is boring and what is fun. They present parts and dimensions of the world that we ourselves have not experienced directly, and may never come to experience directly. As recipients of all this we simply have to form some sort of opinion about where we are located, so to speak, in the complex landscapes presented to us, about who we are, about who we would like to be – and about who or what we would definitely *not* like to be or become. This complex perception of oneself is called *identity*. It is a problematic word.

The concept of identity

Identity actually means 'one-ness' or 'same-ness'. When we sort out impressions, both from our fellow human beings and the media, we form opinions on the similarities and differences between all the others and ourselves. For instance, we find out early on that some of the people around us are differently equipped between their legs, and this is a decisive discovery. We check out our own equipment and can then conclude that we resemble either mum or dad. Siblings and kindergarten pals can be classified accordingly. But even before we reach such conclusions for ourselves, someone else has done the thinking for us and treated us correspondingly. Whether we are in the boys' team or the girls' team, it will soon be clear to us that we are on the kids' team, which now and then will be in opposition to the grown-ups' team. Gradually it also dawns on us that those of us who live on this side of the bridge are different from those on the other side, not to mention those who live in London or New York or Farawayland.

The mass media may not say very much about the difference between this and that side of the local bridge, but they say a great deal about the differences between those with fannies and those with willies, and also a lot about London, New York and Farawayland. To a greater or lesser extent, the media here also function along with parents, schools and other authorities. At an early age we get to know that the nation-state in which we live is separate from the rest of the world and that all those who belong to 'our' nation-state have something in common that sets them apart from all others. We learn songs and stories we are supposed to love. We learn, if we're British, that people in London are as British as those in Newcastle – they all know the same songs and stories, and speak and write more or less understandable English.

This sort of national community has, since the 1920s, been confirmed and further developed on a daily basis by the institution of the British Broadcasting Corporation (BBC). In other countries, such as the USA, the same job may have been shared by a small handful of broadcasting companies. Locally and regionally, there may be local broadcasting or newspapers that may tell us something about the world at large but that most certainly will keep us updated on the cow that ran loose on Main Street, old Mrs Jones who won in the lottery and the plans for a new road to Cottonfield. The media are, locally, regionally and most obviously perhaps on the national plane, creators of *imagined communities*, to use a term coined by Benedict Anderson (1983). Anderson emphasized the role played, historically, by print media. The daily press provided the first impressions of a national community of people that not only live in the same defined geographical space, but also make up a community of experience within or *at the same time*. Broadcast media, and especially their live programming, very much strengthened this function (cf. Johansen, 1997). Such imagined communities can in certain situations make us feel, perhaps surprisingly, quite strongly tied to people we have never actually met, who are very different from us in many ways and live far away from us. The strength of the imagined community, 'the nation', is, as Anderson points out, ultimately demonstrated in people's willingness to kill or be killed in war for its sake – even if the nation for the most part might consist of people we otherwise would not care very much about even getting to know.

One could say, then, that the media assist other social institutions in telling us what it means to be a boy or a girl, what it means to come from Los Angeles or Bournemouth, what it means to be American or French or British, what it means to be black or white, to be a child or a student, and so on. Our 'identity' is thus actually a patchwork of identities, a complicated set of similarities and differences in relation to other people.

It can be useful to distinguish between two main types of identity. On the one hand we might talk about our *social* or *collective identity* and, on the other, something we can call a *personal identity*. The two are, of course, closely tied to each other, but they are not necessarily completely … identical. Our social identity is, at the outset, the identity we get by way of other people's perceptions of us and the collective contexts we are part of: we come from a particular city in a particular country, we are males or females of a certain age, we have parents with such and such jobs, we have this or that education and a set of hobbies or cultural preferences that lead us to play in a rock band or join the local football team. Other people's perceptions of all of these features will, to a greater or lesser extent, become part of our perception of ourselves, our self-image, that is to say part of our identity. But which parts of this social identity we experience as important to us may vary according to the situation we are in. Sometimes, for instance, at a particular soccer match, the part of town we come from may be important, but which nation we belong to is totally irrelevant. When travelling in a foreign country, preferably one very far from home, however, our nationality may be enough to lead to a conversation with someone from 'our' country, even if the person in question would not be a natural choice of interlocutor back home.

Our *personal identity*, on the other hand, is what we might suggest as an answer when we ask ourselves 'Who am I?' We then ask about what is *unique* about ourselves, what makes us distinguishable from other people we know or know of, what makes our own experiences, emotions and moods special and not necessarily easy to share with others. As many people have experienced, not least when young, that this is a question one may feel it is important to ask, but that it is hard to answer in a totally satisfactory way. There are several reasons for this difficulty, and the complexity of our social identity is not the only one.

In the western world it has been common – at least since the cultural-historical epoch we call Romanticism (roughly the early part of the nineteenth century) – to think of the human psyche ('soul') as something that is *divided* and precisely *not whole* or 'one' (that is, identical). A well-known example of how such a conception is expressed in art and literature is the novel *Dr Jekyll and Mr Hyde*, which Robert Louis Stevenson published in 1886. The physician, Jekyll, drinks a mixture that brings out another and totally gruesome personality he has hidden inside, namely Mr Hyde (Hyde/hide). In the book, Jekyll reflects on his life and finds that he has had to discipline himself so hard while growing up and in his adult life that strong, dangerous forces have built up beneath his civilized surface – forces that are now breaking through in the shape of Mr Hyde. This is a way of thinking that the

Austrian neurologist and psychotherapist Sigmund Freud (1856–1939) was later to give a scientific form in his *psychoanalytic theory*, developed on the basis of his experiences as a doctor and therapist for the Viennese bourgeoisie.

Freud thought that a person's psyche was divided into different parts, to which the will and conscious thoughts only had partial access. The best known of his models for this is the one in which he divided the psyche into *id, super ego* and 'I', or *ego*. The id is the *unconscious* – some psychic processes, more or less shared by all human beings, that go on without our knowledge of them, we only notice them as *symptoms* in more or less incomprehensible dreams, involuntary emotional reactions to certain phenomena and the like. The super ego is a set of norms for right and wrong that we have learned from our parents and other authority figures in society, and which has become a part of ourselves without our conscious control. Between these two – the id and the super ego – lies the ego, the conscious I, trying to find a kind of balance and space for acting freely under pressure from the unconscious forces from 'below' and the external demands from 'above'.

Freud's theories have been tremendously influential in most later psychology thinking, not least in terms of psychological understanding in art and culture, and among most people. It is important to note, however, that his model of the psyche still contradicts just as widespread ideas about the whole and indivisible *individual* with its equally singular *personality*. The idea of a human being's whole, singular personality, which is totally in control of him- or herself and his or her destiny, which controls nature both within and without, has historically been tied to *modern society* (sometimes referred to as *modernity*) and is central to its general system of ideas (its ideology), often referred to as *modernism*. Modernism, in this sense, is something other than the movement of the same name in the fields of art and literature, although the two 'modernisms' are closely related. The modern(ist) understanding of the individual is a precondition for the role of the modern artist as a *creator*. It is also connected to an understanding of history where it is taken more or less for granted that the world, in spite of everything, must *move forwards* – not least through technical advances whereby *the new* in general takes on great value. Such ideas are also central to artistic modernism.

Certain types of leftist and feminist theoreticians have seen modernism and its understanding of the individual as representing the interests of the social class known as the *bourgeoisie* and, more specifically, the *men* of this class. The many varieties of the sort of social and cultural theory called *postmodernism* all share the idea that the subject or personality today is fragmented (divided), complex and partially contradictory. It is thus assumed that the (masculine?) 'identical' subject has collapsed. Hence, we live in *post-* or after-modernity – modernity and its subject has ceased to exist. However, at least as a historical thesis, this idea is quite problematic. As we have just seen, there are split, complex subjects both in nineteenth-century novels and in Freud's psychoanalytic theory, produced in the modern(ist) period. It is probably better to regard the ideas of a totally identical, unified subject as an ideological response to a modern, underlying awareness of splits and contradictions. The 'postmodern' is here, as elsewhere (e.g., in industrial design, where the term designates a more or less playful emphasis on form rather than function), perhaps best seen as an aspect of the modern, an aspect that is more prominent in some periods and some areas than in others. In our day and age, the idea of the unified subject – the strong personality, full of will-power and determination – is very much alive even if philosophers, psychologists, artists and others claim that we are all deeply split and utterly fragmented. These two positions have actually co-existed since at least the early twentieth century.

Identity in complexity

If our psyches are divided and our social identity is decided by a mish-mash of belongings, roles and experiences, how can it be that most of us still feel we are, for the most part, one and the same person? The greater part of our identity has not been chosen by us. One does not, as we all know, choose either one's parents or, consequently, one's social-class background, one's race, gender or mother tongue. Moreover, many of the most important choices we do make – in terms of higher education, for example – are to a great extent conditioned by our backgrounds, which thus also influence our educationally related attitudes, lifestyles and so on. The end result is a quite high degree of consistency in our social and personal identities.

It is, however, also true that these days we also consciously choose certain elements of our identity more freely than was the case in the past. This sort of freedom, which we will return to later in this book, is not something that developed only recently. It is, basically, a central element of modern, as opposed to *traditional,* culture. In the latter case, a person was, at birth, already destined to end up in a certain position and pursuing a certain function in the world. This is, as we all know, no longer the case. In recent years, however, there has been a tendency among some scholars and theoreticians to exaggerate modern (not to mention postmodern) freedom of choice here. It is as if one can choose to be almost anything or anyone at any time – a strict businesswoman in the daytime, an artist experimenting with sex and drugs at night, and a nun every other Sunday. But, just as 'weekend hippies' were easily picked out by the genuine article in the 1960s, the chief executive who plays in an amateur rock band now and then will also be recognizable as a chief executive sort of man in his role as a rock musician. He does not smash up hotel rooms, is a moderate drinker and does not take advantage of young female fans, if he has any. In a later chapter, I will focus on some of the points made by intelligent sociologists on how people's *lifestyles* are actually predictably patterned, even if the elements that go to make them up may at first seem quite random. Our social backgrounds and positions condition us as persons more than we might care to admit.

Still, it is true that modern people are more free to choose who they want to be than were people in pre-modern, traditional societies. We move around more, both socially and geographically, often far away from wherever we started out; we change jobs and professions more often; we change spouses and partners more often, and so on. 'I' may be a girl of 20 who grew up in an apartment near Seattle, who plays soccer, particularly enjoys country rock and whose parents were both born in Pakistan. This imagined, possible person has read classical English literature at school and at home, she is a Muslim and pretty well acquainted with *The Koran* while also a fan of Mike Myers. She likes pizza, tacos, sushi and other wholesome, typically American food, and prefers to watch British drama series on public TV after another tough day at the University of Texas at Austin, where she will be majoring in History. It is the Pakistani element that makes this person's identity appear to be particularly complex; but, in reality, most people are similarly complex creatures. Although one does not have to think of an Australian drug addict who spent most of her life in Kenya before becoming a ski trainer in Sierra Nevada, it will do to consider how anyone may be marked by grandparents from Scotland, a childhood partially spent in church activities, teenage years full of alcohol abuse and sexual desperation, long-term daily reading of the *San Francisco Examiner*, studies in Paris, plus an enormous number of Hollywood movies, and a fascination with British pop music and Russian novels.

In such a cocktail of impulses and so-called roots, several of the ingredients are media products. The media significantly contribute to our personal 'patchwork' identities; one could even say that they may provide a basis for resistance to pressures from forces that would rather have us become totally identical with just one of the patchwork squares. Some may want us to think of ourselves, first and foremost, in national terms; they may want us to be Real Men above all; or they might insist we should be young and trendy through and through. The media may actually offer a bit of balance here. They may, for instance, provide opportunities for an English lad to experience and accept himself as a cosmopolitan, deeply sentimental guy whose old-fashioned main cultural interests are Dante, Beethoven, Baudelaire and Fellini. In other words, one does not understand the role of the media in the formation of identities if one thinks of it as a direct, unconscious influence so that our identities become a simple *effect* of what the media have presented to us. There are, of course, unconscious aspects of our relationship with the media –

almost like habits, which we don't normally stop to think about. Neither do we have personal control over what the media present us with. At the same time, it is important that we also *think* and *evaluate*, both when choosing media products and when using them. (I will return to this in the next chapter, on influence.)

Identity, representation, politics

Even if the media's offerings are plentiful and varied, this does not necessarily mean that they reflect and sustain all the identities and group formations that exist in society. That is why there may be political struggles over the rights to, and forms of, *representation* in the media. It is worth noting here the interesting double meaning of the concept of representation. The word originally meant 'present again' but, in late Latin, acquired the meaning 'stand for', as a picture of a person 'stands for' the pictured person (Larsen, 1993). It is this latter meaning that applies when media scholars talk about 'representation' and 'forms of representation'. What is meant here is a depiction, description or account of fictive or real phenomena. One thinks of texts, images or sounds that stand for something other than themselves. As we will see in Chapter 4, on semiotics, this is also a way of defining *signs*: a sign is something that stands for something else in some way, according to the American philosopher Charles Saunders Peirce. The phrase 'some way' here points to an important aspect of this, namely that 'a sign, or representamen, is something which stands to somebody for something in some respect or capacity' (Jensen, 1995). The actress plays or represents Shakespeare's Juliet on stage, but she also represents her as a hysterical teenager. Representation is also, in other words, always a particular *construction* of that which is represented (that is, depicted or described), and not a complete and totally objective reflection of it.

This is also relevant for the second, related meaning of the word representation, which has been in use since the seventeenth century, where it refers to the function of ambassadors, defence attorneys etc. This use of the word is also found in terms such as 'representative democracy' or, in the USA, the House of Representatives. Members of Parliament in the UK represent their constituencies. These elected representatives are, so to speak, in their seats in our stead. Certain individuals, such as a president, king, queen or top athletes, are often said to represent their nation-state when appearing abroad; and in newspapers and broadcasting there may be interviews with representatives of fishermen or parents of young children. All such representatives may be seen to function, well or badly, in the way they represent (portray and argue for the interests of) large or small groups of people.

Women, workers, racial, ethnic and linguistic minorities, gays, capitalists or, for that matter, people who devote their lives to modern art have all, in different countries, at different times, complained that they are not sufficiently represented in the media's direct and indirect portrayals of the population. They have also put forward sharp criticisms of the *ways* in which they are represented, often leading to public debates. Academic analyses of literary texts, TV shows, films and so on have also often been oriented towards the issue of representation, especially in the context of the type of criticism one might call the *critique of ideology* (see the following chapter, on influence). The strong interest in issues of representation can also be seen in the emotional charge these carry. A discussion of how this or that celebrity or TV show represents 'us' will necessarily also very often involve the issue of who or what 'we' are, or should be (that is, they become discussions of identity, a very personal matter with political implications). Such debates often exemplify the importance of the media in the games and conflicts played out around our identities. If someone is seen in, or acting in, our place, we tend to think that they should behave accordingly.

In some countries, certain ethnic and linguistic minorities have been granted broadcast programmes on the dominant, national channels in their minority language(s), even if they are for the most part living only in particular areas and could be served well by local radio and/or television. The issue here is not just that of being 'served well', however; most of those who belong to these minorities will speak and understand the nationally dominant language perfectly well. The primary motivation for the national broadcasts in minority languages is about granting a symbolic recognition of the minorities in question as citizens on equal terms with the majority population. The programmes are there as representations of the minorities in question, and they serve not least to remind the majority that they are not the only ethnic or linguistic group with fully legitimate citizenship and full civil rights in the nation-state in question.

A thought experiment: in the USA, Hispanic people form the fastest-growing minority group. What if the national TV networks started to broadcast an hour in Spanish every day, possibly with English subtitles, in prime-time, as a form of official acknowledgement of the existence of this rapidly growing, increasingly important ethnic and linguistic group? That this is not very likely to happen is another matter. The point is that such programming would severely challenge the prevailing ideas of what 'American' means, and it would probably also upset a number of other minorities, not least African-Americans, who have struggled for decades to get more and better representation in television.

The question of representation is seen as so socially important that the fundamental freedom of expression has been limited by law in many countries in order to regulate how certain groups are talked about in public (and particularly in the media). It may, for instance, be forbidden to portray women in certain discriminatory ways in advertising, or to portray or speak of people in a disdainful, contemptuous way based on their race, religious beliefs, ethnicity or sexual preference. Such limitations are often subjects of discussion, both because they limit the freedom of expression so fundamental to democracy and because they are often quite difficult to administer in a sensible way. In other words, the concepts of 'representation' and 'identity' lead us directly into important and quite fundamental political issues and debates.

Neither Bostonians, Liverpudlians, Texans, soccer fans, plumbers nor professors have, as groups, any sort of legal protection against unjust or hateful representation in the media. Why not? One can imagine at least two main reasons. First, one's belonging to such groups is commonly considered a less fundamental element in the identity of individuals. Everyone knows that there are lots of different sorts of people in all of these categories; one also knows that it is possible to move, and to change one's dialect and profession. Geographical background and profession are things one can get away from and at least expect to be regarded as somewhat separate from oneself as a specific person. One's sex, sexual desires and looks – in short, one's *body* – are something else. The body is given to us, and we are given to it. Unjust representations tied to our bodily or biologically determined features may therefore be seen as particularly grave or harmful insults, and consequently also particularly important. A person's religious belief is possibly also treated in such laws as something that the person did not choose freely, and as something particularly intimate and fundamental to anyone's identity.

But the fact that religious faith is more protected than professional identity may also have to do with the second reason why some groups are protected and others are not. It is a question of social and cultural *power*. It is not primarily the members of majority or upper-class churches that are protected by the laws and regulations in question. Groups that are commonly seen as large and/or socially powerful will not be regarded as being in need of protection of this sort. A lesbian professor from Gambia will not be hurt by a programme that expresses disdain for professors, but may well be hurt by speeches or programmes that refer to women, lesbians and the black peoples of Africa in a contemptuous or blatantly hateful way.

However, it is not necessarily a solution to limit freedom of expression in areas such as these. The question is not least what constitutes a *crime* and what is only to be counted as a breach of the elementary principles of civility, compassion, good taste and enlightened common sense. It may be a good thing that stupidity and dumb prejudices are let out in the open – they can then be countered and corrected by way of ridicule or serious arguments from a critical public (like the trolls of Scandinavian fairytales, which explode when exposed to the sun). It is also worth reminding ourselves that relatively good-natured humour at the expense of others has always existed and may well be an important safety valve in a social life that is inevitably full of tensions. We need not, therefore, necessarily have a guilty conscience if we tell coarse jokes about those who live in the neighbouring town or country, since we also know very well that there are quite a few good people among them (two or three at least). The same jokes are told the world over about different neighbouring communities or local minorities: the English tell jokes about the Irish that the Irish tell about people from County Cork, while the people of County Cork tell jokes about Dubliners. Swedes and Norwegians tell the sort of jokes about each other that are also told about Polish people in the USA. Most of this is quite harmless, but as some of us will know from experience, humour can also be an unpleasant weapon. It is the social situation in which it is used that decides whether or not this is the case.

Forms of identification

Identification is a concept that may mean a number of things and the term is used in a number of ways. The root of the word is the same as that of identity (that is, one-ness, same-ness). The verb form, 'to identify', then means 'to become (as) one with', 'to become the same as' something else. This can, however, refer to different sorts of processes in different sorts of relationship. If we say we identify with some sports hero, say, it probably means that we *consciously wish* to be or become like the hero in question, either in the sport this person is good at or in terms of his or her stamina, attitude or whatever. We do not necessarily wish or plan to become similar to this hero in every way. On the other hand, when psychologists say that boys identify with their fathers and girls their mothers, they speak of partially *unconscious* wishes, and the desire for sameness is more comprehensive than in the case of identification with sports heroes. Perhaps many young people's identification with film or pop stars is situated somewhere between these two forms. Unconscious components are involved here, and it is more than a guitar technique or a talent for singing that one identifies with – it is not least the star's *personality* (from the Latin word *persona*, i.e. mask). According to psychological theories based on Freud's psychoanalysis, the identifications both with sports and pop stars are versions of the child's primary identificatory processes in relation to its parents. They are about continuing efforts to define themselves in relation to some attractive authorities with whom they have established more or less strong emotional ties.

Our relations with sports, film and pop stars are established by or through the media. Unconscious elements are commonly seen as important parts of, in particular, young people's identification with media stars of various kinds, and this is one of the reasons why some people are worried about the 'effects' of the media. I will return to such issues in the next chapter, but something should be said here, since processes of identification are so central to notions of media 'effects'. The idea is that we *imitate* the heroes of 'action' films and other people, real or fictional, with dubious patterns of behaviour in situations of conflict, dubious attitudes to the opposite sex and so on, just as such things are picked up from parents or, say, siblings. A much more sophisticated version of this kind of thinking is found in media theories (for instance in certain kinds of film studies) that are interested in how the media convey and (particularly) *reproduce and reinforce* certain ideological dispositions in the audience – that is, our already established ideas about right and wrong, what is male and what is female, natural and unnatural, and so on. There are good reasons to take this point of view very seriously.

There are also, however, two reasons why it is far more doubtful that we, who are otherwise 'healthy', pick up obviously unethical patterns of thought or behaviour in the way that some anxious people fear we do. First, as we shall see in a later chapter, *hermeneutics* (the theory or philosophy of interpretation) argues that we are already equipped with a set of norms and values that we use to understand and evaluate real or fictional media heroes. Second, there is, particularly in our encounters with fictional media texts, always an extra 'filter' involved in the experience: we know at the outset that what we read, hear and see is an 'as if' or hypothetical world, a world that appears between inverted commas, quotation marks. A feature film, TV series, novel or, for that matter, a news or current affairs story is not the same as an event in our immediate physical surroundings. The imaginary inverted commas that say 'this is fiction' also become more prominent the further a non-documentary text is removed from recognizable, 'realistic' milieus, characters and actions. With news or other documentary forms the inverted commas are significantly weaker than with fictions (cf., for instance, the notion of the 'photo-effect' in Chapter 4, on semiotics). But even here we often have at the back of our minds a degree of awareness that what we see, read and hear are reports from somewhere else that someone has *made* or *constructed* (the Latin word *fictio* originally meant 'made').

The text might be wildly 'unrealistic' – a far-fetched science fiction adventure, for instance – but we still find that we get 'involved' in the story. Another way of putting this is to say that we experience identification. This is often something other than the sorts of wish-identification we talked about above, in relation to sports and pop stars, even if elements of that could also be involved here. It depends on the sort of text we are reading or viewing. Sigmund Freud did not write very much about this specifically textual or aesthetic form of identification, but when he did, he analysed our relations with quite simple, thrilling adventure novels. He argued that our identification with the hero (an emotionally charged experience of 'being' the hero, living through events 'as if' we were him or her) is related to a wish-fantasy that we are as invincible and immortal as the hero. Such stories flatter 'his majesty the ego' (Freud, 1977). But we are, as we all know, also capable of involving ourselves in stories from the least attractive of circumstances (bottomless slums, violent situations) and stories with basically unattractive, unpleasant characters all over the place. This may, however, also become so painful we can't take it – something that shows the extent to which we actually psychically invest ourselves in the experience.

Not surprisingly, then, Hollywood learnt early on how important a happy ending is to the audience, and to our feelings about ourselves. But we *are* able to get involved in, or identify with, unhappy characters and circumstances. In order to understand this, it may be helpful to return to the identity-forming processes of childhood. Psychoanalytic theory emphasizes that we are shaped as human beings particularly through our interaction with our parents, but it also of course takes into account that our image or understanding of ourselves is also continually developed in our relations to siblings, friends, colleagues or whomsoever we socialize with. *Symbolic interactionism* is the name given to something we might call a sociological approach to (social) psychology. It is clearly related to psychoanalytical thinking, but has a somewhat different main focus. This (originally American) approach developed from the early years of the twentieth century until it got its name in the 1930s, and is particularly interested in how our 'I' is continuously developed through our relations to others or, more precisely, through *how we perceive that others perceive us*. This idea was first formulated in 1902 by the sociologist Charles Horton Cooley, but was further elaborated as a core point in the works of scholars such as George Herbert Mead, Herbert Blumer and others in the sociological tradition known as the Chicago School. Symbolic interactionism maintains that we are shaped by the way in which others see us, by first applying the perspective of others on ourselves and then deciding whether this is a perspective we can share. Applying others' perspective on ourselves is a particular version of the more general ability we have to put ourselves in the place of others, which goes by the name of *empathy*. In children's role-play it is obvious how the ability to act 'as if' one were someone other than oneself is practised or rehearsed, and it is also this ability that is mobilized in children's involvement in fictional stories. One might well regard the ability to 'get involved' in media texts in general as based on our ability to empathize. (It is a good idea to be careful around people without such an ability – they are known as psychopaths.) In this perspective, then, the identificatory involvement in media texts is partially a trying out of different perspectives of ourselves and our own world (since these perspectives are of course also more or less consciously evaluated both during and after the experience), and partially a rehearsal of our more general capacity for empathy.

The term *para-social interaction* was coined by the social psychologists Horton and Wohl (1956) to describe a situation where TV viewers, say, do not actually identify with the people on the screen, but instead relate to them as they would relate to people they had met in the street, café or wherever: they might say hello to them, respond to their dialogue, and so on. This sort of relationship may also be established with the fictional characters that return to your screen on a daily or weekly basis. It is, one might say, a form of (more or less conscious) fantasy, which does not imply (but also does not preclude) identification with the characters in question. In line with the thinking of symbolic interactionism, the empathic form of identification could also be at work here, just as in other forms of social interaction.

The German literary scholar Hans Robert Jauss (1977) suggested a set of different *types* of identification in aesthetic contexts. *Associative* identification is when we allow ourselves to be absorbed into a collective, as in certain types of games or play, at football matches, rock festivals and the like. *Admirative* identification is identification with a heroic figure who is better and/or more powerful than us in one or several ways, be it a divine character or just a common-or-garden superhero. *Sympathetic* identification is the most common form of identification with realist fiction, biographies and the like, where the hero or heroine resembles us to the degree that we feel we experience his or her life 'as if' it could have been our own. As a rule we will here go through experiences that in one way or another *confirm* something we somehow thought, felt or knew already. *Cathartic* identification is also identification with a hero or heroine who resembles ourselves, but who is of a tragic type (that is, a type of person who has some decisive weakness or flaw that inevitably leads to his or her downfall in some sense and to some degree). The word 'catharsis' stems from the ancient Greek theory of tragedy and is usually translated as 'purification'. The idea is that the audience, through a compassionate identification with the destiny of the tragic hero, will experience what may be called 'emotional purification'. The notion of catharsis is also, not surprisingly, important in theories of psychotherapy from Freud onwards. The final category in Jauss's typology of identificatory forms is labelled *ironic*. This is when a text seems to invite a sympathetic identification with a hero or heroine but then, again and again, breaks this identificatory bond by making it appear absurd or otherwise unbearable in terms of our self-image or self-esteem. Ironic identification is, in other words, a type of identificatory pattern that many modernist and socially critical texts will try to establish since it is thought to promote critical self-reflection on the part of readers or audiences.

It is, moreover, an important point in Jauss's way of thinking that particular forms of identification may well dominate in certain genres or certain periods, but they, nevertheless, also co-exist as possibilities and may well be found combined as 'invitations' to readers or audiences in one and the same text. The heroes and heroines of modern popular culture, for example, often invite combinations of admirative and sympathetic identification. They can do great things and survive incredible ordeals, but they are also vulnerable and have difficult relationships with their parents, partners or children.

Young people and the evergreens

The identity of individuals is, as pointed out above, always a patchwork of identities. But these identities, and the whole 'quilt' they constitute, change over time. The media play an important role in such historical changes. One example of this can be found in the category of 'youth'.

The word 'youth' may mean a number of things. Intuitively, however, one would tend to think that it refers to a period in the life of human beings where one is neither a child anymore, nor recognized as an adult. This would be roughly the period between the onset of puberty on the one hand and legal age of majority on the other. But youth is no longer what it once was.

Of course, people were also young in previous centuries, including the first half of the twentieth; but, back then, being young did not *mean* the same as it does now. The French historian Philippe Ariès has convincingly demonstrated the historicity of such concepts in his book *The History of Childhood* (1980). In what is often quite vaguely referred to as 'the old days', boys and girls would, at least in the countryside and in working-class milieus in the cities, be counted as grown-ups as soon as they had passed through confirmation or similar rites of passage in their early to mid-teens. Their new status could immediately be seen from their clothes. Boys, for instance, would change from short to long trousers and could start wearing hats. Special clothes or fashions for young people hardly existed. At public dances, young people might dominate, but many more mature and even middle-aged people would also take part. Dance music was the same for everybody and the musicians might be older than Mick Jagger. (Such social functions can still be found in the countryside in a number of countries.)

Modern media contributed to more marked divisions between age groups and generations early on in the twentieth century. It was not primarily older people who, at least in Europe, had eagerly swallowed lots of western novels from the late nineteenth century. The movie theatres that spread explosively all over the western world from about 1905 were particularly popular among children and adolescents, not least because they were establishments where kids could meet on their own, freed from parental supervision. Young people also constituted the major part of the readerships for new magazines such as the film 'fanzines' that came out from around the First World War, full of film star gossip, fashion and beauty advice, and the like. The movies were seen by many older, 'responsible', people as expressions and causes of a new mentality that seemed to spread among the young, often referred to as self-indulgence, a love of pleasure. There were signs that saving money was now less popular than spending it – an early indicator of the *consumer society* that emerged during the 1920s when workers' wages gradually rose to allow for more than the rent, bread, milk and soap. Young people of that time can be said to have acted as a sort of cultural barometer (as indeed they also did later). They somehow sensed early on what sorts of changes were imminent.

Even clearer than the role of cinema was the impact of jazz music from the 1920s onward. It significantly contributed to a redefinition of the word 'young' so that it came to mean more than simply 'of a relatively low age'. Jazz, on gramophone records or played by local bands, would soon be established as the preferred musical form of, in particular, urban youth. Jazz fans came to represent the sort of youth that many serious people warned against. The music was accused of encouraging self-indulgence and sexual transgression, and of discouraging the formation of a strong will, serious thinking and moral righteousness.

Jazz remained the preferred music of urban youth way into the 1950s, but at the beginning, and particularly around the middle, of that decade something new happened. Through a series of films starring James Dean (*East of Eden, Rebel Without a Cause*) and Marlon Brando (*A Streetcar Named Desire, The Wild One*), and, after a while, movies with rock'n'roll soundtracks (*The Blackboard Jungle, Rock Around the Clock*), adolescence was thematized in a new way. A very important point here is that several media all worked together – film, records, magazines and (eventually) TV shows – and, moreover, so did the fashion and clothing industry, and other branches of business. Special youth fashions began to appear (jeans, leather jackets, greasy hairdos with ducktails) and the motorcycle became the favourite means of transport for young people. The term *teenager* was coined in the USA and was immediately adopted in the rest of the western world.

The media's contribution to the formation of a new youth identity came about, however, in a particular sort of interaction with young people themselves. There seems to have been a new sort of unrest among youngsters, a kind of lack of desire to settle down in the life of responsible grown-ups, an uncertainty as to what one could, or wanted to, become in the world. At the same time many young people had more money than they used to have, and the number of those who pursued education beyond the obligatory minimum started to grow. So many possibilities seemed to open up, so much was uncertain. This could be one reason why *gangs* and the term *gang mentality* were born at the time. Young people of primarily working-class backgrounds formed slightly intimidating, uniformly dressed gangs all over the western world, with names such as 'teddy boys' (England), 'blousons noir' (France), 'halbstarken' (Germany), and 'blackie gang' (Norway).

It is an interesting social fact that it was primarily working-class youngsters that formed such gangs. A British scholarly tradition that has been very influential in media and cultural studies over the last 20 years or so, and sometimes referred to as the *Birmingham School*, conducted some of its most important studies in just such milieus in the 1970s (see also Chapter 2 of the present volume, on influence, and the classic collection of articles by Hall and Jefferson, 1976). The picture drawn by these studies is complex and in part contradictory, most probably because the realities they deal with were like that too. In his *Learning to Labour* (1977) Paul Willis described how working-class boys systematically made choices, not least in relation to education, that would lead to lives and jobs in the class they came from, because they had internalized values that suggested other priorities than those of the educational system. On the other hand, Dick Hebdige showed in his *Subculture: The Meaning of Style* (1978) how working-class kids in many ways created their own group identities. They did this by consciously choosing certain elements from the media and other sources, and combining them in the more or less comprehensive and coherent styles that came to characterize certain subcultures. Examples through the decades include: teddy boys (in the 1950s); mods (in the 1960s); and punks (in the 1970s). The latter is actually the best example, since punks – totally without respect for pre-established meanings – combined crosses, swastikas, leather jackets and military boots according to a principle that might bring to mind the montage techniques of the avant-garde in the visual arts or what has been known as *bricolage*.

From the 1950s on, then, one could for the first time speak of a distinctive *youth culture*, which was partially produced by, or with the aid of, the media – interacting with other social institutions and circumstances. Young people got a new identity *as* young people, not just as 'soon-to-be adults'. Being young became a *lifestyle* in itself, characterized by certain tastes and activities. As such, importantly, it could also be stretched considerably in terms of time. One could continue wearing jeans and leather jackets and listening to rock'n'roll long after moving into a suburban dwelling with a spouse and one's children. This option has been most markedly adopted by those who were young in the 1960s and 1970s – a generation of people who seem to find it difficult to realize and accept that they are adults, or even middle-aged. They'd rather not face it. This is, however, not just some *idée fixe*, and not just a fear of old age and dying: it is related to some thoroughgoing social and cultural processes of change.

The German social psychologist Thomas Ziehe (cf., for example, Ziehe and Stubenrauch, 1983) has talked about the new 'lack of overview' after the Second World War. Children and young people could, in more stable societies at least, learn how to live from their mothers, fathers and other older people. In modern societies, and particularly after the Second World War, social and cultural changes have been more and more rapid. Social and geographical mobility have been radicalized. Industries are shut down and others created. An education that would have provided a decent and secure income in one decade is useless in the next. Expectations directed at boys and girls have changed in a number of important ways over three or four decades. The youth cultures that started to develop in the 1950s can be seen as both an indication of, and a response to, this new uncertainty; the formation of gangs was perhaps an attempt to establish some provisional form of stable identity in a situation where much else seemed to be floating and fuzzy. Since one's identity was now more uncertain, there was more of an emphasis on *choosing* what one was, what one wanted, what one believed in, and so on. The media did not just deliver a youth culture, they also came to present young people with a number of options in terms of identity signs that one could, so to speak, wear or pick up. It was not inconsequential around 1960 to be numbered among the fans of Pat Boone, Elvis Presley, Cliff Richard or Tommy Steele; it was just as important as the choice between the Stones and the Beatles only a few years later. A liking for French New Wave films or hard-hitting westerns would decide who one was in one's own eyes and, importantly, in the eyes of others. Today the more important questions may concern one's feelings about rap, British garage music, skateboards and baseball caps worn sideways. Few will look to their parents or grandparents for advice on what is to be considered important in the lives of young people.

This new 'lack of overview', this new uncertainty, implies that *experience has decreased in value*. When the world is changing continuously, there seems little point in sticking to what was considered acceptable for the previous generation, the previous decade, the previous year. A good example may be found in the area of personal finances. It has, historically, been considered a handicap – and even degrading – to have debts. Those who were young between the two world wars (the parents of those who were born between about 1945 and 1960) were keen to avoid loans and at least to keep them as small as possible if they had to have them. Their children, however, were unable to live by such principles. They would often, in many countries, have to borrow money for a much longer time spent in education, and they could do this because they had reason to expect that they would get good jobs that would make their student loans easy to handle. When finding a place to live, they would also take on the kind of mortgage that would have scared their parents. However, the question of whether loans are OK, even smart or perhaps quite the opposite, has had several answers in the last few decades as economies and policies have changed dramatically in the course of just a few years. When the labour market is filled with people with higher-education qualifications and the price of housing has skyrocketed in metropolitan areas around the world, some people may find the carefulness of their grandparents (or even great-grandparents) intelligent. The experiences of their parents are practically worthless – aside from the main point that, as everything is so uncertain, it might be a good idea to be a bit careful.

Other examples of how the experiences of older people are of little relevance to today's youth can be found in areas related to technological developments, particularly information and communication technologies (ICTs). In the latter half of the 1990s, home computers were becoming quite common in many western countries. Computers are now everywhere in business and the public sector, and most schools have computers with Internet access. Developments in this area have been rapid. As late as 1985 few working in at least European universities had their own personal computers. In 1990, though, most scholars in all disciplines had had such equipment at their disposal for anything between one and four years. The Internet did not exist in its present form then, but the computers brought with them totally new ways of working, and the use of e-mail and, eventually, the net, has in just a few years more or less revolutionized working practices in the academic sector – and elsewhere. It may also have changed ways of thinking, ways of relating to one's work, and most certainly the ways in which one relates to colleagues at other institutions and abroad. Scholars of my generation, with degrees from around 1980, were among the first to experience all this at first hand; we could not look to older colleagues to learn anything about it. They were just as green as we were when faced with the first personal computers. Their experiences with pencils, mechanical calculators and typewriting secretaries were not worth much. Indeed, now we find that children and young people can teach us, their elders, a great deal about chat rooms and downloading music files from the Internet, as well as how to send text messages on mobile phones. This is also what old rockers tell us, with their blue jeans and balding heads with just a few strands of long grey hair: no one is totally grown up any more, no one is finished or complete in the old-fashioned manner, with the indisputably solid confidence of experience in every field. We remain green, even if greying.

I would, however, like to emphasize that some of us will insist that much life experience is still valid and that it is possible to learn from it, both in matters of the head and the heart. This book, for instance, is based on academic and other life experiences – some my own, some those of others, some even of people who have been dead for almost 2500 years – it could not have been written by just any 20 year old.

We are also citizens, members of society

Our uses of the media are not least signs of our wish to live a social life, to feel part of a larger community and context. We do not live in extended families in stable and transparent small societies any more, but the media establish – partially in co-operation with other social institutions – other, more abstract, forms of community. Because we feel that we are members of these abstract communities – and also of course of our much less abstract local neighbourhood – we want to know about them. We want to be informed (again) that the world still exists; we want to know about major and minor events that concern us in different ways – as human beings and as members of society, citizens.

We do not have to be terribly interested in politics to be interested in the morning news. It is sufficient to think of ourselves as adults with a right to elementary information about the situation in the world, the latest tricks played by financial capital, and wheeler-dealing among politicians. Through primary and secondary socialization – family life, education, membership of organizations and use of the media – we have been formed as members of a political democracy. Even if many reportedly feel it a vague sort of 'duty' to keep up with the news (Hagen, 1994), this does not mean that we would rather prefer to go without constantly updated information about the current social, political, economic and cultural situation. Our role as members of society, or citizens, is just as important as any other part of our identity; and, for the existence of democracy, it is absolutely vital.

This is part of the reason why the genre 'news' is one of the key best-sellers for newspapers, radio and television channels alike. News is simply good for business – at least if kept brief and quite superficial. News items can, however, easily become so brief and superficial that we have a reason to feel cheated. We would like to have information about the world because, according to elementary democratic ideals, we are supposed to partake in the processes leading to decisions on how it is supposed to develop. It is then important that we are supplied with information and knowledge that are relevant for such participation. If stories about accidental crime, car crashes, drunken celebrities and politicians at football matches constantly squeeze out material with greater, more direct, social relevance, we are – as members of society with a right to influence important aspects of our own situation – let down, or cheated, by media with such priorities. If such priorities persist, they may eventually lead to a loss of our expectations to be served or treated as active citizens. Our identity as citizens is not given by nature, it is not complete and stable; it is not threatened by the *National Enquirer*, the *Sun* or TV programmes like the *Jerry Springer Show* in and of themselves; but it may be significantly weakened if this sort of material is the only kind of 'information' we are offered or reached by.

The mechanism here is basically the same as in other dimensions of the relations between the media and our identity: We form images of ourselves through interaction with our surroundings. The media offer material through which we understand ourselves.

The media offer identity-strengthening order and therapy

A wish to be updated on the world situation is hardly the only identity-relevant reason why people, for instance, turn on the radio in the morning. Many people prefer those channels that do present brief news updates at regular intervals, but that otherwise basically play music, most often of an uncomplicated sort. The music may work as a kind of light massage; it stimulates circulation and reduces stress. The mix of music, small talk and news can also feel reassuring; it is part of an everyday ritual, marking in a pleasant way that it is morning again and, hey, most of us are on our way to school or work.

Listeners and viewers can now choose between different kinds of morning programmes, oriented towards different kinds of people and thus also, one might say, confirming different kinds of identity. What all broadcasting channels share, though, is that they have a rhythm that follows the phases or sequences of everyday life. Programmes get us out of bed, off to work, home through rush-hour traffic, take us through dinner preparation, and into the entertainment, and possible reflectiveness, of the evening hours – and then to bed (cf. Scannell 1996, Chapter 7). Broadcast media form a 'normal' time scheme for 'normal' lives, they structure each day and give each day of the week a special character. We know we are deviants if we go to bed long after television has signalled that serious people should go to bed, we know we are bad parents if our little ones are not in bed when some violent crime series is on TV. These structures remain, despite the fact that 24-hour broadcasting has been in existence for a while. Indeed, 24-hour broadcasting in itself may be a source of anxiety for those so inclined: there are obviously many people who don't sleep during the night, but during the day! The world is clearly falling apart.

In his book *Television and Everyday Life* (1994) – to which I will be referring and expanding on throughout this section – the British media scholar Roger Silverstone starts precisely from the fact that we do need a certain order in our lives when he analyses how television works in our daily lives. He regards the general need that human beings have for an ordered existence as absolutely fundamental. Internal and external chaos are constant, threatening possibilities that all social life has as a first priority to combat. Silverstone takes this view from both anthropological knowledge, from recent psychoanalytical theory, and from sociology (primarily Anthony Giddens). Habits, traditions, rituals and institutions at all levels, from the morning's brushing of teeth to parliamentary procedures, all contribute when we try, so to speak, to strike some balance in our lives. Television has its place in the interplay between individuals' ongoing construction of identity on the one hand and the general, 'macro', functions of society on the other. As a broadcast medium it contributes, as we have just argued, to establishing a stable rhythm for people's everyday lives in a well-known and much-appreciated mix of programmes and segments, day in, day out, all year round. Television is, as the most central of all media, part of the very fabric of everyday life: it plays a role at several levels, as a material object and commodity, as technology and as provider of programmes.

Television is, first and foremost, something that exists in people's homes. It is a *domestic* medium. Domesticity is a social space that was first developed in what we might term the *bourgeois* period, in the early period of modernity, when the workplace and the home became separated. This separation came to be of fundamental significance to western culture. The home acquired a status as an 'inner', intimate zone, where close relations, human warmth, compassion and sensitivity were paramount, in striking contrast to the cool, rational politeness and cynical struggles outside. But television is, as a phenomenon, a sign that the home is now a much more complex and contradictory place than it at least seemed to be in classical bourgeois times and milieus, Silverstone argues (1994: 25). The relations between public and private spaces and cultures are constantly changing, and television is tied to this in a number of ways. It is involved in power struggles between mothers, fathers and children (who controls the remote when?), and it thematizes The Family again and again, both in factual and fictional programmes, with soap opera as the main genre for this in the fiction category. It also, however, brings politics, economy, commerce and public cultural life into people's living rooms, at a time when there are many signs of the home being celebrated and cherished more than ever as a safe haven for self-realization and healthy experiences, in contrast to the external world's sharply competitive treadmill and the threatening dangers of the streets. Television is, perhaps, the object in which these partially paradoxical tendencies come together; it embodies a domesticity that closes and opens up at the same time.

Changes in the status of the home are correlated to changes in the ways in which public space functions. Silverstone here starts from the British cultural historian and theorist Raymond Williams' now classic description of how broadcast media perfectly fit certain fundamental social features of modernity (Williams, 1975). *Mobile privatization* is Williams' term for the combination of radically increased social and geographical mobility on the one hand, and the tendency towards the social isolation of the individual nuclear family, or any other sort of household, on the other. The suburb is, as a form of urban life, an expression of these tendencies. Radio and television have historically tied together the mobile private units and offered identity and generally relevant information etc. The public sphere and its central media have been shaped to fit the suburb and its way of life, a way of life where it has been said (by the American scholar Margaret Morse, 1990) that experiential parallels exist between driving a car, wandering through shopping malls and watching television – they are all activities we can do semi-automatically and in a 'distracted' fashion, so that they can also be combined with dreaming and social interaction.

The suburbs and other living areas have long been in a process of change in the western world. They are increasingly becoming culturally heterogeneous, and the classic nuclear family is giving way to a number of other sorts of household. At the same time, the number of broadcasting channels has practically exploded. VCRs and other domestic audiovisual technologies, and computers with Internet access have been introduced. All of this has disrupted previously established, and generally shared, daily rhythms and programme menus. Broad political participation is in a sense made easier through transmissions of national and international debates and events, through improved access to information both about the public and personal lives of those who hold power, through daily doses of comments on and analyses of political tendencies and phenomena. At the same time there is less participation in various organizations and other social contexts that used to be the basis for ordinary people's political actions. Bearing in mind this complex background, a discussion may well be worthwhile of to what extent television's typical ways of (re)presenting political issues and actors actually promote rational or sensible political understanding and real possibilities for intervention.

Silverstone also discusses the symbolic functions of the television set. These are also involved in our continuous work to construct and uphold an identity and understanding of ourselves in relation to others. Particularly in the medium's infancy, for instance, sets were clearly perceived as an alien element in the home, possibly a sort of wild animal one might have to *domesticate*. It was hidden behind doors, covered with cloths and topped with a maze of family photos, plants and knick-knacks. In this way the set was not only domesticated, this dangerous mediator of the outside world could become the major sign of a Real Home. Among students in the 1960s and 1970s, the TV set was often probably what most clearly separated the dwellings of couples and families from those of the more or less swinging singles. If it was important for student couples and families to reduce the impression of a petit bourgeois lifestyle and Despicable Conformity lent by the TV, they could, perhaps, paint its teak chassis bright red. Silverstone does not often go into such concrete details, but he points to research that does. One excellent example is Lynn Spigel's fascinating study of how TV became integrated into American everyday life around 1950 (*Make Room for TV: Television and the Family Ideal in Post-War America*, 1992).

But, as I think we all know, television also delivers programmes; it not least mediates an ongoing series of more or less disturbing impressions of a world full of war, crises and catastrophes of many kinds. This adds to an everyday life that is already full of tensions, possible conflicts and, perhaps, fundamental uncertainty – threats of chaos, as Silverstone would have it. The British scholar and TV producer John Ellis (1999) has argued that television programmes in many ways can be said to offer viewers a form of identity-strengthening therapy, in which the anxieties and uncertainties TV itself generates are also treated. News and current affairs segments and programmes may often appear incomprehensible and gruesome, whether referring to natural disasters, crime, various sorts of human suffering quite close to home or in areas of hunger and inconceivable brutality far away. Ellis suggests that a number of programmes in other genres work as treatments, as offers of 'working through' (a term taken from psychoanalysis) these disturbing, often violent, impressions. In anything from chat shows and debates to soap operas and variety entertainment, the problematic phenomena are named, put into words and gradually shaped to fit in to conceptual frames and schemes with which we are already familiar. Thus, little by little, they become less threatening, more manageable.

Even if television provides the most shocking impressions and is also particularly central to any ensuing therapeutic work, these functions clearly apply, to a great extent, to other media too. But after such treatment it is also possible that, for instance, horrific mass murders of particular ethnic groups (such as those in Africa or Kosovo) can become stories about 'those out there' as opposed to 'us back here'. It would be less comfortable, but also possibly politically more productive, if such atrocities were presented as the result of man's general potential for unspeakable cruelty against others, or as (possibly delayed) effects of a European colonialism for which 'we' can be said to share responsibility, to the extent that we think of 'us' as deeply tied to Europeans of all sorts through centuries before our time.

Whatever scheme is used – and there can be several circulating at the same time for each event or situation – the thematization of the disquieting and difficult contributes to some sort of psychological handling of impressions, and thus acts to secure people's feeling of order and balance. This may have its problematic aspects – politically, ethically and ideologically – but, on the other hand, no sensible politics or ethics is well served by a widespread, anxious feeling that the world is incomprehensible and thus impossible to intervene in.

Television's global community

I will end this presentation of some aspects of the media's identity-shaping work by taking a closer look at a certain type of television programme where national borders are transgressed so that a more or less global audience is formed, united in a simultaneous experience of a particular event. Daniel Dayan and Elihu Katz define and analyse such phenomena in their book *Media Events: The Live Broadcasting of History* (1992). More specifically, they describe and analyse the special, ceremonial 'seances' where television puts aside normal programme routines and moves cameras, microphones and employees, often far away from the studio, to convey *live* to an enormous audience an event that, at least in principle, is planned and carried through independently and 'outside of' television. Such events are different from news, even if they are live coverage of, say, catastrophes of various kinds. News events are not planned ahead and are communicated in a different way, in a different kind of language. The murder of President Kennedy in 1963 was a news event, while his funeral was the sort of ceremony that Dayan and Katz talk about. They analyse the kind of TV programmes that give the set a kind of 'halo', where up to hundreds of millions of people set aside other activities in order to take part in a ritual that in some sense or other conveys real or utopian *reconciliation*, community, integration, even if the event itself is about struggle, competition or the like.

Critical intellectuals are, intuitively and for good reason, deeply sceptical about official ceremonies and ritual celebrations of community. That is why it is fascinating to read an intellectually stimulating book that goes a long way towards defending such phenomena. Dayan and Katz know the famous thesis of the German-Jewish critic Walter Benjamin from the 1930s, that aestheticization of politics is characteristic of fascism, but they still argue that no society can do completely without ceremonial, even theatrical, elements in its public life. It is not so much the existence of such elements that is important, it is how these elements are balanced by rational, discursive, debate- and struggle-oriented elements. Katz and Dayan further argue well for the view that well-designed media events not only have conservative functions

– by confirming existing identities, values and authorities – they can also proclaim a new situation, a new symbolical order, and thus change the world, even if they necessarily have to build on (other parts of) people's existing sets of values when doing so. For example, according to Dayan and Katz, the Egyptian president Anwar Sadat's journey to Jerusalem changed the Middle East forever, and it would not have done so had it not been for television's ceremony-like coverage of the event.

The two authors are openly fascinated by the possibilities of television as master of ceremonies. Television gathers the largest audiences in the history of the world for a contemporaneously shared experience of certain events – an at once atomized and immediately socially integrated audience in accordance with the best of 'mass society' theories (see the following chapter). These TV events are also, as a rule, impossible to experience in reality, outside of TV, even if what TV shows is real enough: dozens of cameras in different strategic positions all over London, or whatever location, give the producer and audience a privileged opportunity to 'be' in several different places at once. Television's edited, live version of reality is historically new – and powerful.

These media events not only consist of obvious celebrations of community, such as the opening ceremony of the Olympics or a royal wedding. Such events constitute only one of the three main types, Dayan and Katz suggest.

- They might be *celebrations* or *coronations*.
- They might also be *contests*, such as sports events, certain political debates, congressional hearings or, for example, something like the O.J. Simpson trial in the USA; in these cases, one could say that it is the *underlying, shared norms and principles* that are celebrated, the system of justice, the rules of competition and the community of values they supposedly represent (fairness, impartiality, etc.).
- The third and last main category is that of *conquests*, exemplified by events as diverse as the 1969 moon landing and, again, Anwar Sadat's journey to Jerusalem. In these events, the heroes become incarnations of the values of the audience, and they become the objects of a hefty mixture of admiration and self-recognition.

These three categories will appear familiar to those who are acquainted with structuralist literary theory. The sequence contest–conquest–celebration/coronation is to be found in typical fairytales and adventure stories, and many media events can also be seen in light of such a sequence. The moon landing had its background in the contest between the Soviet Union and the USA, it took the form of a conquest (planting of the flag, etc.), and was thereafter followed by a spectacular celebration/coronation of the heroes. Part of the strength of Dayan and Katz's analysis lies precisely in inspiration from the historical coupling of anthropological cultural analysis and general textual theory, which is a hallmark of structuralist theory. At the same time, they are also very much aware of the specificity of the medium under scrutiny.

In this context, however, it is global, ritual-like TV events that are our main concern. It is not easy to investigate precisely how they influence the colossal, multifarious audience's perception of itself. They may also function quite differently. The Olympic Games may promote national chauvinism rather than international brother- or sisterhood, even if it includes a bit of both. Princess Diana's funeral, on the other hand, provided people in many countries with an opportunity to experience a community of mourning, even if it may have been superficial and debatable (see Robert Turnock's *The Death of Diana*, BFI, 2000). It is, all the same, tempting to speculate that the consequences of global, live TV should be viewed along the same lines as national broadcasting's production of community. It may at least signal clearly that we all live on the same planet, *at the same time*, and that we have to relate to each other, that we do influence each others' lives. Live, global telecasts may contribute to making the 'objective' fact of a global community – in terms of shared ecological conditions, interrelated destinies in economic and ethical terms – a subjectively experienced reality (cf. Johansen 1997).

Despite the abundance of channels and the wide variation of media content in general, the media can, then, still share the ability to influence us and our lives, often in subtle, hardly noticeable, ways. They leave a mark on what we are, what we do and what we think about. It is quite common to say that they 'have an effect' on us, consciously and unconsciously. If this is the case, it is important to note that they do so in a continuous interaction with us, and so their 'effects' on us are comparable to the 'effects' of our interaction with all other factors that are a part of our lives – other people, nature, architecture, means of transport, food or whatever. 'Effects' may therefore be a debatable term to describe the relations between the media and ourselves. In the following chapter, we will look more closely at the question of media influence, as it has been understood in public debates and research throughout the twentieth century, and up until the present day.

2   Influence: the media's power – and our own

Is all media research about effects?

There are those who maintain that the fundamental reason for conducting media research is that the media in some way influence us. As we shall see, this is a debatable view, not least because 'influence' may mean many things. But it is true enough that many of the opinions and much of the research about the media, particularly in the last 100 years, have been about the media's influence on their audiences. Many studies about the production side of the media have also been motivated by the fact that they affect us in different ways. This chapter is about how different kinds of research have attempted to describe and consider such influence. The subject has been so central to media and communication studies that this chapter is almost like a sketch of the entire research history of the field.

The belief that the media affect us lies behind many kinds of professional and organizational activities. Schools choose certain texts that are believed to contribute to making students become decent, tolerant, knowledgeable and socially active citizens. Religious institutions and movements also prescribe a certain media menu that is meant to have a positive influence on spiritual health and daily moral practices. The advertising industry lives quite well from promising sales-hungry businessmen a positive effect on people's spending habits. Political movements have had faith in thoroughly thought-out media campaigns capable of making enormous numbers of people 'see the light', and think and act accordingly. Films are censored in order to prevent psychological damage to cinema audiences.

The media's impact on society and on each and every one of us is clearly one of the main reasons for our need to know as much as possible about the media and what they communicate. But because this seems so obvious, we should remember that studies of the media and their texts – be these religious handbills, poetry, pamphlets, novels, radio, newspaper articles, films or television programmes – need not primarily be conducted because one is worried about the damaging effect on youth and other tender souls. It may be worthwhile for entirely different reasons. It may simply make one wiser. The media's *texts* may be studied because one wants to know more about the world in general or about a particular problem, a certain area of existence – death, love, religious questions and unjust conditions in society. The media deliver very different contributions to experiences, thought processes and ongoing public debate. The questions about *what the media tell us*, and *how*, are still perfectly legitimate points of departure for media research, and only indirectly involve concepts such as influence, impact or effects.

This chapter, however, will be about the serious worries – and also the hopeful expectations – about media's power to influence. We can talk here about two traditions of thought, theory and research – one humanist and one social science. Only as recently as in the last two decades have the two begun to merge or overlap.

Humanistic theories of media influence

In the world of science it is not only psychologists and social scientists that have been interested in media influence. Large sections of twentieth-century literature and film theory are, in fact, marked by ideas about how literature and film respectively can more or less directly affect audience's ways of thinking and acting. Particularly important contributions were made in Russia in the years around 1920.

The *Russian formalists* were a group of ingenious language and literature scholars who, from about 1910 on, developed new ways of looking at their field. They were interested in language both as something that shapes our understanding of reality, and as concrete sounds and written signs organized in certain ways. They were particularly interested in what distinguishes literature as an art form from other uses of language. In 1917 one of these scholars, Viktor Shklovsky, in his famous essay 'Art as technique' (Shklovsky [1917] 1988), maintained that the mark of true literature – what other formalists called 'literariness' – is about breaking away from everyday language. It is a matter of renewing language, for in that way the 'automatic' relationship we have with reality through the commonly accepted, 'normal' language will be broken. Shklovsky coined the concept *defamiliarization* (in Russian, *ostranenie*, 'making strange') as a term for this. When confronted with a new use of language, both language itself and also exterior reality beyond it are made strange or unfamiliar, so that we are able to see both in a fresh, new light.

One of my former teachers, the Norwegian poet and professor Georg Johannesen, once, at the top of a flight of stairs, improvised the following example of the difference between defamiliarizing literariness and everyday language: '"He tumbled down the stairs" is everyday language, while "he tumbled up the stairs" is literature.' The point of the latter statement is that the expression breaks with the commonly held meaning of the verb 'to tumble'. It becomes a *metaphor*, that is to say a comparison between a way of moving up the stairs with the rapid uncontrolled downward movement we associate with tumbling. Consequently we have to take a little break, use our reason and imagination for a moment, before we can 'see' a way of going up the stairs in this fresh light. Simultaneously language, in a way, becomes more visible to us. In a flash we can 'see' how language is both something relatively independent in relation to the rest of reality and also something that influences our perception of it. Language is something with which we can play and experiment, and it may 'create' reality in the sense that it can make us perceive the world differently.

The linguistic techniques that give a text its 'literariness' in this sense are, in other words, intended to 'influence' the reader. The reader is not to be left in peace with his or her habitual, traditional perceptions of the world – new ways of thinking are needed here! It is simply taken for granted that new ways of thinking, seeing the world in new and different ways, is a good thing. It will enable us to make decisions more freely and shape our environment in ever more sensible, stimulating or compassionate ways. This is a markedly *modern* view (which means that it roughly belongs to the period after about 1750), and it is fundamental to the broad traditions of ideas and art called *modernism* (from the latter part of the nineteenth century until the present time). It would have been unheard of in the Middle Ages, when the opinion was that God had arranged the world once and for all, and making important changes was considered blasphemous.

Many artists and art scholars seem to think that a kind of permanent revolution in the arts is a premise for radical changes in society in general. Really good, creative poetry or other art forms are sometimes even seen as a *cause* of social and cultural change. During her revolutionary period in the 1970s, the theoretician of language and literature, Julia Kristeva, who for some time now has had a psychoanalytic practice in Paris, wrote that it was the bureaucratic rigidity of the Stalinist use of language, in combination with the attacks on modernist expressions in the arts, that made Stalin's Soviet regime a terribly repressive machinery (Kristeva [1974] 1988). Many would agree that there is an important connection between rigidity in language and rigidity in worldview as well as conduct. But it is questionable whether the developments in the Soviet Union would have been more democratic had Stalin and his *apparatchiks* been more poetically inventive in their use of language. Perhaps they would simply have been able to invent even more disposable enemies.

In the modernist way of thinking there is thus a strong belief in the ability of language, and therefore the media, to influence people, positively as well as negatively. Film director Sergei Eisenstein was an engineer by education and a central figure in the history of film art as well as film theory. He was convinced that film was superior to all other art forms in its power to influence. In this regard he was in line with Vladimir Illich Lenin, who declared film to be the most important revolutionary propaganda vehicle. Eisenstein is famous for his *montage theory*, meaning his theory that the specific *filmic* quality (cf. *literariness* above) lies in the fact that a film consists of a lot of smaller pieces of film put together in a row (Eisenstein, 1949). Eisenstein's montage theory was inspired by Asian theatre, Marxist dialectical philosophy (specifically ideas about contradictions being what moves history forward) and by quite mechanical concepts about human psychology (such as specific 'stimuli' automatically creating specific 'responses' in our consciousness). Moreover, Lev Kuleshov, the head of the world's first proper film school, had conducted certain famous experiments about how people interpreted the same picture differently according to which other pictures it was presented with. On this basis Eisenstein thought, among other things, that putting together two sequences with radically different subject matter, content and moral value would create a third, connecting and preferably revolutionary idea or insight in people's heads; thus an intelligent film-maker could beat revolutionary messages into people. This view seems quite debatable today. Advertising executives and Hollywood directors alike have long since made use of the aesthetic techniques in which Shklovsky and Eisenstein saw such consciousness-altering possibilities. They are obviously well suited to attracting attention and to providing strong experiences and impressions, but they do not necessarily, in and of themselves, offer any new insight into important issues. On the contrary, one may assume that they more often *confirm* commonly held perceptions.

In art circles there is often talk about the potential for art to influence people and the world by virtue of how texts or works are constructed or put together. Conversely it has been maintained, directly or indirectly, that people are made stupid and/or conservative by reading conventional stories and seeing conventional films. Some of the most solid reasons for this type of opinion emanated from the so-called Frankfurt School – a milieu of critical philosophers, social scientists and art scholars, located at the *Institut für Socialforschung* (Institute of Social Research), founded in 1930 in Frankfurt am Main. Their work is often referred to as 'critical theory'. In 1944, while they were living as refugees in Los Angeles, two of the leading figures, Theodor W. Adorno and Max Horkheimer, wrote the *Dialectic of Enlightenment*, (first published 1947) wherein the famous essay 'The culture industry' was included. One of its main points was that the mechanically *standardized* aspect of, primarily, the *form* of the products of the culture industry entailed a corresponding standardization of the ways in which audiences think and live. The culture industry promotes *conformity* – adjustment to the ruling social system and its norms. Adorno and Horkheimer thought that it made leisure time as mechanical as work on a conveyor belt. Their energetic argument may well lead us to reflect on the long-term effects of exclusively listening to short ditties in four-four time, seeing only a few kinds of quite simple film or viewing only 25-minute TV sitcoms, generally cut from the same cloth.

In the 1960s and 1970s the lines of thought presented in the writings of Adorno and Horkheimer became widespread among critical intellectuals. These thoughts were combined with insights into cultural analysis taken from structural anthropology, primarily from Claude Lévi-Strauss (1966) and the emerging structuralist (i.e. semiotic) textual theory. The idea was that culture industry commodities correspond to the *myths* of simpler societies, that they are stories and concepts that conceal basic conflicts and deliver untenable justifications for the power structure in society (Barthes [1957] 1975). As the 1960s/1970s was also a period when interest in Marxist social theory flourished once again, the anthropological concept of myth was more or less incorporated into the Marxist concept of *ideology* – the (false) ruling ideas that serve the interests of the ruling class. One last important element in this theoretical brew was *psychoanalysis*, which, with its distinction between overt expression and underlying causes, held a related kind of logic (see Chapter 5 of the present volume, on hermeneutics).

All of these elements became the basis for a broad movement in the humanities and some social sciences, commonly referred to as the *critique of ideology*. It did not as a rule work from a simplistic idea about the ability of a single media text to mechanically affect human behaviour. The main objective was to show how texts – from the culture industry in particular, but also in high art – contributed to the continuing reproduction and reinstallation in the public mind of some fundamental forms of understanding that were in conflict with the 'real' interests of the majority. We find a very closely related perspective in film studies of the 1970s and 1980s wherein a special mixture of Marxist, psychoanalytic and semiotic theory (note the absence of the Frankfurt School) held a dominant position. It was called *Screen theory* (from the British journal, *Screen*) or psycho-semiotic film theory. Work in this field was often about how Hollywood films in more or less covert ways contribute to turning each member of the audience into a socially well-adjusted individual, ideologically speaking. These often refined analyses also pointed out how Hollywood movies can contain and handle important contradictions. They broaden our insight into what goes on when we watch a film, and they make us aware of how deeply engrained are the ideological perceptions of such things as what is 'male' and what is 'female' (cf. Mulvey, 1975). Importantly, the theory and the analyses, in line with the general discourse on ideology, took as a point of departure that film works in accordance with what other media and social institutions – school, church, family, and so on – convey. Using a term that stems from the work of French Marxist philosopher Louis Althusser, film studies was well aware that film is not the only *ideological apparatus*. Althusser defined an ideological apparatus as a social institution that addresses us as individuals or subjects, and presents certain ideas about the world and our place in it by way of material structures, 'rituals and practices' (Althusser, 1971). One might think of school, the construction of classrooms and the rituals of the everyday there; but one could also think of the various mass media. They address us as individuals, present certain ideas and perspectives on the world and suggest certain ways in which we should relate to them, use or enjoy them.

The critique of ideology was consequently not about the effects of the media in a simple, mechanical sense – it was about how the media *contribute to the constant reproduction of dominant ways of thinking and prevailing social conditions*. The media are not without power; they do influence or affect us but, first and foremost, by confirming the status quo. This is a very sensible idea; but a few somewhat simplistic contributions to the discourse on ideology seem to maintain that social order would collapse if most people saw other types of film or read other kinds of books. It sometimes feels as though those who are concerned with the influence of the media or the arts exaggerate out of a more or less unconscious wish to portray what they themselves are working on as particularly important to the well-being of humanity. In some instances, and in more banal forms especially, one may also find that the belief in the media's power to influence is related to a deep distrust of, and even contempt for, popular media's audiences: 'Is it any wonder that people live meaningless lives when they read such things?' one Norwegian student asked in an exam essay on popular literature, possibly hoping (in vain) that this attitude would improve his grades.

These critical comments *do not* mean that language, literature, film, visual arts and television are more or less insignificant. They are obviously, as shown in the previous chapter on identity, very important to how we see ourselves and the rest of the world. However, the point is that *their influence on each of us, on groups and society as a whole, is determined by social and cultural conditions that to a large extent are outside the realm of the media and outside the immediate reception of the media's texts, sounds and pictures*. One must take into consideration the total media output and consumption, as well as a long list of social, cultural and psychological conditions. This insight has gradually come to characterize research on media audiences and the media's 'effects' on them.

Old and new research about 'effects', and current debates about violence

Systematic research on the 'effects' of modern mass media was, significantly, first initiated as part of the 'media panic' (see below) that broke out when movie theatres grew explosively in number all over the western world after 1905. It was often organized or conducted by teachers, church groups or other concerned citizens in the USA, UK and other countries. The first Norwegian research about the effect of the media was conducted by the Teachers' Guild in Stavanger, the city where I was born, and since it is typical of these early efforts I will use it as an example.

In December 1910 the Teachers' Guild sent out a questionnaire to all primary school teachers in the city, asking them to investigate how often their students went to the cinema and what such visits led to. It was discovered that most of the children, and everyone in the higher forms, had been to the cinema during the year. Children of poor parents went most often – among other things they had their own income from incidental jobs that they could use for this purpose. It seemed as if the damage was vast and serious. Morality, in particular, suffered. The telling indicator was that all of those children who ended up in the city's reformatory had been eager film-goers. It was also confirmed that moving pictures had inspired various crimes, from the theft of empty bottles for the purpose of obtaining ticket money to more serious offences. In addition, the cinema made the students restless and difficult to engage in anything that was not cinema-like, such as schoolwork; attention difficulties might result in reduced reading and writing ability. By thoroughly examining ten of these eager film-goers a school physician ascertained several eye injuries, some perhaps lasting (see Dahl *et al.*, 1996: 55, 71).

Much of what the above illustrates has been a recurring theme in research about media 'effects' right up to the present time. Both research and debate have generally centred on the visual media of film, comics and TV, but there have also been warnings against crime fiction, jazz music and westerns. Sometimes the reactions to new media are so strong that the term *media panic* has been used. The English researcher Stanley Cohen introduced the concept of *moral panic* in his book *Folk Devils and Moral Panics* (1972). He examined how the media in the 1960s, through its coverage, contributed to the confrontations between the youth groups *mods* and *rockers*, and also created more vague anxieties and corresponding demands to the effect that 'something must be done'. Lately, in discussions related to 'video violence', the media have similarly contributed to an atmosphere of 'panic', for which there is little real basis.

It is striking that in the Stavanger teachers' investigation of 1910 no attention was paid to what kinds of social conditions made the children of the poor think film experiences were so important. It was automatically assumed that the films were the *cause* of many children landing up in reform school, but no attention was paid, for instance, to the fact that drink and poverty at home might drive children both to the cinema as well as to a life of crime – that is, that the two factors, believed to be related, had a common, underlying cause. Similar limitations in perspective and reasoning were found when video recorders arrived around 1980. At that time, one might have found, for instance, a newspaper report on an investigation which purported to show that those who watched a lot of videos, had, among other things, poorer teeth than those who watched fewer or none at all. The opinion would almost make it seem as if videos were the cause of the problem, rather than diet or oral hygiene. The fact that social conditions might explain high video consumption as well as bad diet and lack of dental hygiene, was not mentioned as a possibility, at least not in the newspaper.

Many people were, and still are, worried about the negative impact that violent movies might have on the next generation. This is a reasonable enough human sentiment if one really cares about one's own children as well as those of others, and has a strong dislike for real violence. But if the issue is to be seriously discussed, it is probably useful first to note that the broad term *violent movie* does not make any distinction between different genres. The term may include Shakespeare plays adapted to film, historical war movies, cartoons, westerns and horror movies. The notion of violent movies not only disregards such crucial differentiations, it also *violates the status of each individual movie as a meaningful whole*. The concept leads the attention away from the fact that all the elements in a film, as in all other texts or works of art, obtain their significance in light of the *context* in which they appear, including the genre to which the film or text belongs. 'Violent movie' is therefore a useless phrase for those who realize that films and other texts are cultural products that demand some kind of *understanding* (see Chapter 5, on hermeneutics). 'Violent movie' is an expression that is only relevant to so-called *quantitative content analysis*, which breaks singular texts into separate elements – be they violent incidents or sexual caresses – that are then counted across large numbers of texts, producing results such as the average number of violent acts in all movies screened on television last year. This tells us little about the meanings of any of these instances of violence, and hence also little about what they convey in terms of attitudes to violence.

In public debate it is often automatically assumed that those who see violent acts in film or television will themselves commit them – almost regardless of other circumstances. Teachers, journalists and politicians have been among those most concerned. Today's media researchers, on the other hand, are generally more careful not to say anything definitive about the 'effects' of watching videos, films etc. with strongly violent elements. They have rather warned against blaming the media for violence at home, at school and in the streets of major cities. They have at times been criticized by politicians for this and accused of being 'irresponsible'. Media researchers, though, have good reason to be cautious. Because the debate about violence understandably interests so many people, we will take a look at some aspects of the research in this special field before proceeding to more general research about the media's power over their audiences.

One type of research that has been conducted by (social) psychologists in particular, is the *laboratory experiment* wherein one group of children or students sees portions of film with violent elements while another group does not see them. The behaviour of both groups is subsequently observed in various pre-arranged situations, and the researcher then counts and classifies the 'aggressive' or 'violent' actions that occur. Two types of theory – or, rather, hypotheses – are most common to such research. First, the *stimulation theory*, as it is called, claims that to see violence performed in the visual media 'leads to an aggressive excitement that results in aggressive actions' (Ulvær, 1984: 105). The other hypothesis, often called *imitation theory* or *learning theory*, claims that the viewers – children in particular – *learn* and *imitate* violent behaviour patterns from the characters in films or TV programmes. Experiments conducted in the 1950s by Albert Bandura and his associates are especially well known. For instance, they showed some groups of children a 5-foot inflatable doll being beaten with a bat, in part on film, in part in reality. The doll straightened out after every blow. Other groups were spared this sight. Afterwards Bandura irritated all the children by taking away toys they were playing with, and then he let them into another room with other toys – among them a bat and an inflatable doll like the one the children had seen being beaten. Bandura found that those children who had seen the violent scenes behaved more aggressively than the others – they slapped away at the doll with the bat.

In this way one might (like Bandura) think it had been proven that children become more violent from seeing violent scenes. But it is not that simple. An amusing illustration of how many uncertainties are present in such research comes from a 4-year-old girl who was shown the laboratory for the first time: 'Look, Mom, there's the doll we have to hit!' (Noble, 1975: 134). The intention to produce a situation where all factors are as carefully controlled as experiments in physics or chemistry often falls flat because these are living and intelligent human beings who, for example, understand the purpose of the set-up in spite of attempts to conceal it. One might also wonder about the duration of a possible 'aggressive excitement' or 'model learning' of this type. Broadly speaking, in laboratories only the immediate situation has been studied. Also, a laboratory is something very different from an everyday situation, say, at home in the living room. It is simply an artificial situation wherein it is difficult to discover how things function elsewhere. Besides, not all laboratory research points in the same direction as Bandura's – others have arrived at different results (see Noble, 1975, which also contains a very good discussion and overview of the research carried out until the mid-1970s).

Other types of research have been conducted closer to a natural everyday environment, through observation, questionnaires, interviews and so on. But in these cases it is obviously considerably more difficult to control whether it is the film or TV programme that makes the research subjects (usually children and young people) aggressive. Many studies seem to indicate that children who are already aggressive become *more aggressive* from seeing violent sequences, while more peaceful children are not affected. But what, then, is the cause of the aggressive behaviour? Is it related to hormones? Is it learned somewhere other than in front of the screen? Would the aggressive children also have become more aggressive as the result of watching a Formula 1 race or riding on a roller-coaster? And how long does the 'effect' last?

There is also some interesting research which indicates that it may actually be *healthy* to see movies and TV programmes with violent scenes. This is often referred to as the *catharsis* theory. The word catharsis, as mentioned in the previous chapter, originates from Greek and means 'purification'. It was used by Aristotle to describe the effect the tragedies of antiquity had (or were supposed to have) on their audiences. The catharsis theory is based on a model of explanation taken from psychoanalysis, wherein it is supposed that aggression finds an outlet through empathy with fiction containing more or less aggressive sequences. Feschbach and Singer (1971) performed a large field study of 625 young boys who lived in three schools for middle-class boys and four homes for boys with special needs. The boys in each school were randomly placed in two groups. One group was allowed to watch only TV programmes with violent sequences for 6 consecutive weeks, for a minimum of 6 hours per week; the other group watched only programmes without violence for the same amount of time. The boys went through personality and attitude tests before and after this period, during which the teacher and others who knew them systematically evaluated their behaviour every day. The investigations, generally speaking, showed mostly insignificant differences between the groups that watched 'violent' and 'non-violent' programmes. There was one important exception: in the four institutions for boys with special needs – primarily youths from a working-class background – it was found that those who watched exclusively non-violent programmes became more violent towards their friends (but not towards the teachers). They pushed each other more, fought more often, yelled and shouted more aggressively to each other, and more often broke their friends' things than the boys in the group watching the violent television menu. This clearly points in the direction that, for these boys, watching programmes with a violent content was a way of controlling aggression, by more or less 'purifying' them from such impulses.

Research about film and television violence has been conducted in a number of ways, and in many countries, throughout the twentieth century. So-called *longitudinal* studies have been conducted too; these are long-term studies of the same individuals from childhood to adulthood. Surveys of young people's use of media have been compared to their degree of participation in violent acts. A majority of studies seem to indicate that at least *some people* are influenced in a violent direction by violent sequences on film and TV, but there are also results that do not indicate this. Surprisingly few, but often very good studies, have looked at the effects of *different types* of film with a violent content. Grant Noble, for example, found that documentary and more realistic violent scenes made 6 year olds more anxious, and that it limited their play; while films with more stylized and distanced violent sequences (such as westerns) on the contrary had a positively stimulating effect on the children's play (Noble, 1973). Regardless of this, the methodological problems are so immense that it is difficult to arrive at indisputably certain conclusions regarding the *general* effects of watching violent sequences on film or TV.

For most of us it is probably true that we have seen enormous amounts of violence in the visual media, in everything from news broadcasts to cartoons, from boxing matches to action and horror movies. We have nevertheless not become particularly aggressive. *It is very difficult to influence someone into doing something that runs contrary to his or her deep-seated norms and convictions.* Influencing someone into buying a certain kind of marmalade or trousers – the typical task of advertising – is quite different. This does not mean that *some people* in *certain situations* may not become more aggressive or violent. It is also difficult to say whether or not someone *in the long run* becomes more violent from all the violence they see than they would have become otherwise. Although research cannot ascertain it with 100 per cent accuracy, it may well be unhealthy to see large numbers of very violent films week after week, month after month, year after year. Children, as well as others, may also become anxious, have nightmares and suffer from other related ailments. However, the question remains as to whether all the attention given to 'video violence', for example, reasonably corresponds to the role it really plays as the cause of real violent acts. Compared to the difficult, complex social and psychological conditions at the root of real violence, it is considerably *easier* to point to the media and certain fiction genres with a low social status as the culprit. Most often these media and genres have until recently lacked public defenders. It is worth pointing out that there is no research being conducted about how aggressive one becomes from fine literature, ambitious art films or stage plays with violent sequences. These types of media are certainly less widely distributed than popular films or television programmes, but studying them and their audiences might obviously shed some light on the question of whether violent content in the media *in and of itself* changes attitudes and behaviour. It is not simply breezy polemics to point out that the most widely read book of all, the Bible, is full of strongly violent episodes and other sequences that create aggressive behaviour, and that no one has systematically studied to what extent reading it has led to aggressive or self-destructive behaviour. The fact is that cultural and social conditions also mark this kind of research. It is no coincidence that many researchers, with higher education and from a middle-class background, have not found it worth their time to distinguish between genres or particular texts within the area of popular culture they have studied. Censoring popular film and TV is easier than censoring art or the Bible, and much easier than doing something really effective about all the complicated social and psychological conditions that are involved in the issue.

On the basis of all this it would be reasonable to say that a balance ought to be struck between two principles: on the one hand the *better safe than sorry* principle, which advocates caution because it is not *known* with certainty whether or not violent media texts may be harmful in some form or another; on the other hand, the *freedom of speech* principle, which makes it difficult to curtail or forbid certain expressions, artful or not. By, for example, establishing and enforcing *age limits*, an approximation of balance is achieved between the two. Censorship or total prohibition for all audience groups, on the contrary, are much more debatable efforts.

The simple story of research into the power of the media

We will now take a closer look at some of the main features of more general research about the possible influence relationship between the media and the public. What may be termed 'the introductory course story about media research's perception of the power of the media', traditionally has three chapters. The first is called 'Almighty media' and refers to the time until approximately 1940. During this time media researchers thought that the media could inject values, attitudes and ways of thinking and behaving directly into the heads of the defenceless public. The term *hypodermic needle theories* is often used in this connection, and sometimes the term *effect theories*. Many media researchers in this period thought that clever devices used by the media could make people do almost anything.

The second chapter is called 'Powerless media' and is about the period from the 1940s until about 1970. During this period the prevailing opinion was that the media could not have much of an influence on people unless it played into what people already thought, especially if they did not combine forces with local 'opinion leaders' in the immediate environment of audiences. The so-called *two step flow of communication hypothesis* (Lazarsfeld *et al.* [1968] 1988), wherein the media's influence is supposedly transmitted via local opinion leaders, was based on a study of how people decided how they were going to vote in the US presidential election in 1940. This hypothesis proved to be important to a type of research about the relation between the media and the public called *uses and gratifications research.* Here the main issue for research was not 'What do the media do with audiences?' but rather 'What do audiences do with the media?' The audience was seen as composed of independently thinking and acting individuals who used the media to satisfy their need for information, entertainment, self-realization, and social belonging or identity.

The third and final chapter is, logically enough, a reasonable synthesis of the previous two quite opposite views, headlined 'Mighty media'. The turning point came in the early 1970s as a result of, among other things, an investigation of the role of the media during an election campaign in the USA. It was shown – in line with what Walter Lippman ([1922] 1997) and others had written as early as the 1920s – that the media did not so much determine *what* people were thinking but they had a definite influence on what people were thinking *about* (McCombs and Shaw, 1972). The concept of the *agenda-setting function* was coined in the report from this study, but the point was also known from earlier studies (such as Trenaman and McQuail, 1961). The agenda-setting function implies that the media exercise a highly important form of political power that politicians and certain pressure groups know how to take advantage of.

Another example of the new direction in media research are the American scholar George Gerbner's extensive studies of the *long-term effects* of watching television. Gerbner and his associates made a thorough count of content elements in TV programmes, factual as well as fictional, and found that TV, in the USA, gave a rather skewed view of reality. They compared this with the results of a questionnaire about people's views of the world. They then found that those who watched TV the most had, for example, a tendency to overrate the extent of crime and violence in society. This idea of media's influencing the understanding of reality over a period of time is called *cultivation theory* (Gerbner, 1973). It is more nuanced than simpler, older influence theories and is less about becoming violent from watching a lot of news and fiction violence than about becoming anxious because of it. It has also been pointed out, however, that many of those who watch TV the most live in poor areas where there is, in fact, considerably more real violence than elsewhere. These studies also have other methodological problems, but cultivation theory remains an interesting hypothesis that it is difficult to falsify (dismiss) or to verify (confirm). Similar investigations in other countries have not produced the same results, perhaps quite simply because television programmes there have been differently put together.

Within the social sciences a more focused approach to issues of power and lines of social conflict, generally speaking, became important to a renewed interest in the power of the media. Simultaneously, critiques of the history of research in the area, and a number of other insights, made it clear that questions about the 'effects' of the media are highly complicated.

Background: mechanical psychology and the theory of mass society

The story of the simple introductory course may lead many to believe that media researchers were terribly wrong, up until the last two decades. This is not necessarily the case. There has always been research with other methods and results than the mainstream tendencies presented above. Uses and gratifications research originated before 1940 and is still conducted in various forms. The above-mentioned laboratory experiments about violence are examples of the continued presence of injection theory thinking.

When evaluating how correct or incorrect the injection theory proponents of the inter-war period may have been in their thinking, one should remember that it is difficult to ascertain how strongly the media may have influenced people 60, 70 or 80 years ago. Several historical sources indicate that people were less blasé regarding strong media impressions during the inter-war period, so that they were, for example, more easily moved emotionally by black and white film with poor sound than we are. The inter-war period was the heyday of direct propaganda, particularly in the Soviet Union and Germany, but also in many other countries. In the planning for its 1930s election campaigns, the Norwegian Labour Party openly learned a lesson from the German propaganda minister Goebbels, who, it was said, was the most intelligent of all the Nazi leaders (see Gripsrud, 1981, Chapter 14). To us, Hitler appears a screaming madman, but for most Germans in the 1930s he was obviously very moving and inspiring. Consequently, it can be seen that human emotions, assessments and psyches in general are historically changeable entities.

During the inter-war years, mainstream research used a mechanical *stimulus-response model* as a basis for its conception of the power of the media. This was related to what was considered the most advanced contemporary research in psychology. Russian researcher Ivan Pavlov's experiments with conditioning are a well-known example of such research. He served food to his laboratory dogs after having rung a bell and, after a while, the dogs began to salivate as soon as the bell rang, whether there was food or not. It was thought that a corresponding unconscious 'incarnation' of reactions to certain stimuli would also be possible in human beings. If cinema-goers see irritating persons shot dead often enough, one might think, as did Albert Bandura, that they would carry over such reactions into everyday life.

This type of thinking has survived in psychology in various forms of so-called behaviourist therapy, in laboratory experiments such as those mentioned above and in various experiments with (and including attempts at) so-called *subliminal influence*, particularly in advertising. The idea in the latter is that the brain registers things of which we are not conscious, and the unconscious impressions might then direct our behaviour. A film might include a lightning-fast encouragement to buy a soft drink, or a TV ad for the drink could include extremely brief sexually appealing shots so that we, without knowing why, are filled with an enormous desire for the soft drink when we see it at the supermarket. Although such effects still have no real basis in bona fide research, their use was still attempted by a well-known manufacturer of sports shoes and clothing in TV spots before the 1998 world soccer championship.

Stimulus-response psychology was one of the general sources of inspiration for the simple 'effect' way of thinking. Another is called *mass society theory*, which is related to theories of the *social psychology of the masses*. These were attempts to understand the particular traits of modern society and the mentality of its people. The transition from agricultural, rural societies to industrial, urban ones has, since the middle of the nineteenth century, been a main theme of sociological thought and empirical research. Industrialization and urbanization involved a transition from stable and close human relations in villages and rural communities to great conglomerations of people in cities who were thought to have been deprived of stable norms and close ties to neighbours and other fellow beings. The German sociologist Ferdinand Tönnies created still important concepts by labelling this a transition from *Gemeinschaft* to *Gesellschaft*, from community to society. According to mass society theory, individuals in the big cities – particularly those of the lower classes, of course – were regarded as 'atoms', easy to move with different forms of demagogy. These individuals might suddenly gather and begin to act precisely like a mass, in which individuals would act in unison out of some sort of herd instinct. The absence of a solid system of norms based on traditions might lead them to do terrible things. Masses everywhere are characterized by feminine traits according to the French physician and sociologist, Gustave LeBon, who in 1895 published an influential book on mass psychology, claiming that the masses easily move into 'emotional extremism' (LeBon [1895] 1981).

The concept of 'masses' is a metaphor that is telling in terms of how social elites regarded the rest of the population. A mass is something that may swamp and drown you; on the other hand it may be fenced in, shaped and controlled. Social masses may be shaped by propaganda, and controlled by the police and the military. In the first Norwegian novel with a clearly revolutionary message, Per Sivle's *Streik* (*Strike*), published in 1891, there is a famous metaphorical sequence wherein the workers are implicitly likened to pieces of gravel that suddenly gather together and fly through the air against their oppressors. Right up until the present time, radical and revolutionary intellectuals all over the world have also used the concept of the 'masses', and they have been quite preoccupied with shaping them, and setting them in motion through propaganda and agitation. This tells us something about how a certain relationship between leadership or elite on the one hand and the nameless masses of people on the other is inherent in certain types of political theory.

The ideas about the masses are part of the political and cultural history of the entire twentieth century. It is consequently no wonder that these have also influenced media research and concepts about the power of the media. In the powerful collective movements of the inter-war years, on the political left and right, the 'masses' were strongly and openly celebrated and choreographed in huge political rallies, theatre performances with 'movement choirs' and 'speech choirs', sports events, mass gymnastics and so on. The fascination with large numbers of people gathered with one purpose in mind is still to be found in demonstrations, parades, marathons and soccer games. We may see this as a reminder that the theoreticians were not necessarily out in left field, at least not all the time. It is obvious that the transition from relatively stable and tight peasant community to more mobile and distanced city community – from *Gemeinschaft* to *Gesellschaft* – represented a fundamental social change with far-reaching consequences in many areas. In this book there will be many references to this transition and other aspects of what is known as social *modernization* – as was the case in the previous chapter, on media and identity.

Pre-1940: more than 'injection research'

Returning to media research prior to 1940 we may begin to gain a more diverse impression than that of a one-sided focus on the 'almighty media' and their 'injections' into defenceless heads. Although studies like that carried out by the Stavanger teachers prevailed internationally, other kinds of work were also being done.

In 1914 young Emilie Altenloh presented her doctoral thesis in Heidelberg, Germany. It was empirically based on the statistics of cinema owners and 2400 questionnaires distributed in Mannheim and Heidelberg. The questionnaire gave respondents the opportunity to say in their own words what kinds of films they preferred and why. Altenloh's investigation is in many ways still very interesting. First, she considers the entire film business – from production and distribution to experiences in the cinema itself. Second, she compares films to other cultural presentations and asks people what interests them about those. Third, she places films and the strong interest in them in the historical context of the modernization process. Last but not least, she examines how profession/class background and gender in particular influence genre preferences and experiences. Precisely because she was not primarily interested in film's influence on morality, she gives a fascinating and many-sided picture of what the movies *meant to the public*. She found, for example, that while men's tastes varied quite a lot according to social group, women's were strikingly similar regardless of background. The women even had a tendency to prefer the same kinds of documentary sequence – pictures of waterfalls, ocean waves and drifting ice floes. Things had to be flowing and moving – somehow metaphorically connected to the fact that their tastes in fiction were for romantic melodrama (Altenloh, 1914; Gripsrud, 1998).

In the 1920s several studies were published, in the USA and other countries, which showed that the film medium could not have such hugely far-reaching effects as many worried and furious anti-film activists thought it could. But these studies had relatively little influence on the public debate. During this decade social science methods were refined in various ways, through the flourishing of market studies, among other things, in step with the emergence of the consumer society.

In 1929, through the initiative of a parson, a gigantic research project was started about the impact of film. It came to mark a new step in the development of media research, perhaps also for social science research in general. The project – the Payne Fund Studies – took its name from the private charity fund that financed it. The data was gathered from 1929–32 and, from 1933 onwards, 12 books were published containing the results. A journalist, hired by the project directors, wrote a popular science summary entitled *Our Movie Made Children* (1933). It had great impact on the public debate about the moral effects of Hollywood films, which in the summer of 1934 resulted in the detailed rules of decency in film (the Production Code) finally being ruthlessly enforced. In reality, the Payne Fund Studies were considerably more varied in their conclusions than the journalist's summary had implied. The popularized version was an expression of the employers' intentions, intentions they even attempted to force on the researchers. They tried to directly interfere with the researchers' conclusions.

Many of the studies showed that film 'influenced' children's play, that young people learned ideas about how to relate to the opposite sex, about what modern dress and customs looked like. They showed that children's perceptions of Chinese people, African-Americans, war and criminal behaviour could be affected by films that presented either a positive or negative picture of the phenomena in question. It is important to note that the children who were being researched, in small towns around Chicago, had barely seen or experienced any of the phenomena of which their perceptions were changed. But as far as influence on immorality and criminal attitudes was concerned, the results were, in 1938, summarized as follows by one of the participating researchers, sociologist Paul G. Cressey (1938: 518):

> 'Going to the movies' is a unified experience involving always a specific film, a specific personality, a specific social situation and a specific time and mood; therefore, any programme of research which does not recognize all essential phases of the motion picture experience can offer little more than conjecture as to the cinema's net 'effect' in actual settings and communities.

These insights are still highly valid. But, as we have seen, they hardly influenced research practices in the first few decades after they were formulated.

The Payne Fund Studies were also diverse and varied with respect to methods or procedures in research. Two of the most interesting studies present the material, so to speak, in the raw. They are primarily based on, and quote at length, so-called movie biographies, written by 1500 young people in one case and hundreds of young criminals or 'problem youths' in another (Blumer, 1933; Blumer and Hauser, 1933). Here one finds young people's own unostentatious and in part very entertaining depictions of their own relationship to the cinema and movies, their thoughts on how movies have affected them and so on. In terms of methodology this use of a 'soft', qualitative method (as opposed to quantitative survey methodology) perhaps points towards current media research. But the Payne Fund Studies also developed advanced techniques in everything from measuring attitude to laboratory experiments wherein the electric tension in the palms of the hands of the movie viewers was measured (see also Gripsrud, 1998).

Another example of an investigation that ran counter to the 'injection theory' is Herta Herzog's (1941) classical study of American women's relations to radio soap operas, still one of the most interesting contributions in the field. Instead of questionnaires with predetermined answer choices, Herzog used a more flexible form of interview with so-called 'open' questions, where those who are being studied are, as much as possible, allowed to speak for themselves. With such methods it becomes clearer that the use of media takes place in the many-faceted lives of concrete human beings in ways that make simple conclusions about 'effects' considerably more difficult to formulate.

In traditional research history, however, it is a far more comprehensive study of the formation of political opinion that has been seen as a major turning point in thinking about the ability of the media to influence us.

Developments after 1940: the two-step hypotheses, and uses and gratifications research

We have already touched on the book by Paul F. Lazarsfeld *et al.*, *The People's Choice: How the Voter Makes Up His Mind in a Presidential Election Campaign* ([1944] 1968); it was based on a large research project that Austrian-born Lazarsfeld and his associates conducted in Erie County, Ohio, in connection with the presidential election in 1940. The project involved a representative sample of as many as 3000 people and attempted to discover which factors determined people's votes. Quite a way into the work it was discovered, however, that there was an important factor the design of the study had not considered: people *talked with each other* quite a lot about the different elements of the election campaign and its coverage in the media. Researchers then thought they could see that ideas and information went from radio and print media to local 'opinion leaders' and then, from those, to 'less active segments of the population'. This discovery of the importance of people's talking with one another, and the role of the opinion leaders, meant that mass society theory with its image of atomized individuals required revision, and that the same was true of the 'injection theory' regarding media influence.

This unexpected discovery was the point of departure for a study by Lazarsfeld and his young associate Elihu Katz, conducted during the summer of 1945. It involved 800 women in the small town of Decatur, Illinois, and the question was how they related to 'media messages' in four areas of everyday life where they had to make decisions: shopping (daily provisions), fashion, public affairs and cinema-going. The main focus was precisely on small, tightly knit communities (primary groups) and how these related to the mass media messages in the mentioned areas. The book, entitled *Personal Influence: The Part Played by People in the Flow of Mass Communication* (Katz and Lazarsfeld, 1955), in which the results were presented explained how different people behaved as opinion leaders in different areas (in the field of public affairs, for instance, they were almost never women). The book was also a contribution to small-group sociology in general. The study of smaller groups was quite fashionable in the 1940s and 1950s, and a foundation was established for a whole tradition that, in later years, has flourished in studies of the sociology of everyday life – and media use. The main point was that the two-step hypothesis was confirmed. Media influence was not only dependent on the form and content of the message, and not only on each individual's personality and mental capacity. Henceforth it could not be understood independently of local social relations between the individual members of the audience.

But these conclusions were not without problems. The Katz and Lazarsfeld study presupposed that 'power' or 'influence' is something that takes place on certain, limited occasions. Media's long-term, structurally determined power or influence could not be captured in such a study. Also, media influence was defined as 'measurable change of behaviour or attitude', thereby excluding the media's possible *confirmation of the status quo* from the categories of 'influence' or 'effect' (Gitlin, 1978). This is particularly problematic for those who assume that precisely presenting the dominant interpretations of the world, and thereby contributing to harmony, peace and quiet in society, is perhaps the most important function of the media.

The simplest and most effective objection to Katz and Lazarsfeld's reduction of media power to a minimum is the following: what happens in situations wherein both the public and the so-called opinion leaders *have no other sources than the media when forming an opinion about something?* (See also the Payne Fund Studies, above, on the effect of movies on children's perceptions in areas where personal experience was lacking.) In his article, Todd Gitlin used the so-called Cuban crisis in 1962 as an example. At that time there was hardly anyone in small-town America who knew anything about Cuba. In order to form an opinion, every single opinion leader was therefore as dependent as everyone else on what the media could convey. In such a situation the media defines the world. A closer example for us is the Gulf war wherein the US military, based on experiences in Vietnam, had learned to carefully control what the media should convey about what was going on. Although there are opinion leaders, the media has the upper hand in such situations (except when, for example, the Pentagon, as again was the case during the Gulf war, quite directly rules the media).

There is, then, also a somewhat naive optimism in the two-step hypothesis: People live in close proximity in societies where wise neighbours filter the media's messages for them. People think for themselves, at least millions of opinion leaders do. This optimism also exists within the type of research that became dominant from the late 1950s onwards, called *uses and gratifications research*. Here the main question is, as mentioned above, more about what people do with the media than the other way around. This view was in part related to the discovery that direct media impact was more modest than presumed earlier, and also in part to the realization that the function of the media had to be studied in a larger context, seen in light of people's everyday lives. But what perhaps primarily characterizes uses and gratifications research is a certain, relatively simplistic, implied psychological view. An important source of inspiration was the social psychologist Maslow's so-called 'hierarchy of needs', a theory about human beings first satisfying certain basic needs for food etc., and only then, on a 'higher' level, worrying about things such as self-realization and social contact. Researchers attempted, primarily with the help of survey methodologies, to discover which needs people sought to satisfy with the use of media. As mentioned above, it was found that a need for information, a need for social belonging (identity) and self-realization were reasons to choose different types of media and media content.

Using the concept of *need* in this way is problematic for at least two reasons – needs are conceptualized as historically stable and attention is only paid to *individual, psychological* needs (Elliott, 1974). One may also say that there is a somewhat naive optimism in the presumption that people really know their needs and seek to satisfy them with conscious, purposeful behaviour when faced with what the media offer. It was in other words presumed that people have a full overview of their psyches and full control over *what* they read, listen to or watch – and *why*. There may be reason to point out that this sort of belief in individual, totally free choice in a sort of 'media supermarket' is not only somewhat naive, it also has certain ideological overtones that were quite important in the Cold War situation in which this particular way of thinking originated, and it is now recognizable as a fundamental element in liberalist belief in the blessings of a 'free' market. This image of audiences' relationship to the media is present every day in all the talk that goes on about *ratings*. People freely choose how to satisfy their needs; the media must only give people what they want – and of course we all know exactly what we want.

But there are reasons to doubt and modify this view of audiences as sovereign rulers. First of all the disregarded fact is that we can only choose between offerings that the media have decided for us. We cannot choose what is not available. Perhaps there are needs that cannot be satisfied by what is currently offered; perhaps one could imagine that certain needs would be *better* satisfied by programmes or texts other than the existing ones. Equally important to a critique of uses and gratifications research, however, is the fact that people also have an unconscious dimension to their psyches and quite often act irrationally or in ways that are difficult to justify. It has been claimed that the so-called 'sixty-eighters', i.e. the generation to whom the tumultuous year 1968 holds special significance, have 'a life full of good reasons' (Nielsen, 1984: 13), since they have had to politically legitimate anything from their choice of underwear to their preferences in entertainment or holidays. But not even this particular generation can explain and provide the reason for everything they do, dislike or want. While I was writing my book on the US soap opera *Dynasty*, I often met highly educated people who more or less secretly had followed the series, and who were unable to give a good explanation for the fascination they felt. In uses and gratifications research there is a tendency to pose questions that the researchers themselves perhaps would not be able to answer in a clear and convincing way.

The primary merit of this research tradition, in terms of shedding light on the question of influence, is however that it simply grants people a modicum of reason, independence and authority, even though this confidence may be carried a little further than warranted. In principle it cannot consider the existence of influences of which the research subjects themselves are not consciously aware – and willing to talk about to researchers. Neither is the approach well suited to illuminating broader power conditions in the area of the media, because it has a tendency to overlook larger social structures or shared, collective conditions. Uses and gratifications studies have nevertheless produced (and still produce) much useful, basic information about the population's use of the media.

In the 1970s, then, the foundation for new kinds of media and audience research was created. In part it absorbed older traditions (often unconsciously), and in part it brought something entirely new into the picture: stronger attention to the media texts (the programmes, the films and so on) and what these mean in terms of what kind of *meaning* people get from them. In was in this phase that humanist and social sciences research began to overlap and merge.

The controversy over positivism and social science media research

In order to understand what went on in international media research in the 1970s, it is necessary to know a little about the situation in society in general and in the universities in particular, from the middle of the 1960s onwards. It was a time of strong radical and clearly Marxist-inspired currents among young and not-so-young people, particularly students and young researchers.

Centred in Germany, a heated debate started in the late 1950s about the organization and methods of social science research; it was known as *the controversy over positivism*. To put it briefly, it was a settling of accounts with the uncritical idealization of the natural sciences as a model for all scientific research. Critics of the then reigning types of social research were of the opinion that the objectivity that was being cultivated was, in reality, false. It was tied to the emphasis on quantitative methods that provided research results in the form of statistical correlation and tables, wherein the conclusions appeared to be practically untouched by the researchers' hands, just as in physics or other natural sciences. As the Norwegian philosopher Hans Skjervheim convincingly argued in the German debate, the social science researcher, in contrast to the natural science researcher, is *a participant* in what is being studied – society – not just an impartial observer. Moreover, the methods preferred by 'hard data' social sciences turned fellow human beings into objects in unethical and professionally untenable ways – professionally and scientifically untenable because an adequate understanding of society presupposes that its members' own understanding of their existence be included (Skjervheim [1958] 1974). The philosopher and social researcher Theodor W. Adorno claimed, in a publication that started the whole controversy, that the focus on quantitative investigations of 'variables', in carefully delineated areas, resulted in the society *as a whole*, of which various specific areas are parts, being lost to view. Moreover, questionnaires and survey methods in principle only summarized the subjective opinions of smaller or larger numbers of people. They did not give insight into the underlying and overarching objective social forces and structures. In this way social science research would only be a 'collection of facts for administrative purposes', not real critical science (Adorno [1957] 1972).

It took approximately 20 years from the time Adorno formulated this critique until the 'controversy over positivism' really hit social science media research. This obviously says something about this research not being exactly in the forefront of the social sciences as a whole. In 1983 the *Journal of Communication* published an issue entitled *Ferment in the Field*, in which appeared a series of articles that, in various ways, called to account traditional media and communication research, which was quantitatively oriented and imitated natural science methods. A distinction already made by Paul F. Lazarsfeld in 1941, between 'critical' and 'administrative' communications research, was again brought to the fore.

The latter was exactly the kind of research Lazarsfeld himself conducted – empirical research in the service of any institutions (with money) that wanted to know how they could use the media more effectively for various purposes. According to Lazarsfeld, critical research, on the other hand, was characterized by being more theoretical or 'speculative' in its way of studying historical tendencies in the development of media and communications, and it also broke with natural science ideals about 'objectivity' by openly asking whether these tendencies were positive or negative. One of Lazarsfeld's main points, soon forgotten, was that 'administrative' research needed the 'critical' – otherwise it would face intellectual death. Some will agree that, to a large extent, he was right (Lazarsfeld, 1941).

In two slogan-like formulations, the American sociologist, Robert K. Merton summarized the differences between the predominantly American 'administrative' research and the predominantly European 'critical' research. The American administrative research says: 'We don't know if what we are saying is interesting, but at least it is true.' The European, critical research says: 'We don't know if what we are saying is true, but at least it is interesting' (quoted in Madsen, 1975: 112f.). Although one might discuss the concept of truth in this connection, the formulations fairly accurately characterize two types of orientation in media research; and what happened from around the middle of the 1970s was that critical research took the offensive – and was joined by important new trends in the humanities, not least in literary studies.

The development towards media studies in literary studies

In the 1960s the field of literary studies was refreshed by theoretical impulses from structuralism. Structuralism is a way of thinking about social conditions and texts that is based in linguistics, but which, from the 1950s onward, came to significantly leave its imprint on philosophy and social sciences, particularly in France. We will return to this in Chapter 4, on semiotics. Suffice it to mention here that structuralist theory provided the foundation for a new way of placing literature in the context of social conditions and psychology. Literary texts were 'opened' to their surroundings in various ways. Structuralism was a 'democratic' literary theory in the sense that it used the same methods and concepts to study the classics, pop lyrics and advertising texts alike. It was interested in the basic principles of construction of *any* text, and completely uninterested in celebrating the Great Writers that children are destined to hear about from their very first day in school.

Such perspectives were in tune with the rediscovery in the 1960s of Marxist and psychoanalytic theory. With these theoretical tools different texts were pounced upon, texts that were understood to be ideological constructions contributing to the maintenance of unjust and oppressive social conditions. In line with what we have already said (above) about the critique of ideology, one could claim that a particular kind of 'effect theory' was underlying these ideas on how texts influenced readers. The ambition was precisely to launch a critique of ideology, meaning that one aimed to 'reveal' the hidden, conservative, false ideological messages in classical literature as well as in advertising texts. The critique of ideology influenced by structuralism took it for granted that readers, or the audience, of various media and art forms necessarily were influenced by what they read, saw and heard.

It was from another quarter, Germany, that the question of the readers' own activity, their interpretative activity in the reading of literature, surfaced in a theoretically influential way for the first time after the Second World War: in a lecture by Hans Robert Jauss at the University of Konstanz in 1967. Jauss pointed to the simple fact that it was through people's *reading* that literature was, so to speak, realized, and gained significance and influence. He suggested that the traditional history of literature should be traded in for a history of reading. One should study how literary works were *understood by their readers* – when they were first published and later. Understanding obviously varied over time and among different reading groups. Jauss coined the concepts *reception history* and *aesthetics of reception* on this basis. The word 'reception' was chosen to indicate that readers or the public are not just passive 'receivers' (as they are called in traditional mass communications research), but active *producers of meanings* in their encounters with different kinds of text; and, Jauss maintained ([1970] 1974), they produce meanings on the basis of their specific literary experiences as well as their social experiences or conditions in general.

We will come back to this way of thinking too. The point in this context is that 'the aesthetics of reception' was an idea that caught on internationally and led to comprehensive and creative research in literary history subjects that had not noticeably been touched upon previously, such as studies of library lending, of literary criticism in newspapers, of ordinary people's letters and memories of reading experiences, and so on. In the USA, this 'readers' entry into literary research' received support from other types of literary theory, such as 'pragmatism', which we here could define as a theory about texts receiving their meaning from the situation or context in which they are read and are part of. A particularly prominent representative of this tradition, with links back to American philosophers such as John Dewey, has been Stanley Fish, with his theory of groups of readers as 'interpretative communities', which he sees as enjoying near total freedom in their readings of texts (Fish, 1980). But in continental Europe and Scandinavia, Jauss was particularly important, along with his colleague at the University of Konstanz, Wolfgang Iser (there was talk of the 'Konstanz School', cf. the 'Frankfurt School' above).

In the mid-1970s a situation therefore existed in the humanistic studies of texts wherein there was (a) a general interest in 'sociological' questions based on political involvement and Marxist theory; (b) a text understanding and theory, strongly influenced by structuralist ideas, often called 'semiology' or 'semiotics' and (c) a new interest in readers' role in literary communication and in the history of literature. In order to understand the role and function of literature in society, people in Germany and other non-Anglo European countries, such as those of Scandinavia, read Jürgen Habermas's book *Structural Transformation of the Public Sphere: An Inquiry into a Category of Bourgeois Society* (Habermas, 1962; Norwegian translation 1971, English 1989). (See also Chapter 8, on the public sphere and democracy.) Advanced students and younger scholars alike embraced the study of popular literature, including weeklies, journals, library lending, newspaper literary critique and other hitherto uninteresting material. Increasing numbers of people studied pictures and visual media, inspired by structuralist theory. Parts of literary studies were, in other words, about to become a discipline for more general *media studies*.

The Birmingham School: 'English cultural studies' and public resistance

In the mid-1970s important ideas for both the humanistic and social sciences also came from a dynamic, interdisciplinary research milieu in England, more precisely the university in the industrial city of Birmingham. In order to understand how this milieu could become important to research about the power of the media, it is necessary to look at its history.

In 1965 the Centre for Contemporary Cultural Studies opened and was associated with the Department of English at the University of Birmingham, under the direction of Richard Hoggart. Shortly after the Centre opened, Hoggart employed a young sociologist, Stuart Hall, with a Jamaican background. Thus co-operation between the humanities and the social sciences was established at the Centre right from the start. Hall became the leader of the centre in 1970 when Hoggart went to work for UNESCO in Paris. A third important name in this type of research, still known as *cultural studies*, was Raymond Williams. A professor of English at the University of Cambridge, he became something of a father figure in this area of study.

In 1957 Richard Hoggart published the book *The Uses of Literacy*, a study of English working-class culture, in part intended as a warning against the 'Americanization' of this culture, which Hoggart felt was going on. With books such as *Culture and Society* (1958) and *The Long Revolution* (1961), Raymond Williams became known as a creative historian of literature and culture, influenced by Marxism. He also was particularly concerned with the English working class (he came from a working-class environment in Wales) and its culture, which he described as *a whole way of life*. Consequently 'culture' to him was not just certain objects and texts, but a whole set of practices, ideas and values. Williams thus more or less uses a concept of culture associated with social anthropology. In both a social and geographical sense, Hoggart, who was from Yorkshire, Hall and Williams all came from the periphery of British 'high culture', including university milieus, and it is important to bear this in mind when trying to understand the direction of their work. Within a general orientation towards social and cultural history, they were particularly concerned with ordinary people's everyday lives and with cultural activities, in a more traditional sense, that were part of that life – not least the use of mass media. Their backgrounds made them see the working class and people in general not as passive victims of media influences of one sort or another. They knew that these people, in many ways, created their everyday culture on the basis of their own values and norms, and the resources at their disposal. The latter meant that they were not at all indifferent to what people were offered, for instance through the media.

Stuart Hall's contribution at the Birmingham Centre was decidedly important to the development of theoretical perspectives. He was particularly concerned with two kinds of continental European social and cultural theory influenced by structuralism: first, Louis Althusser's Marxist theory of society and ideology; and, second, *semiotics* as a way of understanding communication (see Chapter 4 of the present volume, on semiotics). A third theoretical impulse was also introduced: the Italian Marxist Antonio Gramsci's *hegemony theory* from the inter-war years. This deals with how social power in a modern capitalist country is dependent on the dominant social classes and strata keeping their positions through the fact that those who are being dominated recognize the legitimacy of this arrangement – that is, the *hegemony* of the rulers. If one were interested in changing the power structure in society one must look for signs of *resistance* to the hegemony and the social values and practices on which it rests. This was in tune with the thinking of Richard Hoggart and especially Raymond Williams.

The concept of 'resistance' became a key word within the field of cultural studies and resistance was found in various youthful *subcultures* in English society. These were studied with the help of participant observation and other methods taken from small-group sociology and social anthropology but also through the analysis of the texts these groups related to and created. In the previous chapter, on identity, I mentioned studies by Paul Willis and Dick Hebdige as examples of this sort of research, and since their time many other analyses have been made of everything from Rastafarians to soap fans, in short the whole spectrum of popular culture phenomena. The main point has always been that popular culture audiences relate *actively* to the media that surround them, and pick what they need for their *own* cultural activities, based on their own values, norms and interests.

Two contributions to the study of the socially most central mass media, especially TV, and its relationship to the public, became particularly important. One was an article published in 1973 by Stuart Hall entitled *Encoding and Decoding in Television Discourse*, in which he argues for a semiotic understanding of media communication (Hall, 1980). Hall's two main points were quite simply that the programmes transmitted by television are 'encoded' (formed, constructed) on the basis of certain social and cultural perceptions that, first of all, give the programmes a certain intended or desired meaning (a 'preferred reading'), but that, second, are not necessarily shared by those who sit in front of the screen and apprehend ('decode') the programmes. Inspired by the sociologist Parkin (1972), Hall differentiated between the preferred or (socially) *dominant* 'reading', a partially critical or *negotiated* reading and an *oppositional* reading. Therefore not only are *misunderstandings* of the intended 'message' theoretically possible, as they have always been in traditional communication models, but also *other interpretations and evaluations* on the side of the audience than those intended by the producers. In this way the simplest perception of the communications process as a linear, direct transmission of a message was undermined, and the same goes for the simplest effect models.

The second particularly important contribution was an empirical study by Charlotte Brunsdon and David Morley of the TV programme *Nationwide* (a UK current affairs programme) and some of its viewers, inspired not least by Hall's article. It included an analysis of the programme (Brunsdon and Morley, 1978), and the programme was also shown to some small groups with different social backgrounds. The reactions in these groups were then analysed. Morley found that the same programme was perceived differently in the different groups, in line with the aforementioned three-part model. Some understood it in the way it was intended ('the dominant reading'), some objected to the intended meaning ('oppositional reading') while a third group could be placed in the mixed category ('negotiated reading'). They all obviously understood what was going on in the programme; the differences were in the *interpretation and evaluation* of what was going on. Active union members, for example, had a critical attitude towards statements by 'experts' who were supposed to appear as unproblematic, objective authorities (see Morley, 1980 and 1992).

During the 1980s cultural studies became a varied and rapidly growing area of research, and in a long list of English, American and Australian universities, *cultural studies* became part of the curriculum. In the USA, cultural studies has long since, to a great extent, lost its connection to empirical social science and has rather become a form of politically motivated, 'post-structuralist' textual analysis (see Chapter 6 of the present volume, on rhetoric). Cultural studies is especially concerned with how race and gender are represented in the media, but also conducts 'readings' of everything from Disneyland and supermarkets to body piercing (see, for example, Fiske, 1989). In the USA, as well as in other countries, the idea of audience resistance has gone too far in the opinion of many, almost to the point of caricature: it is as if, the dumber, more simplistic and reactionary media offerings become, the more creative and sharp the audience's resistance. John Fiske – an ex-pat Englishman who came to represent this tendency – subsequently changed his ways and published a book entitled *Media Matters* (1996). Its main point is to demonstrate that what the media – and television in particular – serve up is not without social significance, even though the audience does not passively let itself be 'influenced' by just anything.

Status

Media researchers continually receive phone calls from journalists wanting to know if, for example, soap operas have a negative effect on young women or if the latest Schwarzenegger or Van Damme movie might make young people violent. Newspapers obviously see such issues as good headline material, just as anything else that is considered dangerous and sensational. While it is in and of itself encouraging to find that a form of critical attention to media content exists, there is a tendency to focus mostly on questions of more or less unconscious 'effects' with more or less strong negative consequences. The overview of the history of research in this chapter has hopefully demonstrated the need for a more complex understanding of the relationship between the media and the public, in order to understand the complicated interaction between the many factors of this relationship. The subject is not particularly suited for tabloid presentation.

The introductory statement in this chapter (that we basically conduct media research because the media 'influence' us), is problematic because concepts such as *influence* or (in particular) *effects* can so easily give a skewed understanding of the role of the media in society and for each of us – in the direction of mechanical, direct 'response' to 'stimuli'. But the media are of course an important part of the social and cultural milieu in which we live. They are the main sources of information, well-considered knowledge and a variety of experiences. They provide a forum for public debate and the formation of opinions. They serve up daily representations of real and fictitious situations in which values and ideas figure in various ways, without necessarily being noticed. It is therefore also clear that the media in all of their functions influence how society and human beings develop and understand themselves – but we need to underline that this happens through complex processes.

A great deal of research about the relationship between the media and the public is still being conducted, in which all of the methods and theories mentioned in this chapter are in full swing. We will come back to this research in later chapters – not least those in Part 2 that deal with different perspectives on media texts. The 'absolute truth' in this area is not to be expected, however, as so many factors are involved and as these factors (the media texts themselves, human beings and social conditions) are so manifold and constantly changing. But new contributions are constantly being made that may shed light on certain instances and parts of this complex of problems. A better understanding of these questions requires perspectives, theories and methods developed for the study of culture, texts and communication. Also needed is a thorough and varied knowledge of social and cultural conditions, and differences in general. The latter is the subject of the next chapter.

3 Distinctions: social difference, lifestyle and taste

There's something for everyone

It is just common sense, that 'there's no accounting for taste', or *chacun à son goût*, as the French expression imported into English goes. We simply like and are interested in different things – football, embroidery, cars, flowers, classical music, hip-hop, Shakespeare, soap opera, pine furniture, chrome and leather furniture – and various varieties of all of these. We can find many such differences within a group of friends or within one and the same social milieu.

Statistically speaking, however, it is not equally likely that all individuals will develop a particular liking for, say, classical music. Interests in this and other forms of art do to a great extent follow the divisions between social categories. Accordingly, a greater part of some social groups than others are really devoted soap opera fans. For example (and as mentioned in the previous chapter), in 1984 I carried out a simple survey of the audience for the US soap opera *Dynasty* in my country (Norway), which then had only one TV channel, and discovered the pattern shown in Table 3.1.

The figures are extremely high in all categories, primarily because of Norway's single-channel situation and there are of course a number of methodological uncertainties with all such surveys. Still, the pattern is so clear that some real tendencies must underlie these figures: women are clearly more interested than men, and people with fewer years of formal education are more interested than those with more. This result is hardly surprising; it is confirmed not only by common knowledge (and prejudice), but also by lots of similar studies. The interesting question is, however, why do the choices we make between different media and cultural offerings – *choices that we make as, in principle, free individuals* – still, when analysed, yield such statistical differences between various social categories.

Table 3.1 Episodes of *Dynasty* watched in Norway, 1984, by gender and years spent in formal education

	Watched more than 50 per cent of episodes	Watched more than 75 per cent of episodes
Gender	Per cent	Per cent
Men	60	37
Women	80	62
Years in formal education		
Up to 9	85	59
10—12	75	59
13—15	65	40
Over 15	59	39

(Gripsrud, 1995: 113)

This chapter will attempt to sketch a basis for answering this question. It is necessary, then, to start out with some quite fundamental sociological concepts and issues. After this, the emphasis will be on the work of French sociologist Pierre Bourdieu, for two reasons: first, Bourdieu has for a long time been a dominating figure in the area of cultural sociology; and, second, we can understand both processes of media production and processes of media reception with the aid of Bourdieu's concepts and perspectives. Bourdieu has not least been influential where sociology meets aesthetics, i.e. in questions about taste and the estimation of quality in cultural matters. As you will see, the topic of this chapter is closely related to the issues of identity we wrote about in Chapter 1, while it also points forward to the topics of the final three chapters of this book, on media production, 'the public sphere' and various media and cultural policy issues.

Differentiations and hierarchies

A number of the 'classic' sociologists, such as Émile Durkheim, Max Weber and Georg Simmel, were very interested in what distinguishes modern society from the older social forms from which it developed. The historical changes known as processes of modernization have many aspects. Various types of *pre-modern* societies are, as a rule, characterized by being relatively simple and, in a sense, transparent. If one thinks of, for instance, medieval Europe, one can roughly say that society was organized as a quite simple pyramid, with a small, powerful elite on top and a sea of peasants at the bottom. This social order was considered to have been created by God, just as nature, and so everything was part of a singular, divine scheme. Social critique was blasphemous. One of the most important aspects of modernization is that society becomes more complex through a *social differentiation* (the establishment of differences) of two kinds.

First, differences are established between various *spheres* or areas of society, for instance between the private and the public, the religious and the mundane or secular. Scholars have also talked about the development of differences between *spheres of value*, i.e. areas where different sets of criteria are applied when evaluations and decisions are made. Science, art and morality were thus separated, so that science concentrated on *truth* and art on *beauty*, while the question of what was *good*, the area of morality, was in principle kept separate from the other two. In pre-modern societies these three areas were more or less one and the same: what was true was also both good and beautiful. Nowadays we all know that all that is beautiful is not necessarily morally good.

This implies, then, that separate institutions are developed to administer different types of values and evaluations. The division between different social spheres is thus also linked to the *second* aspect of social differentiation in processes of modernization, which is the increasing *social division of labour*. The pre-modern society consisted largely of more or less self-sufficient farmers. In line with the development of trade, crafts, industry, health care, a system of education and a 'service sector', the spectrum of jobs and professions has expanded enormously. An ever more detailed social division of labour is a main part of the basis for a similarly detailed system of social differences between groups of people. The relatively stable, self-supplied agricultural society also had such differences: it had a basic division of labour between the sexes; there was a clear difference between those who owned land and those that didn't, between rich and poor. But the social differentiation was quite simple compared to the situation today.

The differences between different sorts of work are not just differences between more or less equally valued jobs. To say that 'there are differences between people', is to refer to *systematic differences in terms of economic and social resources and power between different groups* – that is, it refers to a *hierarchical* social structure. Some speak of *class differences*, others prefer to speak of *social stratification*. In the theoretical traditions of the social sciences there is a historically important opposition between those who speak of classes and those who speak of stratification.

The concept of *class* is largely tied to traditions oriented towards *social conflict*, most often connected to Marxist theory. Marxism emphasizes economic factors when social classes are defined. The main question is, simply put, whether one makes a living from placing one's labour power at the disposal of others for a certain pay (a wage, or salary), or whether one owns or controls a business and its means of production. Society is here regarded as fundamentally marked by different categories of people having principally opposing interests, that are either reconciled through negotiations leading to series of compromises, or that, under certain circumstances, can lead to rapid and radical changes in power relations, i.e. revolutions (cf. notions such as 'the class struggle'). The term *social strata*, on the other hand, is as a rule defined by criteria such as income, education, profession, type of housing and for that matter the number of telephones in a household. The term is often linked to so-called structural functionalism in social theory, i.e. a perspective in which society is regarded as a sort of machinery where there may well be malfunctioning bits and pieces now and then, but where there are no irreconcilable (antagonistic) conflicts of interest between social groups.

This is not the place for a more thorough treatment of these concepts and their backgrounds. It is enough to note that there are different ways of defining and regarding systematic social differences in resources. The two perspectives sketched above can also be combined in certain ways, and as research traditions they can benefit from each others' empirical results. A conflict-oriented class perspective will need notions of strata or subgroups within and between the larger and relatively simple (main) categories of class. Class theories may also leave out or put in brackets the typically Marxist idea that class conflict contains the embryo of fundamental social upheaval. A predominantly structural-functionalist perspective may probably acknowledge the existence of principally irreconcilable conflicts between certain social groups, but only award them a subordinate or modest significance for social conditions at large and their development.

For the moment it is enough to say that systematic social differences in terms of resources and power are a fundamental feature of modern societies. We all know this from our own social experience, and the social sciences have in different ways striven to decide its implications. Differentiations between classes or strata are usually thought of as having mainly to do with economic conditions and factors more or less directly connected to them, such as education and income. But as we shall see in this chapter, such differences also have consequences for how individuals think of themselves, how they behave in certain situations, what they like and what they don't like.

In such matters, however, other social divisions than those between classes are highly important. *Sexual difference* or, in social and cultural contexts, *gender difference* is, as it always has been, an absolutely fundamental social difference. Factors such as age, race, ethnicity, geographical background (centre/periphery) and *the meanings we assign to them* certainly also contribute to important divisions among us. All such differentiations tend to not only order people in 'boxes' at the same level, they also place these boxes on top of each other, i.e. order them hierarchically. The fundamental ideals of equal worth ('all men are created equal') must all the time collide with obvious differences in income, power and status. Differences can vary in size among societies with different social, economic and cultural traditions and systems, but there is hardly any society that does not have them.

All of this is, of course (because it is fundamental), of great significance for how we are to understand the role(s) of the media in society. One can, for example, from a class-theoretical point of view ask whether the media actually support some class interests more than others and investigate the ownership and contents of various media from this point of view. Here, however, we will concentrate on a sociological perspective where an interest in differentiation between social spheres is combined with an interest in social hierarchies. This perspective sheds light on the production side of the media while also improving our understanding of what matters most in this part of this book – that is, social patterns in people's choice, use, understanding, experience and evaluation of mass media.

Habitus and social fields

How are we actually to understand that 'external' social circumstances – such as the professions of our parents and our own jobs, their and our own education and income – somehow become parts of our ways of thinking and acting, and that this is the same for every individual? This is one of many ways to phrase one of the most fundamental problems in the social sciences, the so-called structure/actor problem. What are the relations between general social structures on the one hand and the freedom of thought and action of individuals on the other?

One of the most interesting answers in our context comes from the above-mentioned sociologist Pierre Bourdieu. In the 1950s he studied the peasant community in Kabylia, Algeria. One of the things he noted, and that puzzled him, was how people there intuitively seemed to 'do the right thing' in various social situations (the right thing according to highly complex rules of conduct, which Bourdieu himself had to learn as one learns a totally foreign language). The rules in question seemed to be almost built in to people's bodies, rather like the knowledge we have of how to swim or ride a bicycle. This is automatic knowledge. We do not reflect upon it. We don't go through in our minds the principles and movements of swimming before jumping in the pool. Social rules can, in a similar way, be 'stored in the body' as a set of tendencies to act in a certain way in certain situations, a set of *dispositions*, a sort of attitude to the world. Bourdieu compares such a set of 'dispositions' with a set of hypotheses we have about social reality and about what it is possible and impossible *for us* to do in it (Bourdieu, 1992: 54); he has, since the latter part of the 1960s, referred to this as a *habitus*.

This concept can be said to have a long pre-history in rhetoric, philosophy and classic social scientific work. Bourdieu was also inspired by the art historian Erwin Panofsky and his use of the term *mental habit* in an article on gothic architecture (cf. Broady, 1990: 244ff.). Bourdieu maintains that we have all had a habitus installed through the life we have led under certain social circumstances. It is a product of our socialization (see also Chapter 1 of the present volume, on identity) and, consequently, it is never quite finished and never without traces of our background. The habitus is formed of internalized social conditions – that is to say, social conditions in an individual version.

Bourdieu thinks of the individual, with his or her habitus, his or her set of socially conditioned set of dispositions, as faced with a given set of social *positions*, a set of 'places' within the complex and hierarchical structure of society. The habitus then guides, it does not simply determine, how the individual thinks, chooses and acts. It will, for instance, influence one's choices of education. Choosing an education at a university will seem more 'natural' to children of academically trained parents than it might to others. Educational statistics in any country demonstrates this. Similarly, the offspring of artists or other people with a marked interest in high art may feel less like outsiders at the opening of an art exhibition than people with other backgrounds, while they may feel more lost than their friends with a working-class background at a pub catering for football fans. A habitus is, in other words, something *relative*, something that becomes apparent *compared with something else or someone else*. It is furthermore important that even if family background gives our habitus some decisive features, both education, work experience and other social practice will also contribute to shaping it. The habitus is 'inert', but never totally 'completed'.

The habitus will influence where we 'end up' in life, what social position we occupy. Social positions exist within what Bourdieu calls *social fields*, i.e. *social areas where certain activities take place in accordance with certain rules and where there is a continuous struggle over status or recognition among those involved*. One can speak of the educational field, the literary field, the journalistic field, the scientific field, the field of art and so on. Fields can be large or small, comprehensive or subfields within a larger area. Both the French term *champ* and translations such as 'field' have a certain military ring to them (cf. 'battlefield', 'field manoeuvre', 'field artillery' etc.) and this is quite to the point. According to Bourdieu, 'battles' go on within all social fields: struggles over scarce resources; recognition and power. The precondition for these struggles is an agreement among those involved concerning certain values and attitudes, not least an agreement that whatever one does within the field in question *is important*. For the participants, these fundamental values, attitudes and ideas are self-evident, they form a sort of common sense or, to use Bourdieu's Greek term, the field's *doxa*. In the literary field, for instance, one does not ask whether or not literature is important, and all involved will agree that it is better to publish one major, aesthetically ambitious novel every other year than ten 'pulp' novels every year. There are similar unquestioned ideas in, for instance, the fields of both journalism and science.

At certain times individuals or groups will come along who break with parts of the field's doxa; they are 'heretics' or *heterodoxic*. They challenge people or groups who dominate the field, for instance by maintaining other criteria for what is to be counted as valuable literature, real journalism, solid research or interesting theory. More or less drastic upheavals may result from the entry of new groups to a field, such as when the market for cultural products grew immensely in the mid-nineteenth century and a substantial growth in the number of writers and (other) artists provided the basis for what is known as the 'Bohemian' milieu in Paris (Bourdieu, 1996: 54f.). Another example could be that the 'educational explosion' in France and other countries in the 1960s meant that a great number of students from previously excluded backgrounds were admitted to universities and this was part of the basis for the student rebellion in May 1968 (Bourdieu, 1990: 143ff.). But what decides whether such heterodox rebellions succeed, as well as those that take place under more normal circumstances, is not least the extent to which the heretic rebels manage to give the impression that they are the true representatives and custodians of the fundamental values of the field. This presupposes that they have qualities that the other participants in the field will acknowledge as valuable. In the literary field this could be that they demonstrate solid knowledge of the classics of world literature, including highly respected philosophical writers and traditions, and that they are distinguished by a particular gift for argumentation and style. So not just any person's habitus is suited for successfully challenging the reigning notions of what constitutes valuable literature, or which authors (dead or alive) are particularly interesting.

Different social fields touch on and influence each other, but they still have a form of 'self-rule', a *relative autonomy*. It is the players in the field who decide what the field is about and what counts there. Bourdieu maintains that this autonomy is a precondition for the ability of the various fields to continue to produce something that is valuable more generally, to people outside of the field in question. The autonomy of the literary field is a prerequisite for the continued existence of literature as an art form. The autonomy of the journalistic field is a prerequisite for the maintenance of journalistic ideals and corresponding practices. For instance, in his short book *On Television* (1998), Bourdieu argues that the autonomy of journalism is severely threatened by a 'colonization' from the field of economy. Demands for increased profits from owners and a greatly increased interest in circulation figures in the press and audience figures in broadcasting media make for greater influence for forces that are alien to the field, that break with its fundamental goals and functions. Similar tendencies of a 'colonization' can be found in other fields: the educational, the scholarly or the greater cultural field. Bourdieu's point would be, then, in his own terminology, that the fields' own understandings of what is important and what isn't must be mobilized to resist the corruption of the fields represented by the demands from owners and marketing departments.

Forms of capital and the social space

The people of Kabylia could further their own or their families' interests with varying competence or luck without breaking the rules internalized in their habitus. Securing one's own interests mainly meant to protect and increase one's *honour*, something that was understood and recognized by other people. Recognition is something one can collect in various ways – and lose. In Kabylia, honour was the most important form of what Bourdieu calls *symbolic capital*, and since it became apparent primarily in people's conduct, not in things outside of people themselves, it was at stake in every social situation. This is different in modern societies.

With writing and an educational system a new form of symbolic capital arrived, *cultural capital* (that is, the amount of *socially recognized* and therefore valuable knowledge and competences of a cultural kind that a person has). This implies that there is cultural capital in having solid knowledge about the established, 'legitimate' art forms, but not in being the world's best informed on country music or ice hockey. The latter sorts of knowledge could win one a high status among the fans of the two cultural forms in question and, within these and other areas of popular culture (and also so-called youth culture), there are mechanisms at work that make it possible to regard these areas as kinds of social field in the sense of Bourdieu (cf., for instance, Bjurström, 2000). But knowledge or competences appreciated within the various subfields of popular culture are not awarded with the sort of general, *official* recognition to which the term cultural capital refers. In fact, this kind of knowledge sometimes attracts derision, and accusations of 'nerdiness'. In contrast to the symbolic capital of traditional, pre-modern societies, cultural capital can in societies like ours be apparent in objectified forms such as academic degrees, titles, prizes and the like. As these objectified forms indicate, it is on the whole a set of institutions that ultimately guarantees the value of cultural capital. Bourdieu also talks about *educational capital*, a particular form of cultural capital, and graduation papers, the PhD diploma etc., are the visible forms of this capital.

In this way Bourdieu modifies the often quite one-sided emphasis of

Marxist class theory on *economic capital* as decisive in terms of where one is positioned in the social hierarchy. In modern western societies, cultural capital is important in determining the degree of recognition a person enjoys, what 'social status' he or she has, and thus also what social resources and power. The amount of cultural capital is of course particularly important for those who want to be upwardly mobile in the official or legitimate cultural fields, such as that of literature. The precondition for a successful heterodox 'rebellion' is, as mentioned above, that the rebels are well equipped with cultural capital, i.e. knowledge and competences that the others in the field recognize. A favourable habitus is then one that provides the individual with a 'nose' for what it is important to know or know of, what it is important to have read, in order to know the traditions, views and common assumptions so well that one can formulate one's own, 'rebellious', ideas in a persuasive, convincing way (cf. Chapter 6 of the present volume, on rhetoric). A favourable habitus, which is often tied to family background, is in other words not enough, it is just a great advantage.

In addition comes, and this is decisive, a great *investment* of time and energy in working long and hard to acquire the right sorts of knowledge and skills. This will in most cases also cost money – in the form of student loans or, perhaps, an inheritance, or courtesy of the backing of rich parents – so that one can take the time needed. Especially in an old, large and solidly established field like that of literature, it may take a great deal of serious study to, say, 'make it' as a successfully heterodox critic. But what Bourdieu calls *social capital* may also come in handy. Social capital is, briefly put, one's network of resourceful friends, acquaintances and contacts, which may be bigger the better you are at socializing or 'being around people'. As the saying goes, 'a man is known by the company he keeps'. Finally, it is worth mentioning that there may be forms of capital not mentioned by Bourdieu that may be important in countries other than France, where he has carried out most of his empirical work. Scandinavian scholars inspired by Bourdieu's form of sociology have, for instance, suggested that there may be a form of 'organizational capital' at work in their countries, since a number of popular social and political movements have served as routes to positions of power for people with quite small quantities of both economic and cultural capital. This 'organizational capital' would, then, be experience and recognition accumulated through years of organizational activity. So Bourdieu's notion of capital, just like his other terms, must always be thought of as something *relative*, something that varies with the specificities of circumstance.

Using Bourdieu's way of thinking, one can, for example, come up with a thought-provoking explanation for the fact that so many students are particularly interested in media such as film, photo and comics as art forms. Students may through their backgrounds, and/or long educations and years spent in a university milieu, have understood that art is a good thing for society and the individual – and that an interest in art is one of the things that tends to characterize people in higher social positions. Media such as film, photography and comics allow more individuals to feel like, and pretend to be, specialists in them because they have relatively shorter histories and consequently less extensive scholarly and critical writing about them than literature and the visual arts in general. These latter fields demand more or less in-depth knowledge of over 2000 years of complicated history, and the quantity of scholarship and criticism may seem totally overwhelming. If one chooses instead to concentrate on, say, comics as an art form, one can get by with a much smaller investment in terms of time, money and energy; and on top of that even get to enjoy the feeling of being somewhat cheekily heterodox in relation to the field of art as a whole, in opposition to all those old-fashioned idiots who don't realize that the times they are a-changing. Moreover, on can also feel that one is on the side of The People, that is those who live their lives more or less totally outside the institutionalized field of art.

The concept of 'cultural capital' is a metaphor (cf., again, Chapter 6 of the present volume, on rhetoric) that implies a comparison between capital in the original, economic sense and knowledge of (legitimate, official) culture. According to Bourdieu, some groups (such as executives at large corporations) have high status and power in society primarily because of the economic capital they control or own, while others (such as successful university professors and artists, managers of significant cultural institutions and the like) have status and power because of the amount of cultural capital they have accumulated. Since these latter categories as a rule do not have much economic capital to speak of, and economic capital (still) carries *most* power, they (the 'intellectuals') are 'the dominated part of the dominating class'. They, therefore, see money and the power it brings as not very important at all. Correspondingly, the dominating part of the dominating class, mainly rich business people, will often find much of the work that, say, university professors do quite uninteresting and insignificant, not 'useful' at all, and therefore, to them, of little worth. Secretly, though, the two groups may envy each other on some points and, to people further down in the social pyramid, the two categories may in many ways seem hard to distinguish.

Distinction ([1979] 1989) is still considered Bourdieu's most important book. Here he sums up a large number of empirical studies conducted by himself and his collaborators in France in the 1960s. In line with the thoughts presented above, and with the aid of a particular statistical method called *correspondence analysis*, Bourdieu has constructed a model of (French) society, or, as he prefers to call it, *the social space* (see Figure 3.1). The various positions within this space, marked as professions, are decided by the amount of economic and cultural capital they, statistically speaking, have at their disposal.

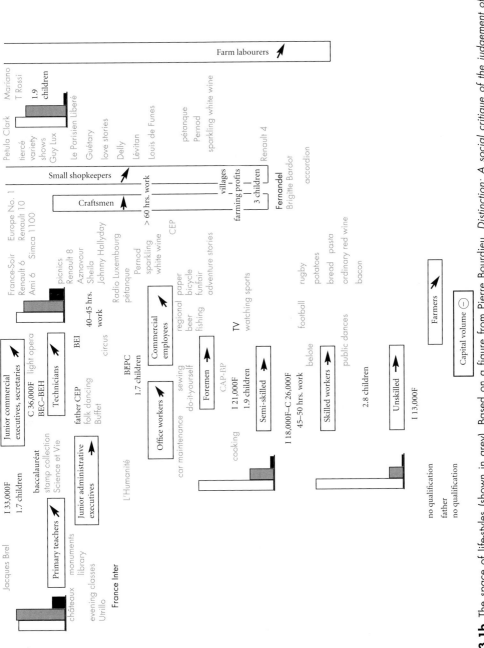

Figure 3.1b The space of life-styles (shown in grey). Based on a figure from Pierre Bourdieu, *Distinction: A social critique of the judgement of taste*. Routledge 1986. Used by permission.

At the top of the diagram we find those social positions that have the largest amount of capital (both economic and cultural), and at the bottom are those positions that have the least of both. But the left-to-right dimension of the diagram is also highly important; this indicates the relationship between economic and cultural capital within the total amount of capital that is characteristic of the various positions. In the upper right-hand corner we will thus find those positions that are high ranking primarily due to the large amount of economic capital they have; in the upper left-hand corner we find those positions that are high ranking primarily because of the large amount of cultural capital they have accumulated. Correspondingly, somewhere near the middle of the vertical axis, we find primary school teachers on the left-hand side (more cultural than economic capital and otherwise roughly in the middle) and certain skilled craftspeople, owners of small businesses etc. on the right-hand side.

Both this and similar diagrams constructed in other countries, based on the same sort of empirical data and statistical procedures, demonstrate that the left-to-right dimension is to a large degree a reflection of the differences between the public (left-hand) and private (right-hand) sectors. Such studies indicate, in addition, that those with more cultural than economic capital also tend more often to be politically more or less left-oriented and have cultural values in line with such an orientation (cf., for instance, Rosenlund, 2000). When we examine such connections, we are, however, talking about something other than the social space as such. We are talking about what Bourdieu calls *the space of lifestyles*. In these diagrams one representation of this space is put, so to speak, on top of the other on a transparent sheet. The result is interesting, if not necessarily surprising: we largely find our everyday prejudices and qualified guesses confirmed. But before we go into this in more detail, we will take a closer look at the term *lifestyle* – a word that is frequently used, not least in the advertising industry.

Lifestyles

As a sociological concept the term 'lifestyle' goes back to the German scholar Max Weber, one of the founding fathers of modern sociology. He was, in general and simplified terms, interested in the connections between the economic and the ideological, between objective social conditions and people's subjective understanding of their situation. More specifically, he was interested in the fact that some of the first great capitalists in Europe had a very thrifty, puritanical way of thinking, which encouraged the accumulation of capital instead of generous spending (consumption). Was this economic practice a result of their ideas, their view of life – or was it the other way round? It was in this context that Weber first spoke of the *Lebensführung* – 'life conduct' – of social groups. The concept refers to the systematic way in which people think and act in everyday life. The basis for the systematic character of this 'life conduct' was, for Weber, to be found in the (religious) view of life in various groups. It must be remembered here, though, that it was his study of Protestant sects in the seventeenth century that made him think along these lines, studies he sums up in the famous work *The Protestant Ethic and the Spirit of Capitalism* ([1904–5] 1992). These groups, of course, had a certain explicit, religious view of life as a fundamental and community-forming element in their lives.

Today there are relatively few social groups that have explicitly formulated, principled worldviews of this sort guiding their everyday practices. On the contrary, people may often say one thing and do something quite different, as when they declare themselves to be strong believers in individualism and then proceed to dress, act and think exactly like everyone else in the same social group. An example of this could be the millions of 'youth rebels' in the 1960s and 1970s who demonstrated their anti-conformist individualism by uniformly wearing long hair, jeans, etc. A related example would be the later creative individualists who, at least for a while, all dressed in black and sported the same types of cool glasses and hairstyles. This systematic character of our 'life conducts', or *lifestyles*, now typically springs from some principles of which we are *not* consciously aware and which we are therefore unable to express directly. These principles only become apparent – to an external, analytical eye – in our *practice*. Since we like to think of ourselves as free individuals, we will tend to resist when impertinent researchers take away our individuality and reduce us to exchangeable members of a certain social category. There might, then, be some comfort in the fact that we can use another of Max Weber's classic concepts to label categories for social groups and their lifestyles *ideal types* ([1922] 1997). Ideal types are empirically based tools for thinking that we can use to understand social phenomena. They are 'concrete abstractions' that precisely refer to *super-individual patterns* more than specific individuals and their multitudes of individual peculiarities.

In Chapter 1 of this book, on media and identity, we saw that people's identities are composites in various ways. Some of our identity has been given to us through our sex, family, geographical location and so on, while other elements can be more freely chosen. It is the same with lifestyles. Some fundamental traits come unsought, through background, education and work (for example, fishermen rarely play tennis); other elements one can choose. *Choosing elements of one's lifestyle is often also choosing elements of one's identity – and vice versa.* Such choices say something about who we are and, especially, about who we *want* to be – as opposed to, as different from, others. Some lifestyles appear more attractive than others because they *signify* or 'mean' something that is supposedly attractive or valuable. Bourdieu says that *lifestyles are the systematic products of the habitus* (1989: 172). The 'system of dispositions' that we have internalized through our background and experiences, i.e. the habitus, will largely shape our lifestyles, both the elements we do not choose ourselves and those we more consciously choose. The habitus leaves its mark on our lifestyle through the aspect of it that Bourdieu calls *taste*, defined as our 'tendency and ability to acquire (materially or symbolically) a certain class of classified and classifying objects or practices' (Bourdieu, 1989: 173). Taste is the principle for the choices we make on the basis of our socially determined dispositions, and that results in the systematics of lifestyles. The habitus guides what we find attractive, not through a completely mechanical and direct form of determination, but through the operations of taste. Taste governs what we regard as lifestyles and positions within reach and which lifestyles and positions we absolutely do *not* wish to be associated with.

The media, and advertising in particular, are constantly proposing images of identities and lifestyles that we can choose between and buy (if we have the money). Shampoos and clothes, homes and cars, everything is presented as *signs of lifestyles*. Which of these signs are attractive to whom is decided more by social conditions than strictly individual factors. University professors would most often not buy a Mercedes even if they had the money, and in spite of it being a very good car. French or Swedish cars will often be found more suitable; they signify something else, such as 'good taste' and 'social responsibility', as opposed to 'mechanical perfection'. Among certain kinds of student it may be very important to have seen the latest experimental film or theatrical performance, to have read the most recent issue of some intellectual journal and to be able to say something apparently sensible about both. Other parts of the student body and people in general couldn't care less about such things, but instead feel a deep urge to follow a certain soap opera and read this week's *National Enquirer* or, in the UK, *Hello!* or *OK!*, and have qualified opinions on both. Individuals in both of these groups may well (secretly?) disagree with these priorities, but they will nevertheless have to respect the norms of their respective milieus – if they wish to belong there. Patterns of consumption, including the consumption of media and cultural products, are important parts of the *space of lifestyles* in Bourdieu's diagrams or maps of society.

The notion of taste in philosophical aesthetics

Before we can look more closely at Bourdieu's theory of taste, we should attempt a brief overview of developments in the philosophical discipline of *aesthetics*. We should do this because the term 'taste', like other terms in the sociology of art and culture, stems from aesthetics and because many of the fundamental criteria for the understanding and evaluation of artworks – which can also lead to a ranking of audience groups – do the same. It is not by accident that the subtitle of Bourdieu's book *Distinction* is *A Social Critique of Judgement*. This refers directly to the aesthetic philosophy of Immanuel Kant in his *Critique of Judgement* ([1790] 1987).

In the context of aesthetics, it seems that the notion of 'taste' has, as so many other things, its origins in the Renaissance, in Italy, roughly in the fourteenth and fifteenth centuries. In a widely distributed book on education from 1404, for example, it is said that it is 'suitable for noble men to be able to evaluate and discuss with each other the beauty of both natural and man-made objects' (quoted in Sveen, 1995: 18). The difference between those who really understood works of art and the 'ignorant' who didn't was not least said to be that the ignorant only cared about the colours, while 'the learned' were at least as much interested in the arrangement and proportions. In accordance with this, one could distinguish between painters who mostly painted to 'amuse the eyes of the ignorant' and those who rather painted to 'please the intellect of the knowledgeable' (1995: 19). Art and the understanding of it was, then, already a *means of distinction*, something that contributed to the marking of differences between people, between the well informed or educated on the one hand and the uninformed or uneducated on the other. At the same time, it is well worth noting *what* was preferred by the 'learned' and the 'ignorant' respectively: an emphasis on intelligence and form was contrasted to an emphasis on amusement and (pretty or striking) colours.

It was, however, not until the seventeenth century that the word 'taste' began to be used in relation to the ability to differentiate between good and bad in art. To begin with, the meaning of the word was also a good deal broader than that – art had not yet reached a status of institutional autonomy (cf., above, the section about social differentiation in relatively autonomous spheres of judgement). To, for example, the Spanish Jesuit Baltasar Gracián, writing in 1647, having 'good taste' more or less meant being able to conduct oneself properly as a gentleman or man of the world (Gracián, 1995). It had to do with rationality and moral choices just as much as with the ability to judge works of art. Good taste in the latter area depended on general reason but also on a specific competence that was necessary in order to be able to identify and value the qualities of artworks. According to this line of thinking, then, beauty is not 'in the eye of the beholder', it is rather a quality of certain objects that can be 'discovered' by those who understand about these things.

It is often said that the Scottish, empiricist philosopher David Hume in his *Of the Standard of Taste* (1754) argued, in opposition to this view, that judgements of taste are entirely individual or subjective and that 'beauty' thus is not a quality of the object but something the spectator-subject ascribes to it. Such a view can be said to be in line with Hume's general epistemology (theory of knowledge): knowledge is based on experience, but if we observe that B again and again follows A, it is only in our heads that A can be made the *cause* of B, so that we can count on B *always* following A. The causal relationship is, in other words, a kind of logical connection we *ascribe* to that which we observe, it does not reside in the observed itself. The same would go for beauty, or, as one would probably say today, an object's artistic or cultural value.

Hume did not, however, think that all works of art are 'actually' equally good and every judgement equally valid. He says that even if beauty and its opposite are not qualities of the objects but entirely belong to the perceptions of the subject, it has to be admitted *that there are certain qualities in things that have the ability to produce the feelings of beauty or ugliness* (Hume, 1994: 83). These qualities in things can be so small or so intertwined that not everyone can discern them and experience the feeling of beauty in them. Those who can do this better than others are those with good taste or a sufficient 'delicacy of taste'; and, Hume adds, while having a delicacy of taste for food can be a burden for a man and his friends, a delicate taste for art and wit is a clear advantage since it opens the way to the finest pleasures a man can have (1994: 84). Hume thus seems to reckon that there is something in the mental apparatus of all human beings, analogous to our sense of logic, that makes certain things or aspects of them appear 'beautiful'. Logic is a general human capacity, but it is also a capacity that is present and developed to varying degrees in different individuals. The capacity to identify beauty, or 'good taste', could be thought of in a similar way.

It may well seem to be splitting hairs to discuss whether 'beauty' is something that exists in the object or in the subject. For those who are in favour of placing it with the subject will have to acknowledge that there must be something in some objects and not in others that releases or produces the experience of 'beauty' in the subject. 'Beauty' will always be a matter of interplay between the subject and the object. Yet the question of whether 'subjectivist' or 'objectivist' theories are the most adequate is still very important. The more the subjectivist element is emphasized, the closer one gets to a position where it is maintained that all objects are of equal worth and all judgements equally valid. The more the objectivist element is emphasized, the more emphasis must also be placed on the (presumed) competence of those who judge. The question is, for example, whether any old person's opinion on hip-hop or drum'n'bass records is equally valid as that of those who take these cultural forms seriously.

The balancing of the subjective and the objective is also a central problem to epistemology, the theory of knowledge. How much of what we think we know about the world have we actually *ascribed to* the object we think we know something about, on the basis of language and other aspects of our mental apparatus, and how much is in fact qualities of the object that in fact exist 'out there', independently of us who observe it? There are, in other words, close ties between epistemology and *aesthetics*, the 'theory of beauty'. The very word 'aesthetics' etymologically (i.e. in the history of the word) stems from the Greek word *aisthesis*, which meant purely experiential, sense-based knowledge about reality. This was opposed to theory and its insights into the *essence* of things, since the senses could only give access to the unreliable, fleeting surfaces of things. The first philosophical work with 'aesthetics' in its title was the German A.C. Baumgarten's *Aesthetica*, the first volume of which was published in 1750. Baumgarten wanted to make a case for 'sensual knowledge', to contribute to the experience of art being recognized as a special form of knowledge. Art did not provide a poorer or lower form of knowledge or insight, it did not just consist of and produce fuzzy and confused ideas that had to be purified and clarified by intellect and logic; it provided, according to Baumgarten, a *different type* of knowledge or insight, valuable in itself.

This could be seen as the introduction of a philosophical perspective that corresponded to the roughly contemporary development of art as a separate institutional sphere in society. This development is especially evident in the philosophy of Immanuel Kant (1724–1804). His major work was 'the three critiques': that is, *Critique of Pure Reason* (1781), *Critique of Practical Reason* (1788) and *Critique of Judgement* (1790). One might say that these three volumes correspond to what we have previously referred to in this chapter as the differentiation of society into separate spheres for questions of truth, morality – and beauty.

Kant can be said to prefigure or introduce Romanticism by, among other things, awarding aesthetic experiences or insights, relying on *feeling*, an autonomous role besides the knowledge of nature, relying on the intellect (*Verstand*), and knowledge of morality, relying on reason (*Vernunft*). It has therefore been said that Kant's ideas about the aesthetic have, in many ways, been constitutive for the prevailing understanding of art and the aesthetic in modern, western culture. For this reason, and because Bourdieu's work refers so directly to Kant, we will say a bit more about the ideas in his *Critique of Judgement*.

Aesthetics is a part of Kant's theory of knowledge where feeling as opposed to intellect and reason is the decisive basis for judgement. This form of knowledge, and the way of getting it, is actually not specific to our encounters with works of art. Kant, for example, refers frequently to experiences of nature. Here we have, in other words, a starting point both for a very wide conception of the area of the aesthetic, and for a focus on the aesthetic as a contrast to the areas of reason and intelligence.

Kant's aesthetics is 'subjectivist' in the sense that he ties it to the subject's experience, perceptions, mental categories, intellectual and emotional registers. A certain phenomenon is, in that sense, as with Hume, not in itself aesthetic, it is our experience of it that is aesthetic or non-aesthetic. Still, as we shall soon see again, Kant also maintains the idea that there are 'adequate', universally valid criteria for the beautiful, and that these have their basis in human capacities that we all actually share. This may also be seen as a parallel to Hume.

First, Kant thought that beauty is something we experience with what he calls a *disinterested delight or pleasure*. 'Disinterested' here means something in the direction of our not finding a picture of a bowl of fruit 'delightful' or pleasurable because we are hungry, but because the picture of the fruit in the bowl is beautiful *as a picture* – not as an unworthy replacement for the real thing. The experience of beauty presupposes that one looks at the picture without such a non-aesthetic interest, in a contemplative and distanced way. In a storm, the ocean can be beautiful in a somewhat disturbing, even terrifying way – *sublimely* – when you regard it in a safe and thereby relatively 'disinterested' way on shore, in striking contrast to the highly engaged, interested way in which you would regard it were you *on* the stormy ocean in a tiny rowing boat. Kant, in other words, privileges a *distanced* approach.

Kant also formulates thoughts about an *innate sensibility* in certain individuals, which provide a basis for ideas about *geniality* in the production of artworks as well as in the appreciation of them, i.e. that particular individuals are born with a particular gift for either producing great art or appreciating it. Such ideas might make art a more or less exclusive domain for a minority of people with highly specialised genetically based equipment. But this sort of thinking is actually contradicted by another of Kant's ideas, which is that the aesthetic experience is based in a *sensus communis* – yes, a 'common sense', a sensual capacity shared by all people. Aesthetic experience is, according to Kant's way of thinking, to be formulated in *aesthetic judgements*, that is to say evaluations that are critical (discerning) and that rank (as bad, good, better, best) the particular case. Now, aesthetic judgements are necessarily subjective, but, says Kant, they also *make claims* to be universally valid. If this latter part is to be accepted, one must presuppose the existence of a *sensus communis* and an agreement on certain criteria, so that the judgements can be sustained or motivated by referrals to these criteria. Herein lies another type of limitation to the entry into the aesthetic field: it is not only open to those born with certain capacities, it is open to anyone who, on the basis of universal human capacities, makes the necessary effort to acquire the relevant competence. In other words, with Kant there is a contradiction, or at least a tension, between the idea of innate qualifications as a prerequisite for passing valid aesthetic judgements and the idea of more generally available insights that also qualify for such an activity.

The subjectivist, individualistic character of Kant's understanding of the aesthetic, as well as his definition of it as a separate area of experience where qualified judges of taste evaluate various phenomena or products, both point to the specifically modern, European cultural context within which Kant lived and did his thinking. Kant's aesthetic philosophy is – with all of its internal tensions – *fundamental* to the western institution of art and all traditional ways of speaking of art, from philosophical and other academic writing on aesthetics to newspaper reviews and conversation in cafés. Several central positions in modern debates on art and culture can be recognized in the above points. It is also for these reasons that Kant's aesthetics have been an important point of reference for the critical cultural sociology of Pierre Bourdieu – especially his theory of *taste*, which we will now go on to look at in more depth.

Pure and barbaric taste

Bourdieu once said that he was 'wholly and fully ready to admit that Kant's aesthetic is true, but exclusively as the phenomenology of the aesthetic experience of all people who are the product of *schooling*' (quoted in Østerberg, 1995: 157). The capacity for the sort of aesthetic experience that Kant talked about is not 'natural' – it is a product of social conditions, not least education. In Bourdieu's terms it presupposes a certain habitus, and a central aspect of the habitus is *taste*.

Bourdieu bases this view on a series of extensive empirical studies he conducted with various collaborators in the 1960s. These were, among other things, concerned with the uses of photography and art museums. The study of the art museums, *L'amour de l'art* ([1969] 1997) was based on a survey conducted in 21 French museums and 15 in other countries, with a total of 15,000 respondents. In addition 250 people were interviewed and, in a separate study, 700 people were followed and observed while wandering around in museums. The most interesting results were not actually the figures showing how the public visiting the museums was socially skewed – 1 per cent were farmers or agricultural workers, 4 per cent workers, 23 per cent belonged to various parts of the middle class while 45 per cent came from the upper classes (*classes supérieures*) – more important was what the researchers found concerning people's very experience of the museums.

Two-thirds of the farmers and workers ('the popular classes') could not, after their visit, name a single one of the artists whose works they had just seen, and they told the interviewers that they had problems seeing any differences between the pictures at all. Others had only coarse categories into which they could place the pictures (all abstract paintings were 'like Picasso');

and those with a little further education would tend to operate with almost similarly inclusive, coarse categories. But art-historical competence covers more than such simple and 'superficial' things as rough epochal categories, it also makes possible the identification of meaningful elements in pictures that are simply not spotted by those without such competence. Any unskilled wanderer in, say, the Uffizi Gallery in Florence, with its endless rows of Madonna-and-child paintings will know what we are talking about here. The competent spectator can identify not only certain standard symbolical elements in religious pictures, but also meaningful differences in colours, brush strokes, and so on. Knowledge about such things means having a language for elements and aspects of various artworks that makes possible the naming of differences and thus the establishment of meanings and, possibly, pleasures that are inaccessible to other people. This is basically the same as the difference in the experience of a game of soccer between a European who is well acquainted with the sport and an American who is not or, vice versa, a game of American football or baseball. Without an adequate language, one simply does not see a number of important features of the 'object'.

Since so many of the artworks in the museums were incomprehensible to those of the lower classes in Bourdieu's study, one might think that they would reject them as uninteresting or being of low value. But because these people knew their place in the social hierarchy and were well aware that the pieces in question were artworks with a high cultural status, they instead expressed their more or less humble *respect*. They found their own ways of making the works valuable, ways other than those artistically relevant. They would, for instance, underline all the *work* that must have gone into the making both of the art and the museum itself. They pointed out how *old* the artworks were, and said they particularly liked the pictures that showed something they regarded as (morally) good and valuable, such as Christ. The less-educated visitors, in other words, had a tendency to bring with them *points of view and parameters they would use in their daily lives*, not criteria specific to art. They wanted artworks to portray something they recognized and understood, and something that was worth painting and exhibiting. Good pictures would show good things and preferably have bright and pretty colours. These are the central characteristics of what Bourdieu ironically – with reference to Kant's description of a taste that has not yet freed itself from 'barbary' – calls *barbaric taste*. The taste of those best educated is, also with reference to Kant, called *pure taste*. It is, first and foremost, characterized by its being based in *criteria that are specific for the aesthetic area*. The motif of an artwork is here often practically irrelevant; the main thing is formal qualities, judged in relation to other pictures, the tradition and so on. Pure taste presupposes a distanced, 'disinterested' approach, in line with Kant's idea of 'disinterested delight' as characteristic of the experience of 'beauty'.

The lower-educated were in favour of museums having pointers showing the way around the collections, and explanatory texts posted here and there. The higher-educated thought differently about these things; most of them were very much opposed to such ideas. They rejected such an interference in their experience of art. To them, the experience was primarily dependent on an ability to regard the artworks in an open, curious way – then their artistic qualities would become apparent by themselves. Museum visitors from the higher classes thus had a tendency to disregard or forget about all the competence they in fact had or made use of. Instead they seemed to prefer to think that their experiences of art resulted from a 'natural' ability they had to see and experience art. In line with such ideas, much art pedagogy has built on the premise that if people just get to see art, and look properly, the art experience will come of itself – to those with a talent for it.

There is a clear connection between these ideas of the higher educated and the emphasis they place on having *personal* taste. When naming their favourites they would tend to shun the most well-known, canonized artists and rather mention lesser-known people they would claim had been at the forefront of developments. Bourdieu regards this not only as a sign of self-determination or cultural independence; such independence presupposes that school-like knowledge is so solidly apprehended that one can dare free oneself from it. When one does so, and for instance goes for the lesser-known artists when mentioning favourites, one also marks the difference between oneself and those who more timidly try to repeat the standard perceptions they have struggled to learn.

The area of art is in these ways thoroughly marked by class differences, right through to the subjective experience of art. This social area also contributes to the visibility of class differences, since certain forms of art and practices linked to them are generally perceived as signs of one's belonging to particular social categories. As mentioned, the main title of the book in which Bourdieu sums up much of his research is *Distinction*, and it is precisely distinction, the marking of social differences understood as rankings, that social life both in the field of art and elsewhere is to a great extent about. For differences in taste with regard to art are tied to more general differences in habitus, and thus to extensive differences in lifestyle.

Lifestyles in market research

According to the Danish sociologist and market researcher Henrik Dahl, a 'nerd' can be recognized as follows: 'When asked "Would you like a whisky?", he answers "No, thank you, I'm not thirsty." A nerd thinks we only drink because we are thirsty, dress to keep warm and buy a car to get from one place to another' (Dahl, 1997: 85). The rest of us know that there is more to it than this, not least a desire to signal to other people what kind of human being we are, or want to be. More or less systematic differences in lifestyle are visible and most modern people, particularly urban and younger people, can determine quite precisely 'what sort of people' will choose this or that type of clothing, car, house, cultural activity, TV programme, book or whatever. This is, of course, exploited by the advertising industry when it targets specific parts of the population. Certain car models are made particularly attractive to younger professional women; others are aimed at the well-off middle-aged man who 'still has a boy inside him'; a third group – those who like to signal proper breeding – drive 'discreetly elegant' cars.

'Signal' is a pertinent word here. All goods that can function as *signs of lifestyle* are also *signs of identity*, i.e. they tell others who we are or, rather, who we want to be. That commodities can function like this, is actually an old theme in sociology, as illustrated by the American sociologist Thorstein Veblen's concept of *conspicuous consumption*, which is over a century old (Veblen [1899] 1953). What we consider to be attractive identities depends on our habitus and the composition of our capital. Even if there is significant space for our conscious play with signs, the limits to that space are thus to a considerable degree decided by social preconditions on which we have had little influence. In principle, anyone can dress in proper art appreciator's clothes and go to the opening of an art exhibition, but not just anyone can drop the 'correct' comments on the exhibited pieces.

Since so much of this is common knowledge, part of our everyday practical knowledge, people in advertising and the sales departments of the mass media can go a long way simply by relying on what 'everyone knows'. However, partly because they want to motivate their choices of strategy in a convincing way, and partly because they wish to detect and relate to changes that might be going on in people's priorities, the advertising industry and its clients have long been researching all the factors that form people's patterns of consumption, including the use of media. Modern media constantly survey their audiences. They want to know what kinds of people read which newspapers and books, watch which TV channels, visit the cinema, etc. This type of audience investigation is known as *market research*.

Market research makes use of any available social scientific method – surveys, focus groups, participant observation – and a whole battery of sophisticated statistical techniques. The information provided by these procedures deals with how audiences are composed in terms of age, gender, education, work, income, values and lifestyle. Bourdieu's work has been a source of inspiration for this type of research, both theoretically and methodologically, and it is in part a form of sociological research that may be of general interest. It is also geared to finding out what different types of audiences want from the media, what they like and dislike. The idea is that the information it gathers will make it easier to make the products that audiences want. Commercial media often boast that they work hard to give the audience exclusively what it wants (something we will return to several times in this book).

But they do not necessarily give all parts of the audience what they want. To commercial media, small groups and groups of poor and elderly people will be less important than large groups and groups of young and well-off people. According to normal commercial logic, the point is to gather as large as possible an audience of people with *spending power* – and a willingness to use it. What 'as large as possible' means may of course vary with the sort of medium or media product in question. Those who publish a fashion magazine for women do not care what type of content men would like to see there, and are not particularly keen to know what women above 60 or below 15 think either. Market research for the media is a necessary tool when one wants to reach particular parts of the population and to adjust the profile of content in order to maximize reach within a particular target group. Solid market research will also provide more general information about the audience, their opinions on this or that, their values, attitudes and preferences in a number of areas. This is very useful when the media come to approach potential advertisers: 'Our readers are particularly interested in what your company produces, 86 per cent of them love animals at least as much as human beings and 57 per cent have a dog or cat; 52 per cent have above-average incomes so an upmarket style would be good.'

This sort of thinking is not only found in the commercial media, it is in a sense just a modern interpretation of an old insight drawn from rhetoric of antiquity, that one must adjust one's speech to one's audience if one wants to be persuasive (cf. Chapter 6 of the present volume, on rhetoric). The question is, though, whether one also lives up to the equally old criterion for good rhetoric, namely that one should speak truthfully.

'Targeting' has increasingly become important, both for various cultural institutions and the (in principle) non-commercial public service broadcasters of Europe and other parts of the world. Radio and TV channels are constructed so as to address and please particular segments of the audience in terms of their programming. Where these channels offer broad, comprehensive schedules in terms of programme categories, one will find that their programmes assume that lifestyles are systematic so that there is a kind of unity to the choice of anything from hairstyles and furniture to musical preferences and favourite holiday spots. Stereotypical characterizations of audience types can then be generated – for example, using 'typical' types of clothing, as the Norwegian public service broadcaster did when referring to its radio channels as the 'knitwear channel', the 'leather jacket channel' and the 'beret channel' (the latter referring to a long-dead custom among intellectuals who wanted to look a little French). A particular mix of programme formats and musical styles was appropriate to each garment.

These clothing terms were chosen as a 'fun' way of marketing the new channels, but the channel profiles were actually constructed with the aid of systematic and far-reaching continuous market research conducted by a private company that serves a number of major media and other businesses and organizations. The company divides the population into categories that in part resemble those of Bourdieu, but that focus more on 'values' and 'attitudes'. It uses the same statistical method as Bourdieu – correspondence analysis – and so also produces diagrams or 'maps' of a kind that is reminiscent of those of Bourdieu. Their main axes, however, are 'materialist' vs 'idealist' and 'modern' vs 'traditional'. One thus gets four main categories: 'modern materialists', 'modern idealists', 'traditional materialists' and 'traditional idealists'. Modern materialists are interested in money, consumption, status, speed and fun. Modern idealists are interested in self-realization, various 'soft' values, including art, and the latest thing in every area. Traditional materialists give priority to safety/security, material well-being, common sense and conformity, while traditional idealists think that saving and safety are very important, along with puritanism and religion, respect for the law and patriotism. (These are just a few of the characteristics listed for each of the four categories of people.) The 'knitwear channel' was to serve the two traditionalist categories, the 'beret channel' was to serve the modern idealists, while the 'leather jacket channel' was to serve (young) modern materialists. In Britain, radio channels are constructed and diversified according to similar principles, though the appropriate symbolic garments may be different. Radio 2: The cardigan channel?

Whatever else this kind of ordering of broadcast and other media offerings can do, it may help ensure that none of us will ever be seriously surprised at anything we encounter in the media (or at least that we will never be surprised to find that we actually like something we never expected would be anything but dull, or indeed that we didn't even know existed because it was intended for 'the others'). It is a practical system, since it tells us what we will get from various channels or magazines, or whatever. But how does it work in terms of social and cultural democracy?

The social mapping based on the values and attitudes referred to above is different from Bourdieu's maps because France in the 1960s and Britain or the USA at the beginning of the twenty-first century are very different. Nevertheless, there are also important similarities. The 'modern materialists' resemble those with more economic than cultural capital (the top right-hand box in Bourdieu's diagram), the 'modern idealists' resemble those with more cultural than economic capital (the top left-hand box), while the traditionalists are distributed in the lower parts of the diagram, some to the left (idealists), some to the right (materialists). More important, however, is that both types of social maps refer to the systematic character of lifestyles and thus also underline that the concrete manifestations of lifestyle may change over time while the divisions themselves remain. 'Modern idealists', or those in the upper left-hand corner of Bourdieu's diagram, were in some countries, for a decade or two, consumers of folksy pine furniture and other somewhat nostalgic styles. But the people in knitwear also, later, filled their homes with pine furniture in imitated rural styles 'from the old days', so the 'modern idealists' decided to start buying furniture in other sorts of wood, or even stainless steel. *The main point is that the system of distinctions is maintained.*

Market research is mostly conducted by private companies that, as a rule, pay their employees far better than publicly owned academic institutions. They can, as a result, hire competent people with solid educational backgrounds and research records. The interaction with the scholarly field may, however, actually be quite well developed in many ways. Market research can, theoretically, be updated and can produce many interesting results – from a scholarly point of view. Still, it is not counted as truly scholarly, 'real' social-scientific work. A main reason for this is that the results are not published in the ordinary way so that they are immediately freely available to the community of scholars and possibly a wider, more general public. The results of market research are instead for sale, at a very high price, to those who ordered them, possibly through some form of subscription. This is a fundamental breach of the *ethos* or spirit of scholarly endeavour. It is furthermore not in line with the traditional and highly important principles of academic freedom, in that market research in principle only deals with the problems its clients' business interests dictate, not those problems pointed out by independent scholarly work. This latter principle is, however, constantly undermined these days, where 'commissioned research' in various forms is more or less the norm at universities and independent institutes, and where whatever other research exists is expected to demonstrate its immediate usefulness to society all the time.

But market research is still a particularly clear example of what Paul F. Lazarsfeld called 'administrative research' – empirical research at the disposal of anyone who can pay for it and who wants to know how to make use of or shape the media more 'efficiently' (cf. the previous chapter). There is nothing immoral about this in itself; and if ethically dubious commissions are proposed, one can just say no. But it is still worth asking if there isn't something problematic about research that maps the composition, preferences and values of audiences with the sole purpose of making it easier and cheaper for media to become better tools for advertisers through their contents. This means that the goal of research is to help media owners, advertisers and manufacturers make more money, while the satisfaction of the audience is only a *means* to achieving this goal. Does this research, then, contribute to making living human beings pure and exploitable objects for capitalist interests? And what about the use of market research to 'target' particular audiences with particular media offerings such as radio and TV channels? Doesn't that, as suggested above, contribute to a fixation of social and cultural cleavages and hierarchies?

These are important critical questions, but they do not only apply to market research. They could more or less concern all research that maps social and cultural structures and relations: its results could also be used for manipulative purposes. A defence could be that all valid and reliable information about social conditions is valuable in itself as long as it is freely available to anyone, and that it cannot be an important concern for scholars that their work may be misused for more or less manipulative financial or political purposes. This is a relevant argument, but it may still be worth keeping the question of the *social functions of research and scholarship* at the back of one's mind when problems are formulated, concepts and approaches defined, methods and forms of publication chosen. *For whom* or, better, *in line with which knowledge-interests* is one's scholarly work conducted?

Is having cultural capital and 'pure' taste an advantage?

There are many, not least in the USA and the UK, who believe that Bourdieu is arguing that 'high' art and the understanding of such art is 'only' socially constructed as 'high' and therefore nothing but snobbery and that the 'barbaric' taste of the popular classes is 'actually' just as good as the pure one. This is a misunderstanding.

That something is 'socially constructed' does not mean that it is 'unreal' or exists without justification or substantial reasons. Snobbery is, on the other hand, always unjustified. It can here be defined as the flaunting of a cultural capital one has too little of. Cultural capital is, one could argue, in itself a good and useful thing to have. But not everyone has the advantage of having it as part of their habitus baggage through primary socialization. The main target of Bourdieu's critique is not the knowledge and competence that constitute cultural capital, or the fact that cultural capital can contribute to a high position in society; he once said that he himself has the taste that is adequate for his position (at the very top of the left-hand part of his diagram), and he is clearly interested in and knowledgeable about high art. He most energetically opposes the idea that the world of art is open to anyone with the right sort of attitude and talent. As we have seen, his main point is that one does not gain real access to high art and its traditions without some more or less hard work in terms of education, work that is less hard for people with the 'right' sort of background, people who have had a positive attitude installed early on and started learning at an early age. As has been demonstrated in the previous brief overview of the history of the concept of taste, it is already over 500 years since the distinction began to be made between those who had a more thorough knowledge of art and those who more or less lacked it. With this distinction came another: between art that was designed to please the many without particular competence; and art that *connoisseurs*, those with 'good taste', would appreciate most.

What Bourdieu calls 'pure taste', is first and foremost, characterized by a distanced, analytical approach, and it presupposes a well-developed language that can sharpen one's perceptions and strengthen the ability to communicate to others what one has seen, read or heard. Pure taste is therefore related to more general cognitive, intellectual competences, such as the ability to think abstractly, reflect – and analyse. Such general competences are clearly useful when one wants to understand the world and oneself, to understand social situations and relations, or when one wants to acquire *any* sort of abstract knowledge or way of thinking. Pure taste is also tied to a considerable amount of cultural capital – that is to say, lots of useful knowledge about history, geography and social conditions, plus of course knowledge of art and philosophy that most serious thinking on society and culture constantly refers to. Economic capital is money and money is, as any political economist will tell you, just generalized, abstract exchange value, with no concrete use-value in itself (unless you use notes to make roll-up cigarettes or go swimming in cash, as Disney's Uncle Scrooge does). Contrary to this, cultural capital has a use-value as a basis for self-reliant, critical thinking, besides the fact that it has an 'exchange value' that can be traded for certain social positions.

But the notions of 'pure' and 'barbaric' (or popular) taste are, of course, also *ideal types*. Few people, if any, have a cultural taste that is exclusively and at all times absolutely 'pure'. An art historian I know has, for instance, publicly 'admitted' that she regards her taste in visual art as quite 'pure', while her collection of CDs on the other hand is quite barbaric. The situation is most probably of a similar kind with most people in the upper left-hand part of Bourdieu's diagram. Few people could justifiably call themselves 'connoisseurs', or something to the same effect, of all art forms, even if we only think of, say, literature, music and visual art. Most people who are really fond of and attend concerts with classical music are without particularly 'deep' knowledge of the theory of music and they do not experience well-known romantic or baroque pieces in a distanced or analytical way. And, even if they do have the necessary qualifications and could have listened in accordance with the principles of 'pure' taste, they may not *want* to do so all the time. Sometimes they just want to immerse themselves in the music, to feel and enjoy. Even with the best-educated lovers of film and literature, one can sometimes hear them say they had a really good time with a movie or a novel they do not really consider a work of art.

'Pure taste' can, then, also be seen as a competence that one can choose whether or not one wants to use. Many academically educated people with lots of cultural capital will appreciate 'barbaric' phenomena in various media, such as football matches, action movies, Hollywood TV series and straightforward pop music. Some of these – possibly professors of cultural and media studies, but also professors or students of any other subject – may be eager to argue and demonstrate that what they like of these sorts of thing is *actually* incredibly deep stuff with an aesthetic quality one really has to be highly qualified to spot. They may claim, for instance, that they watch a football match on TV, in a very enthusiastic way, only because they so much appreciate the aesthetics of the game, not because they, for somewhat murky reasons, hope that 'their' team will beat the other team to a pulp. Or they may try to convince themselves and others that they watch *Baywatch* every week because this show is a sublimely ironic commentary on the postmodern condition.

Nowadays an ironic, distanced way of speaking about and enjoying popular culture products, such as soap operas and other officially low-status phenomena, is widespread, not least among students. This is obviously a way of legitimating and thus 'saving' the pleasures of these products. By letting the world know through one's use of irony that one knows these are not exactly culturally respectable things, one can secretly still savour the kind of pleasures one's new or desired social position in principle forbids. One thus also indicates that one belongs to a different class and knows better than those simple-minded idiots who straightforwardly love soap opera or the music of Aqua or Boyzone, without feeling the least bit ashamed. Such use of irony may often be regarded as snobbery, in line with our definition above – the flaunting of a cultural capital one has too little of. The more real cultural capital one has, the greater one's self-confidence, so that one has no problem saying that one likes barbaric pleasures *as barbaric*.

It is often said that the borders between popular culture and art have become unclear, fuzzy, broken down. This is also true in many ways, both in terms of how the products or texts in question are, and in terms of audience overlaps. This is principally because of a new openness towards 'barbaric' products among well-educated people. It is worth noting, however, that this openness occurs far less in the other direction. People with considerable amounts of cultural capital may well enjoy popular arts and various 'barbaric' activities more than ever before (cf. Peterson and Kern, 1996), but those with relatively little cultural capital cannot just as easily enjoy modern visual art, demanding novels, serious music and so on. One might say that those with more or less solid cultural capital and more or less 'pure' taste have a *double access* to cultural life; they can move more or less freely across the boundaries between its higher and lower sections. They can, moreover, develop analytical, critical concepts to describe, analyse and evaluate their experiences of popular culture. (People with academic degrees in media and cultural studies may be very good at this, and may even make a living out of it.) Other people will be confined to a 'single access', i.e. only have access to popular culture forms, and will also, as a rule, be without a specialized language for their experiences (Gripsrud, 1989). Even if one can, of course, have a great life without such a language, it is hardly sensible to see the lack of it as an advantage.

'High' and 'low' culture in historical perspective

The close ties between social class differences and differences in cultural preferences or taste that we have dealt with in this chapter imply that the cultural distinctions are as old as class differences. Only societies totally without class or other hierarchical ordering of their members can be totally without a hierarchical ordering of cultural or artistic products and practices. This is not to say that such hierarchies have always been of the same sort and have always had the same structure.

The British cultural historian Peter Burke (1978: 302) has claimed that Europe around the year 1500 had a two-culture system. There was a learned, 'high' culture for the upper classes (the nobility, clergy and associated groups, wealthy merchants and the like), and a popular, 'low' culture for the rest of the population. This popular culture was, however, at the same time *a common culture*, in the sense that it was shared by everyone, including the upper classes, and everyone took part in its feasts, ceremonies and so on – everyone knew its narratives and songs. After 1500, however, came times of exploration, scientific discovery and more rapid social development in general. All of this revolutionized the learned culture so that it came to differ much more markedly from the popular, more stable culture in terms of worldview, forms and contents. Around 1800, then, the distance was so great that representatives of the educated upper classes could explore the rural and peripheral areas of their own countries, looking for a really 'authentic' popular culture among the people they themselves had lost contact with. Such explorations were an important part of the epoch of cultural history known as Romanticism, and were often motivated by theories about a *national popular or 'folk' spirit*, most influentially formulated by the German philosopher Herder (as *Volksgeist*) in the late eighteenth century. This 'folk spirit' was thought to be 'stored' in its authentic or original form in the language, traditional narratives and music of rural areas. People such as the Brothers Grimm in Germany and many like them in other countries therefore collected many folktales and folk tunes.

This interest in unspoiled, authentic *folk culture* manifested itself just at the time when worries were expressed that it might be lost. Capitalist economy was growing rapidly, resulting in industrialization, expanding international trade and quite dramatic growth in urban populations. In cities and industrial areas, traditional folk culture was about to be replaced by a new, more or less industrially produced, market-based culture: the modern, commercial *popular culture*. New songs were sold in prints and performed by professional singers; narratives were written by professional authors and sold by travelling salesmen or in shops; different sorts of theatres appeared, providing stage entertainment for quite broadly composed audiences, not just for the nobility and the royal courts. It was not least as a contrast to this urbanized people and its popular culture that rural folk spirit and its traditional culture could be idealized as something 'deep' and 'authentic'. Popular culture was regarded as a downfall from the noble old folk culture, just as the proletariat of the cities represented a lower type of people compared to the proud peasants of the old school.

The institutions of 'high' culture – museums, symphony orchestras, concert halls and prestigious theatres – can in many cases be regarded as means to ensure that the upper classes could be on their own in their encounters with the art forms they favoured. The American sociologist Paul DiMaggio has shown this, among other things, in a study of developments in Boston in the nineteenth century (DiMaggio, 1986). Public concerts in the first part of the century would most often have a socially mixed audience and a repertory where the 'Railroad gallop' would be played (sometimes with a miniature steam locomotive moving across the floor of the concert hall) along with the best of European art music. The establishment of symphony orchestras as private organizations, without any public support, ended such practices, and the same sort of process took place in other art forms. The result was a narrowing, both of musical styles and social groups represented. It is true that museums of fine art might organize open days for members of the middle and lower classes for what were, at least officially, educational reasons; but in light of Bourdieu's findings about lower-class people's respect for the art they did not really understand, this could be regarded, as it is by DiMaggio, as a way of ensuring a broader recognition or social legitimation of the supremacy of high art. Apart from genuine educational idealism, such (possibly more or less unconscious) motives could also be part of the reason why upper-class people of various sorts supported what I have referred to as 'group excursions to the world of art' (i.e. efforts to bring working-class people into high art institutions in groups organized through trade unions or other organizations) (Gripsrud 1981). This was a quite widespread practice, particularly between the two world wars, in many European countries. It was not, however, necessarily popular among the regular patrons of these institutions, who worried about workers spitting on the carpets and generally disrupting the finer, civilized atmosphere.

All the informal markers of high art institutions as places for the upper social classes have lasted much longer than the direct, financial barriers presented by high membership fees or ticket prices. Nowadays it is often more expensive to go to a pop concert than it is to buy a ticket for concerts given by local symphony orchestras. It is those tightly knit entities – habitus, cultural capital and taste – that decide whether one visits high art institutions and feels more or less comfortable there. At the same time, a greater part of the population do this than ever before. The central institutions appear much less exclusive now than they did 100 years ago. A main reason for this is the so-called educational revolution that started around 1960. What used to be elite educations have become quite common, and this means a much wider distribution of cultural capital. Consequently, many more people will feel less like strangers *vis-à-vis* the institutions of high art than was previously the case.

The generations of mass education have, at the same time, grown up with modern media and are familiar with (and even fans of) the popular culture of these media. This is why they have, and make use of, a 'double access' to both the high and low sections of cultural life. Such a practice must have consequences for the ways in which we think about notions of 'quality' in the field of media and culture.

The question of difference in quality

Disparagement of, or outright contempt for, certain cultural products will often be combined with disparagement of, or contempt for, those people who prefer such products. At a time when professors of philosophy actively seek the pleasures of simple crime series from Florida on TV, and professors of literature declare themselves fans of rock music and action movies, such stupid prejudices become even more stupid. This does not mean, however, that the question of differences in quality between different types of media and cultural products has become totally anachronistic. In this, the last section of this chapter, I will depart from Bourdieu's thinking and instead present some of my own ideas on this subject. I do not think they contradict Bourdieu, but they do draw on other sources.

One might argue that the discussion of quality has actually increased in importance the more media production expands, and our whole consumption of cultural products grows. In the real world (i.e. outside of academic theorizing) evaluations of the quality of journalistic and aesthetic products go on all the time in a great number of places all over the media and cultural sector. They also go on in a number of related businesses – decisions concerning the production and sales of clothes, furniture etc. are made not least after judgements of quality, both in aesthetic and other terms. In the media field alone, there are many people whose jobs are all about deciding whether something should be produced, published or distributed according to criteria that may well include the question of whether there is an audience or a market for the products alongside a number of other parameters. At least as important is the constant evaluation of quality that is performed by those who write, produce radio programmes, pictures, films, television shows or music while they work. They have to ask questions such as these: 'How do I or we solve this problem?' 'Is this a good idea?' 'Is this beautiful, appalling, funny or whatever?' Such assessments of quality are mirrored by those performed by each and every one of us when we begin a book, listen to music, watch a film and so on. Is this worth our time and attention?

Even if all such assessments are 'subjective' in the sense that they rely on the perceptions and more or less emotional reactions of individuals to the objects they evaluate, they are not conducted in a social vacuum. In principle, all quality assessments should be *arguable*, and the arguments used must necessarily refer to a set of more or less complex *aesthetic norms* for what is good and what is bad. As, for instance, the Czech literary scholar Jan Mukarovsky ([1931] 1970) once pointed out, such aesthetic norms vary with time, place and social class, but some of them are, according to Mukarovsky, at any given time the norms that dominate in a certain society, an idea Bourdieu would evidently agree with. (Bourdieu might, for all I know, on the other hand be more reluctant to accept Mukarovsky's idea that the norms of the dominating classes will 'trickle down', so that norms abandoned by the upper classes later live on in the lower parts of the social hierarchy.) The point here is, however, that all aesthetic norms of quality must be capable of being defended through some sort of argumentation, and so they must refer to a more general foundation than the 'purely subjective' perceptions.

The question is, then, whether this more general foundation is the same for all sorts of art or cultural products. It evidently is not. Novels and newspaper features are not evaluated by the same norms and the quality of film, TV and music is assessed by yet other sets of criteria. The characteristics of different media vary, and consequently the criteria for their evaluation must be different. More interesting are, however, the differences in criteria for the evaluation of pop music in comparison with serious music or those applied to a novel by Barbara Cartland in comparison with a novel by Dostoyevsky. One can also imagine that people will compare the quality of an episode of *ER* with that of Jim Jarmusch's film *Down by Law*, even if this is a comparison across media. Such comparisons are relevant, for instance, when one is deciding how to spend an evening.

A key to an understanding of such assessments is provided by the Italian scholar of literature, media and culture, Umberto Eco. He has argued that the value of a cultural product is dependent on how, or for what purpose, we use it. The same person who listens to pop music in the middle of the day may well prefer Beethoven or Stockhausen or some other relatively complex music at night (Eco, 1984: 54f.). This imagined person will not be seeking the same sort of experience in these two choices. The pop music could, for instance, be chosen for its stimulating, mood-lifting or relaxing effects (as could 'light' classical music); while one of Beethoven's symphonies, say, would demand more concentrated listening and provide a more complex, possibly intellectually stimulating, experience. In both cases the musical experience will be valuable, but in a different way. If one is to evaluate pop music, one will have to first compare it with other pop music and the functions pop music usually has (i.e. assess its quality *in view of the genre in question*). But then one might, of course, also imagine that one can evaluate the pop music product in question in light of more general, overarching criteria for what is valuable art and what is less valuable. The statistical probability that a pop tune will then be competing with Beethoven, or that an average crime novel will compare with James Joyce's *Ulysses* is quite minimal, even if the former of these alternatives sells millions more copies than the latter. Beethoven's music and Joyce's literature are, one might say, counted as more valuable than most pop tunes and popular novels because they are more suited for purposes or functions that our society and culture regard as more valuable than the experience of pleasure in dancing at a club, or feeling the adrenaline pumping while watching an exciting scene in an action movie.

This could be so simply because a few dry academics, with 'pure taste', control the institutional power to decide what is really valuable and what isn't. It is true that much popular culture is more complex and thought-provoking than many academic dry sticks have realized, and that these academics may have difficulty validating the everyday pleasure and other emotional experiences that popular culture provides for its audiences. It is impossible to decide beforehand, a priori, where the limits should be drawn for what a particular genre can do in relation to the general, overarching norms traditionally used to distinguish between the really good and the more mundane. Now and then there might be a pop CD or a soap opera or even a piece of tabloid journalism that invites concentrated apprehension and reflection. But the fact that many of these traditional norms still exist and function, even if the border between 'high' and 'low' culture is now more unclear than ever, in my opinion has to do with their foundations in basic, broadly accepted values in our type of modern society.

Most of Ingmar Bergman's films may, for instance, be said to be more valuable representations of human relations than all soap operas to date, not least because they are more nuanced or complex and go far deeper into the problems they are about. They are, in a word, more *serious*. They treat human problems in a thorough, serious way, and one could therefore also say that they take humankind and its problems in earnest, treating them with the respect they actually deserve. Tragedy has historically been regarded as more valuable than comedy, and this may result from the seriousness and dignity with which tragedy handles the human condition. This is in keeping with how most people feel that fundamentally important questions ought to be treated. This does not, of course, preclude that comedies too may acquire a status as highly valuable, but they do this precisely when they in some way communicate a sort of insight that in itself is not particularly hilarious. If one, as I do, breaks with tradition and regards the comic perspective on human beings and their world as at least as important as the tragic one, this view may be put across in a comic way, but it still has a highly serious motivation. The very best comedies are precisely those that convey a serious, and possibly even painful, insight in a comic language or form. 'Insight' is, moreover, an important notion here because it points to the connection that, historically, has existed between serious art on the one hand, and philosophy and various sciences or other forms of scholarship on the other. Reflection and knowledge is generally regarded as valuable, and the artworks or (other) media products that are directly or indirectly tied to various traditions of learning and other advanced treatments of fundamental problems will consequently have more than just 'seriousness' as a basis for their value.

In modern societies it is furthermore a culturally fundamental premise that anything can be improved, from work and sports achievements to technical appliances and marriages. The ubiquitous celebration of *the new* in all areas is related to this; the new is in principle expected to be better than the old. Renewal tends in itself to be thought of as something good. This certainly also applies to the fields of media and culture, where 'renewal' and 'creativity' are always seen as positive. It is, for instance, regarded as a good thing when some product can be said to renew its genre. Such renewal can sometimes be just a whim of fashion, a gimmick of some sort, at other times it could be seen as a contribution to keeping sensibilities, imagination and intellect alive so that we can also more easily discover, say, possibilities for social improvement.

The sort of seriousness that is a prerequisite for a high general cultural value is, for instance in the films of Ingmar Bergman and other great directors, also most often expressed in the fact that they are produced with great consideration for all details and are marked by highly qualified professionalism in all or most functions that go into the production of a film. If one produces one 25-minute episode per day of a TV serial, or two 50-

minute episodes per month for that matter, it is simply impossible to achieve the same sort of quality (cf., for example, Gripsrud, 1995, Chapter 1). In films like Bergman's one can simply say that more work, and as a rule also more qualified work, in terms of thinking and craftsmanship, is invested per minute and per hour than in most or all TV series or serials. This point is in line with the core element of truth in the 'barbarian' respect for things that obviously took a lot of (competent) work to produce. Still, this is not, of course, to be taken to mean that the value of a piece of art is simply decided by the number of hours it took to produce it, even if one adds that one is thinking of highly qualified work. Great things have been produced very rapidly, springing from a brilliant idea, resulting from luck, accident or whatever. Even if such things will usually have had some basis in extensive preparations and solid experience with the medium in question, there is still an important space left for the sudden revelation, the perfect line that 'just appeared', the rare light conditions that just happened to be there when the photograph was taken, the interviewee or actor that unexpectedly produces magic in front of the camera, and so on.

There are, however, also artworks and other media products that are technically very competent, that obviously took a lot of work to produce, that are serious in contents and philosophically relevant, but that we still would condemn. This is the case when the texts or products in question appear unacceptable in terms of ideology or values. Leni Riefenstahl's Nazi propaganda film *Triumf des Willens* (*The Triumph of the Will*) is one example of this. The film is, in many ways, a masterpiece – but for all people, other than Nazis, it is still 'bad'. A TV series like *Ally McBeal* is commonly regarded as a quality show, which has renewed its genre, but to many feminists it still isn't a good series since, to them, it in many ways appears highly problematic in ideological terms. Values and convictions of all sorts – even the relaxed liberal ones in the middle ground – play an important role in discussions of 'quality'. This is one central reason why no one should expect absolute agreement on all judgements of quality. But the fact that even anti-fascists can see that Riefenstahl's films are competently made, and that they also have great value as historical documents, demonstrates how one can distinguish between different kinds and levels of evaluation. An agreement between professionally competent 'judges' is more easily reached on some accounts than others, including an agreement on which products are more worthy of discussion and disagreement than others.

Most of us will find it difficult to register differences in quality between two professional symphony orchestras' performance of Beethoven's Fifth Symphony. In all media and arts, including the popular ones, there is a difference between the most competent specialists and us ordinary listeners, viewers or readers. It takes more than general cultural capital to function as a competent evaluator of certain art forms, for instance as a critic who is to publish her or his views. The role of the critic, which developed with the institutional autonomy of the arts and the general, bourgeois public sphere, is ideally to function as the competent spokesperson for the public or audience *vis-à-vis* the artists or producers, and as educator and guide for the public. Those who fill this role should, consequently, have a thorough knowledge of the medium and the genres they are to evaluate, and also an amount of general cultural capital that enables them to regard the products they assess in a more general perspective. The best critics supply us with a better understanding of the media or art forms in question and also contribute more generally to making us a bit wiser.

Luckily, though, we still have a right to disagree with even the best of critics. Our disagreement will, however, only be of interest to others (except sociologists, market researchers and other ethnologists) to the extent that we can come up with real arguments in favour of our view. Having a bit of cultural capital is, then, helpful. One might, say, have the pleasure of quoting Bertolt Brecht whenever it feels appropriate: 'Even when there is talk of higher and lower forms of amusement, art does not care, since it wants to move high and low and to be left alone as long as it can entertain people by doing so' (Brecht [1948] 1973: 111).

PART 2

Perspectives on media texts

4 Semiotics: signs, codes and cultures

The 'railway model' of communication

Most people who have gone through elementary school will be familiar with the simple, basic model of communication:

sender → message → receiver

'Communication' is what goes on when a 'sender' sends a 'message' to a 'receiver'. This *linear model* contains the three most important elements in all forms of communication and it also indicates the *direction* of the process. It is logically valid, but it is very simple. One could call it the railway model of communication. The railway is, as we all know, also a form of communication. Of course, when a place is said to have 'good communications', this does not necessarily mean that people often chat peacefully there. It means the place is well connected to other places by way of roads, railways, flight paths or ferries. The simple, linear model of communication actually compares the communication of writing, sound and pictures with the transportation of a parcel by rail. The parcel that someone wraps and posts will usually arrive safely and unchanged to the addressee, who will know exactly what to do with the contents. This is not necessarily the case when the media do the transporting, and when the parcels are various types of text.

The media actually most of the time do not communicate simple, unambiguous 'information' such as 'the time is now 6.30pm' or 'Rock star so-and-so was arrested for possession of heroin last night'. Such messages can easily be transformed into yes/no-type questions. They are either true or false. But what is the meaning of the little video vignette that opens the main newscast every evening? And when Tony Blair or George W. Bush appears on the TV screen, do their pictures mean the same to all viewers? And what about the direct, interpersonal communication between people in everyday life? Even the most common of sentences, such as 'the weather is pretty good today' or 'I love you when you are like this' can be more or less enigmatic.

Both interpersonal and media communication is therefore a lot more complicated than the transport of parcels by railway. We need a more complex understanding of what goes on. But still, we do in everyday life feel we understand most of what is said both in the media and among people we meet. This chapter is about how both understandings and misunderstandings can be regarded, and at least partially explained, by a *theory of signs*, or *semiotics* (from the Greek *semeion*, sign).

The cultural competence of everyday life: signs and codes

Imagine turning on the TV and the first thing you see is the frame shown in Figure 4.1, from the opening credits of a feature film. What sort of film would you think this is? Most students will spend about a second deciding that it is a

Figure 4.1 Still from *The Sons of Katie Elder*, Henry Hathaway, 1965.

western. There are several reasons for this. We see an old steam locomotive, which will place the scene at least a century back in time, possibly more. The train passes through a wild mountain landscape. Both of these elements could well belong in a film that is located in Switzerland or Norway, or any other country with mountains and railways, but the text on the screen has words and names that we associate with English-speaking countries, and the USA dominates film production. So we might assume that the film is set in the USA at least 100 years ago. What visually decides that it must be a western, however, is the shape of the letters used. They somehow appear to be roughly cut in wood, and this sort of graphic form is a *sign* we have learned to associate with fictions from the Wild West. The steam locomotive and the landscape are compatible with this interpretation, and the same goes for the sound we hear: Elmer Bernstein's music, with prominent brass sounds in a symphonic orchestration of a piece expressing will-power, optimism – and horse-manship, i.e. a sort of galloping music we know from innumerable scenes of riding on the prairie and thereabouts.

In just a second, then, reasonably competent film and TV viewers will have 'read' what sort of movie this is from the picture and, possibly, the sound. It is a philological point worth mentioning that the word for 'read' in German, *lesen*, and in French, *lire*, are both etymologically derived from the Latin *legere*, meaning the putting together of diverse elements to form a new whole (etymology = the history of words). This is basically what we do when we read – we put together letters to form words, and words so that they form more or less meaningful sentences. But, as we have just seen, a similar process may take place with pictures and sounds. We see some figure we identify as a steam locomotive. We *link* this to a notion of 'the old days'. We see letters reminiscent of pieces of wood. We *link* this to a fictional genre, the western. The wild, mountainous landscape can also be linked to this. These elements mean different things, but they can all be brought together in our ideas about the western genre.

Each of these visual elements can thus be said to function as a *sign*. According to the Swiss linguist Ferdinand de Saussure (1857–1913), who coined the term *semiology*, a sign is a whole consisting of a *material signifier* and an *immaterial signified*. The signifier can thus be dots, lines, shapes, sound waves or whatever physical, concrete entity that *we* link to, or associate with, some idea or notion. We hardly ever stop to think about such associative connections, since they are established in accordance with a *rule* or *code* that we learned long ago. These rules are not in any book of law. They are *conventions*, that is to say 'agreements' established by way of habit in a community of users of the same language, the same sorts of pictures, music and so on. *A code is a rule or convention that associates a signifier with a certain signified or meaning.*

The relations between signifiers and signifieds: arbitrariness and motivation

As just mentioned, Ferdinand de Saussure was a linguist and consequently primarily interested in speech and writing, i.e. verbal language. One of the things that characterizes verbal language in relation to pictures is that the relation between signifiers and signifieds is accidental or *arbitrary*. There is nothing about actual dogs that determines that the sound 'dog' is used to refer to them. This is why the animal in question can be called *Hund* in German and *chien* in French. Same animal, different words. Some small children may, at pre-school age, wonder why 'hill' is not called 'butter' and why are the plants we can climb called 'trees' and not 'ball'? The answer is of course that this is simply the way it is. It is something speakers of English somehow agreed upon (established a convention on) a very long time ago. There is nothing, in principle, to prevent us from shifting to call cats 'dogs' and dogs 'cats' as of tomorrow. ('But wouldn't it confuse the animals?', the hero of David Lodge's novel *Small World* asked when he heard the latter sentence conclude a brief introduction to semiological thinking.)

Visual signs are different. If we on the TV screen see some shape that looks like a dog, we might say that what we see is a signifier that refers to the signified 'dog'. While the signifier 'dog' in the sentence 'The dog came running across the lawn' at least at first has no meaning other than a general 'dog-ness' attached to it, no particular breed and certainly no name, the visual dog sign on the screen is far more specific. At least as long as we are talking about a photographic sign or a 'realistic' drawing. It is a collie (Lassie, perhaps?) or a German shepherd (could it be Rin-Tin-Tin?), for example. Some would argue that photographs and realistic drawings are also coded signs. They are shaped in accordance with the *codes of perception* that we have, i.e. certain rules for the interpretation of visual or other sensory impressions that we routinely use in everyday life and that may not be shared by all cultures. In this case, they might not be known in cultures where the 'dog' phenomenon – wherever that may be – is unknown. As soon as one leaves behind photography and the most 'realistic' of drawings etc., it also becomes more clear that visual signs are also based in codes or conventions. A circle with scattered lines stretching outward around it is a conventional representation of, or sign for, the sun. We accept that this figure means 'sun' in, for instance, children's drawings, even if the sun does not actually look like that when one looks at it in the sky. The same applies to all simple drawings and other stylized, more or less abstract visual forms, such as road signs and the signs on the doors of public toilets that are to inform us whether they are intended for men or women. The latter do not much resemble real men and women, but we recognize them precisely as conventional signs for the sexes that are also sort of humanlike shapes and thus partly motivated.

The relationship between signifier and signifieds in signs can, in other words, be *more or less conventional, more or less motivated* – from the totally arbitrary and consequently conventional in verbal language to the minimally arbitrary or clearly motivated in straightforward photography. We will return to this in a slightly different context below.

The two steps of signification: denotation and connotation

Some readers may have noticed that, in our description of the video still from the opening credits of *The Sons of Katie Elder*, above, we tried to signal how an audience, in effect, perceives what the screen shows – the signifiers – in two steps. We first identify a steam locomotive, and we then link or associate this phenomenon with 'the old days', history, a long time ago etc. We first see that the letters are reminiscent of pieces of wood, and then we link or associate this with the western genre. Such a sequence is, however, not really noticeable in real life. It is primarily an *analytical, logical or theoretical distinction* between two sorts of signification; in reality we perceive both meanings more or less simultaneously. The first of the two meanings – the first, most 'immediate' one – is, in the semiological theoretical tradition based in Saussure's work, called *denotation*; the second, 'indirect' meaning is known as *connotation*. Con-notation (cf. chilli con carne – literally, chilli *with* meat!) is a 'with meaning', an additional meaning that is clinging to the first. The scholar who coined these concepts was the Danish linguist Louis Hjelmslev, who between the two world wars further developed the 'structural linguistics' that Saussure was trying to establish *as a foundation for the more general semiology that was his ultimate goal.* This general semiology was to study 'the life of signs in social life', as Saussure once put it. The French literary scholar and cultural critic Roland Barthes was then central among those who in the 1960s presented theoretical and analytical contributions both on the relations between denotation and connotation, and other themes within semiology.

An important part of the reason why the distinction between denotation and connotation was introduced, was the fact that the meanings or signifieds of signs tended to change with time and place. They are not absolutely and finally determined once and for all. The same signifier can mean different things for different people at different times in different locations. Signs that once had positive connotations can, for example, later come to have negative connotations. Certain symbols related to the Vikings were, for instance, commonly regarded as having positive meanings 'attached' in the

Scandinavian countries in the 1920s; but since Nazi organizations used them before and during the Second World War, it is now impossible to see them without the presence of a 'Nazi' connotation. From a totally different area one could think of how 'glam rock' star Gary Glitter stood (in his platform heels) for a kind of 1970s innocence, until he was convicted of downloading child pornography from the Internet (cf. the *Guardian* 12 November 1999). One could consider also how the traditional imagery of trades union solidarity (muscular men and heavy industry) appears after the impact of feminism, Thatcherism and the so-called new economy. In fashion, one can easily notice such changes in connotation over time. Clothes, shoes and haircuts that once connoted an attractive lifestyle now signify something backwards, 'hick' or stupid. Platform shoes were the thing to wear in the 1970s, looked incredibly naff for almost 20 years and then returned in the late 1990s as the preferred footwear for millions of young women all over the planet.

We can also illustrate the significance of the distinction between denotation and connotation by looking, say, at the visual signs that represent (signify) certain nation-states. Take the American Eagle: one might wonder why the land of the prairie and the wild west would not instead choose a cow or a horse as its animal. Eagles are not commonly seen where most Americans now live, while dogs and cats are ubiquitous. The choice of the eagle was made, of course, for certain historical reasons, similar to those that also made an eagle the visual symbol of Germany. The eagle is a bird that connotes pride, power – and a willingness to use violence if necessary in order to defend and feed itself. It is a predator. A cow is not. The figure of the eagle is on the first level a motivated, visual sign for a particular kind of bird – it *denotes* this bird. At the second level it *connotes* pride and power (and, to some, violence), so that it can be used as an *arbitrary or conventional symbol* for the USA.

It is furthermore worth noting that connotations in semiology are often seen as different from 'associations'. Connotations are culturally established, codified, shared 'associations' within a certain community, while 'associations' otherwise are individual, personal. If the American Eagle reminds me of a certain teacher I once had, this is an association. To media scholars it is primarily connotations that are of interest. Associations are primarily relevant for psychotherapists, family and friends.

Varieties of meaning: connotational codes and cultural differences

The notion of connotative meanings demonstrates how the semiology developed by Saussure, Hjelmslev and others has acknowledged that the meanings of signs can vary according to the contexts in which they appear.

This is part of the *pragmatic* dimension of semiology. 'Pragmatic' here means 'determined by the specific situation' (that is to say, determined by the place, time and purpose of communication, the specificity of both senders and receivers). Signs of all sorts are always used and perceived in concrete historical, social and cultural situations, and even if most denotative meanings are more or less constant the variation of connotative meanings is of great importance to all sorts of communication. Connotative meanings are, just as denotative ones, regulated by codes, the conventions that link signifiers to signifieds. The notion of 'code' is therefore the key to the pragmatic dimension of semiology, since it is tied to certain cultural communities that share the conventions in question. *Culture* can, at least in this context, simply be defined as a *community of codes*. If one moves to a new place, and particularly to another country, it will take quite a while to get to know all the local codes, even if one may claim to 'understand the language'. Certain words, expressions, images and objects have a significance of which newcomers will not be aware. Even if one has moved to a country that is, culturally, closely related (say, from England to the USA or Canada, or from one Scandinavian country to another), one will soon notice that there are songs, names, stories and places one's new friends and neighbours know well that one has never heard of, that words one thought were quite innocent actually may cause embarrassment because they have somehow acquired, say, a politically incorrect meaning; so late-night conversations in bars or at parties may become problematic or even tiresome.

The notion of codes and the related definition of culture thus have important consequences not least for all sorts of international communication, both interpersonal and through mass media. Connotative codes that are peculiar to one culture can, for instance, make it hard to understand what goes on in an imported TV serial. In the 1980s the Danish researcher Kim Schröder (1988) interviewed groups of American and Danish viewers about the prime-time soap *Dynasty* after screening a particular episode for them. He asked his interviewees, among other things, to recount the events of that episode, in which the show's 'bitch', Alexis (played by Joan Collins), who spoke with a British accent, was threatened with the line 'Remember the Boston Tea Party!' A middle-aged Danish couple remembered that there was talk about some tea party in the episode, but could not really recall that there had been any tea parties in either this episode or any other episode they had seen. So they just supposed that such an event had taken place, possibly in an episode they had missed. In other words, they lost a point that was certainly picked up by all American viewers and probably by most British as well: the Boston Tea Party was, of course, the beginning of the American War of Independence and involved Americans dumping a shipload of tea into Boston Harbour. In order to understand that the line was a threat, without resorting to tone of voice or facial expressions, one would have to know this historical reference – and thus know that it connotes war against the British – and also to perceive that Alexis spoke with a British accent (of a sort that connotes the arrogant upper classes). The Danish couple could not make these connections, and neither could most of *Dynasty*'s audiences in over 90 countries.

Knowledge of codes is often, as in this example, directly tied to factual knowledge. But it is also a more vague sort of knowledge of conventional meanings in a certain culture, which one could call a knowledge based in *familiarity*, established through living within the culture. In a now classic analysis of a magazine ad for pasta products – the article 'The rhetoric of the image' – Roland Barthes demonstrated how different elements in the ad had 'Italian-ness' as a shared connotation. Barthes also pointed out how an apprehension of these signs for 'Italian-ness' would be dependent upon a previously established knowledge of, or familiarity with, certain tourist clichés that Italians (or Chinese, or Senegalese) do not necessarily have (Barthes [1964] 1977a).

Signs and what they refer to: language as a system of differences

We can also see the connections between semiology's understanding of the sign on the one hand, and notions of culture and cultural differences on the other, if we have a closer look at Saussure's theory of how signs actually acquire their meanings. As already mentioned, Saussure was primarily interested in verbal language and basic elements in his 'semiology' must be understood in light of that. One such element is the idea that there is an arbitrary relation between the signifier and the signified of a sign, as evidenced in the fact that different languages have very different words for the same phenomenon; even so-called *onomatopoeic* words, words that imitate sounds (such as meow, growl and splash) are different. Anglo-American pigs say oink-oink, Scandinavian and Russian ones speak differently, it seems. But things are further complicated because the sign as a whole, both signifier and signified, is separate and different from the sign's *reference*, i.e. the external reality it is supposed to name or say something about.

The *signifieds* divide the world into categories – categories of 'content'. These categories or ideas of how the world is ordered, are not always dictated by the physical realities themselves; they are often culturally specific. The colour category 'brown' does not, for instance, exist in certain cultures, and the colour 'orange' did not exist at all a couple of centuries ago. The English language has fewer words for 'snow' than does the language of Inuits ('Eskimos'), while Arabic may have a particularly well-developed set of terms for camels. These are examples of how the signifieds are also to some extent culturally determined, relatively 'arbitrarily' organized. Anthropologists are familiar with such differences. They may even be so profuse and fundamental that different languages imply significantly different perceptions of the world and our existence in it. In the 1950s the anthropologist Whorf, in co-operation with his mentor Edward Sapir, developed what is known as the *Sapir-Whorf hypothesis* or *Whorf's hypothesis of linguistic relativity* (Whorf, 1956). This hypothesis is precisely about the close connections between the way in which a language is organized and how the users of this language perceive or experience the world. The empirical basis for the hypothesis was primarily in Whorf's studies of the language of the Native American tribe the Hopi. This language is not least grammatically extremely different from European languages. It has almost no nouns, and verbs are inflected in very different ways. Such radical differences obviously make it difficult to translate from one culture to another.

Saussure imagined that since the meaning, or the signified, of a verbal sign (such as the colour 'orange') does not spring from the 'thing' (here, colour quality) itself, it has to be explained as resulting from the principle that *the sign acquires its meaning through its relations to other signs*. The meaning of the sign 'orange' is determined by its relations to 'red', 'yellow', 'brown' etc. The signified of a verbal sign is, in other words, determined by its opposition to, or difference from, other verbal signs. *Language is a system of differences*. What is 'light' is determined by what is 'dark', what is 'hot' by what is 'cold'. This could be formulated as the principle that *meaning is constituted by difference*. At the level of the signifier in verbal language one can think of the way in which every word is composed of sounds that *differentiate meanings*, so-called *phonemes*. A person that lisps is fully understandable in English, but there may well be languages where a lisping 's' and a straight 's' may give otherwise similar words different meanings. To find out whether two sounds are phonemes, linguists will use a so-called *permutation test*; b and p are two closely related sounds, but the difference between them is important in English. You can demonstrate this by replacing the 'b' in 'bass' with a 'p': 'pass' means something other than 'bass' and hence 'b' and 'p' are meaning-differentiating phonemes in English.

The logic of the permutation test has been transferred to other areas in order to investigate whether some element in a complex entity has any significant role in the whole thing. Could one imagine Woody Allen playing the hero in the *Terminator* films instead of Arnold Schwarzenegger? Hardly – it would have made them parodies. But what about Bruce Willis or Steven Seagal? Would that have changed the meanings of the films, and if so, in what way? What would *Desperately Seeking Susan* have looked like with Celine Dion playing Madonna's part?

In more philosophical terms, *the role of difference in our way of thinking* has attracted a lot of attention in the last couple of decades, and this is also the case within media studies. As mentioned in the previous chapter, the name of Pierre Bourdieu's most important book is itself *Distinction*, and this is one of many indications of how Bourdieu's work is marked by the *structuralist* tradition in the humanities and the social sciences that is derived from the structural linguistics or semiology of Saussure. It is, however, not least in relation to the problems of identity, which we dealt with in Chapter 1, that the notion of *difference* has been central in recent years. Since we tend to think in terms of differences, understood as *oppositions*, we immediately also think in categories that tend to render the imagining of gradual transitions, in-between things or states, and any interconnections between the two poles of an opposition quite difficult. The fundamental example is the opposition between male and female, which through enormous networks of connotations is used to order anything from sexual preferences to clothes, cars, behaviour and ways of thinking. Another example could be the racial opposition between 'black' and 'white'. 'Black' here tends to cover everything that is not absolutely 'white', thus radically polarizing and simplifying an enormous variety of skin colours and other so-called 'racial' attributes.

If our systems of differences or oppositions are seriously questioned or challenged, this may cause anxiety and even aggression since it may appear to threaten our identities. Open gayness can thus provoke discomfort, anxiety and aggression in some (bigoted) milieus. At the same time the play on gender differences in drag shows, the interest in sex-change operations and all the androgynous acts in the worlds of pop and fashion, clearly demonstrates how fascination and titillation can also be produced by 'dangerous' transgressions of these cultural borderlines.

The sign according to C.S. Peirce

So far in this chapter we have largely kept to the Saussurean tradition in the theory of signs, i.e. semiology. The most frequently used term for the theory of signs these days, however, is *semiotics* (hence the use of this term in this chapter's title). This term was coined by the American philosopher, physicist and mathematician Charles Saunders Peirce (1839–1914) who, independently of Saussure, had related ideas. His definition of a 'sign' is different from Saussure's, and he has other ideas as to the components of the sign. According to Peirce, *anything that in some way or other stands for something else in some respect or capacity* is a sign. It is thus already clear at the outset that Peirce does not take verbal language as his point of departure. For him, signs are something much more extensive – in fact, *'everything is signs'*, to the extent that it means something to us.

Because 'everything is signs', a consequent semiotics in Peirce's sense will have it that when we see a horse, at three feet distant, it is a horse sign that we see. We see forms and colours, and may hear sounds and recognize smells that we associate with the meaning 'horse'. If we go over and touch the horse, we will perceive more signs of the same, such as soft hairs over strong muscles, a mane and so on. If we are still in doubt, we may get some final sign evidence when the horse kicks us in the backside! Peirce's semiotics is, in other words, a theory of perception and a theory of knowledge (epistemology) at least as much as it is a theory of communication. It is, moreover, radically pragmatic, in that it makes the meanings of signs dependent on the situation, down to the variations on an individual plane: what is a sign for me need not be a sign for you. Thus the distinction between individual associations and collective connotations disappears, as does that between denotation and connotation.

This can also be seen if we look at a graphic representation of Peirce's model of the components of the sign (see Figure 4.2). The 'sign' is that which stands for something else, and the 'object' is that which the sign stands for. The interpretant is the signification or meaning that the sign has for someone. A simple, stylized drawing of the sun may be the sign. The object is then the sun we (sometimes) see in the sky; and our thought, '[this is] the sun', is the interpretant. ('Interpretant' is of course derived from the word interpretation, and does not refer to the interpreter but the interpretation.) An important point here is that the object is not the thing itself, not 'the actual sun'. In line with the example of the horse above, the object is also a sign, i.e. certain phenomena (light in the sky, heat) that we interpret as signs of 'the sun'. And it is not only the object that is a sign in its own right, the same goes for the interpretant – the word or term 'sun' in this example. The interpretant may

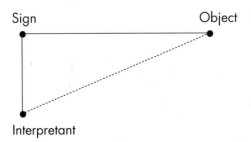

Figure 4.2 Peirce's model of the sign.

itself result in a new interpretant, in a new triangular sign. The sign 'sun' may for instance be interpreted, associated with or perceived as 'star', a radically more distant and possibly extinguished sun. The new object will then be 'a star (in the sky)'. The term 'star', the new interpretant, may then by some be taken to mean 'movie star' – and a series of new interpretants is then made possible. Such processes of ever new interpretations or signs are called *unlimited semiosis*. They may be reminiscent of how conversations may develop at more or less festive occasions where various associations made by participants can lead far away from the subject first discussed. In media studies it may be more relevant to think of how literary texts or films are interpreted again and again, including reinterpretations of previous interpretations. In the field of political communication one might think of how terms such as 'environmental' or 'environment friendly' have gone through similar chains of interpretants and signs, *mediated by or produced by the media*.

Peirce's model of the sign and the idea of 'unlimited semiosis' imply that *it is impossible to determine the final and absolute meaning of signs*. This way of thinking is highly dynamic, i.e. oriented towards the shifts in meaning according to specific situations and a high degree of flexibility in the sign systems that cultures consist of – and that the media produce and mediate.

Peirce's three kinds of sign, and a discussion of photography's relation to reality

Peirce distinguished between three kinds of sign, according to *the logical relation between the sign and that which it stands for*.

1. Signs where the relation is *arbitrary* and totally *conventional* (cf. the discussion above) are called *symbols*. Verbal language belongs in this category, as do the colours of traffic lights, certain logos and other phenomena we must have learned a certain code to enable us to grasp the meaning of.
2. A second group of signs are *icons* or iconic signs. These are signs that *resemble* what they stand for. They are simply pictures, or sculptures, i.e. two- or three-dimensional representations of a more or less photographic or 'realistic' type. A photograph of the US President is an iconic sign for the US President.
3. Making up the third and last group of signs are *indexes* or indexical signs. 'Index' is the Latin and English word for the first finger of each hand, frequently used to point at things, and an indexical sign, so to speak, points at that which it stands for. It does so in the sense that there here is a *causal* relation between the sign and that which it stands for. Smoke is an indexical sign that something is burning and snot indicates (i.e. is an

indexical sign for) a bad cold. The *symptoms* doctors look for when arriving at a diagnosis are indexes of disease or injury. The *clues, leads* or *traces* that detectives look for are indexical signs for the murderous activities they are investigating.

These categories can actually become key terms in interesting theoretical debates with practical consequences. Photographs are, for instance, clearly iconic signs, but it has been disputed that they also are indexical. The first problem here is that a sign can belong to more than one of Peirce's categories – in fact, maybe all three of them at once. But the question of whether photographs are indexical signs concerns photography's status as a medium for objective documentation, a technology that delivers indisputable facts. Photography can be said to be indexical because it in a sense is a pure 'effect' of the light reflected by the object(s) in front of a camera when a picture is taken. Photography is accordingly a purely physical-chemical effect, untouched by human hands, so to speak, and consequently an 'objective' representation of whatever was in front of the camera. The counter-argument is that the photographer has to make a number of choices – of framing, point of view, lenses, lighting, film speed etc. – plus another set of choices when developing a picture in the darkroom. Taken together, all of these choices provide the photographer with so much space for his subjectivity that photography is no more indexical than is any drawing.

This sort of thinking can lead to a quite provocative conclusion when the issue is whether computer-manipulated photographs in the media should be explicitly marked as such (e.g. 'This photograph has been digitally manipulated'). The Danish philosopher and media scholar Sören Kjörup (1993) has, for instance, argued against such a procedure, since it would imply that the public is encouraged to regard ordinary photographs as *not* 'manipulated', as pure and objective documentation. Kjörup was not surprisingly met with the argument that it in fact *is* a direct physical-chemical reaction that imprints an image on the light-sensitive film, and that whatever manipulative possibilities the photographer has, this simply means that photography has a documentary potential that is of a totally different kind than that of any artist with a pencil, however clever. Defending the indexical character of photography is also a defence for prevailing notions of *truth* – the idea that there are certain facts, especially concerning physical reality, that are objective, i.e. indisputably correct information about an objective reality existing independently of those who study it and their approaches to it. To present as ordinary photographs computer-manipulated pictures where the alterations made are not detectable is, according to this view, to tamper with notions of truth that are fundamental to modern science, politics, law, and a number of other social and interpersonal domains.

The question of whether computer-manipulated photographs should be marked as such in the (journalistic) media is, then, just a small part of a larger discussion on the status of photography and photographic media in general as providers of objective representations of reality. This is obviously of central importance to the question of how we are to regard the footage and still photography that are so integral to television news, current affairs and other documentary programmes. I would, for my own part, suggest that even if we maintain that photographic representations are indexical signs, this does not have to mean that we believe they deliver totally objective, indisputable renditions of what went on, or goes on, in front of the camera. There are good reasons to sympathize with those who warn against an unproblematic faith in photography.

This question and issues related to it are central in many media contexts. They also point to the importance of understanding semiotics in light of, and in combination with, the other perspectives on media texts that we will deal with in subsequent chapters. We will, therefore, return to the question of photography and truth in the final section of this chapter.

Code-shifting and codes that delimit sign systems

I said above that a code is a rule that links a signifier to a signified, but the same signifier can also be linked to different signifieds. There is, moreover, also another important meaning of the concept of 'code'. We will approach these issues by way of one of the first scenes from the film *The Sons of Katie Elder* (see Figures 4.3 and 4.4).

The sheriff stands on the platform as a train arrives at a station somewhere in the American west, and a guy wearing black clothes, black hat and a four-day beard gets off. The stranger asks about directions, and the sheriff points out the way he should go. The guy in black then disappears and the sheriff's deputy asks the boss if he knows the newcomer. 'No,' answers the sheriff and looks, slightly worriedly, in the direction in which the stranger has disappeared, 'but I know the type, and I don't like'm.'

An audience already acquainted with western movies will, of course, know very well why the sheriff answers as he does. The stranger is obviously a bad guy; *he is wearing bad guy signs all over him* – the black clothing and the four-day stubble. But today's audiences also know that these features are not *always* signs of badness. The pop star George Michael was in the mid-1980s a sweet and well-groomed boy, as part of the duo Wham!, and in the video for their single 'Wake me up before you go go', he was seen jumping around in a white polo shirt and white shorts. But then Wham! broke up and George Michael decided, after a while, to appear as a mature, serious artiste. Consequently

Figure 4.3 Still from *The Sons of Katie Elder*, Henry Hathaway, 1965.

Figure 4.4 Still from *The Sons of Katie Elder*, Henry Hathaway, 1965.

pictures of him began to appear, showing him dressed from head to toe in black clothes and sporting four-day 'designer stubble'. Instead of a black hat, though, he wore dark sunglasses. This attire did not mean that he wanted to portray himself as a 'baddie'. On the contrary, he rather wanted to present himself as totally *honest*, as fully *authentic* in what he was now doing. In the pop world, then, black clothes and four-day stubble growth has another connotative meaning: they stand for a sensitive soul, a thoughtful sort of character, a 'deep', melancholy and quite introverted personality that, all the same, has a strongly felt need to express himself. The code here is obviously different from that used in the western movie.

In the 1980s, large sections of the younger generation began to dress in all-black clothes, directly inspired by the codes of the world of pop music. They rarely had black hats, but they would quite often dye their hair black instead. Dark sunglasses also went well with this style, since they might signal an introverted nature and, perhaps, 'bitter experience', 'depth' etc. (Some readers may remember the ironic pop refrain 'The future's so bright I gotta wear shades'.) Millions of younger people signal in this way that they are deep, sensitive and melancholy, and have a strong need to devote themselves to creative self-expression.

There are, however, interesting connotative links between the two meanings of the same signifiers. The bad guy is someone who tends to live on the other side of the law, and so he stands in opposition to well-ordered society and ordinary people's trivial, law-abiding lives. The artist has been seen, since the nineteenth century, also as a bohemian, someone who breaks ordinary rules of conduct, stands in opposition to mainstream norms of decency and lives on the outskirts of established society. It is this figure that George Michael and other people in black and with four-day stubble refer to. The bad guy and the artist are still different meanings, and the point here is that *it is the context in which the signs appear that determines which connotations are relevant*. The codes on the level of the single sign are replaced *in accordance with codes at a higher level*. These higher-level codes define which types of sign belong together – they are codes that define *sign systems*. For westerns, a particular *western code* applies; for the world of pop music, there is a *pop code*. Such codes regulate which signs are admissible into the systems in question and decide the meanings, or signifieds, of these signs. 'Black clothes' are a sign that is part of both the western code and the pop code, but is assigned different meanings within the two systems.

Some people may prefer the term 'rock code' to 'pop code', since the traditionally more colourful, bright and 'simple' top 40 pop music is perceived as different from more ambitious and 'serious' rock music, where blue or black denim and leather dominate the attire of both stars and fans. The word 'pop' in the term 'pop code' is, however, used in a more inclusive way here, covering popular music in general, so that it also provides a space for that country music artist who always dressed in black, Johnny Cash. In his case, the colour black actually referred both to his background as a 'bad guy' (prison experience) and his status as an artist of a slightly melancholy kind.

What we have here called a pop code is a code that regulates the meanings of various sorts of appearances in the world of pop music, but there are also musical pop codes, and these regulate, say, which instruments might be used and combined, which rhythms are acceptable within this sort of music, what styles of singing are permitted and so on. Such musical codes – varying with the ever-expanding spectrum of styles within the field(s) of popular music – constitute the *genres* of popular music.

Genres as codes – historical and theoretical genres

In a semiotic context, one can define a 'genre' as *a code that regulates which kinds of signs can be combined in which ways within a certain category or 'family' of texts*. The word 'genre' is derived from the Latin *genus*, which means 'family'. The word 'text' is related to the word 'textile' and its original meaning is 'tissue', i.e. a set of individual elements closely knit to become a whole. A text, then, is a tissue of signs.

Genre codes are relatively stable, but not at all unchangeable. They are, just like all other codes, determined by cultural conventions, agreements among people within a culture. Screenwriters and film directors, for example, sometimes try to change genre conventions by removing old and/or adding new elements to the traditional mix. The audience will sometimes accept such changes, sometimes reject them. Those that are accepted will then become part of what one might call the 'vocabulary' of the genre in question, if they concern elements such as typical locations, typical characters, objects (such as weapons) and so on. One example could be the change that took place with western heroes in the 1960s, which was particularly obvious and influential in Sergio Leone's so-called spaghetti westerns such as *The Good, the Bad and the Ugly* – the hero was now not necessarily particularly moral any more. But changes could also relate to the 'syntax' of the film, the chain of events that make up its narrative; in the 1960s and 1970s, for example, a number of westerns ended up with the death of the leading character(s). Both of these developments were departures from what has often been considered the classic western code, where a fundamentally good hero rides into a community of pioneering farmers and gets rid of their enemies before riding, totally unscathed, into the sunset.

The notion of genre is highly important to the understanding of all sorts of media content, and we will return to it several times throughout this book. Journalists' knowledge of the genres of news media ensures that they know how to create reportage or an article. Their familiarity with the genres of their trade enables them to work quickly within certain predetermined forms, and the audience's familiarity with these forms also makes it easy for them to identify what is being communicated in journalistic texts. In many media, genres also work as informative tags for consumers. Video rental stores arrange their stock in a few, rough genre categories (such as 'action', 'comedy' and under the catch-all 'drama'). At cinemas films may have slightly more nuanced genre tags: 'action comedy', 'romantic comedy'. These are examples of what the literary scholar Tzvetan Todorov, who lives in France, has called *historical* genres, i.e. genres that are, or have been, operative in the communication between media producers (such as journalists, the film industry, authors and publishers) and their audiences. Todorov also talks about *theoretical* genres, however. These are classifications that have been constructed later, by scholars or critics, but that were not originally used in the communication between media producers and audiences.

The most frequently used example of such a theoretical genre is the film-historical concept *film noir*. This refers to a large group of Hollywood films from the 1940s and 1950s which, at that time, had other generic tags. But certain French critics in the 1950s thought they could identify certain important common features of these films – specifically filmic devices such as lighting and camera angles, certain favourite settings (wet city streets at night, sparsely lit rooms), certain characters (the frayed, cynical detective, the beautiful and dangerous woman), and certain types of recurring themes and ambiences. These critics, therefore, implicitly referring to the French literary genre *roman serie noir* (a name these novels were given because they were published with black covers), coined the term 'film noir', which ever since has been the object of research and teaching, and has become part of every film fan's vocabulary.

One could say of film noir that this genre is a code that was *constructed* some time after the making of these films, and so is, in a sense, less 'authentic'; but one might also say that later critics and researchers merely *exposed and named* a code that was in fact operative at the time the films were made – even if neither Hollywood nor film audiences were consciously aware of it. This is actually the way it is with most codes in our culture. We are not consciously aware of them in our daily lives, they are just parts of the taken-for-granted-ness that is characteristic of how we, most of the time, relate to the world we live in, including the media. Codes are much easier to spot at a distance, in time or space. The term *critical distance* refers to this fact. 'Critical' means *distinguishing*, the ability to distinguish one thing from another, and that requires a certain distance – at least mentally, as a conscious effort. This point not only refers back to the notion of 'pure taste' in the previous chapter, it is also something we will return to in the next chapter, which focuses on hermeneutics, the theory of interpretation.

Syntagms and paradigms

Genre codes and their changes can theoretically be understood by way of a central pair of concepts in semiotics (actually, in structural/structuralist linguistics). We have already in a sense demonstrated this in a somewhat loose, metaphorical way by speaking of changes in a genre's 'vocabulary' as opposed to changes in its 'syntax'. A syntagm is normally the same as a sentence, but one may also think of it as something more extended, as referring to the *linear dimension of a text*, its 'sequenciality'. Grammar lessons at school might have taught you that different languages have different patterns from which correct sentences are made; in the place of the subject, say, one might place nouns, not verbs. This gives us wide, but not unlimited, sets of possibilities when constructing sentences. The categories from which we make choices when filling the designated places in the sentence pattern, can be called *paradigms*. There are verb paradigms, adverb paradigms, and so on, that consist of all verbs, all adverbs and so on respectively. *Paradigms may be thought of as 'storage shelves' where one finds and takes out the words one needs to fill certain places in the syntagms.*

If we then move from grammatical analysis to a semiotic analysis of signification, similar or analogous conditions apply. All sorts of signification can be thought of as organized in 'syntagms' where the components are selected from paradigms, which here will be groups of verbal or other signs *with a similar or related meaning*. The relation could either be of the type called *parasynonymy* (i.e. semi-identical meaning, as between 'warm', 'hot' and 'boiling') or it could be of the type called *antonyms* (i.e. contradictory pairs such as 'hot' versus 'cold', 'light' versus 'dark' and so on). The main thing, according to the French film semiotician Christian Metz, is that paradigms consist of a number of units that compete for the same place in the syntagmatic chain, and that any chosen unit (word, picture, sound etc.) gets its meaning *through a comparison with those that could have appeared in the same place* (Metz, 1982: 180ff.).

There is a noticeable inspiration from Saussure's idea of language as a system of differences here, and it is precisely the extension of this idea to cover *all media and forms of communication* by way of analogy that is important. A stereotypically French pedagogical example of a syntagm could be the menu at a restaurant. It is ordered in accordance with a culturally specific sequence of various types of dishes that make up a decent meal: starters, main courses, cheeses and desserts. This sequence can be regarded as a culturally specific *syntagmatic code*. If someone orders the courses served in the reverse order, it will at least be met with raised eyebrows. (In Britain, however, the cheese course usually follows dessert in the menu order in many restaurants, and in the specific ritual of port and stilton cheese beloved of Oxbridge colleges.) For each element in the syntagmatic chain, each course, there are paradigms from which one makes selections. Not just anything will fit as a starter, and what fits as a starter will not be found in the paradigm of desserts. Another example could be clothing. There are paradigms for headwear, upper- and lower-body garments, socks and shoes. Wearing a pair of knickers as a hat will be a breach of a paradigmatic code – and also of a syntagmatic one. For there are syntagmatic codes for combinations: a tuxedo, say, does not go with jogging trousers. It is a breach of the code, as is ski boots worn with a ball gown. Such breaches of codes can, of course, be designed to attract attention. They may therefore also be used successfully in humour or advertising.

In film and television we might therefore imagine lighting, camera angles and the like as selected from 'storage shelves', or paradigms, full of more and less adequate alternatives; and every selection will contribute to a meaning that would be changed if other selections were made. One problem with such a transfer of the idea is that words are *discrete* – i.e. clearly separated entities – while selections of filmic elements, such as lighting and camera angles, will most often be made from continuous scales where the differences will be gradual. Still, the idea that those who make a film or any other text continuously make choices among alternatives that have consequences for the meaning of the final 'syntagm' or product is clearly both sustainable and important.

The paradigmatic dimension of texts is, then, the selection of elements for the places in the syntagmatic chain, and the relations between the selected elements and the alternatives. This is a key to the *theme* of a text – that is, what it can be said to be about at a deeper level, and how it treats its subject(s). One can, for example, think of the choice of characters for a fictional story in a particular medium. From the paradigm 'women', one can choose from a variety of possibilities – and the same is, of course, the case for the paradigms 'men', 'human relations', 'settings', 'conflicts' and so on. The prime-time soap *Dynasty* – which I refer to often due to the fact that I wrote a book about it (Gripsrud, 1995) – had a couple of female lead characters who were clearly older than probably all other leading ladies in US prime-time TV fiction – in their forties or so. The show therefore came to thematize women's ageing and the question of what this process is supposed to mean. When action movies have female 'heroes' instead of the usual muscular men, they thematize the notions of femininity in our culture. In both of these examples we are talking about conscious choices made by producers. The *unconscious choices* – those that have been arrived at 'automatically' – may be even more interesting, since they will be related to (be indexical signs or symptoms of) norms and understandings that are so engrained that one does not even stop to think about them.

The 'character paradigm' of American soap operas was once described as follows by an American critic:

> Soap opera people belong for the most part to the socially and professionally successful. They are well-groomed and cleanly limbed. They live in homes with no visible mops or spray cans that yet wait shining and ready for any unexpected caller. At the same time, almost all of soap opera's characters are drawn from the age group that spans the late teens into middle-age. They constitute what might be called the legitimately sexually active portion of the population. And the great majority come from the generation that reaches from the mid-twenties into the mid-forties. That is to say, they suggest a sexuality that has transcended the groping awkwardness of adolescence but that never goes beyond a commerce of bodies which are personable and smooth – even the older men are clean older men.
>
> (Porter, 1982: 126)

This characterization of the genre code that guides the selection of characters by the writers of American soaps obviously says something about the dominant American culture. The British code tends to provide a paradigm of characters that is radically more inclusive in terms of looks, ages and degrees of success in life. Paradigms such as these, and the selections made from within them, can thus often tell us something about underlying, not necessarily acknowledged, features of a society and a culture, or a way of thinking. They become *symptoms*, and a clever textual analyst may be able to formulate a diagnosis. Such analyses are therefore sometimes called *symptomatic readings*. These diagnose not so much the psyche of the individuals who created the text, as the society, culture or milieu that they are part of, and share values and ideas with. A symptomatic reading is an *interpretative strategy*, and we will return to this and related issues in the next chapter.

Images and verbal language: *relay* and *anchorage*

Up until now I have mostly talked about the sentences of verbal language and other types of texts where the elements follow each other in a time sequence, or along a sequential axis. But what of singular images or still photography? Is it also possible to speak of syntagmatic and paradigmatic dimensions in such cases? My earlier examples from clothing would suggest that it is.

Images are composed of elements that are not as clearly distinguished as the word signs of verbal language. The meanings of images are therefore also most often more unclear, fleeting, plural. This is one central reason why images are most often combined in some way with verbal language. In film and television they are accompanied by dialogue, writing (graphic signs) and/or music. Press photos are accompanied by a caption and/or article or story. Images in advertising are accompanied by a text, at the least the logo of the company or trademark in question. Art pictures as a rule have a title, but at times artists may wish to say that spectators can interpret their piece as they like, and thus the title is 'No title'. In the above-mentioned article by Roland Barthes, 'The rhetoric of the image', he distinguished between two types of function that verbal language can have in relation to images: *anchorage* and *relay*. The term 'relay' (French = *relais*) originally referred to the change of horses at posting stations in the (very) old days, but it here, accordingly, means that the text adds something that is not actually present in the image, i.e. adds some new element of meaning to the whole. A fresh horse takes over. A caption in a dialogue-bubble in a comic is a much-used example of this. Anchorage is, however, perhaps the more fundamental function, which is to point out *which of the many possible meanings of an image are thought to be the most important*. This is in a sense also what the relay function does – it draws attention to certain possible interpretations and specifies them by way of additional information. But at the same time – and Barthes overlooked this in his analysis – *the image will also anchor the verbal text*; that is to say, it will influence or shape it to some degree, in some way. We will now look at a particular example.

Relatively simple images may be thought of as syntagms where all elements are presented and perceived simultaneously. The individual elements can be thought of as chosen from paradigms in such a way that they form a 'sentence', statement or utterance. The caption or title can put us on the trail of this utterance. But in, for example, film and television, the verbal text that makes up the title of the film or programme will be known to us before we get to see the images. The images may then help us understand what an often quite enigmatic or ambiguous title is supposed to mean.

In the mid-1980s I, quite by chance, saw a late-night programme called *The Very Hot Gossip Show* on public service TV. The television announcer declared that this was going to be a really hot show with the dance group Hot Gossip. It was then up to the actual programme to provide an explanation of this somewhat strange description.

The still shown here as Figure 4.5 is the first image in the show's introductory sequence, before the title has appeared on screen. What we see here is the lower part of a pair of legs, with fishnet stockings and high-heeled shoes. The street has cobblestones and there is a reflection of light from a lamp

Figure 4.5 *The Very Hot Gossip Show* (1).

off screen – otherwise, it is quite dark. This is all there is to see. The soundtrack consists of very low-volume disco-like pop music and the sound of heels clacking against cobblestones.

If we regard this image as a syntagm, we can say that the signs are chosen from paradigms for location, lighting, road surfaces, shoes and stockings. From the paradigm of 'locations' one has chosen 'city street' instead of farmland, forest, desert or kitchen. The light is not daylight or twilight, it is a street lamp in the darkness of night. The road or street surface is cobblestones, and that is mostly associated with small streets, possibly back streets, in European cities (where the main streets are of asphalt and the pavements concrete). The shoes are not football boots, shoes made for jogging or just plain walking, they are high-heeled shoes. Such shoes are used when women dress up to look particularly stylish and attractive – they result in a particular walking style that many men find erotically and aesthetically appealing. Finally, there's the fishnet stockings – not tennis socks or leg warmers. Fishnet stockings are historically associated with risqué women's performances in more or less indecent circumstances; they are not 'sensible' legwear, they are made for the erotic exposure of women's legs. If one now puts together the connotative meanings of the visual part-signs in this image, one arrives at a syntagm that, in verbal language, can be formulated roughly like this: 'erotic exposure of a woman's body in a city back street at night'. One may thus suspect that *The Very Hot Gossip Show* is to be about prostitution.

Later sequences confirm this interpretation (see Figure 4.6). The woman's face (or the very feminine transvestite's) is heavily made up and, walking towards her comes a pair of military boots and uniform trousers – a very manly man, in other words – with whom she quickly establishes a rapport under a street lamp before they disappear together, arm in arm. (It is also interesting to note that the sexual difference is further underlined by a racial one – she is an extremely pale white, he is a black man.) The analysis we performed of the first frame of the show can be said to have 'anchored' the show's somewhat enigmatic title, pointed out which of its many potential meanings applies.

This show also makes the notion of codes relevant in another way. Judging from the explicit sexual nature of the dancers' presentations in various numbers (including suggestions of sado-masochism and various other 'kinky'

Figure 4.6 *The Very Hot Gossip Show* (2).

sexual pursuits) and the ways in which they were filmed, the programme was one of the most pornographic ever to be shown on public service TV anywhere (pornographic is a Greek word that originally meant 'portrayal of a whore'). But it created no public debate, most probably because the dancers kept their clothes on. 'Pornography' is coded as the display of *naked* people in sexual postures and activities.

Semiotics and interpretation

We have already defined 'culture' as a *community of codes*, i.e. a set of ideas about what signs mean and how they may be put together, which is shared by a large or small group of people. 'Communication' is a Latin word that originally meant 'making (something) common (or shared)'. Communion, commune, communism, communitarianism – and, of course common – all have the same root. The concepts 'code', 'culture' and 'communication' are thus closely related in many and complex ways. It should also be obvious from all we have been through in this chapter that a model of communication that likens the communication of meaning to the straightforward sending of a parcel by train cannot be used as more than a minimal point of departure. Culture understood as a community of codes is both a *prerequisite* of communication – as a shared condition for the process – and a *complicating factor*. The model must be lowered into the cultural sea of codes, to put it poetically. In addition, this sea of codes is also surrounded by other social, material structures and processes – institutions, technologies, markets, social classes, gender relations, racial relations and so on. We have talked about such things in the first chapters of this book, and we will return to them later, for instance in the next chapter, which focuses on hermeneutics.

Semiotics – understood as a joint term for the traditions of both Saussure and Peirce – deals with dimensions of the process of communication that social-scientific research in the field has traditionally overlooked. This is why the sociologist Stuart Hall, then at the Birmingham Centre for Contemporary Cultural Studies, could create a sort of watershed in the history of media research simply by introducing the notions of signs and codes in his article on en- and decoding (see Chapter 2 of the present volume, on influence). Semiotic theory is mainly developed with a view to the understanding and analysis of texts, i.e. the entities that are 'transported' in a process of communication. But, as we have seen, semiotics is also a highly important aspect of a more general theory of culture. It therefore also provides a productive approach to what goes on when the media's texts are produced, as well as when they are received, used and understood by audiences.

Semiotic theory is important in discussions of the relations between reality outside of media texts and these texts' representations of that reality. We have already talked, in several sections of this chapter, about how both Saussure's and Peirce's versions of semiotics render the relations between language and external reality, between signs and that to which they refer, problematic and variable. Even if photographic signs – photographs, film and video footage – can be awarded a special status as indexical signs in the sense of C.S. Peirce, semiotic theory still contributes to an understanding of the uncertainty that may well arise when one is to decide what such photographic signs actually *mean*. It is, in particular, the notions of 'connotation' and connotational codes' that can do this, since they refer to the variability of all meanings.

One example (which, I admit, is of particular interest to me as a Norwegian, but still useful as a general illustration) can be taken from the soccer World Cup, which took place in France in 1998. In the final minutes of Norway's match against Brazil, the referee awarded Norway a penalty. It was unclear to most people, both in the stadium and in front of millions of TV screens, whether he had good reason to do so, even to those of us who had been glued to the screen when the Brazilian supposedly committed a foul. According to the English writer Julian Barnes, in *Time* magazine, the global TV audience agreed that the Norwegian player Tore André Flo just 'unexpectedly sat down', that he was faking it and 'collapsing for no good reason'. All available footage from any camera angle and all studio experts seemed to agree that the referee had been tricked, and so the Norwegians were consequently considered 'lucky bastards' (Barnes) to win the match with the aid of the penalty, while the Brazilians were considered victims of a fraud.

However, after 'everyone' had been talking about this for a couple of days (still according to Barnes), 'an obscure Swedish video clip' emerged which showed that Flo's shirt had actually been (illegitimately) pulled, to the extent that he ended up on his behind (see Figure 4.7). This saved the honour of Flo and the Norwegian team, while confidence in television's total overview and precise rendering of facts was left a little tarnished.

The interesting thing here is that trust in television's coverage was weakened by a video clip – in which everyone, including Julian Barnes, chooses to have full confidence. And, judging from this Swedish video clip, it does actually seem reasonable to argue that the penalty was justified. But, had the Brazilians hired a few top American lawyers, things might after a while have looked different, at least to Brazilians and others with a reason to distrust the moral stature of Norwegian soccer players.

It is indisputable that the Swedish video clip shows that Flo's shirt is pulled by a Brazilian player, so that it stands out 'like a sail', as Norwegian coach Egil Olsen put it at the time. This was the objective, indexical signified of the photographic sign. But it was hardly this alone that resulted in the penalty. Shirt-pulling is not allowed, but it has become so common in football that

Figure 4.7 World Cup 1998: the Flo shirt-pulling incident.

hardly any referee in an international match at this level would blow the whistle because of it, and especially not within the penalty area. The reason for the penalty was that the referee and, later, everyone else, assumed that it was the shirt-pulling that caused Flo to sit, quite suddenly, on the ground. Our imagined American lawyers might have claimed that this experienced professional player with the British club Chelsea had simply chosen to *pretend* that he was pulled so hard that he fell when he just felt his shirt pulled. It would be very hard to prove them wrong from the video images alone. The persuasive power of the video clip depends on how one perceives Flo as a player and person. To Norwegians, he is simply a great guy from the tiny village of Stryn in fjord country, and so he has a non-photographable moral disposition that makes calculated dirty tricks unthinkable. To people from other countries, such as the referee and Julian Barnes, it may be that ideas of Norway as a peripheral, well-ordered, quite innocent and in some ways slightly backwards country (lots of nature, only four and a half million inhabitants) would have a similar effect when assumptions were to be made about Flo's morality. Interviews with him and so on could also have supported the assumption that this sort of country boy would not be capable of dirty tricks. These, then, were the connotative codes at work when the video clip was seen as demonstrating beyond doubt that the penalty was correct. But, as our American lawyers might have suggested, Flo could instead be regarded as an experienced, enormously wealthy player in one of the toughest soccer leagues in the world – the British, a cynical sports circus. Then the indexical document might easily appear, at best, to be dubious evidence of the correctness of the penalty.

Another, and more serious example – which is also much more well known – occurred in Los Angeles in 1991. When the African-American Rodney King was arrested in March of that year, a man by the name of George Halliday was standing nearby with his video camera, taping what went on. He sold the tape to a local TV station for US$500. This was the basis of something the American film scholar Michael Renov (1993: 8) described as follows (to paraphrase his words): disagreement over the interpretation of a video tape resulted in a violent rebellion and damages estimated at about US$700 million.

Holliday's 81-second take shows, in unclear, badly lit pictures, that a man lies on the ground while a group of police officers stands around and above him, hitting and kicking him. This is the indexical information the images provide. The disagreement that (somewhat surprisingly to most people) arose, concerned the question of what this scene actually *meant*. Most of the roughly one billion people around the globe who saw this piece of video thought they saw an example of brutal and, in policing terms, totally unnecessary violence. One might say that the overwhelming majority of TV viewers spontaneously applied a moral connotational code for the interpretation of fights, which awards sympathy to the underdog – a person lying on the ground while attacked by several enemies, the guy who is alone against many. But the white jury from the white suburb in the ensuing trial did not apply such a code, not after the policemen's lawyers had completed their analysis of the footage in court. Through innumerable repetitions, uses of new framings, slow-motion, reversals and stills, the video sequence was in a sense emptied of the moral and emotional significance perceived by most TV viewers. The spontaneous code was replaced with another, which it (finally) became possible to use. A space was opened up for moral and emotional connotational codes that members of the jury and many in their social category have readily available: black Americans in confrontations with the police are connotationally interpreted as dangerous, violent, drug-intoxicated criminals; thus the police officers' claim that the abuse of King was necessary because he was aggressive became believable.

Both of these very different examples show how semiotics provides concepts and ideas that may seem very abstract and far removed from actual experience and current public issues, but that become highly useful and meaningful if applied within some larger context of interpretation. They therefore point in the direction of the next chapter, which is about hermeneutics, the theory of interpretation; but we can also find such a pointer from another angle.

Semiotics may function very well in historical studies, but it is basically a *synchronous* (contemporary) sort of approach, not *diachronous* (oriented towards time that passes). This is due to its links with structural linguistics, which is principally about describing language as a *system* rather than a historical *process*. It cares little about the origins and historical developments of words – it is, rather, interested in how language is organized *now*. Similarly, the theoretical offspring of structural linguistics in the humanities and social sciences more generally, *structuralism*, is also primarily interested in society as a particular set of relations between contemporary elements than in the historical processes that resulted in the current situation. Saussure called the fundamental set of principles in language *langue*. The concrete, endlessly varied *use* of language in society, called *parole*, has its precondition in the system. The system, precisely because it is fundamental and underlying, can only be studied through analyses of *parole*, i.e. concrete uses of language. In literary and film studies, inspired by such ideas, a lot of work was done, especially in the 1960s, to identify the fundamental principles – *langue* – of each of the two arts or media. Correspondingly, anthropologists such as Claude Lévi-Strauss and his followers tried to identify the underlying system of ideas in a great number of narratives (myths) in various societies; and sociologists have tried to identify the system that underlies and is shared by concretely varying social relations and situations in different countries.

These structuralist efforts that, as we have said, are closely linked to semiotics in terms of a shared point of departure in structural linguistics, can also be seen as implementations of a certain *strategy of interpretation* – they are all looking for something more fundamental underneath the confusing, complex surface of appearances, a surface that nevertheless carries symptoms or traces of what is hidden underneath. A scholarly tradition that is particularly preoccupied with such strategies and the nature of interpretations in general is *hermeneutics*, and it is this that my next chapter will be about.

5 Hermeneutics: interpretation and understanding

The point of view of the audience

In this chapter we will approach the process of communication from an angle that differs slightly from that of semiotics. We will in particular have a look at what happens when we make use of, or appropriate, media offerings according to *hermeneutics*. One might say that this theoretical tradition primarily regards the process of communication from the standpoint of the audience, the readers, viewers and listeners, but it also clearly concerns the process as a whole.

Mass media texts appear to the audience as separated from the sender and her, his or their intentions in a different way than is the case with interpersonal, face-to-face communication. When in a movie theatre, few people will bother or think to ask what the hard-working screenwriter or director in Hollywood may have meant 'at a deeper level' with regard to what we see and hear. The same would apply to most readers of novels. In principle, it also applies to newspaper articles and chat shows on TV. The point is that if we are sitting in a chair or on a sofa getting a 'message' by way of electronic shadows on a screen or whatever, we are relatively 'free' when answering the question 'What does this mean – to us?' The person or persons who address us cannot control that we have understood their utterances in line with their intentions. We don't call up some Hollywood studio to ask what on earth that car chase or heroine's line was supposed to mean, and Shakespeare and Ibsen have both been dead for a very long time so we can't check with them what they intended their plays to 'actually' mean.

The word 'free' is between inverted commas here since we are not, of course, totally free when trying to understand some mass media text or other. On the contrary, we are restricted in lots of ways by our culturally determined prior knowledge of signs, genres, media and the world at large, before and now. This is one of the absolutely central points in hermeneutic theory. Our *pre-understandings* are necessary prerequisites for our perceptions and understandings of new texts – as well as other phenomena. So, in this perspective, our *pre-judices* are not generally subject to condemnation. If we were totally without them, we would not be able to understand anything.

Hermeneutics and research

Hermeneutics means 'theory of interpretation', and was originally more or less a methodological discipline in forms of scholarship such as theology and law, i.e. scholarship aimed at determining the 'actual' or 'real' meaning of certain texts (the Bible and the law, say). However, hermeneutics also has roots all the way back to antiquity, where hermeneutic questions were integral to epistemological reflection and, more specifically, central to the methodological problems concerning the understanding of old texts that were more or less difficult to comprehend.

At the same time, humankind as a species is constantly busy trying to understand, to find meaning in the things that surround it. When we encounter something incomprehensible, we may get angry or try to invent some sort of meaning to give to it. One of the reasons that death is such a taboo subject in our culture may well be that its meaning has become quite uncertain for people of our day and age. 'Incomprehensible' works of art are probably extremely irritating to people more because they appear incomprehensible than because they are 'ugly' or possibly 'immoral'. Hermeneutics is thus more than a methodological tool for clergymen and lawyers.

At least since Romanticism, it has also been seen as an increasingly plural philosophical tradition, that one may find includes names as diverse as Wilhelm Dilthey, Martin Heidegger, Hans-Georg Gadamer, Paul Ricoeur and Charles Taylor. All of these emphasize different things and may have different opinions on a lot of subjects. But in general, epistemological issues and the theory of science have been central to many of them. The German Wilhelm Dilthey, for instance, introduced the famous distinction between the sciences of *understanding* (the humanities and 'cultural sciences' such as history, psychology, philosophy) and the sciences of *explanation* (the natural sciences). The social sciences have had a hard time deciding which of these categories they belong to – some disciplines and traditions have emphasized interpretation and understanding, others the emulation of the methodological and epistemological principles of the natural sciences. Actually, both the social sciences and the humanities combine the two aims and procedures related to them. Max Weber, for instance, pointed out early on that sociology 'is a science concerning itself with the interpretive understanding of social action and thereby with a causal explanation of its course and consequences' (Weber, 1968: 4).

After the Second World War, perhaps the most important of hermeneutic philosophers was Hans-Georg Gadamer, particularly well known for his book *Truth and Method* ([1960] 1975). In it he discusses the conditions for valid historical knowledge and, very influentially, how we actually come to understand texts from other historical periods or situations than our own. Gadamer made the point mentioned above, that interpretation is something that marks humankind as a species, but he is especially interested in how we make sense of, or establish the meaning of, the texts and events of the past. This is where the above-mentioned 'pre-understandings' come in: we can never escape our own historical conditions when interpreting history or texts from the past. We cannot hope to find an answer to what an author such as Shakespeare 'actually meant' by a play. All we can do is to try and establish a meaning through what Gadamer sees as a 'dialogue' with the text in question. The text is seen as an 'answer' to 'questions' we ask on the basis of our own historical (social, cultural) situation – but it may also pose 'questions' we ourselves have to 'answer'. Through the act of interpretation, a fusion takes place between what Gadamer calls the 'horizon' of the text and the 'horizon' of the interpreter – and the result is something new, a new perspective of some sort. The text enriches and changes the interpreter and thus also, to some extent, the world in which the interpreter lives. This, in a sense, implies a form of relativization of the meaning of texts (and, also, historical events), since it will change over time. Gadamer's work and way of thinking formed the basis for the movement in literary theory known as *reception theory*, where the role of the reader in literary history is emphasized, and to which we will shortly return. But, as we shall also see in this chapter, hermeneutic problems and concepts are also central to scholars as diverse as the theorist of science Karl Popper and the philosopher and sociologist Jürgen Habermas.

Hermeneutics is, then, about what it means to understand something and how one arrives at an understanding, a meaning, which is also a form of knowledge. Two relatively simple concepts I have already introduced in previous chapters can serve as clues to what a process of interpretation or understanding involves: *text* and *reading*. A text, we have seen, is a 'tissue' of signs with multiple possible meanings, combined in ways that can also add to the potential meanings. Most texts therefore have a greater or lesser degree of *polysemy*, a plurality of significations or meanings. Words and other signs also vary in meaning as time passes, and are differently understood in different societies and cultures. To read, as we pointed out with reference to the etymological meaning of the Latin basis of the German and French word for this activity (*lesen, lire*), is to combine different elements to make a (new) whole. To perceive or appropriate the meaning of a text through reading it is, in other words, an *activity*, not simply passively 'receiving' finished meanings. We are served with a plurality of *signifiers* with a plurality of possible signifieds, and we use our acquired knowledge of codes to determine what they are saying (to us).

Reading is thus a process in which meaning is created through the encounter between the elements of the text and the reader's head. In this head lies our experiences, knowledge, opinions, attitudes, unconscious desires and disgusts. The meaning we get out of a novel or required reading in a university course is consequently, in a sense, a mix of elements we brought to the act of reading, and the signs and sign structures we found in the text. Gadamer's hermeneutic term, which covers all of the preconditions and presuppositions we have when trying to understand a text, is *horizon of understanding* ('Verstehungshorizont').

When we encounter a new text, be it a novel, a film or today's issue of *The New York Times*, we do so on the basis of previous experiences not least with texts of a similar kind. We start reading the newspaper with certain expectations as to what a newspaper is, what it is supposed to contain, and how it should look. Such expectations are decisive for how we perceive and understand what we read. They are also tied to more general expectations as to how the world appears and works. The hermeneutic literary theoretician Hans Robert Jauss (1974) speaks of the *horizon of expectations* of readers rather than horizons of understanding, but the meaning of the two terms are pretty much similar. Reading is to Jauss a process where the reader's horizon of expectations meets the 'horizon' of the text, i.e. the register of signs, traditions, values, views and attitudes carried by the work or text. This encounter is, as in Gadamer's more general hermeneutics, thought of as a 'dialogue' where the reader and the text take turns in 'asking questions' and 'answering'. Our questions could be anything from 'what will happen to the hero' to 'what does this ridiculous textbook have to do with *my* life', and texts that behave properly will at least give us a clue or two in the direction of an answer. The questions that the text asks the reader may probably best be thought of as various challenges it presents us with: 'How would you have reacted in a similar situation?' 'Do you agree that life in the countryside is really this bad?' 'Does it really make sense that language actually only refers to itself?' The idea that reading is a form of dialogue along lines such as these is a reflection of the general status of the term 'dialogue' as absolutely central to hermeneutical thinking.

The term 'horizon of expectation' is in fact also used by Karl Popper to designate the pre-knowledge and presuppositions of some field or problem. Social scientists cannot, for example, simply go out and observe society. (Neither can journalists, if anyone thinks that they could.) They have to know *where* they are to do their investigations, and *what to look for*. And that which they look for will have to be understood on the basis of what they already know, and the theoretical assumptions with which they are equipped. One cannot do serious research according to what I once heard referred to as the 'Vasco da Gama method' (i.e. with reference to the Portuguese naval explorer who supposedly did not know where he was going when he set out, did not know where he was when he was there, and did not know where he had been when he returned). Still, there have been research projects that resemble this. And journalism.

This also applies to the sort of research that is the study of texts. One must necessarily know something about the text one studies beforehand (the minimum is knowledge of the elementary meanings of the signs employed), and have some idea of what to look for. It goes for all sorts of research that the *knowledge-interest* that drives one's investigations is, as pointed out by Jürgen Habermas, of fundamental importance to the results one may arrive at and how one does so. Habermas differentiates between three categories of knowledge interests:

- the technical-instrumental one, which underpins the natural sciences
- the hermeneutic one, which he sees as fundamental to interpretative disciplines such as history, social anthropology, literary studies etc.
- and the 'emancipatory' or critical one, which may be said to characterize critical inquiries in the humanities and social sciences aimed at exposing power structures and enabling human freedom.

The latter would also be 'hermeneutic' in our sense here, but a critical hermeneutic that breaks with traditions that a 'mainstream' hermeneutic discipline would tend to respect and further.

For any sort of research it is important that one manages to be open to possible *surprises* in the encounter with some concrete material, whether texts, human actions or whatever one studies. Our horizons of expectations can collide, so to speak, with observations we make in the material. In such cases, the philosopher of science Karl Popper says that the observations may:

> have an effect upon our horizon of expectations like a bombshell. This bombshell may force us to reconstruct, or rebuild, our whole horizon of expectations; that is to say, we may have to correct our expectations and fit them together into something like a consistent whole. We can say that in this way our horizon of expectations is raised to and reconstructed on a higher level, and that we reach in this way a new stage in the evolution of our experience; a stage in which those expectations which are not hit by the bomb are somehow incorporated into the horizon, while those parts of the horizon which have suffered damage are repaired and rebuilt.
>
> (Popper, 1979: 345)

This way of thinking is completely parallel to that of Hans Robert Jauss when speaking of how literary texts may make readers reconsider both their ideas about literature, and their notions of right and wrong in various fields. Literary texts that can do this may become watersheds in both literary and cultural history. Artists of all sorts – and possibly also quite a few journalists – dream of producing texts or artworks that may have such a life-changing influence on their audiences.

Karl Popper's description above is also closely related to the historical and theoretical arguments of another philosopher of science, Thomas S. Kuhn (1971). He demonstrated that scientific *paradigms*, defined as systems of findings, procedures and theories that regulate research in a given scientific field for some period of time (i.e. a sort of horizon of expectations) can be fundamentally challenged and collapse when certain new, 'groundbreaking' discoveries are made. While Kuhn took his examples from the natural sciences – physics in particular – we may rather think, for instance, of how disciplines such as literary and film studies were changed forever by the structuralist influence in the 1960s; the objects, the questions asked and the common analytical procedures became different. Pierre Bourdieu's analyses of 'rebellions' by heretics or 'heterodox' actors in various social fields are actually about quite parallel processes – both inside and outside of academia. An interesting media-historical research topic could, for instance, be to identify and analyse 'paradigm shifts' within the field of journalism.

The hermeneutic circle

But how does the act of interpretation, the construction of an understanding, proceed? The fundamentals may be exemplified by how we read a single sentence, such as this piece of graffiti (which is actually, I believe, a quote from the US feminist Gloria Steinem): 'A woman without a man is like a fish without a bicycle'. We understand such a mini-text in several steps, one might say: each word individually, and gradually, cumulatively, the sentence as a whole. The precondition is, of course, that we know the graphic signs (writing) used and understand the language in question, but the whole that this particular sentence makes up, is slightly absurd, and can only be understood if one uses what one has of more general cultural, political and historical prior knowledge to regard the text as part of a larger, contextual whole. The sentence is a sort of a feminist manifesto in a very brief, humorous form, which would have been practically unthinkable before the 'new' feminist or 'women's lib' movement of the 1960s and 1970s. This example may illustrate, then, how our understanding is developed through a movement back and forth between parts and wholes on various levels. *One must understand the part in order to understand the whole and the whole in order to understand the part.* This principle is called *the hermeneutic circle.*

It should be quite easy to recognize this from our reading of, say, Agatha Christie-type detective novels. We read the first few chapters and form a preliminary idea of what is going on and who is involved, but the final chapter(s) will, if the novel is any good, make sure that characters and events we thought we had understood early on will have taken on a new and very different meaning. What we regarded as an innocent aside in the novel's second chapter turns out, in light of the novel as a whole, to be an important clue as to who the murderer is. Or, when reading a poem, watching a film or TV drama, enigmatic elements become meaningful only in light of the whole, and the discovery of new meaning in particular elements may influence our perception of the whole.

We do, however, already have some idea about the whole at the outset (cf. the notion of the horizon of expectations), even if this may be more or less thoroughly changed as we read, watch or listen. We might say that this, our idea of the whole, is *projected* from our heads and on to the text; it is continuously used to give meaning to what we read, while we read. A main element here is, of course, our previous experience with this particular sort of text. Our *genre-consciousness* or *knowledge* is, as we pointed out above, a central part of our horizon of expectations. It applies to detective novels as well as newscasts, James Bond movies, textbooks and plays written by Ibsen.

But in our graffiti (slogan) example, we also saw how a real, thorough or 'deeper' understanding of it depended on our placing the whole of the sentence as part of a *larger* whole – a specific historical and social *context.* As we have already seen, context literally means 'with text' (con-text). This is about how the social surroundings of the text resonate in it so that knowledge of these surroundings is often a prerequisite for understanding the text at all – something we touched upon when speaking of the pragmatic aspects of semiotics in the previous chapter. The specific situation in which things are said or communicated is often of decisive importance for a comprehension of the utterance, whatever it may be. But the term 'context' may also refer to more specifically *textual* 'surroundings', i.e. other texts, old or contemporary, that the text refers to or even quotes in some way. Any western film refers to other and previous westerns, and no new poem is written without resonances of previous poetry. The semiotician Julia Kristeva (cf. Chapter 2 of the present volume, on influence) has dubbed this phenomenon *intertextuality.* In her perspective, any given text is part of a gigantic 'total text', where all texts of all times are parts, even if any text will be closer to some other texts than others.

The principles that apply to the process of understanding in reading, do, according to hermeneutics, apply to *any* process of interpretation and understanding. We move within the hermeneutic circle whether we like it or not, whether we know it or not, when trying to understand something, be it today's newspaper, the media in general, history, society – or ourselves.

Hermeneutic self-reflection

A literary scholar once said that the need for interpretation 'springs from the situation that arises when a reader suddenly realizes that the meaning of a text is not self-evident, does not present itself to an immediate perception' (Kittang, 1977: 19). Obviously, this scholar here thought of interpretation as a specialized, conscious activity, not simply a part of being human, something we do all the time. He was primarily thinking of an experience one might have when reading certain types of literature. A main problem with conscious interpretations of the most typical mass media texts (journalism, advertising, TV chat shows), their functions and meanings, such as media students are expected to make, is that they are so 'commonplace' or 'usual' – i.e. trivial – that they appear easy to understand. We do, of course, interpret them all the time in an elementary sense, but largely in an unconscious way, without thinking about it. With this in mind, I often quote one of my teachers, the poet and professor Georg Johannesen, who once said that ' in order to understand what goes on in a concert hall on a festive occasion one must imagine all participants wearing grass skirts'. One must, in other words, consciously try to distance oneself, take the position of a social anthropologist from some faraway country or an intelligent alien from outer space. One must *make strange* what appears self-evident (cf. our presentation of the Russian formalists in Chapter 2). We must try to regard the common, trivial, and everyday as something conspicuous. This implies consciously trying to replace the usual, everyday codes or categories with which we routinely understand reality, and instead trying to grasp the meaning of phenomena with which we are very well acquainted by way of *another language* (for example, theoretical terms taken from the vocabularies of the social sciences, linguistics or literary studies). Very many of these are, as this book indicates, brought together in the vocabulary of today's media studies.

At the same time, it is also a central hermeneutic insight that we can never *totally* rid ourselves of our particular historical, social and cultural conditions when trying to understand the meaning of some phenomena. But what characterizes a conscious process of interpretation is not least that the interpreter reflects on her- or himself, and her/his presuppositions and preconditions, in order to lift these out of the more or less unconscious dregs of the so-called self-evident. This is what is known as *hermeneutic self-reflection*. In this concept lies an idea of conscious interpretative activity as a source of increased self-awareness, improved understanding of oneself –

personal growth, if you like. As we shall see, this makes possible a view of studies and research that goes beyond cramming for exams and having a white-collar job.

That such self-reflection is *demanded*, i.e. seen as an inescapable ingredient, places a hermeneutic approach in opposition to other ideas as to what scientific or scholarly knowledge *is*, and how it is produced. Such an opposition is clearly relevant to internal tensions within the field of media and communication studies. But it also applies to all other disciplines or fields within the humanities and the social sciences. It was not least this sort of thing that the struggle over positivism was about (cf. Chapter 2). But the insights of hermeneutics concerning the importance of the preconditions for our knowledge of both texts and all other phenomena also pose questions regarding the truth or *validity* of interpretations. We will return to this once I have presented an example of an interpretation.

Foreign man does the best he can: interpreting the first three pages of the *Mirror*

In late June 2000 I took the ferry from Bergen, Norway, across the North Sea to Newcastle, England. While preparing the English-language edition of this book, I wanted to stay for a few weeks in an English language and media environment. Naturally, I started to work as soon as I got on board the boat. That is, I looked for British newspapers. What I found was the tabloid daily the *Mirror*, the issue from 28 June. I thought it looked interesting, and not only because I know that it is has a very large circulation. I can read English pretty well, and know the country from many, many visits of up to a month in length, going back to my first, way back in 1968. My elementary knowledge of relevant codes, then, should be OK.

The front page of the *Mirror* had the actress Liz Hurley in a very skimpy outfit spread all over the middle section; she had a giant snake coming up from between her legs, headed for her mouth, from which her tongue was sticking out towards it. Above the picture was a small portrait of Hugh Grant, her ex-boyfriend, and a quote: 'Leaving Hugh was like amputating my left arm … but I just had to do it'. The picture of Liz and the snake had the following caption: 'SSSEXY: Liz, who today tells of her love-rift pain, pictured in *Talk* magazine. Picture: ELLEN VON UNWERTH'. Underneath the picture, in bright-yellow capital letters on a dark-blue background: 'LIZ HURLEY OPENS HER HEART', and in smaller, white capital letters: 'PAGE 12 & 13'. The lower fifth or so of the page had 'BLAIR'S NEGATIVE POLL SHOCK' in thick capital letters, plus a very brief introduction to this story, marked 'EXCLUSIVE' in white letters on red background, by the paper's political editor.

The *Mirror* thus presents itself to potential buyers at a news-stand as an unabashed tabloid, giving the top 80 per cent of its first page to celebrities and sex, and the bottom 20 per cent to politics. The bottom section is important, since it indicates that this is not a US supermarket tabloid of the sort that are all about aliens and spottings of Elvis, and grannies having great sex at 97. This paper is somewhat schizophrenic; it has a political agenda alongside (or beneath) the first priority, which obviously is to provide journalistic entertainment. The Liz Hurley story is, since today's public sphere is what it is (see Chapter 8, on the public sphere), a journalistic 'background' story since the couple that split up are celebrities and so their relationship (and certain aspects of their sex life) have been well known to the public all over the western world. But it is hardly the sort of story that is central to readers as *citizens*, i.e. as members of society able and willing to influence its development. The two parts of the front page together may actually provide a pretty good impression of the whole paper: a large-circulation popular newspaper with 80 per cent emphasis on entertainment (often of a somewhat lurid sort), and 20 per cent on politics and other more or less honourable journalistic subjects. It is a paper for consumers of entertainment more than a paper for politically interested and active citizens.

What intrigued me about the presentation of the Liz Hurley story was not that it was on the front page, and not even that Liz was presented in a revealing outfit. Neither of these things is unusual. It was rather the specifics of this photograph plus its relation to the verbal text that struck me as special.

The picture appears highly sexual to anyone who knows anything about psychoanalysis, or nothing about psychoanalysis but something about visual symbolism in general. The snake is, obviously, a symbol of the phallus, here simply the penis, if you like. Liz is on her back, with the snake between her legs while also seemingly preparing to lick its head. The photograph is so explicit that the line 'LIZ OPENS HER HEART' might easily trigger a variety of vulgar jokes. These responses would be examples of *the image anchoring the verbal text it comes with*, in that they point to a possibility of (intended or unintended) irony in the verbal text. Since (perhaps) most people's general voyeurism and curiosity about the sex life of celebrities seem almost insatiable, such an interpretation of the relation between the picture and the verbal text would work as an encouragement to buy the paper in order to 'read all about it' inside. It is more reasonable to believe that the picture has been reprinted from *Talk* magazine as an eye-catcher simply since it is so explicitly sexy without baring any forbidden body parts (cf. the previous chapter, on semiotics on how 'pornography' is coded as sexually explicit representations involving *naked* people). The photo is perhaps even (part of) an explanation of why this particular (actually old) story made it all the way to the top of the front page.

Having examined this front-page presentation of the Liz Hurley story, one might ask what it means as a whole in relation to, for instance, gender politics. The key element here is again the photograph. It is obviously used to sell the paper, i.e. a picture of a half-naked woman's body is exploited for commercial purposes. This could by some be seen as demeaning, as an insult to women in general. On the other hand, the photographer is evidently a woman, and even if Liz is on her back she may also seem to be in control. There is even a metallic-like texture to the upper garment that is reminiscent of snakeskin, and the colours and patterns are not very dissimilar to those of the snake. So Liz may be in control of the situation, i.e. a strong woman enjoying imaginative sex in a luxurious setting (her clothes, the pool above/behind her). What's wrong with that? Moreover, Liz Hurley is a celebrity who lives off her celebrity status and looks, and worked as an extremely well-paid model for a certain brand of cosmetics for years. This sort of press coverage is more likely to boost than break her career. Is this good or bad? The answer would depend on your moral and/or political values, beliefs and principles. You might even have to think twice – do a bit of hermeneutic self-reflection.

For my own part, I was not at all morally outraged or anything like that. But it was, on the other hand, clear to me that this paper doesn't give first priority to socially and politically relevant news, information and comments, and does not have a feminist bias in its editorial. Whichever way you look at the front page, it's another example of the ubiquitous use of younger women's bodies as representations of sexuality for the sole purpose of selling any number of commodities. If not directly misogynist, such a practice is not particularly helpful for the long-term project of altering centuries of ultimately repressive images or conceptions, or signifieds, of the term 'women'.

Turning the page, then, I found a page 2 where 80 per cent (four columns) was filled with (brief) political items, while the remaining 20 per cent (the far-left column) had an overview of the contents of that day's paper plus a weather report. Not bad, I thought, blending a bit of serious stuff in here may mean it reaches readers who will not be spending an hour or more on the likes of the *Guardian*, the *Independent* or the *Financial Times*. I did not feel a need for any interpretative work on this page, even though it might well have been rewarding.

Such a need arose, however, when I turned my head to look at page 3. It largely consisted of portraits of two blonde women with sunglasses. The title at the top of the page is: 'They could pass as twins but Bo has 16 years on Geri'. The two pictures share this caption: 'SISTER ACT: Bo Derek and Geri Halliwell almost pass as twins as they walk through Heathrow yesterday'. Then follows a subheading in capital letters: 'FILM BEAUTY IS STILL A PERFECT 10'. This is, of course, an intertextual reference to the only film Bo Derek is generally known for, *10*, starring Dudley Moore and directed by her late husband John Derek in 1979. A circular-shaped still of Ms Derek from when she was 24 is placed next to the text that the journalist has written after his experience at Heathrow airport.

The two portraits are straightforward, flashlight snapshots of the two women, from their chests up. They are both blonde, with long hair hanging forwards over their left shoulders, and both wear sunglasses. Those are the features they share. That the reporter claims they had 'almost-matching blue-tinted sunglasses' makes a reader worry about his eyesight: The sunglasses are about as different as they can get in material and shape, and while Bo's may be very dark-blue tinted, Geri's are clearly purple. In fact, other than the long blonde hair hanging in a particular way and the fact that both wore sunglasses (they also wore necklaces, not mentioned for some reason – also very different), the two women are about as different as women can be in terms of looks. Their clothes are very different, something that would be just as relevant as their wearing sunglasses. More importantly, their faces are clearly very differently shaped. Bo's is rather long, while Geri's is rather round. Some might say that Bo looks stylish while Geri looks cute. There is no family-like resemblance at all. Geri appears more heavily made up than Bo (more lip gloss and mascara), something that to some would connote a class difference. And what about their heights? These are not mentioned, but anyone who has seen the above-mentioned film will remember how Bo Derek towered over little Dudley Moore even when barefoot, while one suspects that Geri Halliwell would have been closer to Mr Moore in height once she kicked off her old platform shoes. No wonder, then, that the caption moderates the phrasing in the main heading: The two could here '*almost* pass as twins'.

The whole 'twin' idea is thus, of course, nothing but an attempt to create a 'story' out of two observations of female celebrities at an airport celebrities pass through more or less every day. The text is simply a rehash of trivia about the two, which is well known to any reader of the popular press (magazines included), with the possible exception of the information towards the end, that Bo Derek has been 'linked to Jane Fonda's estranged husband Ted Turner'. But, the story says, she 'insists they are long-time friends and nothing more'. The final sentences are marked as quotes, and it may appear as if Derek actually said these words to the reporter at Heathrow. But this is not made explicit, and so they could just as easily have been taken from an interview published elsewhere.

This page seemed to me, in parts and as a whole, simply such a striking example of tabloid journalism that 'a need for interpretation sprang from the realization that the meaning of the text was not self-evident', to paraphrase the literary scholar Kittang, quoted above. The page, once one has stopped to read it and then started wondering about it, more or less asks to be interpreted – and explained – as a text and as a journalistic phenomenon.

First, one may notice how the whole piece revolves around these women's *looks*, related to *age*, and ends up with their *love life* or lack of one. There is nothing here about Derek's acting after 1979, and that film was all about her looks. There is nothing about Halliwell's current career as a singer. The piece is thus another contribution to the upholding of an actually very old-fashioned and more or less one-dimensional image of women's lives and purposes. It refers to the frenzied discourses elsewhere in the media world about the need, especially for women, to preserve youthful looks forever, and it continues also the connected idea that a husband is the absolutely central thing women actually need. This page is a far cry from the graffiti slogan 'A woman without a man is like a fish without a bicycle'. From a feminist point of view, its underlying system of values is ideologically reactionary.

Second, it is obvious that the reason why articles such as this are prominently placed in one of the UK's best-selling newspapers, is to sell papers by entertaining readers with celebrity gossip. But as I have just pointed out, there is nothing new in this story, no saucy rumours or anything like that to spice up the lives of ordinary voyeurs. Moreover, and more important, *the 'twin' idea will appear unfounded to anyone who actually studies the photos and reads the text properly*.

So, the conclusion to my interpretation of these first three pages of this issue of the *Mirror* is that this seems to be a newspaper that, at least in terms of gender politics, is clearly reactionary and assumes that its readers prefer undemanding journalism. In order to find out if this is really a fitting description of the paper, I would have to perform similar interpretations of several whole editions to see if there is a match between the part I have dealt with here and the paper as a whole. One would not necessarily need to examine very many editions to reach a conclusion that would be valid: newspapers are quite stable in their chosen formats or styles and political tendencies from day to day and year to year.

Such a conclusion would not and could not be accepted as the absolute, objective truth, but it would be *arguable*, and if my interpretation above was confirmed as representative, it might be hard to refute it for those who would like to do so. Hermeneutic knowledge is not the same sort of knowledge as that which goes into the construction of bridges (even if there is a lot more hermeneutics there than is normally conceded by engineers and natural scientists). It is always *inviting discussion, dialogue*.

I would, for instance, not try to eliminate the influence on my interpretation exerted by my professional pre-knowledge of how commercial media work, the role of my political leanings in the 'horizon of expectations' with which I encountered this particular newspaper issue. It is also possible that my Scandinavian, specifically my Norwegian background had something to do with my results, as well as my being male. Such afterthoughts are examples of a hermeneutic self-reflection, and such reflection is part of the interpretative work. While the traditional positivist ideal is to try to eliminate or forget about the specificities of the researcher, the hermeneutic practice is rather to include and discuss them in the course of the analysis and even sometimes in the eventual presentation of the interpretative analysis. The ideal is not, then, to write whole essays on oneself based on introspection. Only the clearly relevant factors are worth mentioning, and *the validity of the interpretation always rests solely on the evidence taken from the text or object analysed*. An allegation of misogyny is not more valid if the interpretation or analysis leading to it is done by a woman. Likewise the interpretation cannot be legitimately refuted by pointing to the sex, personal history etc. of the interpreter, but only by pointing out weaknesses in the argument itself, demonstrating that, in some way, it is not in keeping with the nature of the material, text or object.

On the other hand, the response could be *so what?* After radical German students in 1968 had worked for a long time on a very critical analysis of the totally dominant German tabloid *Bild Zeitung*, they concluded that the paper was reactionary through and through in every possible way. This was not a big deal to the newspaper's editors – they knew this already, since their market research had for a long time revealed that it was precisely the reactionary profile of the paper that sold several million copies of it every day. I suspect that the *Mirror* would respond likewise to a similar analysis: its editors most probably know what they are doing.

It would be tempting now to say a few words about how the *Mirror* relates to the greater whole of the British press, the even greater whole of the British media system, and then to the whole of British society where, according to official data, 'the number of people living in households on less than half average income rose from 16.9 per cent to 17.7 per cent [in the Blair government's first two years in office], as the incomes of the rich grew three times as rapidly as those of the poor' (the *Guardian*, 14 July 2000). But I will leave that to others. Except for mentioning that the largest-selling so-called 'quality' newspaper, the semi-tabloid *Daily Mail*, has a circulation of almost 2.4 million copies, while my own British favourite paper, the *Guardian*, has a circulation of just below 400,000 per day (*Daily Mail*, 17 July 2000) in a population of 58 million.

Little wonder, then, that many of my British friends and colleagues are so concerned with the quality of British broadcasting, I thought to myself when I first saw these figures. But actually, I was later informed, the per capita sales of national newspapers in the UK are among the highest in the world. 'The magazine market and the market for regional newspapers are correspondingly smaller,' a friend and colleague told me. 'We don't have the equivalents of the *Newsweek*, *Time*, *Paris Match*, or *Der Spiegel* type of weeklies. This is to say that newspapers in Britain have a particular structural position in the popular reading market, spreading far wider and covering more different interests than in most other countries. Circulation x 4 = readership is the formula used.' I stood corrected, reminded once again that factual knowledge is a prerequisite for correct interpretation.

Interpretative strategies

I have in the above example actually employed what the French hermeneutician Paul Ricoeur has called a *hermeneutics of suspicion*. This term refers to types of interpretation that are oriented towards *latent* meanings that a text conveys 'underneath' its *manifest* plane – a *critical interpretative strategy* that is characteristic of, for example, theoretical traditions such as psychoanalysis and Marxism. It presupposes as a rule that those who speak, write or produce various types of text are not always (or maybe, perhaps, not as a rule) fully aware of what the text they form actually carries in terms of meaning. In this sort of thinking it is assumed that 'society', 'the dominating ideology of femininity', 'the worldview of the West' or 'the unconscious' will be expressed in the text, with the author, the journalist or the film-maker as a more or less unwitting mediator.

Consequently, such a form of understanding may not only be called critical, but also (and perhaps more precisely) *symptomatic*. The text is a manifest symptom of some latent condition (cf. the previous chapter, on semiotics), often some form of conflict or 'disease'. In this tradition, the criteria for truth or validity of an interpretation is that it is *internally coherent*, that it *covers the structures of the text* and that it is *in keeping with certain theoretical assumptions concerning the conditions of language, psyche or society to which the text is supposed to relate*. Both textual and extra-textual matters are, as a rule, understood on the basis of theoretical traditions that are rarely questioned in a particular textual analysis. Theories are instead treated as tools in the interpretative work, as 'keys' that can be used to 'unlock' the 'closed' dimensions of the text. This may be a problem if it means one overlooks or violates the *individual specificity* of a particular text and its possible potential to critically illuminate the preconditions or unquestioned assumptions of the interpreter.

In contrast to this symptomatic interpretative strategy or reading, the *sympathetic* form of reading can be called a 'positive' or *confirmative* interpretative strategy. It aims to discover, as loyally as possible, what can be assumed to be the original *intention* of the producer of the text, or, possibly, to demonstrate how the text in question can be placed within a particular, more or less valued tradition. These two ambitions often go together very well in the traditional writing of film, art or literary history. Here the author, and not 'society', 'ideology', 'language' or 'the unconscious', is the originator of the text. The interpreter should therefore try to read the text *sympathetically*, i.e. try to place him/herself in the position of the author and thereby try to identify an intended meaning. The interpreter is as far as possible to 'eradicate' him/herself and his/her particular preconditions and instead *identify* with the author when deciding and presenting the meaning of the text.

The sympathetic interpretative strategy is thus a form of reading that, in practice, centres on *the individual*. It is the subject that actually puts together the text that in a way constitutes and guarantees its presumed unity and coherence. Because one in this sort of thinking principally regards the *subject* as a coherent and unified entity (cf. Chapter 1), one also tends to be oriented towards the unity and coherence of the text – much less towards glitches, gaps and contradictions in it. In film studies this sort of approach to film texts is called *auteurism*, after *auteur*, the French word for 'author', a term used from the 1950s onwards to designate film directors in order to award them the status of Individual Artist behind the collective product a film actually is. In this way film could be elevated to the same status as the other arts that, since Romanticism, have officially been produced by creative 'geniuses' (see Chapter 10 of the present volume, on production). *Auteurism* is, in other words, a sympathetic approach to film analysis and film criticism, which regards the director as the creative subject that expresses him/herself in films. A question to think about: why has it become customary for journalists not only to sign their contributions to papers, but often also to add a picture of themselves next to their names (in the same way that TV news reporters always repeat their names, which have already been mentioned by the newsroom, at the end of their segments in newscasts)?

The criterion for whether an interpretation is valid or not is, according to the tradition of sympathetic interpretation or reading, that it can be said to be in keeping with the *intention of the originator*, the more or less conscious expressive will behind the text. The text is, in other words, seen as having an *expressive* relationship to the creator-subject or, in more positivist terms, the *cause* of the text is the originator or author. One will still find that textual theory and analytical interpretation of this sort often operates, in practice, with a notion of the 'I' behind a text that is different from the empirical author-person. A great poet, director or painter is as a *genius* precisely in a certain sense larger than him/herself, s/he is in some way *representative* of humankind or at least certain parts of it.

A third interpretative strategy or form of reading is *objectifying*. The text is here seen as an autonomous or independent entity, whose relation to a concrete, creative human being is more or less irrelevant. Two things are central to different varieties of this approach: the text's relations to its predecessors in its particular textual tradition on the one hand and, on the other, the text's internal relations or structures. The latter focus is most typical of the literary criticism that in the 1940s and 1950s was termed *new criticism*, and it is due to this focus that the objectifying interpretative strategy developed very thorough *close readings* of literary works. In the objectifying form of reading, it is the *coherence* of the interpretation and its degree of correspondence with the (presumed) coherence of the text that is the decisive criterion of validity.

The techniques of *close reading* were in many ways taken over and carried on in the structuralist and semiotic approach where, however, the analytical terms were marked by the insights of the theory of signs. Purely 'objectifying' readings of poetry were, for instance, produced by leading structuralist theoreticians such as Roman Jakobson and Claude Lévi-Strauss, sometimes working together. These two gentlemen at one time compared the meaning of a poem with a crystal that appears only when the dross that covers it is chipped away (Jakobson and Lévi-Strauss [1962] 1971). It was on the basis of such thought that the fictional professor of literature Morris Zapp in David Lodge's novel *Small World* had fantasies of textual interpretation as *strip mining*. One pushes soil aside with a bulldozer, and thereby exposes the golden ore below – the indisputable, absolute Meaning of the text. Zapp did for a while envisage himself doing something like this to the collected works of Jane Austen, so that he could have the pleasure of putting a number of colleagues out of work because the meaning of all of these texts had been determined once and for all. But semiotic close readings have more often been conducted with ambitions characteristic of the symptomatic interpretative strategy, thus in many ways opening up the text to the world around it.

Debates over these various strategies of interpretation or forms of reading and their criteria of validity have often been quite intense since they are tied to various more general political or philosophical ways of thinking and values. The foundation of the sympathetic form of reading in ideas of the genius, the creative, coherent subject, breaks with understandings of society, psyche and language that emphasize our shared inheritance in these areas, together with the gaps, differences and conflicts within and between them. The objectifying way of reading implies that texts, and particularly those categorized as art, live their lives in isolation from social life in general. According to some, this invites, as does the sympathetic approach, an elitist and more or less asocial (and thus im- or a-moral) understanding of what art and the production of texts are about – namely various forms of communication between people.

A more reasonable position is probably an *eclectic* one: that there is something correct in all the three approaches and the assumptions on which they are founded. The emphasis may shift from one strategy of interpretation to another according to the sort of text we are faced with and what we decide the purpose of our interpretative work to be in a particular instance. It is not, of course, insignificant to a text's signifiers and signifieds who or which concrete human beings produced it, where and when. It is similarly clear that social, semiotic and psychological dimensions of textual production exceed or escape the conscious control of individuals. It is finally obvious, as mentioned in the introduction to this chapter, that we as audiences encounter the texts of mass media in isolation from their producers, who for that matter might have been dead for hundreds of years. We are then obliged to perform some sort of 'objectifying' reading, which in fact also has the advantage that it demands heightened attention to what the text actually contains – no matter what the producer of it may originally have intended, and no matter what we might have expected beforehand.

Melodrama as a genre and as a form of understanding

A genre can be seen as a code (see the previous chapter, on semiotics). But from a hermeneutic point of view it is important that a particular genre also constitutes a perspective, a way of understanding the world and our existence within it. Different genres will focus on different dimensions of social and personal life. A brief introduction to theories on the genre of *melodrama* may illustrate this. As we shall see, melodrama has been said to be related to what we, above, called the *hermeneutics of suspicion*, i.e. a form of understanding that distinguishes between a manifest surface and something (more important) that is latent, underlying. An important reason for having a closer look at this is moreover that melodrama is an extremely important 'supergenre' in all media: a large number of media genres, both factual and fictional, may be said to have melodrama as a shared basis.

Melodrama was originally the name of a particular theatrical genre that arose quite precisely in the year 1800 in the commercial theatres of Paris. As indicated by the Greek prefix *melo-*, the term referred to a type of play that was accompanied by music, and that included song and dance numbers. The Swedish historian of theatre and film Rune Waldecranz described melodrama in his 1976 book *Så föddes filmen* (*How Film was Born*) as 'an emotionally engaging tragedy with a happy end'. Waldecranz had actually read all the plays written by Pixérécourt, the man who first formed and named the genre, and found that all (and they were many!) had certain features in common. Most central among these were that all the plays were based on a bourgeois, puritan understanding of morality, and told a story of the struggle between innocence and virtue on the one hand, and immorality and evil on the other. The contrast between the light and bright Good on the one hand and the darkness of Evil on the other was also very much emphasized in the stage decor, lighting and, not least, in the music and an 'exaggerated' style of acting. Every play also had to have at least one dramatic scene with thunder and lightning, flooding, an avalanche or the like, most often in connection with the final, dramatic battle with the evil villain.

The melodrama genre thus often demanded an elaborate stage machinery. It was not easy to create realistic illusions of thunder, lightning and earthquakes in times that had no electricity. Experiments were also performed with shifts between simultaneously ongoing scenes in ways that prefigured the editing techniques of film. Much about the melodrama prefigured the medium of film and its most typical narratives – which should be obvious from this description. Movie theatres also in many ways took over the functions and audiences of the melodrama theatres when they emerged in the early twentieth century (cf. the aforementioned title of Waldecranz's book). At that time, however, the sociocultural status of melodrama had sunk to a definite low. With the advent in the second half of the nineteenth century of realist and naturalist drama, the heavily emotional melodrama with its stereotypical characters and weightily underlined conflicts had become something 'vulgar' and 'feminine' to the upper classes who frequented the better theatres.

Not surprisingly, then, film – and later television – scholars have been particularly interested in melodrama and its development. As early as 1972, Thomas Elsaesser published an article in which he proposed an entirely new interpretation of this area. He regarded melodrama as an *expressionist* genre, in the sense that it was oriented towards uncovering some forces, conflicts and relations that were imagined to be 'under the surface' of characters and the(ir) world (Elsaesser, 1986). This is also an important idea in a book by the literary scholar Peter Brooks from 1976 (reprinted in 1984), entitled *The Melodramatic Imagination*. Brooks – who seems never to have read Elsaesser – argued that melodrama was more than a genre, it was a 'meaning-making machinery', *a way in which to understand the world*, which is closely tied to *the conditions of modern society*. Before the French Revolution, at the end of the eighteenth century, everything had in principle been understandable since everything in the last instance was part of one and the same divine order. But following the Renaissance, a new perception of the world had gradually been established, in which God had, so to speak, retired to His Heaven. The French Revolution in a sense completed this process. Now nothing was absolutely certain; everything was up for debate in a 'humanized' world, from political matters and natural phenomena to interpersonal relations and morality. This made for a deep feeling of uncertainty and insecurity and, according to Brooks, melodrama offered valuable existential assistance in this situation. The 'message' of every melodrama is that *underneath the surface of existence there is a universe of strong moral forces and laws to which we must learn to relate.* Every single melodrama would try to present these moral forces as clearly as possible in a concrete, personalized form. The characters were incarnations of moral principles (e.g. good or evil), not psychologically realistic figures. Brooks ties the 'melodramatic imagination' to a widespread scepticism towards the 'surface' of things, a general idea that the more real, the more true and important factors are located 'behind' or 'beneath' what we immediately see or hear (or smell etc.). Thus he argues that great authors such as Dostoyevsky and even Kafka are 'melodramatic' in various ways. In our context, however, it is probably more important that he demonstrates how the 'expressionism' of melodrama, its emphasis on laying bare that which is hidden or latent, ties it to the hermeneutics of suspicion I talked about above (i.e. a form of understanding represented by Marx, Freud and many others). Melodrama wants to present the latent in a direct, concrete way so as not to let us be confused by the manifest, the apparent, the more or less chaotic surface of reality.

Such a view also makes it possible to understand some of melodrama's historical development. The modern psychological understanding that was formed during the latter half of the nineteenth century was based on a parallel distinction between a latent and a manifest plane in the human psyche. *Dr Jekyll and Mr Hyde* by Robert Louis Stevenson, which I mentioned in Chapter 1, has this distinction already in its title – the decent doctor had a terrible monster inside him. Sigmund Freud later proposed, as I have also mentioned, a contested but, over time, widely accepted scientific version of the same basic understanding. The melodrama genre followed this development by no longer only presenting an underlying *moral* universe, but also a *psychological* one. Psychological entities or figures – such as the Evil Father, the Good Father, the Good Mother, the Evil Mother etc. – could now also appear on stage incarnated in the form of quite 'flat' fictional characters. The melodrama genre is now often seen as identical with the *family melodrama*, i.e. texts that are about the intimate and conflict-ridden relations between people in a family or couple, between parents and children – often traditionally women-oriented texts. The family ties between melodrama and soap opera should be clear from this. But if one bears in mind the history of melodrama and the interpretation of the genre as a particular kind of 'imagination', one can easily see melodramatic features in genres such as westerns (baddies in black clothes taking on clean-shaven goodies in white; bad ranchers against good farmers). One can also easily spot elements of melodrama in crime fiction, not least movies of the *film noir* category. The same goes for most American TV fiction, other than comedies.

Melodrama has always been about strong emotions and has appealed equally strongly to the emotional involvement of the audience. From Peter

Brooks' point of view the audience's identification and involvement is to be regarded as a sort of pedagogical aid or tool – the point is to teach the audience a lesson about the basic, underlying forces and rules. Even if the stylization or simplification of characters and conflicts has been important, the ambition to create identificatory involvement in the narratives has always also led to an emphasis on realist credibility in the form of presentation. Characters in film melodrama have, at least since the 1930s, normally had a degree of complexity – for example, by having a conflict between two principles built into them, such as the tough guy with a soft centre – a Humphrey Bogart speciality. (Typically, this may be explicitly pointed out, as in *Casablanca* where the police chief says to our man: 'Underneath that hard, cynical shell you're at heart a sentimentalist'.) The borders to psychologically realist drama are consequently fleeting, and have been so at least since Henrik Ibsen, say, made use of melodramatic elements in his plays.

So it is not surprising that factual genres are also marked by melodrama. The material from 'real life' must also be formed in some way by journalists and documentary film-makers. They will, then, often employ simplified constructions or models of conflict; they may want a strong emotional appeal etc. – devices that belong to the melodramatic 'supergenre'. This is clear in the use of photography in the popular press, with its emphasis on intensely emotional close-ups, simple visual symbolism etc. Journalism is, in general, geared towards concrete presentations of social structures and forces that are actually quite abstract. The simplest approach is then to personalize them, tie them to the actions and appearances of individuals. Thus it also becomes possible to morally judge the people in question; they can be divided into good guys and bad guys. Such a melodramatic perception of the world can also be used by the actors in global politics to legitimate their actions. In American foreign policy, for instance, it seems that the USA is strikingly often called upon to take on Pure Evil; a similar sharply polarized worldview is also a trademark of certain states and political movements elsewhere.

Melodrama and its form of understanding may work well as long as it is about presenting fundamental moral and psychological principles. But it is problematic when real, complex social conditions are presented in the same form. Society at large, nationally as well as globally, is governed more by anonymous, abstract social forces (such as the laws of capitalism) than by individuals and their moral characters; and it can rarely be understood in an adequate way if one only distinguishes sharply between the all-good and the all-bad. The melodramatic understanding can, in a journalistic context, often be considered a misunderstanding.

Hermeneutics as a critical perspective

If communication is about production of meaning, then the hermeneutic perspectives I have outlined so far in this chapter must be central to all studies of media and communication, from the bottom up. One main point is the same as for the semiotic approach – the relatively simple and well-ordered models of communication are 'exploded'. They are opened up to a surrounding ocean of history, society and culture, and this goes for both the 'sender', the 'message' and the 'receiver' boxes. In the 'sender' institutions, one interprets the world or a particular segment of it on the basis of general values and ideologies in society, as well as norms and ideas that are specific to such institutions. The text or message will include meanings that more or less unwittingly get there through the complex process of production. At the receiving or 'reception' end, a similarly complex production of meaning through interpretation takes place, also involving unconscious elements.

This means that everything becomes more complex and hard to get a grasp on methodologically. It also, importantly, means that it is impossible for any of us to regard the field of media and communication as outsiders, as a chemist regards a process she is not involved in. It moreover means that a *holistic* perspective, one that in principle has the whole of the communication process in view, is absolutely necessary. Both with 'senders' and 'recipients', processes of meaning-making go on, on the basis of a historically produced reservoir of signs, codes and forms of understanding, contained, so to speak, in verbal language and its genres, in visual traditions, forms of presentation, and so on.

One can also suggest some critical perspectives that may result from a hermeneutic way of thinking in media studies. A first example could be hermeneutics' potential for a *critique of science* (where 'science' would also include humanistic scholarship). This is best understood with reference to the historical struggles within the field. In the chapter on influence (Chapter 2) I referred to the American sociologist Robert K. Merton's characterization of two main traditions within the field by way of two mottoes. One of these, a predominantly American, 'positivist' or 'empiricist' tradition, operated, in Merton's view, according to the motto 'We don't know if what we say is particularly important, but it is at least true'. The other, a predominantly European, philosophically inflected tradition, operated in accordance with the motto 'We don't know whether what we say is true, but it is at least important'. What we did not discuss in Chapter 2 was precisely Merton's notion of *truth* here. The positivist or empiricist way of thinking tends to reserve the notion of scientific truth to that which can be empirically confirmed by way of procedures that produce quantitative, statistical representations of reality. This has two problematic consequences.

First, one might end up measuring something other than that which one intended to study by way of these preferred methods. This concerns the problem of *operationalization* of the theoretical notions one necessarily starts out with when formulating the question to which one seeks an answer. Theoretical notions tend to be of a qualitative nature. Such problems are, of course, well known, and there are established ways in which to handle them. To hermeneutically oriented researchers, however, operationalizations will appear much more difficult. There will always be a drastic leap from qualitative, theoretical thinking about the complex reality that we have to understand by way of language, to quantitative representations of it in figures, even if hermeneutically inclined researchers also make use of quantitative methods.

The other problem is this: if the notion of truth is limited to 'findings' derived from that which it is possible to investigate by way of (ever more refined) quantitative methods, this will also limit the sorts of questions scholars may legitimately work on. The areas of research will be limited to the questions that can be answered by way of the methods that are officially recognized as 'scientific'. Method comes to define the issues worth studying. One may thus end up answering questions few see any reason to care about, while fundamental, perhaps less 'operationalizable', issues are left alone. A hermeneutic sort of approach is more free in its choice of problems to investigate, since the criteria of validity or truth are different here. An absolutely objective understanding is, in principle, impossible since the interpreting subject is always inscribed in historically, socially and culturally specific contexts. So in a hermeneutic approach, what is true or valid knowledge is decided through a continuous dialogue, where the 'pre-scientific' – moral, ideological – preconditions for understanding the phenomena in question can be discussed. As mentioned above, the ideal of empiricist or positivist research has been to 'eliminate' the influence of such preconditions methodically – rather than to acknowledge them and include them in the research process and the presentation of its results.

But hermeneutic ideas not only inspire a critique of science; they can also inspire critical social theory more generally and, in that way, form a basis for, say, media research. The most central name here is Jürgen Habermas, Professor of Philosophy at the University of Frankfurt, Germany. A main subject for him, which he has dealt with in various writings over more than 20 years, is the relationship between two types of rationality, two ways of thinking with different criteria for truth or validity that imply different relations between people. The following is a brief, simplified presentation of some of the main points that are central in particular to his *Theory of Communicative Action* ([1981] 1984 and 1989).

One form of rationality is the *technical-economical*. This rationality has an absolute criterion of truth such as that of the natural sciences and school mathematics: A proposition is either true or false, and it should be as exact as possible. This is evidently the sort of rationality that is useful when constructing aeroplanes or power plants; but questions concerning meaning, ethics etc. are, in principle, impossible to answer in a satisfactory way within this rationality. A technical-economical form of rationality orients one towards the measurable efficiency of this or that plan or action. Terms such as *goal-oriented rationality* or *instrumental rationality* are also used about this type of thinking, and in political discussions one often speaks of *economic rationalism*, referring to the twin ideas that market mechanisms are preferable to government intervention, and that government should take economic considerations as the totally dominating criterion when making decisions about policy. The social consequences of the dominance of technical-economical rationality are many. They will, for instance, imply that it is difficult to find acceptance for an argument on political matters that cannot immediately be supported by 'exact figures', which demonstrate the technical and economic efficiency of a certain policy. It is not enough to say that polluted air is detrimental to people's health and that it should therefore be cleaned; one needs rather to calculate that a 50 per cent reduction in air pollution will save £x million in reduced sick leave, hospital costs etc.

The British educational system is in the process of a transformation from elementary to university level, where technical-economical rationality totally dominates the language in which education (and research) is understood and the ways in which goals are set for this sector of society. The standard of education is presumed to be measurable through identical national tests; teachers and schools are to receive resources according to how they fulfil goals of the sort previously encountered in the manufacture of goods such as cars and electrical appliances; the quality of research is measured in terms of the number of books published, and so on. In summer 2000 it was revealed (in the *Guardian*) that this may lead to teachers filling in tests for their students in order to comply with the required standards of 'productivity', and British university researchers speak of how they need to rush the publication of a book before the end of the year, even if this reduces its quality, simply because their department will otherwise risk suffering budget cuts. These examples show not only how this form of rationality privileges 'exact figures' as a particularly effective form of *rhetoric* (see the following chapter), they also indicate how there may be a counter-productive mismatch between this rationality, and the social and cultural areas it is allowed to 'take over'.

Habermas labels the other form of rationality *communicative*. He could possibly also have called it hermeneutic. Habermas argues that this sort of rationality is to be found, for example, in people's everyday lives, and in various more or less popular organizations and movements, primarily those formed around issues such as ecology, feminism, and so on. The criterion for truth or validity is here, one could say, closely tied to ethics, and *dialogue* is the 'medium' of this form of rationality. While the technical-economical rationality tends to be authoritarian in the sense that its notion of truth is absolute, objective, indisputable, communicative rationality is in principle open and democratic since truth is decided through ongoing discussion. Habermas argues that there is an orientation towards mutual understanding and the establishment of some form of consensus inherent in human communication or 'communicative action', and so the nature of human communication (as dialogue) can provide a normative foundation for social critique. He suggests that each of the two forms of rationality dominate in one of two different social spheres, termed *system world* and *life world* respectively. However, the system world is expanding, colonizing areas that traditionally belonged to the life world. This expansion is, though, met with resistance, for instance from more or less spontaneously formed popular movements such as those mentioned above.

All of this should illustrate how the languages, procedures and understandings of science and scholarship are not necessarily totally 'innocent' or neutral in themselves. They can be tied to different sorts of rationality, different notions of truth and various general, basic social interests.

Finally , it may be worthwhile pointing out how hermeneutics also can provide a basis for what one could call a *critique of education*. Hermeneutics is a theory of interpretation, but it is fundamentally a theory of what knowledge is and how it is achieved. It may thus be of importance to how we understand society and how we imagine society *ought to be*; but, bearing in mind the matter in hand, hermeneutics is highly relevant in terms of how we understand university studies – for instance, of media and communication – and what such studies *ought to be like*. One of the central themes of hermeneutics is, precisely, the relationship between the one who interprets, understands and knows, and that which he or she interprets, understands and, after a while, knows something about. The notion of hermeneutical self-reflection actually points to the necessity of forming a *relatively independent, personal understanding* of whatever one studies. From what one reads and hears as a student, one must form one's own thoughts and opinions, on the basis of one's own situation and interests. When really learning as a student, one not only forms a personal conception of a particular academic field or subject, one also, at the same time, changes oneself. It was put like this by the French philosopher and historian Michel Foucault:

> ... knowledge is a spiritual adventure and a spiritual transformation. The one who knows is not only different from the one who does not know by the

simple fact that he knows about certain things, but by the fact that he or she is no longer the same. In other words: knowledge is that which changes the very subjectivity of the one who knows.

(Foucault, 1979: 7)

These are thoughts one might well call hermeneutical. They tie education to development of self or personality. They make studies and research – an advanced form of education – into personally, existentially relevant activities. To study is to orientate oneself in the world in order to understand oneself and one's own position in various contexts. Since the media are so important and take up so much time in our everyday lives, media studies is an excellent field for the development of such improved self-understanding.

6 Rhetoric: language, situation, purpose

Semiotics, hermeneutics, rhetoric

Referring to the simplest, linear model of communication, one could perhaps say that semiotics has the text as its primary object, and hermeneutics the relationship between recipients and the text, while rhetoric in particular focuses on the relationship between senders and texts. Rhetoric could, with a view to some traditional conceptions of it, be defined as 'a theory of communication from the point of view of the sender'. But this is very much a simplification. So much so, in fact, that it misrepresents the actual relevance of the three approaches.

Semiotics, as we have seen, is about signs and sign structures, the material of the communication process, and how this is handled at each end, both by senders and recipients. In a similar way, hermeneutics may be about interpretation, and especially the interpretation that takes place on the part of recipients, but it is also conducted all the time in innumerable ways among senders, journalistic or artistic, since any subject must be interpreted both before and during the production of a text about it. Interpretation is also simply a necessary part of being human. Any text always carries or represents an interpretation of something.

In a similar way, one can show how rhetoric is highly relevant to, and indeed an aspect of, the process of communication as a whole. In this chapter I will try to illustrate this by moving between classic concepts of rhetoric and examples from the present time.

The field of rhetoric: from antiquity to poststructuralism

The rhetorical theoretical tradition has its origins in ancient Greece, roughly about 400 years BC, as (a theory of) the art of speech. In the Greek 'democracy' of that time free men (women and slaves were not invited) met to discuss political issues, juridical conflicts and other business of collective interest. Rhetoric's next period of flowering was Roman antiquity, especially around discussions in the Senate. In such contexts it was obviously very useful to be able to argue one's views and interests convincingly. Rhetoric as a theory arose as a reflection on what characterizes *good* speeches, that is to say speeches that appeared convincing to the assembled public and which were, in that sense, 'effective'.

This is also precisely the point of departure for a fundamental conflict concerning the role of rhetoric. We know it early on from one of Plato's dialogues, *Gorgias*. Gorgias was one of several men who had specialized in the art of speech and practised as teachers of the discipline, the so-called *sophists*. What characterizes the sophists as teachers of rhetoric, and as practitioners, was that they thought they could speak (and teach others to speak) persuasively *in favour of any view or opinion*. To the sophists, it was all a question of the devices or techniques employed in speech. Plato condemned this way of thinking because the sophists did not care about what was *true* and (morally, ethically) *good*. They only cared about *the effect on the public or audience*, not about whether the speech presented the case or matter under discussion truthfully or whether the opinion they presented was ethically defendable.

Modern, and especially tabloid, journalism has been criticized as representing a form of sophism (Skjervheim, 1987). Creating an attention-grabbing, engaging form in terms of layout, stories or reports has, the argument goes, become more important than producing a reliable, adequate account of the events covered. The prioritizing of stories is similarly decided upon more with a view to the sensational and emotionally engaging than with a view to what it is important to present so that readers or audiences can get a truthful, adequate picture of the world situation.

It was sophism that first gave rhetoric a bad reputation. 'Sophistry' is still a pejorative term used to characterize empty arguments and quibbling. But the term 'sophistication' is also derived from 'sophism', showing that the practice of the sophists was also marked by elegance and refinement. 'Rhetoric' has to a considerable degree been associated with the negative side of sophism, as is demonstrated in expressions such as 'pure rhetoric', 'just rhetoric' and the like, with regard to ways of speaking that may be eloquent but are, actually, shallow and evade the facts of the matter. It has also often been tied to *demagogy*, a term that originally meant to 'stir people up', i.e. a form of speech, most often highly emotional, directed at seducing the audience by appealing to its 'baser instincts', as some have put it. Rhetoric is thus identified with agitation and *propaganda*, i.e. argumentation for certain causes or ideas that is lax about facts, one-sided, strongly emotional and aimed at large audiences. Rhetoric has also been associated with *embellishment*, i.e. what may also be referred to as 'flowery' language, a form of speech or writing where artful expressions and imagery dominate at the expense of matter-of-factly adequate meaning. One then tends to forget that embellishment occurs all the time in editorial comments and TV documentaries. Television news and documentaries too may often contain visual segments with no other purpose than to be something agreeable or interesting to watch while something totally different is talked about on the soundtrack.

Rhetoric has become a pejorative term because of the widespread view that matter-of-factness and truthfulness are ideals that are more or less alien to a rhetorical practice and way of thinking. This view is wrong on two counts. First, it is assumed that a form of speech that in a 'neutral', more or less non-emotional fashion presents factual matters in a way that at least appears to be correct, is non-rhetorical. This is wrong since this sort of language is also rhetorical. In our day and age, such a neutral, matter-of-fact language may, in fact, be *the language best suited to persuading an audience*.

This point may be expanded upon by saying that *any use of language is rhetorical*, in the simple sense that it attempts to make someone else accept, realize, understand, experience etc. something the speaker ('sender') means, understands, knows, feels, thinks etc. Aristotle was in favour of such an inclusive, more or less totalizing, view of the field of rhetoric. Another way of putting this is to say that there is *a rhetorical dimension in all forms of communication* or, as some would have it, that there is an inescapable 'rhetoricity' in language and, indeed, in any form of communication. The rhetorical point of view will thus be important to the study of all forms of communication, but *rhetoric as a discipline in its own right* is probably most useful in understanding those forms of communication that clearly try to present certain material or certain views as persuasively or convincingly as possible. Typical examples of this might include lectures (and other forms of teaching), feature articles and leaders in newspapers, political speeches and interventions in discussions, and advertising. All of these are more or less conscious attempts to persuade an audience to listen, learn and accept, and the means are, to some extent, carefully chosen.

The choice of rhetorical means must be adequate to the *topic,* which is an essential part of the *situation.* Classical rhetoric put great emphasis on the fact that rhetorical communication always takes place at a certain occasion, at a particular time, directed at a particular audience, with a particular purpose. Rhetoric is, in other words, fundamentally *pragmatic* (cf. Chapter 4 of the present volume, on semiotics) in its orientation. This is also why it is obvious that a 'neutral', matter-of-fact language will, in many situations, be the only viable one for those who wish to persuade someone of something. The Greek term for the rhetorical situation, *kairos,* also had a dimension of 'timing' or 'suitability'; good rhetoric 'suits the occasion', is correctly 'timed'. This means, among other things, that the good rhetorician knows *when it is time to speak, and for how long* – and when it is time to be quiet and think.

Other classical theories of rhetoric emphasize truthfulness and other ethical values. After Plato's critique of the sophists came his student Aristotle's book about the theory of rhetoric. It is there emphasized that *good* speech is *truthful (ethically, morally) good and beautiful*. Classical rhetorical theory, then, as formulated by Aristotle, sees as intimately linked three areas that, in modern societies, are separated and handled by different institutions. Now science (and perhaps journalism?) takes care of truth, the courts and the church take care of morality and ethics, while the institutions of art decide what is beautiful. In classical rhetoric, however, bad speeches were those that were lacking in one or more of these areas. This actually still applies to a considerable extent in our everyday judgements. We speak of a bad speech, a bad article etc. when we find it untruthful (contrary to the facts), ethically dubious or condemnable (it promotes, for example, racism), or lacking in style or 'beauty' (clumsily formulated, overly repetitive, dull etc.). The main point here is, however, that the demands for truthfulness and ethical standards do not come to rhetoric from the outside, as an 'external control' of rhetoric, they are built into classical rhetoric itself.

Especially after the Renaissance, from the seventeenth century onwards, rhetorical theory was increasingly reduced to a technical teaching of eloquence so that it gradually appeared mostly as a set of catalogues of linguistic 'devices'. Such a reduced meaning of the term rhetoric is not only found in the widespread devaluation of the discipline, it is also found in modern literary theory, which is very preoccupied with rhetoric – but primarily in the sense of what we have just recognized as linguistic devices. Various kinds of literary sociology have studied the socioculturally determined situation (*kairos*) in a wider sense, but such efforts have largely appeared to be marginal within literary studies. However, in contrast with the everyday understanding of the term 'devices' as a set of 'tools', literary scholars have not regarded 'linguistic devices' as tools lying, ready to be used, in an imagined toolbox for speakers or writers. We cannot choose or reject them at will; they are instead regarded as *inescapable elements in, and prerequisites for, any kind of linguistic or communicative practice*, since they are, in fact, nothing but signs and sign structures. This notion of rhetoric, which in itself does not really break with classical rhetoric, except by being a limited version of it, is in other words closely linked to a semiotic understanding of language and communication. It is also a central element in the broader tendency within textual studies that has been referred to as *poststructuralism*. As this term suggests, poststructuralism is, in a sense, built on structuralist sign theory, semiotics, but at the same time certain insights and elements of semiotics are radicalized and have become a main focus. Roland Barthes, who we referred to in Chapter 4 as a leading structuralist or semiotic theoretician, embodied this transition as a scholarly writer by becoming a leading poststructuralist from about 1970.

The fact that the denotative and connotative signifieds of signifiers can change with a change of context is one such element, which potentially undermines ideas of sign systems or languages as stable wholes. They are in constant movement, meaning is never finally determinable, neither in the individual text nor in the world at large. While structuralists were content to demonstrate how a text was 'actually' built on an underlying thematic opposition between 'nature' and 'culture', or between 'male' and 'female', poststructuralists are more interested in how the text, in various ways, and primarily in more or less inconspicuous details, actually shows elements of meaning that have been excluded or marginalized in order to make the basic thematic elements appear clearly separate and in opposition to each other. 'Strength' may be used as one of the defining features of masculinity, and is thus barred from being a defining feature of femininity; 'compassion' is regarded as feminine and is thus excluded from the list of features associated with masculinity. Still, the text may contain examples of women showing strength and men showing compassion, and the whole system of oppositions that defines masculinity as opposed to femininity may thus be questioned (cf. Chapter 4). The task of the analyst is to present such a *deconstruction* of the seemingly stable meaning of the text, a deconstruction that is already present as a potential interpretation in the text as it is. This has especially been a main point for the French philosopher Jacques Derrida. The word 'deconstruction', or *deconstructionism*, has accordingly been used to refer to a significant proportion of poststructuralist work. One might also consider how the notion of intertextuality (cf., again, Chapter 4) implies that the idea of the individual text as a clearly delimited and autonomous 'work' is deconstructed.

Derrida has often been referred to as saying that 'there is nothing outside the text', and this has been variously applauded or strongly rejected – often due to a misunderstanding of terms. Saussure imagined the sign – both signifier and signified – as separate from the referent, i.e. the reality external to the sign. Peirce regarded anything that might mean something to someone as a sign, and so his theory too excludes an accessible reality beyond the signs (see Chapter 4 once again). This does not, of course, mean that nothing *exists* outside of signs and language, only that it is not *accessible to us* other than through signs. In theories favoured by literary studies the signs of verbal language are normally awarded status as that which shapes us as human beings and our perception of the world – 'because language is the very air I breathe, I can never have a pure, unblemished meaning or experience at all' (Eagleton, 1983: 130). Since language's relation to a reality external to itself is both indirect and fundamentally unstable, such ideas might lead to the practice of always placing notions such as *reality* and *truth* between inverted commas. Reality and truth become functions of language, and constructions that rely totally on the position from which speech (or writing) comes and in which situation. When the notion of truth and the understanding of knowledge in this way becomes fundamentally *relativized*, then a thread or link back to the rhetorical tradition of antiquity is also broken, since a notion of *intersubjective truth* was central there.

This does not mean that the notion of truth in classical rhetoric was the same as that which now officially dominates in science, politics and the media. The field of rhetoric is the field where 100 per cent certainty is impossible to achieve – it is the field for the *more or less probable*. When truth is to be decided in the sense of rhetoric, it is therefore a question of argumentation, discussion, dialogue. One may well note the parallel to hermeneutics (see the previous chapter) here. Truth is what those who are well informed agree upon. There are more or less certain *facts*, and these may well be part of the argument, but the same applies to a number of *assumptions* that one will simply have to take for granted, even if they are not scientifically proven or even provable. In practice, this is how things work in our day and age too. Not only in the fields of politics and art, but also in the humanities and social sciences – truths and opinions are constantly up for discussion. There are even tough discussions going on about the degree of absoluteness one should attribute to the truths of the natural sciences. The field of the more or less probable, the field of rhetoric, is – probably – larger than we are inclined to imagine.

The rhetorical work

No one simply speaks; those who speak always do so in a certain situation and with a certain purpose. Classical Greek rhetoric, i.e. that of Aristotle, reckoned there were three main sorts of speech situation and three corresponding types of speech.

- *Judicial speech* is about something that took place in the past and decisions on guilt or innocence pertaining to these events, as in a court of law but not necessarily only there.
- *Epideictic speech* ('demonstrative speech') is about the present and aims to present praise or blame. Aristotle was probably thinking of public festivals or funerals as typical occasions for such speeches. In practice, *encomium*, or eulogy, is the most important variety here: speeches that aim to praise something or someone (*panegyric*), such as speeches at jubilees, opening ceremonies, birthdays etc. Another feature of such speeches is, as one may

have experienced, that they serve, not least, to demonstrate how clever the speaker is – this may be the most 'demonstrative' thing about them.

- The third type of speech is *deliberative*. It is about the future and about persuading an audience that this or that particular action is the wisest.

One might sum all this up by saying that the judicial and the deliberative forms of speech address audiences that are to decide about a particular action, while the epideictic speech, or rhetoric, addresses an audience that is not expected to act in any particular way. It has, however, been suggested that Aristotle's category 'epideictic' should be expanded to cover 'any discourse that does not aim at a specific action but is intended to influence the values and beliefs of the audience' (Kennedy, 1994: 4).

These categories are not immediately adequate for all the genres that are rhetorically relevant today. One can, of course, say that crime novels and the coverage of crime in news media are reminiscent of judicial speech, that speeches in parliament and newspaper editorials are most often deliberative, and that newspaper articles celebrating some famous person's birthday are examples of epideictic speeches of the panegyric variety. But what about the story of a football game in the sports pages? A philosophical article in a scholarly journal? A documentary about the lives of supermodels? Such examples may include an element of all the three main types.

Classical rhetoric's categorization of the phases of work on a speech may be more interesting. Many of these phases will be well known to anyone who has ever prepared an essay at school or college. Rhetorical theory says that there are five such phases or steps, and each is the subject of a particular subdiscipline. In Latin, the first phase is called *inventio*, and is simply the gathering of material for the speech – that is, the elements and arguments that are relevant to the subject of the speech. Based on experience, one might create long lists, called *topics* (from the Greek word *topos*, which means 'place'). These lists could function as a sort of 'map' of the mental 'places', *topoi*, where elements and arguments for a speech are to be found.

A topos may, to begin with, be thought of as a *question* one asks about a particular subject. The choice of a particular question concerning a subject is a choice of a way of approaching the subject, and thus also a choice of what aspect of the subject one wishes to focus on – a choice of subject. So the concept of *topos* covers a sliding scale from question to approach to subject or theme.

Aristotle had four 'key questions' one could ask about any subject, even if some were more important in some of the speech situations we talked about above than others. These concerned what is possible and not possible, what has happened and what has not happened, what will happen and what will not happen, and what is more or less, say, important than what else. He also listed

28 other questions for general use. These were general, formal topoi that were used in a *dialectical* way (through a sort of dialogue, a going back and forth between questions and answers) to produce a clearer idea of the subject and thus of what would be valid arguments.

But there were also other, more specific, 'content-related' topoi that, in a similar way, can be thought of as questions or approaches to a subject or to the material one is to say something about. These were mainly drawn from the reservoir of generally accepted opinions, insights, ways of understanding and verbal standard formulae (such as sayings) known in Greek as *doxa* and, in English, as *common sense* (cf. Chapter 3, on the distinctions in Bourdieu's use of the term doxa). Such a content-topos is called *locus communis* in Latin and *commonplace* in English. It is, by definition, a *cliché*. In literary studies, the term topos is therefore also used as a term for cliché-like situations, motifs and themes. A cliché is a metaphor taken from typography where it meant something durable, something that could be used over and over again, without the negative associations the word now connotes (i.e. something that is well-worn, not *new*).

In the context of modern media, one finds 'topical' devices and ways of thinking in, for instance, what journalists refer to as 'angles'. These are precisely about which kinds of question one asks concerning a given type of subject, or material, a collection of types of information one has at one's disposal and is about to present. Journalists sometimes try to evade responsibility for the topoi they use by claiming to ask questions 'on behalf of the readers/audience'. In practice, this means that they ask questions that they, for various reasons, *assume* the readers are particularly interested in. They may thus risk assuming that the readers are more stupid than they really are, and they also risk not asking those questions by which it is possible that the readers would have been better served. Certain 'content-topoi', or commonplaces, are particularly frequently used: 'The little man against the bureaucracy/experts/powerful people' is a favourite (the obliques used here illustrate that it comes in several varieties). Such journalistic topoi can also have a basis in the everyday common sense of sayings and myths, such as 'You have to take the rough with the smooth', 'Everybody is the architect of his own fortune', and the like. That the list of journalistic topoi is not long, can quite easily be confirmed by looking at a selection of newspaper and television reports or stories – they often appear to be variations on well-known topoi such as those mentioned here.

On closer inspection, there are also topoi in other businesses, such as research or scholarship. Historians must, for example, know which sort of causes they should look for if they want to explain historical developments: divine intervention, other spiritual forces, class struggle, technological progress, market forces or whatever (Lindhardt, 1975: 63). In media studies there are also, in addition to those shared with, say, historians, many topoi of this sort: the passive/active TV viewer, the power of media moguls, the evils of tabloidization, and so on. This also goes for most academic disciplines; publications should include, for instance, certain verbal clichés of a sort one could call *topoi of modesty* (of the type 'I do not in any way pretend to have solved the problem …', 'The following may be a small contribution to …', and so on), ritualistic accounts of previous work in the area and many other standardized approaches and forms of expression.

The second phase of the rhetorical work is called *dispositio* and is simply the ordering of the elements and ideas one found in the *inventio* phase. The speech was to start with the *exordium*, which aims to 'win the audience in the same way an appetizer whets the appetite without satisfying it' (Fafner, 1992: 19). There then followed sections where the material and the arguments for one's view are carefully presented, until the *conclusio* part is finally reached, where the, by now, not very surprising conclusion and, if adequate, a recommendation of a certain form of action, are formulated. As some readers may have heard in school, a good speech or essay should have 'the shape of a fish', with a head, a body and a tail (i.e. a beginning, a middle and an end). Those who become journalists will soon have to learn a different *dispositio*: news items should be shaped like a 'pyramid on its head', i.e. the main point and all the central information and arguments that sustain it should come first – thereafter one can keep filling in less and less important material. Those who edit the final newspaper product can then do this in the simplest and fastest way possible, i.e. by simply deleting from the end up, until the desired story length is reached.

Once a structure has been arrived at, it is time for the actual preparation of the speech; this is called *elocutio*. *Elocutio* means 'style', and this is the field within rhetoric that was the most extensive and that, also, has dominated the perception of rhetoric in the last couple of centuries. *Eloquence* is, in a sense, also the subject of rhetoric, albeit in a wider sense than that directly referred to under *elocutio*. In this field we find a huge collection of terms for various types of verbal expression and 'devices' plus ideas on where and how they work (we will, therefore, return to this later). Also included are rules pertaining to the material aspect of language – the signifier, if you will – i.e. things like the sound of a voice, rhyme and rhythm. The ideal was a speech that was as clear and influential as possible: true, good and beautiful.

The fourth phase may appear to be of less interest today; this *memoria* phase was simply about learning the speech by heart, so that one could perform it without a script and thus more easily appear totally focused and committed to what one was saying. Nowadays it is mostly actors who need to learn long texts by heart, and they may well find useful some of the mnemonic tricks employed by the rhetoricians of old. The idea that a speaker who is very much tied to her or his manuscript does not function well is just as valid today as it was then, and this is something to which students and others will probably be able to testify. The practice of 'reading a paper' at academic conferences or as a visiting speaker at a university is often a ludicrous travesty of human communication. It is why the tele-prompter (or auto-cue) was invented; this is the machine that TV presenters read from when they appear to be looking straight into our eyes, particularly in newscasts. News anchors should, in perfect keeping with the insights of antiquity, appear as if they really mean and stand for what they are saying; and TV journalists reporting live, on the spot, must for the same reason be able to remember at least a few sentences when they are on air. So maybe *memoria* is more relevant to today's media than it might, at first, have appeared.

The fifth and final phase of rhetorical work is also particularly relevant to the medium of television; it is *actio*, the act of presenting the speech to an audience. Not being tied up by a manuscript is part of this, but it is only a precondition that enables all the other elements to function properly: an adequate, carefully planned use or modulation of the voice, an emphasis on certain words and sentences, mimicry, looks, body movements (experienced speakers may move around the podium) and gestures: fingers or fists in the air, the waving of arms etc. Actors are, in other words, absolute professionals in terms of the *actio* part of rhetoric. But we know that actors are playing a part when they appear on stage or screen. Anyone who appears in public will in some sense also be playing a part, but these days it is considered *bad rhetoric* if play-acting is a rather too obvious feature of the performance. It has even been convincingly argued that a bit of clumsiness and stuttering may now be a good thing for a politician on TV, because the person in question will then appear human and *honest*. It is often forgotten that what one says is not necessarily *true*, even if one is totally honest (Johansen, 1999). We will return to the historical causes for, and some theoretical perspectives on, these matters in the chapter on the public sphere and the media's roles in it (Chapter 8).

Means of persuasion

According to rhetorical theory, there are three means of persuasion available to the speaker when an audience is to be persuaded or convinced of something: *ethos*, *logos* and *pathos*. The basis for this triad is the three elements in the simple model of communication we saw at the start of Chapter 4: sender, message, receiver/recipient. At the same time, however, all three are to be understood as *elements in the speech or text*.

Ethos is an emotional means of persuasion tied to the character of the speaker, more precisely the *impression* the speaker makes concerning what sort of human character he or she is. What we said above about the memoria and actio phases is, in other words, primarily relevant for this means of persuasion. Is this person trustworthy? What about his or her judgement? Is he or she really devoted to the best interests of the audience? It is of course an advantage if a speaker is known beforehand to be an honourable or even admirable person. The use of sports stars and other celebrities in advertising is an attempt to use the respect for these people's efforts in the arena, on stage or screen, as a persuasive force in a totally different field. This is of course bad rhetoric in the sense that it is irrelevant to the case and ethically problematic – athletes or movie stars are not particularly knowledgeable about cars or food. The press may sometimes be eager to get a professor or some other expert in a certain area to make statements on a subject on which they are supposedly particularly well qualified to comment, but sometimes also on subjects that anyone who knows them will tell you they are not particularly familiar with. This is a conscious use of the ethos that is tied to titles such as 'professor', 'researcher' etc. The specifically rhetorical form of ethos is, however, the impression that is communicated *in the speech* – that is, in the nature of the argument, the choice of verbal 'devices', in the actual performance.

The physical arrangement of the speech situation may also, however, contribute to a favourable ethos. A rostrum or 'speaker's desk' may in itself furnish the speaker with authority. In visual media, such as television, one often sees background and surroundings used to give presenters or hosts authority and credibility in other ways (we will return to this idea shortly). When politicians choose to campaign on city streets, face to face with the public, informally dressed, this is to emphasize that they are 'one of us' and hence not to be suspected of not wanting the best for everyone.

The word *logos* means word, speech and reasoning. It is, in this context, the term for the intellectual or rational means of persuasion. This is of course particularly central in judiciary and deliberative speeches. There are two main types of intellectual means of persuasion in rhetoric – the *enthymeme* (deduction) and the *example* (induction).

The enthymeme is a simplified version of the logical or dialectical *syllogism*. A syllogism consists of a major premise (a general rule), a minor premise and a conclusion: for example, 'All men have hair growing on their face. John is a man. Therefore John has hair growing on his face.' The enthymeme is most often a shortened syllogism, where the major premise, the general rule, is omitted, so what remains is just 'an assertion supported by a reason' (Kennedy, 1994: 58): 'Tony can't be trusted anymore, he's become a politician.' The major premise or general rule here is that 'no politicians can be trusted', but this is not made explicit – because it is presumed to be well known and accepted by the audience. The enthymeme is, in other words, a form that does more than save space or time, it invites *the audience* to supply the major premise, the basic presupposition for the conclusion. This implies, on the one hand, that the enthymeme presupposes a cultural community, a community of knowledge, experience and values; on the other hand, since it invites and requires a contribution or 'filling in' from the audience, it may also at times make the audience feel flattered because they are *able to* identify the general rule that is presupposed and thus understand what is said.

The enthymeme is an everyday version of deduction from the general to the specific. The *example* is, similarly, what corresponds to scholarly *induction* from the specific to the general. An example is a reference to a parallel, known particular case, which serves to indicate that a general rule applies. The example implies a comparison between what one speaks of and the case one refers to, and this may at times take the form of a direct, explicit comparison: 'Such an attitude to Iraq is like Chamberlain's to Hitler.' But the comparison may also be more indirect, such as 'The new series from David E. Kelley will certainly be of miserable quality, remember *Chicago Hope*?' The latter example demonstrates how important it is to choose one's examples in light of who one is speaking to – the imagined speaker quoted had better be addressing an audience with similar peculiar tastes in TV entertainment.

Pathos refers to emotions, but primarily to emotions (such as passion) that are so strong one almost feels overpowered by them, a victim. Pathos is the (use of) feelings that are more or less overwhelming, more or less beyond conscious control. Ethos is also an emotional means of persuasion, but milder, as in varieties of respect, trust, feelings of community etc. Pathos is more powerful stuff, such as joy, anger, grief and the like. A good speaker creates pathos in an audience in the right places. Compassion is, for instance, an emotion it is important to mobilize either in a plea for aid to victims of a famine somewhere or when speaking in defence of the accused in a trial. But in good rhetoric this is not a question of manipulation. The Roman rhetorician Cicero said that:

> … there is so much power in the thoughts one has and the views one presents in the course of a speech that there is no use for simulation or cheating, since what one takes to in order to make an impression on others has an even greater influence on the speaker than on anyone in the audience.
>
> (From *De Oratore*, quoted in Andersen, 1995: 40)

In antiquity one thus more or less imagined that pathos resided in the thoughts, images and ideas that made up the material of the speech. Pathos was, in other words, not something that only belonged to the *elocutio* part of the rhetorician's work, it also clearly belonged to the *inventio* part, the very subject. This must not least be seen as resulting from the fact that one did not have a modern, individualistic conception of emotions. Emotions were in a different way objective phenomena, present in us as sources of knowledge and engrained as elements of language. They were thus not in diametrical opposition to reason, but assisted it in the establishment of knowledge and understanding. Emotions could also be valued as good or bad, adequate or inadequate, in quite a different manner than that which is now, in our therapeutic culture, commonly accepted.

Anyone who has ever seen courtroom scenes in American movies and TV series has seen how the lawyers there mobilize pathos so the audience, often the jury, is moved to tears or rage. The same happens in real courtrooms, both in the USA and elsewhere. In the perspective of classical rhetoric this is not necessarily a manipulatory device to be condemned. It is rather a question of mobilizing the emotions of, say, the jury as a source of insight into the nature of the crime in question, the situation of the victim or, for that matter, the miserable life history of the criminal, and his or her strong feelings of remorse or guilt. A good lawyer must appear as if he or she believes in such emotions, and they might arise as a result of them being 'carried away' by their own speech. A lack of pathos in both courtroom and political speeches might simply weaken the speaker's credibility: 'What a cold fish this guy is!' 'Does he even believe what he's saying himself?' There is thus an important link not only between the logos and pathos means of persuasion, but also between pathos and ethos. If, on the other hand, the use of pathos is contradicted by obvious weaknesses in the logos part of the argument (say, clearly contrary to indisputable facts) or contradicted by aspects of actio/ethos (the delivery of the speech shows that the speaker is not really committed), then pathos can return to the speaker with a vengeance, i.e. severely increase the audience's distrust and irritation.

On the basis of all this, those who wish to might, for example, question whether the totally detached, neutral, rational, fact-oriented journalistic coverage of wars and (other) disasters is necessarily the best, or most helpful. On the other hand much consciously subjectivist *new journalism* may also appear problematic. While the journalist's private, personal feelings are, in principle, irrelevant to the public, the emotions that, so to speak, lie in the material or subject itself are another matter. They are relevant to an understanding of the case.

'New journalism' as rhetorical practice

News journalism has traditionally had as its aim to answer the questions 'who, what, where, when, how and why' in the most neutral and truthful way possible. The ideal has been a sort of objectivity that is closely related to the ideal of objectivity in science, especially in the way that positivism understood it (cf. Chapter 2 of the present volume, on influence). But in the mid-1960s a form of journalism emerged in the USA that was dubbed *new journalism* (even if it actually had forerunners in, for example, the creative reportage style tried out in Germany between the two world wars, in the movement known as *neue Sachlichkeit,* 'new factuality' or 'matter-of-fact-ness'). The material foundation for *new journalism* was the plethora of financially strong, more or less serious magazines that exist in the USA, such as *Esquire, Harper's, The New Yorker, Playboy* and (eventually) *Rolling Stone.* They had both the money and the space needed for the often extremely long reportage supplied by the pioneers of new journalism, with Tom Wolfe in the vanguard. But many of the political and cultural features of the 1960s were also important preconditions. Previously established truths were up for debate in a situation marked by the Vietnam War, black people's struggle for civil rights, and youth and student rebellions. New journalism was hip. The critique of positivist notions of objectivity in the sciences was, not surprisingly, paralleled by a critique of journalism's version of them. This situation offered possibilities for journalists with literary interests and ambitions. They consciously used forms and devices in their journalism that had hitherto been the privileged resources of literary fiction.

Tom Wolfe (1975) has pointed out four basic techniques of new journalism:

1. the construction of the story by way of *scenes*
2. use of *complete dialogue*
3. use of *third-person point of view and inner monologue*
4. emphasis on *symbolic details.*

The first and second points here imply that the story or reportage is written as much as possible in the manner of a drama, or a series of dramatic scenes, which will approach the form of realist theatrical plays or films by representing the dialogues of the people involved in what appears to be a complete way, not just by way of a few carefully chosen lines. The use of a third-person point of view and inner monologue means that the journalist will be using the traditional novel's 'omniscient' narrator (see the next chapter, on narratology) and will thus implicitly appear to know the inner life of the people, or characters, that his or her story or reportage is about. The emphasis on a wide selection of 'symbolic details', i.e. details that shed a connotative light on that which is described, is also a very literary sort of device. The cumulative effect of all this is, in rhetorical terms, that the pathos-appeal of the text is radically strengthened compared to ordinary news reporting. New journalism aims to produce entertaining texts, texts readers can identify with and get emotionally involved in – texts that will make them smell and experience what is described or recounted. While this is not in itself suspect, one can at least say that it may create problems in relation to the journalistic *ethos*. Readers might ask how important the empirical *truth* is when the literary ambition becomes so dominating. Which possibilities will a consequent new journalism text provide in terms of *alternative views* of the events or situations described? Such questions might become even more pressing when the new journalism text places the reporter him/herself and his/her psychic life in the leading role, such as in Hunter S. Thompson's so-called 'gonzo journalism'.

A not unreasonable view would be that new journalism neither can nor should replace the more sober (!) news journalism. It can still retain its position as a source of inspiration for other forms of journalism. These other journalistic genres offer a possibility for editorial staff that are tired of being 'news bureaucrats' to productively make use of the joy to be found in writing for its own sake that may originally have led them into the journalistic profession. Readers may thus enjoy both a certain literary pleasure and also a more colourful, nuanced picture of the world. New journalism's literary ambitions make it, however, a very demanding genre, both because of the extensive work that needs to be done in the preparation of the pieces and, not least, because writing something that can really live up to literary criteria of quality is very hard.

The speech situation in television news and other programmes: enunciation analysis

We have already talked about how the notion of *ethos* implies that a speaker must address us in ways that inspire confidence. Both what is said and how the speaker looks and behaves may be important. We also mentioned how a sense of the occasion or situation, *kairos*, is essential – a good speaker will not address a funeral, a wedding and an office party in the same style. These old, general rhetorical principles indicate how a speaker can establish certain kinds of relationship between him/herself, the audience and the subject of the speech.

Television programmes are for us a 'text', even if they involve living people speaking (or having spoken, if it's a taped programme) to us, or, more precisely, to a camera. The rhetorical relationship between a speaker, an audience and a subject is therefore also built into the text, so to speak. In principle, this applies to *all* texts – the narratives of novels, the reports and notices of newspapers, advertising boards and radio programmes. Semiotic theorists have been very interested in such rhetorical relations. They prefer to talk about *the relations of enunciation*, building on a distinction between the *enunciated* or 'expressed' (French = *l'énoncé*), i.e. what is said, and the act of saying or expressing it, *enunciation* (French = *l'énonciation*). The world's first analysis of the role of enunciation in television news was conducted in the early 1970s by a Dane, now for many years a colleague of mine at the University of Bergen, Peter Larsen (Larsen, 1974). His analysis may be seen as an analysis of this aspect of the rhetoric of television, an analysis where the semiotic theory of signs and connotations is employed in the interpretation of how TV news speaks to us about the world. The following is largely based on Larsen's analysis.

The world over, TV news tends to open with a little video vignette showing the globe in some more or less stylized form. What is signalled here is that what is to be said in the programme that is just starting comes from a position of global overview, assuring us that we will receive a truthful impression of what the world is like at this moment. We might say that one perceives what has been called an *olympic* overview (referring to Mount Olympus, home of the Greek gods). This vignette is, then, the first element in the construction of the programme's ethos, a work that continues in the studio sequence that follows.

The newscaster is quite formally dressed. If it is a man, he will wear a good-quality jacket, shirt and tie; if it is a woman, she will also wear a suit or something with similar connotations of a formal occasion. One does not host TV news programmes in T-shirts or, for that matter, tuxedos or daringly low-cut dresses. The main presenter is commonly called the 'anchor' or 'anchor-person', a term which signals that this person is to be a figure of authority, someone to trust and safely hold on to. The studio background in most western TV-channels has traditionally been in shades of blue, grey or other rather cool colours, connoting 'hard' facts, 'cool' reasoning, neutrality and authority. The BBC and channels in some other countries have changed this, going instead for warm colours such as yellow, orange and even red. This is an interesting twist since it suggests that the programme comes from a warm, cosy and probably caring kind of place, where the emotional, the compassionate etc. will not be excluded. This idea may have been adopted from the formats of breakfast TV, perhaps, which in most countries has always had a deliberately homely atmosphere. Britain's Channel 4 has chosen a studio design that is strikingly 'arty', somewhat reminiscent – to a foreigner – of a trendy nightclub, with a number of different colours cleverly arranged. This solution may have been chosen to connote 'creativity' and 'modern' or 'style-conscious' as characteristic both of the channel and its news programme.

But the main evening newscasts cannot move too far in these directions without risk of losing authority, seriousness. That is why those news presenters on the BBC and other channels that have opted for warm colours are not sipping tea or seated on peach-coloured sofas, surrounded by house plants; that is why Channel 4 also has elements that signify 'hi- tech' and other 'serious' meanings. Channel 4 also includes glimpses of another feature of news studio backgrounds that has spread to many channels, having probably first been introduced by CNN: viewers catch glimpses of a working editorial staff in the background, and/or a number of screens showing pictures from various parts of the world, i.e. satellite television. This is a way of underlining that the news programme comes from a place that is continuously linked to all parts of the globe, continuously working to stay on top of the eternal stream of news bulletins. One may interpret this as marking a new type of authority in news programmes, corresponding to a more general devaluation of traditional forms of authority. It is no longer possible for the individual TV institution to claim authority (and thus credibility) based solely on its long and solid traditions, and its supposedly high level of knowledge or expertise. People in TV newsrooms are no longer to be considered *wiser* than us, the viewers, they are, however, *better positioned* in relation to the events of the world. The importance of a *comprehensive understanding* is thus reduced in favour of an emphasis on the presentation of a number of disparate *events* (Gripsrud, 1989). Some channels also choose to underline that the news is also about speed, action and excitement by, say, placing a fast tracking shot or zoom-in on the presenter at the beginning of the programme, and using it again a few times during the bulletin. This might weaken the impression of seriousness and credibility were it exaggerated, but it rarely is. It is still clear that those who speak to us are far better informed than we are, and take their jobs seriously.

These people speak to *us*, talking *about* something or someone else. There is an almost flattering recognition of us, the viewers, in this: these well-informed people seem to think that talking to us is worthwhile, they take for granted that we too are seriously interested in the state of the world, and they look us straight in the eyes. The news programme's 'first person' – its *I*, so to speak – establishes an alliance with the programme's 'second person', its *you* – i.e. us, the viewers – in its speech about the 'third person', the *it* or *they* that the news is about.

A news programme consists, as do many other TV programmes, of a mixture of studio segments and outside reports. There is thus a possibility that it may appear to fall apart, that the programme does not speak to us in a coherent, trustworthy voice. Any text – in any medium – that does not speak with one coherent voice, expressing a coherent, underlying *reason*, may risk appearing 'schizophrenic', according to some (Brandt and Dines Johansen, 1971); schizophrenics are not, perhaps, considered the most trustworthy among us. This is why it is important in newscasts that the transitions from the anchor-person in the studio to the different reporters in the various external reports are as smooth and as seamless as possible. The reports will most often get a short introduction from the studio, so that the voice of the reporter seems to carry on a speech or utterance already begun; alternatively, a fraternal conversational situation is established where the anchor-person asks the reporter a question which demonstrates that the two of them are on the same team. The close link between the anchor and the reporter is also demonstrated by the rule that *only anchors, reporters and studio staff commentators are allowed to look directly into the camera, i.e. have 'eye contact' with us, the viewers.* If, for instance, interviewees – 'third person singular' in the programme text – try to do the same, they will be breaking unwritten rules and we, the viewers, will tend to regard them as having bad manners or being intolerably self-centred, conceited fools. We do, however, sometimes encounter people who dare to break these rules without our actually condemning them; these are the 'third person plural' – larger or smaller groups of ordinary people who happily wave to mum back home when they are on TV. But those who are to be interviewed seriously cannot allow themselves to say hello to family and friends in this manner without losing whatever dignity they may have.

As viewers, we can of course, in principle, choose whether we want to take on and play the role of the slightly subordinate partner of the anchor and her or his crew. If there are segments concerning things that really matter to us and that we think we know a thing or two about, we might well come to protest – either to those with whom we are watching the programme, by talking back to the screen (the silliest and probably most widespread practice), or by phoning or writing to the TV channel. The arrangement of the TV news programme is still rhetorically efficient – it is a vital contribution to our finding it persuasive. Only those who have their own knowledge-based perspectives on the world, and more or less extensive access to alternative sources of information (national and international), will be able to ask well-founded critical questions concerning the selection of stories, 'angles' or approaches, and so on.

Television's arrangement of its speech situations is thus, not least, created by visual means. The visual, what is said and how it is said, come together to form the *style* of a programme. The notion of 'style' is often more or less synonymous with 'tone' or 'timbre', the characteristics of a certain voice in speech or song. As for all other texts, one could say that *the style of a television programme is its voice,* which is either neutrally authoritative, pleasantly conversational, condescendingly authoritarian, hysterically overexcited, or whatever other descriptive terms one may find appropriate. The generally sober, neutral, serious tone of main newscasts is in contrast to the bright colours and noisier excitement of variety entertainment, and the softer tones of some intimate interview formats dealing with human relations and personal experiences. The style may be different from all of these in, for instance, health information programmes. I once saw a presenter of such a programme recommending carrots and warning of the dangers of smoking while seated behind an impressive desk (connoting counters at public offices, the master's desk at school, the boss's desk at work), with tall, well-filled bookshelves on both sides (connoting masses of accumulated knowledge) and with a curved, Romanesque window behind him (connoting the church, religion). There was absolutely no doubt that an indisputable authority was speaking to us. Those who, for example, lit a cigarette immediately after that would either feel guilty of a sin, or experience an extra bit of 'naughtiness' that added to their pleasure. The speech or programme would, in both cases, have achieved an effect.

Embellishment

As mentioned above, the term 'rhetoric' has often been associated with 'flowery language' and other 'empty gibberish'. This is related to the great emphasis placed on what in Latin is called *ornatus* – ornamentation or embellishment of speech – in the rhetorical tradition. As also mentioned previously, it is the *elocutio* phase of the rhetorical work, where *ornatus* belongs, that has been best preserved in literary studies. But, as the rhetorically oriented poststructuralists emphatically argue, ornatus is not really primarily a question of superficial or 'external' beautification. Good old Cicero had already warned, in his own way, against such a misunderstanding: 'The speech should have a certain amiable elegance. One does not achieve that by smearing make-up on its outside; the fresh complexion comes from a healthy circulation' (from *De Oratore*, quoted in Andersen, 1995: 65). The verbal devices that are involved are, on the contrary, of fundamental significance to what the speech or text is in fact saying – and doing – to the audience.

The rhetoricians of antiquity thought that a good speech should *educate/inform, entertain and move* its audience (*docere, delectare, movere*, as the jingle goes in Latin). Ornatus was not least to serve the 'entertainment', i.e. make sure the audience did not get bored. The speech should be seasoned with various inventive, more or less unexpected, formulations that partly aimed to entertain simply by creating variety, and partly served to make the audience concentrate. This is not, of course, only relevant in the context of verbal language. Various 'MTV-inspired' forms of editing and uses of camera movements etc. in current mainstream television may well be regarded as 'pure' ornatus, i.e. visual surprises of various kinds that primarily serve to keep the audience's attention and entertain it by way of variation. But a central part of the work of ornatus in rhetoric is also *thought work*, i.e. the use of techniques or devices that, say, provide new and surprising points of view and ways of perceiving the case in question or the world at large. Links to standards of 'good language', both in fiction and journalism should be obvious here. The rhetorical ideal is to be understandable, but not banal.

There were three main areas within ornatus. The first concerned the choice of words, where one would be wise to include a few, but not too many, *archaisms* (old-fashioned words, such as 'steed' instead of horse) and *neologisms* (newly created words, often composites, such as one created by my wife this afternoon, 'lipstick feminism'). One could also use words with a certain twist to their regular meanings; these are known as *tropes*, and we will return to them shortly. The other area was *harmonia*, which was about the combination of words – the choice of an unusual sequence, the attention to sound and rhythm. The third, and clearly the most important, area is called the theory of *figures*.

A *trope* is, as we have just seen, a (single) word that is used in a different way than usual, with a different meaning. If someone calls you 'honey', this is an example of a trope so old that people don't normally think of it as one (cf. below). One may speak of a 'transferred meaning' or of a 'figurative meaning' and *figure* is the term both for an expression consisting of several words with some sort of 'transferred' meaning and the term for the phenomenon itself. The theory of figures is thus about both tropes and figures. Another distinction within the theory is what we, with the terms of semiotics at the back of our minds, could call a distinction between *figures of signifiers* and *figures of signifieds*. Figures of signifiers are ways of putting things that are determined by the material qualities of words – sound, rhythm, rhyme. In all types of fictional literature, but especially in poetry, one tends to focus on what may be called 'language as language', meaning, not least, language as a physical phenomenon. When a text appears to have been formed with a view to the sound aspect of language, it becomes evident that language is not a simple, transparent 'window on reality'. The materiality of language marks it as separate from the rest of reality. Not least to a foreigner, it is a striking feature of the British tabloid press that it, to a high degree, indulges in the possibilities of play with signifiers – any issue of the *Sun*, *Mirror et al.* will have an abundance of word play especially in its headlines. These are poetic products, whether the editors know it or not, and are obviously enjoyed by the papers' readers. Large numbers of sayings and formulaic expressions are figures of signifiers. They survive by way of their sound, be it alliteration, ordinary rhyme or whatever (anything from 'bye-bye' and 'too-de-loo' to 'better safe than sorry' and other sayings, as well as 'beat around the bush' and other idiomatic expressions). A figure of signifiers will often be a successful slogan. (Historically, the most well-known of these is probably 'I like Ike', from Dwight D. Eisenhower's US presidential campaign of the 1950s. Roman Jakobson used this as an example when speaking of how the *poetic function* of language could 'take over' and shape a verbal 'message' – the poetic function being language's referral to itself rather than a reality beyond it.) Advertising, of course, often plays on this too.

The figures of signifieds ('semantic figures') are, on the other hand, 'figures of thought' rather than 'figures of sound' (or, in principle, other sign substances). They express some meaning through 'figures' such as irony, comparison and the like. This is such a wide-ranging and important subject that it deserves (at least) a separate section.

Metaphor, metonymy and other 'semantic figures'

The largest and most important among the categories of semantic figures is the *metaphor*. The metaphor is an *implicit comparison*. Just as most other figures, it is constantly used in everyday language, including journalism. Especially frequent are what are known as *dead metaphors*, i.e. implicit comparisons that have been used for so long that no one thinks of them as metaphors any more: sound *waves* are not wet; some people *stumble* when standing still on a podium trying to give a talk; and there are *hurdles* in research projects. Language is, in fact, so steeped in metaphors that it would be totally ridiculous if we tried, say, to mark them all with inverted commas. Those who think that metaphors are just for poets and make 'ordinary' language messy and unreliable, are very wrong.

In addition to this, more or less scholarly language also uses a host of metaphors. Marxists in the 1970s would often say that Marx's famous distinction between society's economic *base* and its cultural or ideological *superstructure* is a metaphor, not a real theoretical concept. This signalled a distance from the dichotomy that was not primarily related to a felt obligation to use a proper, strictly 'scientific' language, even if 'scientistic' fantasies were prevalent in parts of academic Marxism at the time. The most important reason for maintaining that 'base' and 'superstructure' were metaphors, and always placing them within inverted commas if they were used, was an uneasiness about the recognition that the two terms represented the relations between economic and other social areas in a much too simple and mechanical way. Terms such as *productive forces* were never branded metaphors, even if they obviously are. They just sound a bit more abstract (do not suggest an idea such as that of society as some sort of building) and thus seem to be more on a par with the abstract phenomena they refer to.

In fact, most scholarly or scientific terms or concepts were originally metaphors. This goes for the humanities and the social sciences as well as the natural sciences. Concepts are formed by way of *analogies*. The atoms of physics are imagined as solar systems, with electrons in orbit around a kernel. 'Electron' etymologically means 'amber', and the use of this word consequently refers to an age-old experience of what happens if you rub a piece of amber against a woollen cloth: some 'mystical' power is created. The point is that metaphors are eventually normalized through repeated, frequent use and thus lose their metaphorical *effect* in the linguistic community in question. Established scientific terms are, in other words, often what we have called *dead* metaphors – the theatrical 'role' in sociology, the military 'strategy' in economics and a number of other disciplines, the physical 'energy' in psychology.

The metaphorical effect is understood a bit differently in modern theories of metaphor than in classical rhetoric. To Aristotle, for example, metaphor was mostly to be understood as the pure substitution of one word for another, more surprising, one with a roughly similar meaning. The metaphor was *translatable*. It was a device that was intended primarily to increase the beauty and variation of the speech (entertainment, *delectare*), but also the clarity of descriptions and arguments (education/information, *docere*). Certain metaphors could also, more than a directly referential word, influence the audience emotionally (move them, *movere*). But in British theories of metaphor in the twentieth century (I.A. Richards, Max Black, Monroe Beardsley and others) the emphasis was in particular on the idea that metaphor is an *effect* that is produced when a word is used in a certain context, 'where it contrasts other words that are understood literally' (Ricoeur, 1981: 170). A metaphor is of course, at the outset, a word with an established 'literal' or denotative meaning, but when a word is used as a metaphor it is used in a totally different area, and one thus achieves a 'semantic collision', a *logical absurdity*. It thus forces readers or listeners to look for, or rather *produce*, a meaning that is different from the original so that the sentence of which it is a part becomes meaningful. It is this productive activity that makes the metaphor a means of intellectual creativity (see also the anthropologist Clifford Geertz on this, 1973: 211). Through repeated use, the new, metaphorical meaning of the word in question may, then, eventually be included in the register of lexical, denotative meanings it may have. It enters, so to speak, the official polysemy characteristic of the vocabulary of any language. Dead metaphors can, in principle, be translated without any loss of meaning. Living metaphors are, in principle, untranslatable. (Are 'dead' and 'living' as they are used here dead or living metaphors to you?)

Television theory of the last three decades is full of metaphors that, originally, were living. One key example, which we will return to in a later chapter, is Raymond Williams' *flow* as a term for the way in which television's programmes are organized in schedules and the way in which 'an evening's viewing' is experienced by viewers. The production of metaphors was, of course, related to the task of describing and understanding new territory, new phenomena. But, eventually, some of them became normalized, i.e. they died. This happened long ago to the very word television, and the same applies to the metaphor broadcasting, which originally meant sowing seed by throwing it so that it dispersed evenly. Dead metaphors like these may often fruitfully be revived, i.e. analysed *as* metaphors, if one wants to shed some new light on the phenomena to which they refer (cf. Gripsrud, 1998a; Chapter 9 of the present volume, on broadcast media).

Metaphors are not, then, innocent in the sense of being neutral in terms of meaning – simple synonyms. George Lakoff and Mark Johnson have shown how metaphors shape both our everyday ways of thinking and political perceptions in particular ways in the book *Metaphors We Live By* (1980). Here they point out, for example, that it affects our understanding of public discussions that they are constantly referred to and understood by way of metaphors of war and aggression – from the above-mentioned use of 'strategy' to 'devastating arguments', from 'the party leader hit back' to 'they defended themselves to the best of their ability'. In 1991, George Lakoff published an article on the Internet where he demonstrated how the Gulf War had been prepared and legitimated through a systematic use of metaphors. Metaphors are often used precisely to emphasize certain positive or negative aspects of whatever one talks about. They can in other words be used to mobilize the emotions of audiences, to serve as pathos arguments. This is also one of the reasons why they are so useful in political language, where they abound for many reasons. They are also, however, as the metaphorical expression would have it, double-edged.

A former Norwegian prime minister, Mr Jagland, tried in the late 1990s to establish himself and his government as visionary by presenting a plan for the building of what he called the 'Norwegian House', to be raised on four political 'pillars'. The idea was that this visual metaphor would suggest that his government aimed to be constructive and that its goal was to build a secure and good *home* for the people. These were the intended positive connotations of what I.A. Richards called the *ground* of the metaphor, the shared feature that made the implicit comparison in the metaphor (between 'house' and 'society') possible: 'a limited space in which to live and belong', or something like that. The idea was, basically, to create a new version of the generally respected, positive Scandinavian social-democratic notion of society as 'the people's home'. But most discussions of Mr Jagland's 'Norwegian House' did not focus on what I.A. Richards called the metaphor's *tenor*, its intended meaning or 'direction'. Instead they focused on its *vehicle*, i.e. the concrete meaning of the word 'house'. People queried when houses actually began to be built on *pillars* in Norway; they joked about the 'Norwegian Circus Tent' or they asked who was to be locked out.

Another example might be the political tumult in the UK in the summer of 2000, when an internal memo from the prime minister's 'polling expert' or PR adviser ('Blair's poll pal', as the *Sun* poetically put it), Philip Gould, was leaked to the press. Gould comes from the advertising business and has been closely associated with the campaign and PR people of US president Bill Clinton. In this memo, printed in full in the *Sun* (19 July 2000), Gould gave a number of reasons why he thought 'the New Labour brand has been badly contaminated', and the memo ended with the sentence 'We need to reinvent the New Labour brand.' Peter Hitchens, a right-wing commentator then in the *Daily Express*, and therefore extremely hostile to the Labour government, opened his comment on this leak as follows: 'We do not have a government, we have a "brand". This is the most striking fact to emerge from the trail of leaked memos from Whitehall'; there had also been other, metaphorical, 'leaks' (*Daily Express* 24 July 2000). A drawing that accompanied Hitchens' comment (see Figure 6.1) had Tony Blair appear as a sleazy salesman offering what appears to be a box of soap powder, with a number of angrily dissatisfied customers in the background, exhibiting their badly torn and stained laundry. Hitchens himself ends by asking if the government 'like the makers of grease-packed beefburgers, ... wish to conceal the real stomach-churning contents of their wares behind a brand-name and a grinning face?'

Hitchens immediately contradicts his introductory 'fact' that there is no government, just a 'brand', both by listing a series of what he considers utterly despicable political acts that it obviously takes a government to carry out, and by directly referring to 'the government' he has claimed is non-existent. Also problematic is his use of metaphors: referring to Blair as 'a rather dim bulb who obviously has no grand vision', he forces together two metaphors that do not go together: a bulb, dim or not, may provide a degree of vision, but has not itself the slightest amount of eyesight, however bright it may be. The main point here, however, is that Hitchens uses the metaphorical term 'brand' in a way that *refers to its vehicle rather than its tenor* and, more specifically, refers to the vehicle's *negative connotations* rather than the *positive connotations* one might assume are supposed to form the *ground* for the transferral of the term 'brand' from the area of commerce to the area of politics. The term 'brand' originally referred to a trademark, the name of a particular variety of some commodity. It was later used, metaphorically, to mean something like 'a name that stands for (i.e. signifies) the qualities of a certain variety of something', such as, say, a certain political party.

Gould's use of the term in a political context is not at all original, it is part of a whole set of terms that have been imported into politics from marketing (i.e. the commercial sector). These days it is common to talk about 'selling' politics and presidents, and the trick is to have the electorate 'buy' whatever one as a politician says or does. The common feature of marketing and politics

WE DO not have a government, we have a "brand". This is the most striking fact to emerge from the trail of leaked memos from Whitehall (and why all the fuss about "leaks" by the way? These are not nuclear secrets, just the private political musings of people whose main interest is staying in power).

This raises the most vital question about the Blair project. Does it have a real aim? Is it really just about one man's place in the history books? Is it only about image?

Mr Blair, his own memo confirms, is a rather dim bulb who obviously has no grand vision. He genuinely cannot understand why people think he is against family life (for other people), greedy for more taxes, soft on crime, scornful of thrift and enterprise and anti-British. He seems to believe his own propaganda about the NHS, the schools and transport system, protected from reality as he is by privilege and so-called "security".

Yet a clear thread runs through the actions of the government he heads. It has smashed up the UK, raped the constitution, handed powers to Europe, run down the Armed Forces, insulted the monarchy, ripped up the rule of law, surrendered to terror, flung wide the prison gates to violent crooks, encouraged fatherless families, punished savers, and attacked traditional sexual morality. Given another term in office, it will abolish our independence and squeeze the remaining life out of Parliament.

Are these things accidents which have just happened to take place under Mr Blair's leadership? Or is there somebody, somewhere, at the heart of this government who really *does* have a plan to abolish Britain? And like the makers of disgusting grease-packed beefburgers, do they wish to conceal the real stomach-churning contents of their wares behind a brand-name and a grinning face?

Figure 6.1 Peter Hitchens' *Daily Express* column, featuring 'Blair the Salesman'. Courtesy of the Express Newspapers Group.

can be said to be that they are both about *persuasion* – they are the most central of rhetorical areas. This is the main reason why it seems appropriate to use 'brand' as a term to describe a political party. The act of buying something is seen as similar to that of voting for a political party, and so the goal of marketing's persuasion becomes similar to that of a party's persuasive activities. What gets lost here, though, is the important qualitative difference between politics and commerce, including marketing. Politics is not only about persuading people to vote for a certain party or 'buy' a particular 'brand', it is at least as much about *deliberation*, a constantly ongoing public exchange of ideas and arguments in favour of this or that perspective, principle or action. It involves people as *citizens*, not *consumers* (see also Chapter 8 of the present volume, on the public sphere). Marketing (and thus advertising) is a highly *instrumental* activity; in politics there will also be an element of dialogue or discourse that also carries a different *ethics* (cf. what was said about Habermas in the previous chapter).

The strictly goal-oriented ethics of marketing has historically produced negative connotations of (degrees of) dishonesty and outright cheating that cling to terms such as marketing, advertising, salesmanship etc. Just how deep these negative connotations run can be seen from the way in which the obviously very conservative and hence presumably 'marketing-friendly' Peter Hitchens uses the term 'brand' in the quote above. So, while Philip Gould and his friends in 'New' Labour, may intend the metaphor 'brand' to mean something efficient, rational, modern, goal-oriented (the *tenor* in their use of the metaphor), Hitchens reminds them of how the widespread ambiguity of the term may come back to haunt them, especially in a situation where the negatively charged term 'spin' has come to be seen as one of the main characteristics of the Blair government.

There are texts that are totally metaphorical. They are called *allegories*, and include, for example, the parables in the Bible and other pedagogical texts. But allegories also appear elsewhere. The title of a political commentary by Simon Hoggart in the *Guardian* (19 July 2000), after the Labour government's chancellor Gordon Brown had presented a grand 'spending package' to parliament, was 'Jilted Prudence misses stand-up tragedy routine'. This enigmatic formulation is allegorical in the sense that 'Prudence' is a female name that stands for the chancellor's normal attitude to spending ('Gordon's piggy bank was made of cast iron and bolted to his bedroom floor') and Brown is allegedly (metaphorically) in love with this 'woman' (Brown was at the time unmarried!); but she was not present when he gave his talk in parliament about large spending in the manner of a 'stand-up tragedian': a neologism functioning as a metaphor for his appearance. This whole humorous piece also reveals the family ties between allegory and *irony* – both are about saying one thing and meaning something else. Irony, though, is a humorously intended form, belonging to what the Greeks of antiquity referred to as *urban* humour – i.e. not just coarse or simplistic buffoonery. Etymologically, 'irony' meant 'presenting oneself as (an) ignorant', and that may still be an acceptable description. If someone says 'It was really great fun having my wallet stolen this summer', he or she in principle presents her/himself as an idiot. Both allegory and irony have become terms with extensive and quite complicated significance in literary theory. 'Romantic irony' is, for example, the term for conscious breaches of style and other seemingly misplaced features of a text from the epoch of Romanticism that more or less serve to indicate that what is represented in the text is too immense and/or mysterious to be referred to, or represented, in a direct manner. The interest devoted to allegory and irony in poststructuralist literary criticism tends to have as its main (and constantly repeated) point precisely that (literary) language is forever separate from the rest of reality and always primarily refers to itself, and only highly indirectly (if at all) to non-literary, external phenomena.

It has been suggested (Andersen, 1995) that the various types of trope can be ordered according to the *distance in meaning between the word or words that are used and the meaning that is intended.* (Did you notice the spatial metaphor here?) The metaphor is the trope where this distance is at its greatest, where the *vehicle* of the metaphor is from a totally different area than the *tenor*. At the other end of the scale, where the distance is minimal, we find a number of forms of 'rewriting' or paraphrasing. A *synonym* is, for instance, more or less identical to what it stands for: battle/struggle, ascend/climb etc. A definition is an example of *periphrasis*, i.e. a more wordy version of the same (an example would be 'the windy city' for Chicago). Irony is most often an example of an *antiphrase*, i.e. the opposite of the meaning intended. *Euphemism* is a beautifying kind of rewriting or reformulation, such as 'pass away' for dying and 'mopping-up operations' for killing enemy soldiers trying to hide. Euphemism is consequently a widespread trope in political language. President Ronald Reagan referred to nuclear weapons stationed in space as a 'peace shield'. 'Ethnic cleansing' is a more current, horrible example. In Aldous Huxley's novel *Brave New World* the fictive society of the future has a systematically euphemistic language called *newspeak*. Some of the 'politically correct' language developed by liberal and radical academics, especially in the USA, is clearly euphemistic even if it has the best of intentions, such as instances where 'disabled' is replaced by 'physically challenged'. A form that stylistically often goes together well with, or overlaps, irony, is *litotes*, better known as *understatement*: 'The workers were hardly cheering when they were told that the plant would be closing down.' It is also worth noting that there may be fleeting borderlines between litotes and euphemisms, as when NATO's bombing of Serbia was referred to as 'a limited military operation'.

In between the metaphor and what we have called paraphrasing, or rephrasing, are two types of trope that are closely related but still different. One of these is based on what may be termed *overlapping meanings*, i.e. that the word used has a meaning that either covers the intended one or is part of it. This trope is called *synecdoche*. One of the most well-known varieties of this is *pars pro toto*, i.e. a part representing a whole: 'a cuppa' for (a cup of) tea, 'a set of wheels' for a car. But it may also be a whole representing a part: 'The British [many Brits] are totally drunk all the time when holidaying abroad.' Consequently, exaggeration or *hyperbole* is also a form of synecdoche: 'This stupid textbook is nothing but a boring dictionary.' The trope different from, but related to, synecdoche, is *metonymy*. Metonymy is not about overlapping meanings but *proximity*. It is proximity that provides the link between what is said and its intended meaning. 'I like Tarantino' does not mean one knows Quentin Tarantino personally and likes the guy. It means one likes this director's work. 'I'll have a smoke' means that an effect, the smoke, is used to represent its cause, the lit cigarette. It is also metonymy when something abstract is used to refer to something concrete (saying 'democracy' instead of 'the members of Congress' or 'members of parliament') or, vice versa, 'the car' instead of 'private motoring' in 'the car threatens the environment').

The distinction between synecdoche and metonymy is presented in many textbooks as totally fleeting or even completely erased. One could, of course, say that overlap of meaning is also a form of proximity. Such a view was part of the reason why the linguist and literary scholar Roman Jakobson in a famous article conducted a drastic clearance of the whole complex system of figures in classical rhetoric by reducing it to just two main categories: metaphor and metonymy (Jakobson, 1956). This operation was to have a decisive influence on the later structuralist theory of texts because it was linked to an idea of two basic processes in any use of language, and thus to two fundamental aspects of any language. Jakobson, in other words, established a very important connection between rhetoric and structuralist theory or semiotics.

Two processes in language

The concrete point of departure for Jakobson's article was an empirical study of patients with *aphasia*, i.e. injury to the linguistic capacity of the brain caused by illness or accidents. There were two main sorts of such injury. One resulted in the patients having problems *selecting* the right words. They might say 'table' when they meant 'lamp', and 'fork' when they meant 'knife' (i.e. their choice of words was governed by a principle of proximity or contiguity, that is to say a *metonymical* principle). Other patients had problems *combining* words to form grammatically correct sentences, and made mistakes such as saying 'spy-glass' when they meant to say 'microscope', and 'fire' when they meant 'light'; their choices were, in other words, governed by a *metaphorical* principle of *similarity*. The first group had a problem with linguistic *selection*, not with combination; for the other it was the other way around.

Metonomy and metaphor could in this way be seen as basic processes in language tied to the two axes or dimensions of language that, in the chapter on semiotics (Chapter 4), we called *syntagm* and *paradigm* respectively. Paradigms are the 'storing shelves' of language from which we *select* words or other signs, and syntagms are the connections made when we *combine* the chosen elements. The meaning of a syntagm arises from the combination of meanings that are placed close to one another, in proximity of one another, within it. Paradigms are characterized by some form of similarity between the elements they contain and are, in this sense, metaphorical.

Jakobson thus used the terms metaphor and metonymy for other purposes than those of the old rhetoricians, and he should perhaps have stuck to the terms paradigm and syntagm. But his ideas caught on, so the damage, so to speak, is already done in the tradition of textual theory. Jakobson used his terms not least to define the difference between *the poetic* and *the prosaic*, poetry and prose. In poetry the principle of similarity is transferred from the paradigmatic axis of selection to the syntagmatic axis of combination, he argued. This means that the characteristic feature of poetry is that the linear, sequential dimension of the text, its sequence of signs, is to a great extent ordered in accordance with principles of *similarity* at the levels of sounds, sentences and meanings. It is, in other words, ordered according to principles of analogies, parallelisms, echo-effects of various kinds and (other) types of repetition-with-a-difference (cf., again, Chapter 4, on semiotics).

Those who read poetry, particularly in a consciously analytical way, will tend to look for such features, and for more or less related patterns in the text as a whole. When watching television, we more rarely 'read' in this fashion, but the principle is also operative there. The title sequences of television series or serials – their exordium or appetizer – are sometimes constructed with a beginning, a middle and an end, sustained by the music, so that their form is reminiscent of a miniature narrative. But if one takes a closer look, the various visual elements may all connote a limited number of things, such as money, power and sex (not accidental examples); they are visual metaphors for the same few meanings. Title sequences, even those that, to a degree, mimic a narrative construction, thus tend to be metaphorically or 'poetically' organized rather than metonymically, like prose. Prose, especially the epic or narrative part of it, and, within that, the more or less 'realistic' sort of writing, tends to be based in relationships of proximity between its elements. As Jakobson says:

> Following the path of contiguous relationships, the realist author metonymically digresses from the plot to the atmosphere and from the characters to the setting in space and time. He is fond of synecdochic details. In the scene of Anna Karenina's suicide Tolstoy's artistic attention is focused on the heroine's handbag; and in *War and Peace* the synecdoches 'hair on the upper lip' and 'bare shoulders' are used by the same writer to stand for the female characters to whom these features belong.
>
> (Jakobson, 1988: 59)

There is often, then, an emphasis on 'forward movement' in such novels, narrative progress; and those who read them are, correspondingly, often also most interested in how 'things develop' and, not least, in 'how it all ends' – that is, in the syntagmatic or 'metonymic' dimension of the text.

It is, however, important to remember that this is a question of relative dominance between two principles that are present in all types of text. There are poetic elements in prose and vice versa. Novels, films and journalistic 'stories' also have patterns of repetition-with-a-difference that are, not least, important when we come, analytically, to decide what their *theme* is, what they at some fundamental level can be said to be *about*. To mention a visual medium such as film here is not at all contrary to Jakobson's way of thinking. In the article in question he explicitly referred to how his idea also covers other sign systems than verbal language – he argues, for instance, that the metonymic orientation of cubism in visual art was replaced by the metaphorical orientation of surrealism as a form of reaction. At least since the legendary director D.W. Griffith, says Jakobson, film art has been deeply marked by synecdochal close-ups and other metonymical elements, while the films of Chaplin and Eisenstein are noted for their many examples of metaphorical *montage*. One example is the opening of Chaplin's *Modern Times*, where a shot of a mass of people on their way to work is immediately followed by one of a flock of sheep (on their way to the slaughterhouse?).

Finally, it should be mentioned that Jakobson in his idea that metaphor and metonymy are fundamental processes in any system of signs saw a parallel to the processes Sigmund Freud identified as fundamental in what he called our *dreamwork*. The visual sequences of dreams are, according to Freud, the product of *displacement* or *condensation*. Both serve to give the 'latent' and more or less taboo *dreamthoughts* an indirect, disguised manifest form. Displacement is when a more or less trivial event or phenomenon becomes the centre of a dream sequence, while the taboo, 'dangerous' dreamthought underlying the dream is marginalized, if present at all. Condensation is when an element in a dream represents more than one dreamthought, more than one problematic event, anxiety etc. in the dreamer's life. Jakobson claims that both of these operate according to the principle of contiguity; displacement is metonymic, condensation is synecdochal, while other psychic processes identified by Freud (1988: 60) are metaphorical (identification and symbolism). The French, semiotically inspired psychoanalyst Jacques Lacan, however, without noting his diversion from Jakobson, says that displacement is metonymical and condensation metaphorical (Lacan, 1988: 92).

If one looks at Freud's examples in his book *The Interpretation of Dreams*, however, it seems that Jakobson was right, since the elements that are, so to speak, fused in dream condensations are contiguous in the dreamer's waking life. Lacan, who is famous for saying that 'the unconscious is structured like a language', and was extremely influential in film and literary theory in the 1970s and early 1980s, thus contributed significantly to a conceptual confusion Jakobson can at most be said to have laid the basis for when he used the terms metaphor and metonymy to designate paradigmatic and syntagmatic processes and dimensions in language.

Promises, promises: the rhetoric of advertising

As mentioned above, advertising is one of the most typically rhetorical of genres in today's media world. It usually combines verbal and visual signs, and makes extensive use of a number of persuasive means and rhetorical figures. In the following paragraphs, we will take a closer look at some examples of advertising in order to demonstrate how rhetorical terms and a rhetorical way of thinking may be useful in an analytical context, in combination with insights from semiotics and hermeneutics. At the same time, it will become clear just how complex, or even complicated, the simplest of media texts can be.

We will start by looking at an ad that appeared in one of the *Guardian*'s weekend magazines in July 2000 (it also appeared elsewhere, as part of the ad campaign). Looking at Figure 6.2, one soon finds out that this page is an advert and not an editorial page, though not necessarily at once. Research has indicated that we (in our western culture) tend to establish a first idea of what any page is about by 'reading' it quickly from the top to the bottom, in a zig-zag movement from left to right down the page, in the course of a second or less. This page has a somewhat enigmatic question in the top left-hand corner: 'How can light be strong?' But what we probably notice first is the picture in which the question is placed, showing a girl of about 7 or 8 years old, blowing soap bubbles, and wearing a more or less romantic sweet white dress that stands out against the background. As we look further down the page, we find that she is standing barefoot on a huge bubble she has, presumably, blown herself. This is hardly an everyday occurrence. The picture rather appears surrealistic, even if the medium is supposedly photography, the producer of indexical signs. This manipulated photo or photo-montage is what we first see if just flicking through the pages of the magazine; it is thus, for some – together with the enigmatic question in the top left-hand corner – the

Figure 6.2 The Toyota Yaris ad.

exordium of the advertisement, what is to whet our appetite, not satisfy it. Then, just underneath the picture, which covers roughly three-quarters of the total space, a statement appears, in red letters, divided into two lines: 'The new Toyota Yaris. It defies logic.' To the right of this is a separate photo of what appears to be a quite small car, silvery in colour, placed so that the top of it cuts into the blue (sky) in which the girl floats on her bubble. Underneath this is a text that directly address the reader ('you'), then some extra information in red, and finally some minuscule lines of further factual information. To the right of this block of text is then what our presumed zig-zag search ends up with: a composite *symbol* (consisting of both verbal (symbolic) and iconic signs), which also directly tells us that the car pictured has been chosen as the 'car of the year 2000' in what appears (iconically) to be a European contest; followed by a trademark, accompanied by a slogan ('the car in front is a TOYOTA'); and, finally, the name of this particular model – 'Yaris'.

A first step of any analysis is thus to *look closely* at the text, and then try to produce a *description* of that which is to be analysed.

In fact, another step comes before these two. That is, the identification of *where* the text appears – which medium, which channel, magazine, paper. This is important in order to make a grounded conjecture (a qualified guess) as to who *the intended audience* is. The people who decide where to place ads do so after examining carefully the statistical composition of the audience for the channel, magazine or paper. The Yaris ad appears in the full-colour weekend magazine of the British liberal-intellectual paper the *Guardian*, which, judging from its normal contents, appears to be aimed to a significant degree at well-educated women aged between about 25 and 50. This sort of social category is thus a plausible audience or readership for the ad. So who is the 'sender' of this 'message'? In a sense, it is probably an advertising agency – and in some countries the name of the agency would be placed discreetly in minuscule letters somewhere at the margins of the ad. Not so here. The only 'sender' to be identified is the brand name, Toyota. The sophists hired by Toyota are not named.

We have thus established the elementary context or *rhetorical situation* in light of which this ad is to be seen: the sender, the (presumed) recipients or audience, the subject of the 'message'; the car model, Toyota Yaris; and the medium in or through which this communication takes place. But, in keeping with the principle of the hermeneutic circle, we may also try to place this situation within an even larger context – that of the social and cultural situation at large in the year 2000. The codes, values etc. employed in this text will in some way or other relate to this general, historically specific situation.

Somewhere around 1980, a new sort of representation of women became more and more usual in advertising. Women were more frequently presented in self-assertive postures, in clothes and surroundings that indicated they were in positions of status and power previously occupied only by men. Their eye contact with the audience or spectators was not necessarily just an expression of their awareness of being looked at, primarily by men, as in the tradition of the nude in visual art (cf. Berger, 1972). It, rather, often projected an impression of self-assuredness and strength. This shift was obviously related to the entry of far more women into the workforce outside of the home, the increasing number of women with higher-education qualifications and the efforts of the new feminist movement. Women, at least many of them, now had to be addressed differently. So how does the ad for Toyota Yaris look in this perspective?

First, the exordium is a picture of a girl-child, in very feminine clothing. While this is generally appealing to most people as something sweet, cute and even touching, it is also something that may be thought to appeal to women in particular, with their 'maternal instincts' (largely produced through socialization) and their girlhood images or memories. The surrealism of the picture, its dreamlike quality, adds to its childishness and dreaminess – the angelic girl stands on a bubble, in the same way that angels recline safely on clouds. Second, the introductory question, 'How can light be strong?', childlike in its simplicity, is obviously not being asked by someone familiar with space-age materials and, say, alloy wheels. It is asked by someone more or less technologically incompetent, as not only children, but also most women are traditionally considered to be. (And, as we soon shall see, the question is not answered properly either.) Third, the heading in red underneath the picture says that the new Toyota Yaris 'defies logic', and that is obviously to be regarded as a good thing. It means not only that the car is a wonder, a piece of magic, something that would seem to excite anyone's childish pleasure in such phenomena or ideas. It could also be read as implying that defying or even defeating logic is generally a good thing. 'Logic' is culturally coded as a 'male' value in our part of the world; women are supposedly more prone to rely on intuition, and possibly superstition (magic and the like).

The conclusion to this is, obviously, that the ad addresses potential women customers in ways that are in keeping with quite traditional ideas of 'female' values and characteristics. Most is actually 'said' already in the syntagmatic or metonymical link (contiguity) between the two pictures. The picture of the girl blowing soap bubbles in the sky is overlapped by the picture of the car in a way that also underlines a *metaphorical* link between the two: the car is as cute and magical as the bubble girl. A relation between two signs may, in other words, be metonymical and metaphorical at the same time. The large picture is, in a way, typical of advertising and its normal rhetorical strategy, *euphorizing* in relation to the commodity for sale. It presents a desirable connotation for the commodity: when you see a Toyota Yaris, it would be great if the bubble girl was conjured up in your mind.

All of these elements can be said to be *pathos* arguments for buying a Toyota Yaris, dominated by the sentimentality of the cute girl-and-bubbles picture. There is also an element of *ethos* argumentation built into this, since the 'speaker' is also one who obviously loves children and magic, i.e. is humane and nice like us, not a hardened cynical salesperson. The *logos* part of the argumentation is then presented in the text block under the red letters saying 'It defies logic.'

Yes, this is a paradox. The text in question tries to answer the question of how light can be strong in a logical way, even if it has just been stated that the car 'defies logic'. We are after all talking about a commodity that costs what to most people is a considerable sum of money, and at the end of the day few people will feel reassured of a car's qualities if all the sales representative can do is smile, wave both arms in the air and say 'magic'. Women customers might, for instance, be particularly interested in safety, for themselves and not least their passengers (caring as they are). Many of them might have heard rumours that it is easier to die in a car crash if you are in a small, lightweight car than if you are in a big, heavy one. So the ad's text tries to tackle this after the initial, appetizing suggestions about cuteness and magic. It starts head on: 'You'd think the lighter car is, the more vulnerable it is.' It then does not directly deny this, it says instead 'Not necessarily.' The Toyota Yaris is rather like an exception to a rule. It is, admittedly, light (only 830 kilos), 'but with its tough new body structure, it's also very strong'. This sentence is actually all we get in the way of an explanation. The 're-inforced side impact bars' (that most or all new cars now have) are supposedly not part of this tough body structure since they are to be an added safety measure (also making the car heavier, of course). The other features mentioned may be relevant for safety – airbag for the driver only, up-to-date seatbelts and *optional* ABS – but they have nothing to do with the magic of 'strength' in lightness, they do not make the *car* less 'vulnerable' and they are not even particularly impressive. There is nothing to support the claim that this light car is strong, other than the assertion that its 'new' body structure is 'tough'. Which is like saying it is 'strong'. Light can be strong by being strong. The *logos* argument of this text is a perfect tautology. The text does not 'defy' logic, it is just not very good at it.

The question that would interest Toyota is, of course, if any of the intended potential customers will notice and, if they do, whether they care. The real main argument for the car is, in any case, the main picture: the sweet, cute, dreamlike girl with the bubbles. It says that buying this car will make you experience some of this cuteness and magic, make you remember childhood pleasures, make you also possibly stand out from the ordinary, since few cars are sold with the aid of soap bubbles. The choice of car is to a large extent an 'emotional' one, it is about who you are and who you want to be (see Chapters 1 and 3 of the present volume, on identity and social distinction, respectively), at least once you have decided how much money you want to, or are able to, spend on the sort of car you think you need. It may therefore be a good idea to let images, visual signs, with their often plural, fleeting meanings, take care of the emotional part of the argument and try to counter 'rational' objections to the emotional impulse in the verbal text, traditionally the key medium for intellectual persuasion. The ad fails to prove what it sets out to prove, but it does give enough information for readers to conclude that the Toyota Yaris is at least as safe as any small, light car these days. That may be enough, if the bubble girl works.

In one sense, then, this ad is obviously an example of 'good rhetoric' if it works (i.e. persuades more people to buy the car in question). This view is, however, in breach of the ethical principles that classical rhetoric demands. It is bad rhetoric according to classical rhetorical principles since it actually fails to deliver arguments for its main propositions, that 'light can be strong' and that the car 'defies logic'. These propositions are thus merely 'bait', an exordium that is followed by porridge rather than the exciting meal that is promised at the outset. The exordium, in effect, appears as a trick designed to fool the readers. If the text had really explained how 'light can be strong' and further developed, or possibly totally concentrated on, the illogical 'magic' of the car, perhaps dropping the 'light can be strong' proposition completely, the ad would have been much better. Now, when the *logos* argument boils down to a tautology, the ad as a whole simply (metaphorically) falls apart.

A bit of hermeneutic self-reflection here (cf. Chapter 5, on hermeneutics) would include my admitting that I am generally sceptical towards advertising and its role in the media, and in social and cultural life in general, for many reasons. One of these is that there is, as I see it, an inherent tendency towards the unethical in this sort of discourse. It is quite regularly about covering up (most often indirectly) facts about a product that may be very interesting to potential customers but that would not encourage the purchase of it. It is practically always about claiming fantasy values for a product that are almost impossible to find when you actually see or use it. It is simply, far too often, very close to lying. Even if most of us are so used to these rhetorical devices we are not easily fooled, this is no reason to like the genre. Furthermore, advertising normally seeks to address its targeted audiences in ways that are safely unprovocative, not in any way offensive or bothersome to the group in question's self-image and supposed key values. It tends to be socially and culturally conservative, or at least *conformist*. Advertising is normally a great deal about flattery and adopts a sycophantic attitude, both to the companies it works for and the audiences to which it speaks. These are all reasons for not liking advertising as a genre and for being critical of the ways in which the advertising business has in many ways become a key player in social, cultural and political affairs.

On the other hand, I will freely admit that much advertising shows evidence that there is great talent in the business. The visual craftsmanship is often stunning, both in TV and magazine ads, and verbal texts will often also be very clever. Actually, ads – especially TV ads – may be so imaginative and clever, not least in the UK, that you forget the products they were supposed to persuade you to buy. They are, in this case, great mini-format fictions, but bad rhetoric since they do not do what they are supposed to do. All of this plays in to the way in which I have analysed the Toyota Yaris ad, and so my 'reading' of it is not the 'objective' truth about the ad and its meanings; on the other hand, I have tried to give reasons for my interpretation(s) that will allow anyone to check whether they agree that there is a basis for them in the actual visual and verbal text. Any objections to my reading will have to refer to the 'facts' or the advertisement text in order to demonstrate that I am wrong. Pointing out that I have declared myself critical to advertising as a genre is no argument; it concerns the interpreter, not the interpretation, and is thus what is known as an unethical *ad hominem* argument: going for the man, not the ball (in metaphorical soccer terms).

The notion of truth in rhetoric is about *probability*. Rhetoric invites discussion, or *dialogue*, the medium through which truth is established in hermeneutics. Go on, criticize my analysis if you like.

7 Narratology: the forms and functions of stories

The narratives of the world are numberless. Narrative is first and foremost a prodigious variety of genres, themselves distributed amongst different substances – as though any material were fit to receive man's stories. Able to be carried by articulated language, spoken or written, fixed or moving images, gestures, and the ordered mixtures of all these substances; narrative is present in myth, legend, fable, tale, novella, epic, history, tragedy, drama, comedy, mime, painting (think of Carpaccio's *Saint Ursula*), stained glass windows, cinema, comics, news items, conversation. Moreover, under this almost infinite diversity of forms, narrative is present in every age, in every place, in every society; it begins with the very history of mankind and there nowhere is nor has been a people without narrative. All classes, all human groups, have their narratives, enjoyment of which is very often shared by men with different, even opposing, cultural backgrounds. Caring nothing for the division between good and bad literature, narrative is international, transhistorical, transcultural: it is simply there, like life itself.

(Barthes [1966] 1977b)

One can usually distinguish between three main types of verbal text: narrative, description and argumentation. Some would also add others, but these are the most important. Narrative has a particularly central and interesting position. It is found, as Roland Barthes so eloquently describes in the above quote, everywhere, in all sorts of media and all the time. That is why this chapter is mainly devoted to the theory of narrative (*narratology* as it is called in the structuralist tradition); but we will also look at how narratives are, today, located within more comprehensive textual contexts in the broadcasting media, particularly television, which every day present a host of narratives of various kinds.

In order to understand something of the functions and forms of narrative, it may be suitable to begin, so to speak, at the beginning: young children's learning, use and production of narratives.

A little story-teller

At the age of 3, my daughter told me a story. Here it is, carefully transcribed (and translated):

> I went for a walk and met a boyfriend. And fell in love. Then I had a baby. And when that was young she had one herself, boyfriend.
>
> And then I went for a walk. And then I looked in a zoo store and then I really wanted a dog. And then I bought one. And then the boyfriend didn't like animals. And then she wanted to kill that dog because otherwise she was afraid the boyfriend would move away. Then the boyfriend said that no, no, I like animals after all! And then they were happy and jumped and bounced and went for a walk with him. The dog.

This 3 year old had obviously already learnt a few fundamental things about how a narrative is constructed in our culture. The first paragraph is actually, in itself, a minimal narrative. The film scholars David Bordwell and Kristin Thompson say in their introduction to film analysis, *Film Art*, that a narrative is 'a chain of events in cause-effect relationship occurring in time and space' (1986: 55). But this is a bit too simple. Important additions can be found in the definition once proposed by the French structuralist folklorist Claude Bremond: 'Every narrative is a discourse that subsumes a chain of events – that has a human interest – under the unity of one and the same action.' He adds that 'it is only in relation to a human project that the events acquire meaning and get organized in a structured temporal sequence'. (Bremond, 1966: 22, quoted in Larsen, 1995: 63) On the basis of these forerunners, I would like to suggest the following definition: *A narrative is a representation of a human (or human-like) subject with a project (will, wish, desire) who lives through a series of causally linked events.*

That the links between events are causal means, of course, that the events relate to each other as causes and effects. We find this in the 3 year old's first paragraph: because I went for a walk, I met a boyfriend. Some events are not made explicit, they are just presupposed: when one falls in love, it might easily happen that one behaves so that pregnancy results, and a common end result of pregnancy is that a baby is born. The first paragraph of the 3 year old's text is, then, with a metaphor, a skeleton of a narrative.

But the little story-teller is not quite happy with the minimalism of the first paragraph. We can only speculate what the reasons for this might be. The first paragraph was probably not only too short, it was also too straight or flat, without any clear peak or turning point. It is also quite circular in its form – the next generation has already met a boyfriend, and so we're at it again. No, the little girl must have felt, a *real* story has a dramatic escalation and a turning point before we return to a situation that is marked as different from the one we started out with. Only then can a story be said to have reached its end. This shows how Bremond's formulation above – 'a structured temporal sequence' – can be expanded on with a reference to this sequence's representation of a *project*, i.e. an attempt to change a situation. We can say that *a narrative presents a series of events that lead from one relatively stable situation to another*. Or, as the narratologist Tzvetan Todorov might have put it, every narrative presents *a whole* or *parts of* a transition from an *equilibrium* (a condition of balance) via a *disequilibrium* (imbalance) to a new, different equilibrium (Todorov, 1977: 88). This is also a way of describing the sequence that forms the typical meaningful whole of a narrative. If not all of the moments of this transition are explicitly represented in the text, we will, as readers or audiences, tend to imagine the missing parts as logical preconditions for, or additions to, that which is directly represented.

If we now return to our 3-year-old story-teller, we can see that it is a more expanded sequential pattern she tries to achieve in the second paragraph of her story – the second episode of her serial, or *feuilleton*, if you like. The same main character – who may be missing the now grown-up child – wants a dog. A crisis occurs when it turns out that her boyfriend does not like animals, and a desperate idea about murdering the dog comes up. (This idea is so horrible that the main character is suddenly referred to in the third person!) The boyfriend's love and company are, after all, the most important things. But then comes the turning point, what the Greek rhetoricians called *peripeteia*, and the possible *dénouement*, as a bolt from the blue. The boyfriend declares, without any forewarning, that he actually likes animals – 'after all'! Such solutions to conflicts are called *Deus ex machina* solutions, i.e. a divine intervention in otherwise hard-to-unravel human knots. This has long been regarded as a cheap trick that less talented authors or playwrights take to when they cannot come up with a solution. But, for 3 year olds, it should be acceptable. She gets where she wants with her narrative, and that is to a *happy end* where they jump and bounce about, and go for (another) walk, with him, i.e. the dog, and there may not necessarily be any more children. The two are still together, but happier than before.

In this latter episode or story, then, we find elements we refer to with terms commonly associated with drama theory: *peripeteia* and *Deus ex machina*. But drama is, whether in written form, performed on a stage, as a film or TV drama, actually a way of telling a story, a way of presenting it. It may not be equally easy with all narratives, but in principle any narrative can be dramatized. A narrative is basically a *mental form*, a *cognitive schema*. This is why it can be represented with, it seems, any imaginable means of expression, any sort of signifier (cf. Chapter 4, on semiotics).

News and other non-fictional narratives

Since the narrative is a way of thinking, a cognitive schema, it is also evident that it need not be fictional. The minimal definition of a narrative we suggested above will therefore apply to many news items in papers, and on radio and television. News items are, in English, also often referred to precisely as *stories*. There are reasons to emphasize this: *narratives are not necessarily fictions*. Historians' representations of times gone by are very often narratives, or at least formed on the basis of the elementary structures of narrative. There are probably literary histories one might read as the sort of novel that is known as a *Bildungsroman* ('educational novel'), where the 'hero' – say, 'English literature' – goes through childhood and adolescence, gradually maturing and surviving a crisis or two until he (or she?) finally reaches a state of full bloom, power and wisdom; and things might go downhill after that. In documentaries, currently almost exclusively shown on TV, it has long been important for film-makers to present material from the 'pre-filmic' reality in a narrative form. The Swede Ola Olsson toured all three Scandinavian countries in the 1980s, telling people working in television that virtually all programmes should copy the pattern of *One Flew Over the Cuckoo's Nest*, i.e. the 'dramaturgy' of the classical Hollywood movie: first, an appetizing opening, then a presentation of hero(es) and crook(s) and their conflict, then a part that provides a deeper presentation of (more background information about) characters and conflict, then a 'point of no return', escalation of conflict, climax and dénouement. Anything from quiz shows to documentaries and current affairs programming has tried to follow such a pattern with a few modifications, even if there are other ways of making programmes interesting.

If one reads today's newspaper or watches the news on television, however, there are not many *fully developed* narrative texts to be found. Most news items in papers or broadcast media are probably simple descriptions, in the form of straightforward factual information: '13 people were killed in traffic accidents in Orange County in the month of March.' Or they are brief and simple reports on what someone has said or done at some minimally described occasion: 'At a press conference at the Hilltop Hilton today, Governor Juicy Fruit said his administration regards road safety as a question of values.' But some news items may have more of a narrative form: 'In an attempt to halt the increase in the number of traffic accidents in Orange County, the police have intensified the surveillance of speed this summer. It is now reported that fewer and fewer motorists are prosecuted for violation of speed limits and the number of accidents has been fewer than in July of last year.' This would be an example of a little narrative about a transition from one situation to another, where the decision and action of the police is the cause of the change that occurs. According to Todorov's way of thinking, we will here, logically or intuitively, presuppose or imagine that there once was a situation in Orange County where there were very few or no traffic accidents (first equilibrium), but that there was then an increase in the number of speeding idiots that brought about an unhappy disequilibrium, which the police have finally managed to do something about.

In the continuous news coverage of areas of war, crisis or catastrophe, there will be a shift between short or longer descriptions on the one hand ('NATO planes yesterday bombed four military targets on the outskirts of Belgrade') and reports that present larger or smaller parts of transitions from one situation to another: '20,000 refugees have arrived in Macedonia over the last two days. They have escaped from destroyed villages and say that they have been harassed by Serbian police on their way to the border.' All of this presupposes that the audience is familiar with what may be called the previous history of this part of the world (the *narrative* about how the once quite peaceful Yugoslavia fell apart in chaos and atrocity) and that they place new bulletins and reports as elements in the longer story of (the tragedy of) what used to be Yugoslavia. (The commonly used term in this context, 'tragedy', is precisely a literary or dramatic term, the name of a genre.) In other sorts of news journalism it is possible to show how *journalists*, over time, form a 'case' or 'story' as a *media drama* or, perhaps better, a *media serial* or *feuilleton*. People in various positions of power may, for instance, be played out against each other in a series of interview-stories that, if put together, form a sort of narrative structure where a conflict is worked through and may even find some sort of solution (Eide and Hernes, 1987). In such cases the point of departure is often a real but latent conflict – for example, between the managers of a public hospital and the authorities that decide on its financial resources. The journalist's contribution may then be to select which people should represent the two institutions involved so as to let the bomb explode with maximum impact, i.e. make the latent conflict publicly manifest. In such cases, the journalist primarily acts as a social or political actor, and only secondarily as the author of a 'story'.

The temporal structure or dramaturgy of a narrative is, of course, based on how the projects and conflicts of extra-literary life most often develop. The Greeks of antiquity thought that the purpose of art was *mimesis*: to 'mime' or imitate non-art reality. The traditional conflict curve of a narrative (possibly in the form of a drama) can be seen as a purification and concentration of the wave-like motion that characterizes the form of most real conflicts: your neighbour's handling of his garbage or dog may be irritating for quite a while and there might be a series of small incidents until you finally explode and thus, either clear the air, make the neighbour move or at least end up with a new situation, open, explicit animosity. Political conflicts in Parliament will tend to display a similar pattern of charge and discharge. It is not the media that create this. On the other hand, they may, working on the basis of narrative as a mental or cognitive schemata, make one or other actor the *protagonist* whose project we follow, place one or other actor as *antagonist* or crook, describe the outcome of the events as a happy or unhappy ending etc. Within the structuring principle of narrative as a cognitive schema, the journalist's opinions and values here have significant room for manoeuvre.

Narrative as a culturally fundamental form

So narrative form is learnt at about the same time as language, and is to be found in all sorts of media and varieties. It may be called a *culturally fundamental form*. Why is it so important?

A simple chronological list of events, between which one cannot see any causal link is not a narrative. In medieval times, the history of, for example, the church was most often written as a list or series of events that took place at certain times, so-called *annals*. Things just happened, in a seemingly random order: this happened then, and then that happened next. These annals were, however, more or less a special case when it comes to historical (re)presentations. In a number of varieties they have always been more or less in keeping with narrative as defined above. Events 'must' have some sort of meaningful connection, and there 'must' be some sort of 'subject' that lives through them – be it a human being, an animal, a nation, humankind or whatever one may be able to portray as a human-like creature with some sort of 'project', a will, a desire etc.

If we now consider how everyday life may appear to most of us, it may be easier to see why narratives are so popular and widespread. We tend to lead rather routinized lives, where most elements are repeated on a daily, weekly, monthly, or seasonal basis. Still, every day is full of small and a bit larger incidents: a cup of coffee overturns, a cat runs across the street, the boss yells at you, an old friend calls. One can, of course, make a list of such incidents. It will not, as everyday life in general, show any connection between events. This is different in a narrative. Here, the cup of coffee is overturned, and *therefore* the protagonist is in a bad mood, so he scares a cat off the pavement on his way to work, where his bad mood continues so that his boss gets angry, and nothing really improves until an old friend calls and suggests a get-together in the bar where they used to meet. This is, in itself, a small narrative, where the project of the subject can be said to be regaining the good mood he was in before his cup of coffee overturned. The joy at the call from an old friend can, however, easily be tied to the fact that our man is actually quite lonely and frustrated, and so the small, short narrative may become a full short story, a film or a novel.

The protagonist's project may then be expanded on and made to last a lot longer – he is on his way to a better understanding of himself, life and the world at large. Narratives thus break the patterns of repetition in everyday life and provide representations of more or less *meaningful changes over time*.

This is one of the main reasons for the centrality of narrative in our culture. It is a mental form we take to when we wish to get a grip on changes in our own lives as well as in the world at large. It, for instance, makes it possible to imagine that our lives – or the world – would have appeared differently if we or other people had chosen to act differently in certain situations. *Narrative is the form of experience* – a cognitive schema that enables us to learn from experience. Narratives about other people, real or fictional, can also work as *vicarious experience*. We learn from the experiences of other people, too, not just our own.

We will return to questions of the culturally fundamental functions of narrative towards the end of this chapter. First, we will take a closer look at how texts of the sort called 'narratives' are constructed.

The two planes of narrative: *syuzhet* and *fabula*

Local newspapers are full of short narratives. One day in the summer of 2000 (30 June, to be precise), *The Oxford Times* told the short story reproduced here as Figure 7.1.

This crime story is clearly marked by its function as a news item. Already the title indicates what the central event of the narrative is, and the very first sentence presents the central characters, the criminal act and the most important background information. Readers who are short on time or have little interest in the Oxfordshire crime scene can then move on to other stories or pages. This is the point of the 'pyramid-on-its-head' story form in news media. It seems to have originated in the US press and then spread to the rest of the western world, presumably between the wars.

In literary terms one could also say that the opening is reminiscent of an *in medias res* (i.e. 'in the middle of things') opening to a short story or novel. It has traditionally been considered an effective way of pulling the reader directly into the exciting events and atmosphere of the narrative. One can sense here too that the journalist has literary ambitions: the man who planted the bomb is not simply named or referred to as 'a garage owner', he is 'a jealous lover' whose girlfriend had been 'two-timing him', not just 'seeing another man'. This *exordium* (in rhetorical terms) is intended to be an emotionally charged appetizer that kindles curiosity.

The narrative does not, in other words, start with the beginning of the chain of events it recounts. This, instead, comes just below the middle of the first

Jealous lover fixed 'hoax' bomb to car

A JEALOUS lover booby-trapped an army major's jeep with a hoax bomb after discovering his girlfriend was two-timing him.

Garage owner Mr Robin Debank, 58, placed the device on Major Scott Balda's 4x4 Chevrolet.

Although Ministry of Defence bomb disposal experts found the bomb would not have worked, Debank was jailed for six months at Oxford Crown Court on Monday. Mr John Small, prosecuting, said Debank had been going out with Miss Catrina Valters after meeting her at the Royal Military College, Shrivenham.

The relationship turned sour after the arrival at the college of American, Major Scott Balda. Debank began to suspect Miss Valters was cheating on him with Major Balda.

When the American returned home for Christmas, the relationship between Debank and Miss Valters appeared to improve, said Mr. Small.

He left her a message inviting her to a birthday celebration at his home at Langham's Yard, Gloucester Street, Faringdon, on February 4.

But when she failed to show up, Debank went to her house in the early hours with the bomb-making equipment, found the major's car parked outside, and wired up the electrics to the petrol tank. The next day he phoned Miss Valters to tell her what he had done.

Debank admitted the charge of placing a device likely to cause alarm. An earlier charge of attempted murder was dropped. Mr Anthony McGeorge, defending, said: "The device he attached was harmless and not intended to cause the sort of repercussions that it did. He did not intend to harm anybody."

Figure 7.1 'Hoax' bomb story in the *Oxford Times*.

column: '... Debank had been going out with Miss Catrina Valters after meeting her at the Royal Military College, Shrivenham'. This is the story of a relationship, and it began at the Royal Military College where the two met for the first time. The ending has, then, already been presented to us: 'Debank was jailed for six months at Oxford Crown Court on Monday.' The last paragraph of the story is devoted to the trial and what went on immediately before it ('an earlier charge of attempted murder was dropped'). The part between the information on the start of the relationship and the last paragraph is the straightforward chronology of the relationship that became a triangle and ended up in court.

There are basically two reasons for this moving back and forth in the chronology: first, this is a news item and partially written to comply with the demands of the news genre (key information up front); second, there is an interest in engaging or involving the reader just as in any other entertaining text. Few narratives actually start with the beginning and continue in a straightforward chronological manner. The text we encounter and read may be called the *syuzhet*, and the underlying, 'actual' series of events the *fabula*. (Some theoreticians use the terms *plot* and *story* respectively, but we will disregard these terms here.) One might say that the syuzhet is the way in which we are informed of the fabula. These terms for the two planes of narrative have been imported to film studies from Russian formalism (see Chapter 2 of the present volume, on influence) by the American David Bordwell (1985: 49f.).

Such a simple distinction may be an efficient tool in a critical analysis of media texts. An analysis of a TV documentary about a young woman's trying experiences in hospital is a good example (Mølster, 1996). The woman in question had a very serious, incurable disease. In hospital, she had a number of unpleasant experiences. The documentary's syuzhet was organized so that the absolutely worst of these – surgery where the anaesthesia failed – came as a *climax*, after a number of other incidents of neglect and apparent harassment by the hospital staff, especially the doctors. In the *real* sequence of events, which make up a documentary's fabula, the surgery where the anaesthesia did not work was one of the very *first* things that happened after the woman was admitted to the hospital. Such a horrible experience would, of course, give reason for being very sceptical and even outright suspicious of those responsible and the hospital staff at large. The early, extremely unfortunate encounter with the hospital thus sheds light on later conflicts and the way the young woman and her mother related and interpreted them. The documentary did provide verbal information that made a correct reconstruction of the fabula, the actual sequence of events, possible. But the syuzhet placed the horrible surgery as a climax for dramaturgical reasons – the Hollywood recipe demanded there was a climax just about there. To ordinary viewers, who are not in the habit of analysing a TV documentary after watching it, the sequence of the syuzhet – and not the real sequence, the fabula – would be what remained in memory. There is thus a reason to say that the documentary, in effect, *misinformed* the viewers, even if the correct information was provided in the film-maker's voice-over commentary. A certain interpretation of the young woman's conflicts with the hospital (that they were not least a result of her understandable antipathy and suspiciousness) was made virtually impossible.

If we now return to the story from *The Oxford Times*, we may also see how the altering of the sequence of events may have consequences for the way in which the story as a whole is understood, what it comes to mean. We have already noted how the choice of phrasing in the first sentence is more emotionally charged than strictly necessary ('jealous', 'two-timing'). The ordering of the story events, the syuzhet, may be said to further develop the degree of sympathy for the criminal signalled here. The final paragraph is about events that took place before the garage owner was sentenced to jail for 6 months. First, it is said that he admitted, presumably during the trial, that his action was 'likely to cause alarm'. Then comes the information that an initial charge of attempted murder had been dropped *before* the trial, so what he did was not all that serious after all. And, at the very end, the defence lawyer is allowed the final words: 'He did not intend to harm anybody.' The last paragraph thus piles on events and statements that work as arguments for an interpretation: the garage owner is actually someone to be pitied, or even sympathized with, a man in love who becomes desperate when he discovers that his girlfriend has had an intimate encounter with his rival instead of showing up at his birthday party.

Catrina Valters is curiously silent throughout the piece. For all we know, she may have told a story of an obsessed man who could not accept that their relationship was over, but kept on harassing her for weeks and months, finally planting the bomb on her current lover's car. But as she is not quoted or referred to at all in the report, one would tend to think she had nothing really worthwhile to say in defence of her behaviour. The report is not signed by the journalist. One might wonder whether a man or woman had written it.

Histoire and *discours*: story and discourse

There is another pair of terms that one may run into in scholarly literature and that partly, but only partly, covers the same ground as fabula and syuzhet. In French structuralist theory, inspired by the linguist Émile Benveniste (1966) and the literary scholar Gérard Genette ([1972] 1980), the terms *histoire* and *discours* are used about a plane of 'content' and a plane of 'expression' respectively. Saussure's distinction between the sign's physical, concrete signifier and the mental, non-material signified underlies Benveniste's and Genette's dichotomy. While Genette's 'histoire' is more or less the same as Bordwell's 'fabula', Genette's 'discours' and Bordwell's 'syuzhet' are different. Bordwell's 'syuzhet' refers only to the ordering of the underlying fabula in time and space. He has a third term that covers *everything else in the manifest text* – and that term is *style*. While a fabula and a syuzhet may well be the same in every version of a narrative – the book as well as the film or television version – *style is always specific to a certain medium*. In film, anything that is peculiar to the medium of film will be a part of a narrative's style in this sense – editing, cinematography, sound and what is known as *mise-en-scène* (briefly defined: everything you actually see in the film image).

In literature, such a notion of style would include everything from paper quality and fonts to elements more traditionally referred to as 'stylistic' (rhyme, rhythm, metaphors, *a particular way of writing*). The literary scholar Genette does not have such a notion of style. His 'discours' covers both 'syuzhet' and 'style' in Bordwell. It simply means *the narrative as it appears*.

It is worth noting that the terms 'discours' and 'histoire' have also been used more or less in Genette's way by certain prominent film scholars – notably the French Christian Metz (1982) and the American Seymour Chatman (1983) – in the latter case in the English version *story* and *discourse*. Confusion, then, may easily result.

In addition, the term *discourse* also, at a certain time, became fashionable and widespread, inspired by the French philosopher Michel Foucault's use of it (Foucault, 1970 and 1972) as meaning, roughly, 'the talk about' (something), such as in the discourse of psychiatry, the discourse of sexuality, the discourse of art, and so on. While Foucault in a special way referred to the power of social institutions exercised through language, the basis for all of these different uses of the term 'discourse' is the ordinary, lexical meaning of the word as speech, conversation – an oral use of language where an 'I' addresses a 'you'. There is here, then, a direct link to our analysis of the speech situation in television in the chapter on rhetoric, i.e. the relations between television's 'I' and us viewers in the role as 'you'. A narrative is also an *act* conducted by someone who narrates, and the notion of *discourse* includes this dimension. We will return to this below, after a closer look at the deeper structures of meaning in narratives.

Actors, actants and themes

At least since Aristotle (384–322 BC) wrote his *Poetics* people have tried, in more and less scholarly ways, to construct categories for various kinds of narrative, and to name recurring elements in them. A milestone in such attempts was the Russian folklorist Vladimir Propp's investigation in 1928 of a large collection of a particular sort of Russian folktale, so-called 'tales of wonder'. Propp found that all of these narratives were constructed as a fixed sequence of exactly 31 *actions* (all were not necessarily represented in each folktale, but the sequence was invariable). Propp called these actions 'functions' – the hero leaves home, the hero goes through a qualifying test, etc. – and he found that all 'characters' or actors appearing in the folktales could be categorized into seven 'roles'. His findings were generalized (said to apply to all sorts of narratives) and modified by the structuralists in France in the 1960s, where Algirdas J. Greimas was central to the development of a structuralist *narratology*.

Greimas argued, in line with Claude Bremond's definition of a narrative (cf. above), that the central element in a narrative is that a *subject* has a *project*, i.e. a wish or desire for something. He called this 'something' the *object*. Projects are rarely realized without problems. They are realized through a *conflict* where the subject has both *helpers* and *opponents*. Finally, the object is transferred from something or someone to something or someone else – a form of *communication* takes place where something is delivered from a sender or *donor* to a *recipient*. This may be presented graphically in a simple model with three axes and six roles (as opposed to Propp's seven), which Greimas called *actants*. Figure 7.2 illustrates what this model looks like.

The actants are roles that may be played by several concrete characters in a narrative, and the same character can appear in more than one role. Take a traditional love story where a working-class boy (subject) desires an upper-class girl (object). The girl's father will then be the donor of the girl (when there is a happy ending), but may also appear as one of the boy's opponents, along with the snobbish jerk the girl's parents would prefer as a son-in-law, some of the girl's friends etc. The boy's helpers might be friends of his; and the girl herself, magic birds that sing vital messages or whatever. The recipient will, again if there is a happy ending, of course be the working-class boy.

One may, however, especially in more complex, 'advanced' narratives, also find that more abstract matters belong in the various categories – the subject may, for instance, desire something abstract such as 'self-assertiveness', 'realization of talents', 'political power' or something like that, while the opponents could include 'social prejudices', 'moral weakness' etc. It is also possible to see the concrete characters of a narrative as representing such abstractions, values, ideas, social forces etc. In an analysis, the placing of characters in the six boxes, or actants, may be followed by a second step, where they are replaced by the abstractions they may be said to represent. In our imagined love story the boy could represent 'individual determination and will-power', the girl 'power and love', her father 'social authority' (donor) and 'social prejudice' (opponent) etc.

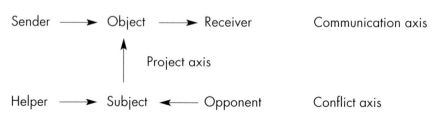

Figure 7.2 Greimas's model of the structure of narrative.

Greimas's model can thus be used as a 'tool' when we want to get a systematic overview of what actually goes on in a narrative. One has to ask who is the story's subject and how one is to term the object of her or his 'project'. There are helpers, and so there must be opponents of one sort or another. By asking such questions, one is actually on the way to an understanding of the narrative's *theme*. The manifest, concrete representation of events and characters is often referred to as the story's *motif*. A more abstract, i.e. *general* determination of what the story is 'actually' about concerns the narrative's *theme*. Again, in other words, we have the distinction between the manifest and the latent. The theme is at a latent plane and so it takes some sort of analysis to reveal it.

If we now revisit the car bomb story (see Figure 7.1), it is quite obvious that the subject of this story is the jealous garage owner, Robin Debank. The object is, then, Catrina Valters, representing True Love. The donor is, interestingly, problematic. There is no prejudiced daddy represented in the story, one who would for instance prefer Catrina moved beyond the level of local garage owners. The donor would in fact primarily be Catrina herself, plus her new boyfriend, the US Major Scott Balda. But these two are also first on the list of poor Robin Debank's opponents. No wonder his project fails – no 'communication' takes place, except in Mr Debank's imagination. The 'recipient' box would therefore have Mr Debank's name – in brackets. Since the subject breaks the law in his pursuit of the object, the police would also be among his opponents. In the subsequent trial, there is a prosecutor who must be included among the opponents, while his defending lawyer is just about the only helper our man has, painting a picture of him that might have made Catrina's heart melt, if she was capable of melting. What all of this leads to is that this is a story of what the French call a *crime passionel*, a crime of passion (note the etymological connection to *pathos* and the point made about the emotional charge of the phrasing of the first paragraph). It is rewarded with months in jail, but the narrative is arranged so that the criminal is regarded with a considerable degree of sympathy. The *theme* of the story can thus be determined as a conflict between the individual's emotions and the law of society or, possibly, *the legitimate vs the legal*.

One could, on the other hand, read the narrative as if Catrina Valters was the subject. This would obviously be contrary to the journalist's intentions, but it is still possible. It may anyway serve as a sort of critique of the way in which the story-as-printed places so much sympathy on Debank's side of the controversy. Catrina Valters' project is to find True Love, and this abstraction is clearly represented by, or concretized in, Major Scott Balda (after Robin Debank has been, so to speak, debunked). Her chief opponent is just as clearly Robin the bomb man. Her helpers would primarily be herself and possibly the Major, plus, eventually, the police and the prosecutor. And since any dad figure is absent, one might see her as the donor as well; or perhaps the reluctant Robin? Such questions indicate how *the actant model is a logical structure* that *produces questions*, not a simple form to be straightforwardly filled in for every concrete narrative one encounters. In any case, it seems that a reading of the story with Catrina Valters as the subject has a happy ending: her main opponent ends up in jail (albeit only for 6 months), she has the support of society and its law, and she is free to live happily ever after with her, possibly balding, US Major Balda. The *theme* in this case could possibly be formulated as a conflict between a woman's pursuit of happiness and a man's possessiveness, a man so obsessive he resorts to violence. The narrative's theme in this case is thus that of *female self-determination vs male domination*.

Both of these readings are possible, but the second one is, as already noted, obviously not in line with what seems to be the journalist-author's intentions. It is a logical possibility that is not sustained by the way in which the narrative is actually formed or *narrated*. This point takes us to another area of narrative analysis: the question of how a narrative addresses us and thus establishes a certain relationship between us and the 'speech' or 'voice' of the text. We last touched on this subject in connection with the notion of discourse above, and before that in connection with our section on the speech situation in television in the chapter on rhetoric. We will now regard it more specifically in relation to the narrative textual form.

Narrative communication: the story-teller and us

A 'narrative' is not just a type of text, it is also closely related to the verb 'to narrate', in the same way that 'writing' is a form of 'to write'. This may act as a reminder of the rather banal fact that a narrative is always also an *act* – someone narrates something to someone. The theoretical term for this is *narration*. On the one hand, the one who narrates is always a real person – or several, as in film, in television or theatre, where a lot of people are involved in the production of the narrative text. But where the mass media are concerned we do not get in direct contact with these people. It is true that we in radio can hear someone narrating and in television we sometimes even see someone. The narrator in the case of radio can be a journalist who tells his own story, an interviewee talking about something s/he has experienced or it could be an actress/actor narrating 'on behalf of' an author. In television we find the same, except that we can also see the person(s) that present(s) the narrative. In newspapers, books, film and television drama, on the other hand, there are, as a rule, no such physical narrators. But we may still sense or get a feeling that a voice, someone or something *in the text* is telling the story, organizing the text and providing some perspectives on what is going on while excluding others.

In literary theory, the physical or 'real' narrator is called the 'author' or, possibly, the *real, empirical* or *historical author*. She or he is logically and physically separated from the text that the reader encounters. The narrator or 'story-teller' we sense *in* the text, who is *a part of the text*, is called the *narrator*. In a literary context especially, this is an important distinction. It implies, for instance, that one can never tell *directly* from a novel, play, short story or, for that matter, an essay, what goes on (or went on) in the empirical or historical author's head. An author may, for example, choose to use a narrator with totally different attitudes and leanings to his or her own. In a novel there may also at times be several narrators – different parts are narrated by different 'voices', for instance, so that different people in the fictional world explicitly narrate different parts of the overall story, or provide different versions of the same.

In much structuralist and poststructuralist textual theory, the distinction between the empirical author and the text as it presented to us is emphasized to the extreme. In my opinion, it is often exaggerated beyond what is sustainable. A sensible critique of an ideology that regards every text or work of art as a more or less direct expression of the personality, soul or 'essence' of the empirical originator has ended up in an equally untenable position. Inspired by structural linguistics and articles by French theoreticians such as Roland Barthes ('The death of the author' [1968] 1977c) and Michel Foucault ('What is an author?', 1979a), many scholars of literature, film and other media have effectively made the question of who actually produced it, and under what circumstances, completely irrelevant to the understanding of any text. The British media scholar Graham Murdock has put it, metaphorically, like this: 'Whereas the ideology of authorship presents authors as ventriloquists who speak through their works, structuralist criticism, led by Barthes, casts them in the role as dummy, manipulated by the hidden hands of language' (Murdock [1980] 1993: 131). A more adequate understanding of the relationship between empirical authors and the texts they produce should avoid both simplifications.

If we now take a closer look at the text-internal narrator, we will find that a number of varieties and aspects of this have been described and categorized in literary and film theory. The area is complex and also confusing. This is partly due to the ways in which artistically ambitious literature and film have made great use of the artistic possibilities offered in experiments with different forms of narration. In popular literature, in mainstream film and television, and in newspapers, things are normally much simpler or more straightforward. But film, television drama and certain forms of journalism can at times, of course, also demonstrate a narrative complexity equal to that one may find in the older arts.

The theoretical complexity and outright confusion in this area are partly due to the still-existing taboo in certain forms of criticism, against bringing the *empirical author* into the analysis. In this context, however, we will try to concentrate on providing a valid, if brief, account of some main terms or concepts that may be useful to analyses of narration.

The narrator in the text can be *overt*, i.e. either a character in the story or 'an intrusive outside party' (Chatman, 1983: 33) who may, for instance, say 'and now, dear reader, we will turn to ...'. But the narrator can also be *covert*, i.e. a more anonymous figure who, we may imagine, 'speaks' to us but who is located outside of the world of the narrative (which he or she is thus interpreting) and often has a hardly noticeable presence in the text. This is probably the most common form in modern, mainstream, so-called realistic novels. Finally, the narrator may be so covert that some (paradoxically, it would seem) speak of an 'absent' narrator, or a 'non-narrated' narrative (I and others would prefer 'minimally narrated'). This is the case when, in literature, a story is told only through dialogue and descriptions of actions, without any comments or interpretative remarks. Most mainstream films will be minimally narrated or 'non-narrated', since they strive to give us the impression that things just unfold before our very eyes. One can further distinguish between *omniscient* narrators (who, for instance, know every detail of what goes on inside the heads and bodies of all characters) and, on the other hand, narrators with more or less limited knowledge. How much the narrator seems to know is closely tied to what is called *narrative perspective*, sometimes also termed the narrator's *position* or *point of view*. This, in other words, concerns from which 'position' the narrator 'regards' the characters and events. (I have put 'position' and 'regards' in inverted commas here because the visual aspect is only part of the phenomenon of narrative perspective. It may also include a certain psychological, moral or ideological 'angle' on that which is narrated.)

In film analysis the term 'point of view' is primarily used to refer to shots in which we as spectators see something from the position of one of the characters – so-called *point of view shots* or 'subjective camera'. In film, such a perceptual point of view may also, however, be juxtaposed with an underlying point of view (often termed *figurative* point of view) in the narrative as a whole. In such cases we may experience a scene from a psychological or moral perspective other than that of the person whose perceptual point of view the camera presents. In the classic western *Stagecoach* (1939) we 'see' or experience a certain scene from the perspective of the prostitute Dallas, even if the camera follows the stern look of the virtuous Lucy (Browne, 1982). Finally, there is a distinction also between *reliable* and *unreliable* narrators. There are, for instance, crime novels and films where the first-person narrator ('I') turns out to be the murderer and consequently has done as much as possible to conceal this for as long as possible.

The narrator is, in any case, always something other than that which (since Booth, 1983) has been called *the implied author*. While the narrator 'speaks', tells us the story, the implied author is silent. The implied author is *an image of the real author* that readers construct on the basis of various indications in the text, that is to say an idea of a *norm, attitude or ideology* that one may sense lies 'under' or 'behind' the text as a sort of governing 'textual intention'. It is important to note that the implied author does not necessarily have much in common with the *empirical* author and her or his views and values. On the other hand, it is hardly possible to describe a covert, withdrawn narrator without also describing the implied author. The distinction between such a narrator and the implied author is purely theoretical or analytical – the covert narrator narrates, and the implied author governs that which is narrated from somewhere in the background.

The Russian linguist and literary scholar Mikhail Bakhtin was particularly interested in what he termed a plurality of voices, or *polyphony*, especially in novels. This occurs when it is difficult or impossible to form a more or less coherent impression of an implied author, i.e. a somewhat clear idea of a governing norm or intention in certain types of novel (or, in principle, other types of text, in various media). Bakhtin was particularly interested in the work of Dostoyevsky and developed the idea of polyphony in this connection. He found that there were several 'voices' representing different norms or intentions in Dostoyevsky's novels. Bakhtin also referred to the relationship between these voices as *dialogical*. He came to develop an extensive theory of language around this notion, emphasizing that all languages, all use of language, form a tension-filled interplay between different varieties and situation-specific meanings (Bakhtin, 1981 and 1984). This way of thinking has also been transferred to the analysis of, for example, film, and has been used as a basis for theorizing multicultural social conditions (cf. Stam, 1989).

In what is called 'narrative communication', then, there are three entities on the 'sender' side: An empirical author *external* to the text, and an implicit author and a narrator *internal* to the text. On the 'recipient' or reader side, each of these have their counterpart: an *empirical reader* external to the text, and an *implied reader* and a *narratee* internal to it. The narratee may be explicit, as when a person in a novel starts narrating to someone, possibly in a so-called frame story; but it can also be more subtle or unclear, as a someone we 'just sense' that the narration is directed at – or it may not be discernible at all. 'The narratee-character is', says Seymour Chatman, 'only one device by which the implied author informs the real reader how to perform as implied reader, which *Weltanschauung* ['worldview'] to adopt' (Chatman, 1983: 150). The implied reader is, in other words, the values, attitudes or ideological perspectives the text seems addressed to, analogous to the implied author being the values or ideological position from which the narrative is narrated.

Umberto Eco (1981) refers to more or less the same idea with his notion of the *model reader*, a term one may encounter in scholarly literature; but as a semiotician, Eco would rather speak of the model reader as a particular *competency in terms of codes*, which is presupposed by the text. Such a competency will, of course, also include components related to values and ideologies. While the narrator and the narratee are thus technical instruments of narration that can be explicitly marked or not marked at all in the text, the implied author and the implied reader concern the fundamental ideological, ethical or political character of the text and they will therefore always be possible to describe. We can, then, summarize the above presentation of the elements of narrative communication in the following model (based on Chatman, 1983: 151), where the brackets indicate the limits to the narrative text and the ordinary parentheses indicate the possibility of the narrator and narratee being unmarked:

empirical author $\longrightarrow$ [implied author $\longrightarrow$ (narrator) $\longrightarrow$ (narratee) $\longrightarrow$ implied reader] $\longrightarrow$ empirical reader

In order to suggest how all of this may be applied in a concrete analysis of a text, we will have another brief look at the car bomb story from *The Oxford Times* (see Figure 7.1). It obviously has some empirical author, but this person is not named. And since this person would be a total stranger to most of us, it will be the *implied* author and the narrator *in the text* that we relate to when reading. The narrator is clearly covert, and not part of the events recounted. We may also notice that the narrator is not omniscient but that she or he now and then uses words that refer to the feelings of Robin Debank ('jealous', 'began to suspect' etc.); but, as we have previously pointed out, some of these words are also signals of a degree of sympathy with the unhappy lover who went to extremes. As we touched upon above, then, the distinction between the characterization of a covert narrator and a characterization of the implied author, i.e. the readers' text-based assumptions concerning the norms or values of the empirical author, is not necessarily easy to make.

There is no marked narratee in this text; but as we have also previously noted, the text leans towards a sympathetic understanding of the crime in question. It signals a degree of support for the legitimacy of strong emotions in a case like this so that the law should be, if not disregarded, then at least practised with leniency or a little compassion. The reader is obviously also expected to share such a perception, i.e. not look at the case from a strict law-and-order perspective. Readers who would feel at home in the latter sort of position will possibly reject the suggested role of the implied reader and thus reject the text, either by interrupting the reading of it or getting upset at the silly 'soft' attitude of the piece, and possibly writing an angry letter to the editor(s). A similar sort of response might be found in female readers who have themselves been more or less severely harassed by men who could not accept that an affair was over and might even have resorted to violence of some kind in infantile attempts to hold on. We have more or less parallel possibilities every time we encounter a text in any medium: accept the implied role we are offered, or resist it by quitting the story or staying on with growing resentment.

Narration in film and television

Most of the above has primarily referred to written texts, but much of it is also transferable to film and television. One important difference is that the empirical author in these audiovisual media is always a *collective*, often with an intricate inner division of labour, while the print media most often have individuals in this role (see also Chapter 10 of the present volume, on production in the media). More important in this connection is that the audiovisual media have five channels through which they tell the story: image, graphics (mainly writing), dialogue, music and (other) sound-effects. In spite of such differences between the media, there are also many fundamental parallels.

According to David Bordwell, films, to a significant degree, lack a narrator. As spectators we do not feel that anyone is telling us anything, we just see and hear a series of events unfold in time and space (cf. Bordwell, 1985: 62). It is we, the audience, who, effectively, construct a story out of what we see and hear, i.e. the syuzhet's mediation of information and what Bordwell calls *style*, the sum of all media-specific elements (camera use, lighting, sound, editing etc.). While it is always, in a sense, the reader or spectator that creates meaning out of any text (cf. Chapters 4 and 5), Bordwell is thinking of a particular *kind* of film when he says that there is no narrator: the realist, so-called 'classic' Hollywood movie (wherever it is produced). Such movies are intentionally constructed so that the audience gets the feeling of directly watching and identifying with a piece of 'reality', effectively unmediated. This is why the French film semiotician Christian Metz once said that traditional film is always presented as story (*histoire*), never as discourse, and that the very principle of its efficiency as discourse is that it eradicates all traces of enunciation, the act of narrating (Metz, 1982: 91). Logically, however, we may assume that there *is* a narrator also in these mainstream films – they are just 'minimally narrated' by a 'covert narrator' – and we may also point out some of the features of this type of narrator.

He or she (or it) is normally very well informed, if not totally omniscient and omnipresent, and also reliable. This often means that the audience is better informed than the characters on the screen and may therefore enjoy the pleasure of feeling smart. Spectators can often provide advice to characters ('Don't trust that guy!', 'Look behind you!') or await, with pleasure, the moment when somebody gets knocked on the head. As Alfred Hitchcock knew, and demonstrated, even the most relaxed of dinner conversations may become excruciatingly exciting if the camera has revealed to us that there is a ticking time-bomb under the table. This sort of thing can, together with surprising camera angles, astonishing crane shots and other more or less striking visual or auditory elements, be regarded as a sign of the presence of a narrator.

When the French director Jean-Luc Godard was making the film *Breathless* (*A bout de souffle*) in 1959, he consciously included indications (indexical signs) of a narrator – such as so-called *jump-cuts* (a form of editing that conspicuously eliminates a bit of time in, for instance, the middle of a conversation). Such devices are in radical opposition to the norm of classical film realism, which requires cuts to be as invisible as possible – so-called *continuity editing*. Marking the presence of a narrator was also a way of marking the creative work of a director, and thus part of the (successful) efforts of Godard and others in the milieu around the film journal *Cahiers du cinéma* to have film accepted as an art form on a level with literature. A precondition for this was that film, like the traditional arts, should have individual 'creators', and so the director had to become an *auteur* (author). Devices with functions similar to those of Godard can now also be found in Hollywood movies. When, in *Pulp Fiction*, Quentin Tarantino suddenly shows us the same time sequence once more, but seen from a different point of view, it becomes obvious that we are dealing here with a cunning narrator. It is easier for the director responsible for such surprises to acquire status as *auteur* than it is for those who stick to middle-of-the-road narrative techniques of the standard formula. A number of films – and a few TV serials – have also been made where the narrator is an 'I', a character in the story, addressing the audience directly in voice-over. This is then a first-person narrative that, just as in literature, has a narrator with limited knowledge of other characters and events where she or he is not present – and who may be interested in presenting her/himself in a more flattering way than might otherwise be acceptable.

One of the most interesting developments in US television fiction since the early 1980s is that the spectrum of narrative techniques has been expanded, in connection with ever more frequent deviations from classical realist form. In line with what happened in French cinema around 1960 this has also resulted in the emergence of television *auteurs*. In the late 1990s, the writer-producer David E. Kelley was established as one of the most central of these, with shows such as *Picket Fences*, *Chicago Hope* and *The Practice*. While there were signs of a more daring, experimental approach in *Picket Fences*, it was primarily in *Ally*

McBeal that Kelley really started to emphasize the presence of a narrator. In the very first episode, Ally partly functioned as a first-person narrator, but it also soon became evident that there was another narrator 'behind' her, one who knows a lot more than Ally. We can thus see and hear things that happen where Ally is not present, while we also get to know what goes on in Ally's head (and the heads of others) in more or less comic and/or grotesque sequences – such as when Ally's tongue hangs out like a tie when she spots a particularly delicious male. This more or less omniscient narrator is obviously prepared to transgress traditional narrative norms. At the same time, we also sense that this show has an *implied author* with a certain set of values who, effectively, regards Ally, her colleagues and friends at a humorous and possibly humanely generous ironical distance. It is possible that the real or empirical author, David E. Kelley, in fact also regards his characters in this way – but we can not, in principle, know this without speaking to him about it. The implied viewer ('reader'), the position we viewers are invited to place ourselves in while watching, is in any case one that corresponds to the implied author's view of what goes on.

Television's sequential structures: flow, programmes and segments

The medium of television is without doubt the most important provider of narratives of all kinds in today's society. Major parts of programming, in many cases well over half of what channels offer, are fiction series or feature films and, in addition, there are documentaries and news items formed as narratives. Television's narratives are parts of a particular textual regime, and *the structure of this regime, the order of this context, marks both the narratives themselves and our experiences of them*. In this section we will therefore go beyond traditional, literary-based narratology and look at what have been seen as some fundamental textual conditions specific to television, before examining television's own narrative genre, soap opera.

When the British scholar of literature, media and culture Raymond Williams arrived in the USA in the early 1970s, he had made the journey from Britain to Miami by boat. Still a bit 'dazed' from the sea voyage, he sat down to watch US television for the first time. It was a strange experience, he later wrote. He started watching a film about a crime in San Francisco, and had problems adjusting to the commercial breaks being much more frequent than they were on the ITV channel he knew from back home. He had further serious problems when the channel also began to show clips from a couple of movies that were due to appear on the channel at a later time. The crime story from San Francisco began to blend not only with deodorant and dog food commercials, but also with a love story from Paris and some prehistoric monsters. In hindsight, he was not really sure what he had understood of the film he was originally watching; he thought he had probably seen some of the people in the commercials as characters in the San Francisco film, and he also perceived some of the scenes from the coming films as taking place in the movie he was watching. The sort of television he experienced here appeared to him as 'a single irresponsible flow of images and feelings' (Williams, 1975: 91f.).

This confused encounter with US television was the original basis for the notion of *flow*, which actually designates two aspects of the way in which television's transmissions are organized: that programmes and sequences follow each other in a constant stream or 'flow' – and that they therefore, in the heads of viewers, are linked to each other, across the seemingly clear divisions into different programmes and sequences. When returning to Britain, Williams found that there were elements of this sort flow there too, even if these were less pronounced than in the USA, and so he figured that 'flow' was a general characteristic of television as a medium. An 'evening's viewing' was obviously planned as a whole entity by broadcasters, and was aimed at grabbing viewers early in the evening and keeping them in front of the screen until it was time to go to bed. To describe the experience of such an 'evening's viewing' would be like describing 'having read two plays, three newspapers, three or four magazines, on the same day that one has been to a variety show and a lecture and a football match' (Williams, 1975: 95). And still, this would not quite be the same, since 'though the items may be various, the television experience has in some important ways unified them' (1975: 95).

Williams no doubt points to something important about television as a medium with his notion of *flow*. We can still easily see a difference between various channels in different countries in terms of how marked the 'flow' quality of programming is, just as Williams had to go to the USA to discover this phenomenon; but there are at least two problematic aspects of the notion and the way in which Williams uses it. First, he claims that it is the 'the central television experience' (1975: 95), i.e. something particular to television and, moreover, the central feature of the television. Second, the metaphorical term carries connotations that are debatable.

As to the first point, Williams himself points to an argument against regarding 'flow' as something particular to television. He says that the 'general trend, towards an increasing variability and miscellaneity of public communications, is evidently part of a whole social experience', meaning that the experience of various processes of modernization such as increased physical and social mobility, the emergence of consumer society and a number of other things. He still claims that 'until the coming of broadcasting the normal expectation was still of a discrete event or of a succession of discrete events' (1975: 88). There are good reasons to doubt this latter claim. Anyone who has read newspapers aiming for a broad audience since the mid-nineteenth century, and particularly since the beginning of the twentieth, has been prepared to find anything from obituaries to entertaining pieces and ads for a host of products in one and the same issue. Variety stage shows have been popular throughout the same period of time, and cinema programmes were, especially in the first 10 to 15 years of the new medium's history, composed in much the same way as television's 'evening of viewing', with a mix of documentary, slapstick, musical items and action in the programme. And, as Williams' own formulation above indicates, it is *broadcasting* more than television in particular that has the 'flow' quality built into it. It is, in other words, *just as characteristic of radio* – while also having similarities with newspapers, stage entertainment etc.

The second problematic aspect of Williams' now classic presentation of the notion of 'flow' concerns the connotational implications regarding the audience's relations to the medium. We remember his phrasing of how US television appeared to him that first time in Miami: as one '*irresponsible* flow of images and emotions' (my emphasis). We may sense in this expression an elderly, academically educated gentleman's resistance to something uninhibited; the metaphor 'flow' also signals that this is something one may be carried away by, passively or powerlessly. Audiences may in accordance with this be imagined as passive, without the ability to distinguish good from bad. Understood in this way, the 'flow' metaphor echoes good old mass society thinking, anxieties about media's ability to form and steer the spineless, easily influenced masses (cf. Chapter 2 of the present volume, on influence).

But people are only carried away by the flow or stream if they, so to speak, fall in to it. The notion of flow can therefore also be relevant to an alternative way of conceiving of the relations between television and its audiences. The river-like stream, or flow, of programmes can also be regarded at a distance, form a position of safety on the shore, only mildly engaged. This is the point of departure for the theory first formulated by the British scholar (and television producer) John Ellis (1982): that television is mainly watched with a *glance*. This is, according to Ellis (and a whole psychoanalytically and semiotically oriented tradition in film studies) in direct opposition to the *gaze* that characterizes audiences' relationship to cinema. Television is, then, according to this theory, not watched in a very engaged way, but rather with quite distanced glances, often in between various domestic activities. The cinematic experience, on the other hand, is deeply absorbing, demanding and achieving the full concentration of the audience.

It is not difficult to see how this can be tied to a ranking of the two media in terms of seriousness and expressive potential. The important question is whether, or to what extent, this is actually true. Television is, no doubt, located at the centre of many people's everyday lives, and since those who produce television have been aware of this for a long time, television programmes are often constructed in ways that correspond to a distracted, not concentrated, form of viewing. John Ellis has pointed out how many TV programmes (and, we may add, radio programmes) are composed of *segments*. He defines 'segments' as 'small sequential unities of images and sounds whose maximum duration seems to be about five minutes' (Ellis, 1982: 112), which are 'following on from each other with no necessary connection between them' (1982: 116f.). A segment is thus, in principle, meaningful and fully understandable even if one did not see or hear what went before or what came after. However, this principle of segmentation does not apply to all television programming, and it is not, of course, the case that television cannot demand and achieve a highly concentrated, deeply involved form of viewing (see, for example, Ang, 1985, and Gripsrud, 1995, on soap opera audiences). It is furthermore not the case that any cinema audience is continuously deeply engaged in what happens on the screen – we all know that there is a lot of necking, cheering and throwing of popcorn going on too.

An important consequence of overemphasizing the flow aspect of television (and radio) is that this view leads to a disregard for the *individual programmes*. They tend to be erased as independent units: either one thinks of flow as something that overpowers the audience and drags it through a number of unrelated, and yet unified, items, or as something that is regarded at a distance, only minimally engaged. This is contrary to how television is actually produced – as discrete programmes by people with certain specific intentions – and also to how most people actually watch television: they watch certain programmes – news, their favourite series, a football match or whatever. Your work colleagues don't ask you whether you were watching television last night (this is what most people do in the evenings), they ask whether you watched *The X-files, Survivor, Big Brother, EastEnders* or a particular newscast etc. It is the programmes that are of interest, not 'an evening's viewing'.

These objections do not mean that the notion of flow is without relevance to the understanding of broadcast media and their texts. They only suggest that the flow aspect should not be overemphasized or exaggerated. It is true that large parts of television's programming are constructed by way of segments in Ellis's sense: news and magazine formats, variety entertainment, talk shows and so on. Segments can be small narratives or of some other textual form. Many of them could be moved to other programmes without having their meaning altered, and without significantly changing the character of the programmes: news segments could, say, appear in a number of other factual programmes. Programme-makers therefore often seem to struggle a bit to make their programme appear as a separate entity. Studio design is important as a marker of the specificity and coherence of a certain sequence of segments, and so is the personal style of the programme host. One might say that the 'programme' category is threatened with dissolution both from 'above', by the flow, and from 'below', by the segmental structure. This is, however, the field of tensions in which every television programme appears and in which it is up to the programme's producers to make their programme stand out.

Soap opera as a narrative form

The notions of flow and segment are clearly relevant to an understanding of *the only narrative form specifically developed for broadcast media*: the soap opera. The genre first emerged as a sort of serial radio drama in American commercial radio in the early 1930s. These serials were transmitted in the daytime and were directed at a female audience of housewives and maids. The original and official name of the genre was daytime drama or daytime serial drama. It was most probably the showbiz journal *Variety* that created the term 'soap opera' in the late 1930s. The first part of this composite term refers to the fact that the serials in question were produced by, or for, the makers (such as Procter & Gamble) of household products, primarily detergents. The second part of the term is more ambiguous. 'Soap opera' will to some appear as what rhetoricians call an *oxymoron*, an expression consisting of two terms that seem to contradict each other (e.g. 'eloquent silence'). Soap is something very mundane and trivial while opera has traditionally been considered something of great cultural value. But opera is also a highly emotional sort of drama, accompanied by music, and both of these features were characteristic of the daytime serials. The term 'soap opera' thus not only contains a contradiction, it also points to similarities between a 'low' and a 'high' genre.

Soap opera made the transition from radio to television at the end of the 1940s. (The oldest soap in the world, *Guiding Light*, started on radio in 1938!) Even if the genre has changed quite a bit in many ways over the years, and especially since about 1980 (cf. Gripsrud, 1995: 165f.) it still concentrates on intimate human relations, even in the most exotic or dramatic of circumstances. The fundamental defining feature, however, is that *it is in principle never-ending, it is written to go on forever*. When the US prime-time series *Dallas* started, in its 1979–80 season to experiment with letting episodes end without resolving all conflicts, the success of this device opened prime-time to soap opera. Since then, we have not only had so-called prime-time soaps such as *Dynasty* and *Falcon Crest*, we have also seen a host of series that are at least partly serials, i.e. they combine the episodic format with the never-ending soap principle. This has even, it seems, become the norm: *Hill Street Blues*, *LA Law*, *NYPD Blue*, *Picket Fences*, *Chicago Hope*, *The X-files* and *Ally McBeal* all contain storylines that extend over several episodes.

The now dominant serial form is thus different both from the *episodic* or *series* form, where every episode tells a new story (or two) about a well-known set of characters in a well-known milieu and setting, and from the *mini-series* or *feuilletons* that tell a single story over a limited number of episodes. These are the three serial forms found in television. The never-ending soap form is most specific for television *since it is the form most closely related to television's flow aspect*. In the same way that television is a daily, and now even 24-hour occurrence, running for as long as we can see into the future, soap opera is also a seemingly eternal phenomenon, served up in daily or weekly doses. These doses are *programmes*. The question is, then, whether the soap opera form also reflects the third level in television's sequential structure, the segments.

It does. It is, as mentioned above, divided into several *subplots* or *storylines*. There are normally between four and seven of these in each episode. They are, of course, loosely tied to one another since, for instance, the same people are involved in several of them, and what happens in one may suddenly influence what goes on in another. But, for the most part, they are relatively independent of one another. In principle, then, one might watch a soap opera much as one watches breakfast TV – taking in the segments that are of interest and otherwise continuing to read the paper or eat. But every episode is put together so that scenes from the various subplots appear in an unpredictable sequence. A scene from story A is followed by a scene from story D and then A returns before we get to see what goes on in E and B. It is also actually quite hard to determine what the temporal relations are between the segments from the various storylines. In some shows the opening scenes in an episode tend to be morning or breakfast scenes, while the final scenes or segments take place at night, so it is suggested that the episode shows events taking place within a single day. But all that goes on between the beginning and the end can, in fact, be quite hard to place in a chronological sequence. We often do not know whether what goes on in one scene happens before, after or at the same time as the scene that went before or the one that follows. *The relations between the syuzhet and the fabula is, in other words, unclear.*

In my own study of *Dynasty* (Gripsrud, 1995) I found that what decided the ordering of the scenes between beginning and end was not time but *their level of dramatic tension*. US series and serials are planned in accordance with the commercial breaks that function as intermissions between acts. There are normally at least four such acts in the course of an hour-long soap episode (which is actually only about 45 minutes in total). Each act has to end on a high point of tension in order to make the audience come back after the break, and the longer the break the higher the tension must be (i.e. the segment before the middle commercial break and, especially, the segment before the episode ends will be peak moments). In accordance with the same logic, the end-of-season episode will be tremendously exciting, so that the audience will remember it all through the break and return for the next season's episodes. A great historical example here is the 'Moldavian wedding massacre' episode of *Dynasty*, where the entire cast was gathered for a wedding in a fictitious European country when masked terrorists opened fire with machine guns. Rumours had it that salaries were being negotiated and that those who were too demanding could not count on surviving the attack.

This structure underlines that the dramatic temperature and emotional quality of each scene (conflict, declarations of eternal love, grief or whatever) in a sense has a value that is independent of its function within the overall story(line). Every scene has as a main function to represent some emotional quality and/or each scene is like a small drama in and by itself. The changes in the overarching story context – the diegetic universe of the soap opera as a whole – are often quite small, or at least reversible: couples that are divorced can be reunited at any time, characters that are evil or stupid can suddenly become kind and smart. These twists and turns are determined by the plot machinery, and the consistency and development of characters in accordance with their experiences is of little importance in soap opera.

> Soap opera is the drama of perepetia without anagnorisis. It deals forever in reversals but never portrays that irreversible change which traditionally marks the passage out of ignorance into true knowledge. For actors and audience alike, no action ever stands revealed in the terrible light of its consequences.
>
> (Porter, 1982: 124f.)

The 'endless' form thus makes it difficult for soap opera to portray how experiences may actually change the course of someone's life forever, change someone's outlook on life, values or character. This is one main reason why it is quite easy to 'get into' a soap opera again after weeks, months or even years: after innumerable divorces and other crises, the characters and the relationships between them are roughly the same as they used to be. The individual scenes, the segments of soap opera, are in some way at least as important as the programmes (episodes) and the overarching, long-term flow or story. The emotional kicks they deliver, in the manner of small semi-independent show numbers, organized in a rhythm basically the same in each episode, is a main aspect of the soap opera experience. An audience without prior knowledge of the soap opera narrative structure would have to learn how to watch it. This was the case for the Norwegian audience in 1983 when

Dynasty arrived on their screens. People were extremely angry when there was talk of taking the show off the schedule 'before we get to see how it all ends'. The Norwegian audience was used to traditional narratives and took the show's *promises* of a long, coherent 'family saga' seriously. Their experience with *Dynasty* could be seen as an exercise in taking television less seriously, in watching TV drama more as one would watch other segmented television programmes.

This is why some people have regarded soap opera as a sign of the *dissolution of narrative*, a sign that indicates how traditional narrative form with its role in the constitution of experience is being replaced by a form that is related to a different feeling for time, more oriented towards the *here and now* than towards longer, life-historical connections – in line with the idea that 'experience has dropped in value' (cf. Chapter 1, on identity, and the following section).

Soap opera's universe of locations and people can moreover be understood as a 'substitute community', somehow existing beside the ordinary, real world and just as ongoing and unfinished as everyday life itself. Every episode, especially when a soap is daily, but also when shown less frequently, is like a journalistic 'update' on the situation in the soap's world. One could thus perhaps say that these serials approach the genres of *information* even if they are, of course, also closely related to traditional narrative.

Soap operas do after all also manage to create an impression that they are long, far-reaching narratives where all subplots and segments are somehow elements of a broad, linear narrative progression. It is true that the segmented structure is a very important feature of these television serials and that the lack of an ending means that we never get to see characters really learn from decisive experiences. On the other hand, they constantly invite the audience to discuss a number of moral and other issues represented in the various storylines and scenes. Watching soaps involves not least passing judgement on characters and the ethical quality of their actions. The audience 'rehearse' their abilities to judge in these areas, where we all tend to consider ourselves experts; and soaps normally confirm that we are, especially compared to the characters on the screen.

The rumoured 'death of the narrative'

The segmented 'show' structure of television texts has, as just mentioned, been perceived as a threat to the central position of traditional narrative form in our culture and thus its role as a cognitive schemata for both personal experience and the understanding of history. However, such an anxiety was also expressed long before television was introduced into people's everyday lives, in, for instance, an essay published by the German philosopher and critic Walter Benjamin in 1936.

'Experience which is passed from mouth to mouth is the source from which all story-tellers have drawn', Benjamin said (1969: 84). The telling of stories was once primarily an oral activity, by the fireplace, at the table or wherever else people gathered. Benjamin thought that there were two main types of story-teller: the sailor, who could tell stories from far away lands; and the farmer, who knew the local area and its traditions through and through. The apprentices in the various crafts were 'travelling journeymen' and the resident master craftsman had also been a travelling journeyman before he settled down. Thus new experiences could be brought in and blended with those that were gathered and preserved in the local community.

The novel represented a significant break with the age-old oral form of narrative. Not only was it written and thereby fixed in its form, contrary to the traditional story-teller the novelist isolated him/herself from practical everyday life when he or she was telling a story. According to Walter Benjamin, this was effectively the beginning of the end for narrative's function as a mediator of human experience. He says, however (and not quite believably), that there is no reason to deplore this development since 'experience has fallen in value' (1969: 83f.). This had become especially clear from the First World War onwards, according to Benjamin. From that time on, it had become impossible to understand the world and our lives on the basis of historical experience: 'For never has experience been contradicted more thoroughly than strategic experience by tactical warfare, economic experience by inflation, bodily experience by mechanical warfare, moral experience by those in power' (1969: 84).

The drastic shake-up of values and worldviews represented by the First World War and the years that followed it has, in a sense, become part of everyday normality. We have touched on this several times in this book already, particularly in Chapter 1. We are forever 'green' (i.e. naïve) to a very different degree than before: young people cannot rely on their parents' experiences; the parents cannot even rely on their own experiences as safe guidelines for the choices they face. 'Wisdom' in the traditional sense has become difficult to believe in. Instead, there is a general condition of perplexity or irresolution. According to Benjamin, there is a new sort of message or text that is in tune with this situation, one that, even more than the novel, breaks with the traditional, oral narrative: *information*. He thought that Villemessant, the nineteenth-century founder of the Paris newspaper *Le Figaro*, characterized the nature of information well when he said that, to his readers, 'an attic fire in the Latin Quarter is more important than a revolution in Madrid' (1969: 88f.). While traditional stories would be about events that took place far away or long ago, information is primarily about the here and now. Traditional stories were often ambiguous in terms of meaning and difficult to verify; information presents itself as immediately verifiable and immediately understandable in itself. Information 'does not survive the moment in which it was new', Benjamin says. A story, however, is different: 'It does not expend itself. It preserves and concentrates its strength and is capable of releasing it even after a long time' (1969: 90).

It is not hard to see that there is something to Benjamin's description of an historical transition from 'the age of the story' to 'the information age', and that this something is related to the reduced value of historically produced experience in modern, fast-changing times. We are every day exposed to a bombardment of easily forgotten, exact information through all sorts of media and, in soap opera, we also have a type of narrative in which the most overwhelming of catastrophic experiences does not seem to produce any significant change in the characters. Still, there is something not quite right about Benjamin's account of the situation. He is simply not talking about stories or narratives as we have defined them in this chapter. When he says that Villemessant's remark about the fire in the Latin Quarter reveals the nature of information, he does not care whether the report on the fire in Villemessant's paper actually is formed as a narrative in our formal, structural sense of the term. What interests Benjamin is rather a particular *social function* this textual structure had in *cultures based in oral communication* – and it is this function he thinks has been lost in modern society. Traditional, pre-modern society awarded a special status to oral narrative as a mediator of experience and knowledge, especially between generations. More or less poetic, 'polysemic' stories presented ways of understanding the world and our existence in it. But oral narrative was marginalized as a textual form and as a practice by a great number of social and cultural processes such as revolutionary progress in the natural sciences and technology, the establishment of a system of education, industrialization, urbanization and whatever else is covered by the term *modernization*. Rational, scientific forms of understanding, prose writing and 'information' in Benjamin's sense took over many of the functions that oral narrative used to have – and of course changed them in the process.

At the same time, however, a need or even a *desire* for narrative was created, seemingly even more acute than that of earlier times. The late eighteenth and early nineteenth centuries produced a number of new forms of narrative, communicated through *media* – melodramatic plays in theatres, *feuilletons* (serial novels) in newspapers, mass distributed novels in book form and, in the 1890s, finally, film narratives. In the twentieth century, books, magazines, radio and not least television provided huge audiences with enormous numbers of short and long stories, some of them *extremely* long. Most of these stories belong to certain less numerous genres, so that they to a considerable extent may be seen as variations on certain well-known patterns. The pleasure of audiences at these stories is consequently to a large degree a pleasure of *recognition*. As Umberto Eco (1985: 164) has put it, the audience rediscover point by point what they already know, and want to know again. Eco regards the great demand for narratives that offer such pleasures precisely as related to the continuous, rapid changes characteristic of modernity. They offer a moment's repose and relaxation, they provide a sense of a certain stability and continuity that contrasts the daily experience of the opposite.

Narrative is also still a basic cognitive form when and if we wish to summarize or organize our highly diverse experiences in some form or pattern. In our time, and especially in the western world, we tend to imagine time as linear, a line along which major and minor events appear one after another. (We also use other conceptions of time, such as a circular one for the understanding of the changing of the seasons, and a punctual one in which we experience certain events as unique, as 'islands' of time cut loose from everything else. But the linear conception of time is still socially dominant in societies like ours.) We are, moreover, individuals with a will, and our actions are as a rule *intentional* in some sense or other, i.e. guided by some *purpose*. We try to plan our lives to some extent, and continuously have smaller and larger projects going on. Even if life is an ever-ongoing process, we can at any time decide to look back and try to summarize what we have been through and how our projects turned out. And narratives are precisely *backward looking*: They are always told from the back end of a sequence of events. The literary scholar Frank Kermode has in his book *The Sense of an Ending* (1967: 50) pointed out something we touched on at the beginning of this chapter, i.e. that narratives may help us make life meaningful by 'cleansing' our everyday sense of 'pure sequence' by establishing meaningful, understandable relations between a point of departure and some ending. They can do this precisely because they cut out a certain 'stretch' in an ever-ongoing process, and then identify – or construct – causal relations between various points or elements in that sequence.

Since stories establish causal links between the events they comprise, their sequence as a whole may take on a sense of *necessity* and thus of more or less pre-determined *direction*. Stories can thus be seen as *teleological*, i.e. goal-oriented (from the Greek *telos* = goal). The so-called 'grand' narratives about the history of mankind tend to be of such a teleological kind. History is presented as a series of events or steps that follow each other by necessity, moving history ever closer to a predetermined ending. One might say that the Christian religion is based on such a narrative: the creation of Paradise, the fall of man, the coming of the Messiah, Doomsday and the establishment of a new Paradise – these are the main events in this story. A quite similar sequence is found in the traditional Marxist understanding of world history: the paradise of primitive communism is followed by slave society, feudalism and capitalism – until it all, via socialism, ends in a new communist paradise. All modern theories of historical 'stages' that follow each other by some degree of necessity may be said to share important features with these grand narratives.

The philosophical or theoretical (and also artistic and to some extent political) movement called *postmodernism* has had as one of its central slogans – taken from the French philosopher Jean Francois Lyotard ([1979] 1984) – that the grand narratives are over. This means that it is thought that it is no longer possible to summarize social developments in one grand, meaningful narrative. From now on only *small* narratives (local, specific to certain areas or, say, problems) can be told. To postmodernists, this is a positive, liberating situation, since it does away with the determinism inherent in traditional 'grand' narratives and, not least, because it makes possible the telling of historical narratives that do not regard history from the vantage point of the old western centres of a world dominated by colonialism and imperialism. There is clearly much to be said in favour of such a view; but, on the other hand, old-fashioned Marxists of the western kind could say that we have seen how things developed in countries (such as Russia) that tried to skip capitalism and move directly to socialism. Such people, and others, could also say that it seems that social and cultural processes of modernization follow a certain pattern once they really get going. Another type of objection is that postmodernism itself presents postmodernity as a necessary new (and final?) stage after (post) modernity and consequently itself operates within the logic of the grand narratives. Finally, one can, as I do, think that there may well be a degree of causality and direction in historical developments, but that this does not necessarily entail an idea of an end in a certain *telos*. One can thus imagine that there is a rational basis for understanding history as some sort of grand narrative, with innumerable 'storylines' or 'subplots', without a necessary ending. Such a narrative form has in fact conquered the world's TV screens: *the soap opera*!

Narrative's usefulness as an experience-summarizing form is, then, one of the main reasons why it still flourishes, in the media and in our heads. The soap opera genre may also remind us of another main reason, which is that narratives have a unique ability to *engage an audience*. Narratives presuppose, suggest or describe characters that act, and the situations in which they act. They thereby invite us to make use of the fundamentally important human ability called *empathy*, i.e. the ability to place oneself in the position of others. This is often called *identification*, a term that actually means that we become one with that or those with which we identify (see Chapter 1). When we read an ordinary story, see a movie or watch an episode of a series on TV we are supposed to imagine the events so lifelike that we to some extent experience ourselves as participants by proxy, i.e. via the fictitious or real characters the story is about. We may notice the degree to which we have been involved by, for instance, the force of the disappointment or joy *we* experience when *they* (the characters with whom we identify) either go down the drain (their partner leaves with someone else and their bank account is overdrawn) or succeed (they finally become world champions, incredibly rich and married to the most beautiful and smartest person around).

Most of us greatly appreciate such experiences in a story world outside, or parallel to our own everyday lives. People in the media are aware of this, and try to offer these as often as possible. Jesus used stories, in the form of parables, to present moral and religious principles in an engaging way, and innumerable clergymen and teachers have done the same since. The story is also a rhetorical device employed to make knowledge and ideas accessible and engaging. One of the world's best-selling novels ever, Jostein Gaarder's novel about the European history of philosophy, *Sophie's World*, could be one example of this. The age of narrative is not over, by any means.

PART 3

Production: contexts and conditions

8 Public sphere and democracy: ideals and realities

We hold these truths to be self-evident, that all men are created equal, that they are endowed by their Creator with certain unalienable Rights, that among these are Life, Liberty, and the pursuit of Happiness. That to secure these rights, Governments are instituted among Men, deriving their just powers from the consent of the governed. That whenever any Form of Government becomes destructive of these ends, it is the Right of the People to alter or to abolish it, and to institute new Government, laying its foundation on such principles and organizing its powers in such form, as to them shall seem most likely to effect their Safety and Happiness.

(From the US Declaration of Independence, 1776)

Congress shall make no law respecting an establishment of religion, or prohibiting the free exercise thereof; or abridging the freedom of speech, or of the press; or the right of the people peaceably to assemble, and to petition the government for a redress of grievances.

(The First Amendment to the US Constitution, 1791)

These two excerpts from documents fundamental to American democracy should be fairly familiar to most readers of this book. The principles they formulate are also found in a great number of constitutions and declarations all over the globe. The Human Rights Act that came into force in autumn 2000 means they are now, finally, even incorporated in British law. They are absolutely central to modern notions of democracy. All human beings are created equal and should have equal rights in society; governments derive their just powers from the consent of the governed, and those governed therefore have the right to change the government if they so wish. The First Amendment, the opening paragraph of which is known as the Bill of Rights is, then, about freedom of expression and related cultural rights, such as religious freedom, the right to assemble or organize, the freedom of speech and the press etc. The social 'space' in which these rights are exercised openly, i.e. not in private, is *the public sphere*. This is where all the (in principle) equal human beings congregate and communicate in a huge variety of ways, not least in order to find out how the government is doing in terms of securing their Life, Liberty and pursuit of Happiness, and what should be done to improve things, if necessary: the formation of a *public opinion*.

These ideas were considered revolutionary when they were first developed in the so-called Enlightenment era of the eighteenth century, and they still are in some parts of the world. Where they long have been part of society's understanding of itself, they remain a source of critiques of inadequacy and injustice of various kinds. They are not totally unambiguous and there are constant debates on how one should actually understand them in practice. Still, they form some sort of yardstick by which the quality of existing democracies may be measured. Their revolutionary character may become clearer if we look at how they represented a fundamental break with the social forms that prevailed in European countries before the French Revolution.

Underlying the ideas expressed in the quotes above and the texts from which they are taken is a sort of 'map' or 'model' of society that suggests a division of society into three main areas: the private, the public and the state. Such a division is characteristic of a *modern* society; it did not exist in the same way in pre-modern societies. A striking and well-known example of this is the court ceremonies surrounding the French King Louis XIV's dressing and undressing every day and night in his chambers. This was only a superficial sign of how state, public and private realms were integrated in absolutist and feudal societies. Louis, and kings like him, had been granted their royal positions and powers directly from God, not from the people they governed. The nobility had similarly received their local powers from God, via the king. They did not have to consider other people's ideas on how society should be governed (except those of the king, of course). Social power in this sort of society had a very clear, simple pyramidal structure; and at the bottom were the masses of people without any rights or powers.

This society did not only lack our division between a public and a private realm or space, it also lacked, for instance, our distinction between the economic and the political. The king's (and the nobility's) power was total, and interventions in economic matters could not be differentiated from interventions in other sectors – the social order was considered as created by God, so everything was part of one Divine plan. Kings and dukes etc. were not kings and dukes etc. between 9am and 5pm, and then ordinary mortals at night and at the weekend. They were kings and dukes etc. all the time, i.e. our distinction between a *person* and his or her social *position* did not exist. This distinction is precisely linked to the distinction between the private and the public.

There were situations in this pre-modern society that can be seen as parallels to or prototypes of the *public sphere* of modern societies. On the one hand there were situations that have been referred to as instances of *representative public-ness*. These were occasions where power was publicly demonstrated or *represented*, most often festive occasions, with verbal and musical panegyric. Decisions were made elsewhere, following discussions that only involved those in power and their closest advisers. On the other hand, there were various kinds of popular gathering where one could hear news and discuss various local issues, such as at fairs, in the village marketplace and outside the church. This has been called a *plebeian public sphere*, after the name given to poor people in ancient Rome. But at none of these sorts of occasions did the people gathered have any say about the decisions of those in power.

The terms mentioned above were coined by the German philosopher and sociologist Jürgen Habermas in his book *The Structural Transformation of the Public Sphere* ([1962] 1989). Habermas here describes and analyses how the modern public sphere emerged historically, and how it developed up until the time at which he was writing, when it appeared fundamentally different from the *classical* bourgeois public sphere. Habermas thought that the public sphere in post-Second World War western countries had acquired the characteristics of representative public-ness again: power is publicly represented, but the processes leading to politically important decisions are not open to the public – the public sphere has been *refeudalized*. In order to understand this idea, we should take a closer look at Habermas's description of the 'classical' public sphere.

The classical public sphere

The engine behind the development of a bourgeois public sphere was, according to Habermas, the *market economy*, i.e. the rise of capitalism. Those who were involved as owners and entrepreneurs in this economy – the bourgeoisie or capitalists, if you like – were not happy with a situation in which kings could introduce whatever laws, customs and taxes they pleased without asking anyone. The bourgeoisie became the social basis for ideas about a democratic public sphere in which the premises for the government's policies were to be developed through public discussion. As private businessmen – *bourgeois* – they competed with each other. In economic matters the amount of capital each of them controlled determined their power. They therefore had, so to speak, to leave the *private* economic area and move into a different 'space' – the public sphere – in order to discuss their *common* interests in relation to the state or king. In the public sphere they were all, in principle, equals; they were *citizens* who shared the ambition to clarify universal or general interests, and no participant in the public discourse could claim any greater importance than others by pointing to his position in other contexts. Only *arguments* were to count here. Modern ideas of universal human rights are closely tied to the idea of the public sphere.

But these people were not only economically active bourgeois and politically active citizens. At home, they were simply human beings. In this private *sphere of intimacy*, they were preoccupied with love and family life, reading and conversation, religious and philosophical issues and, often, various amateur artistic activities. Historically, it was the practices and concerns of the sphere of intimacy that were the point of departure for the first forms of the public sphere, i.e. public and eventually professional versions of home activities. People met to engage in religious activities, readings, theatrical performances and other artistic events, and then they *discussed* their experiences in the cafés of the time (the 'coffee houses'), in semi-public literary *salons*, and in print media of various kinds (pamphlets, journals, magazines, newspapers, books). The *cultural public sphere* (Habermas calls it 'literary', or 'the world of letters') was, in other words, established first; the *political public sphere* came later.

The borders between the two parts of the public sphere were marked in the sense that they centred on different *institutions* – churches, salons, theatres and publishing houses etc. in the cultural sphere, and public meetings and parliamentary assemblies in the political. But, at the same time, the borders were more flimsy then than they mostly appear to be today and, especially in the press, both of them would come together. Front pages might have literary criticism and debates. Theatres were often central political institutions. In the mid-nineteenth century, the first socialist organization in Norway was allowed to say more or less whatever it pleased in print media and public speeches, but when it rented a theatre in the capital and put on a political play, the police moved in. The central position and function of the theatre was a precondition for the work of playwrights such as Henrik Ibsen who wanted their plays to create public debate on political and politically related ethical issues. But the arts were also more generally of great importance as providers of material for ongoing public debates of politics, morality, philosophical and existential issues. Habermas expresses the relations between the sphere of intimacy and the cultural public sphere ('the world of letters'), with particular reference to the reading of novels, in the following memorable way: 'They [the bourgeois strata] formed the public sphere of a rational-critical debate in the world of letters within which the subjectivity originating in the interiority of the conjugal family, by communicating with itself, attained clarity about itself' (Habermas, 1989: 51).

In the cultural public sphere, women, servants and other 'dependent' categories of people were allowed to take part to some extent. This was not the case in the political section of the public sphere. There, two criteria for admission applied: property and education. 'Education' must here be understood in a broad sense, as in the German *Bildung*. This latter term refers to a mixture of knowledge, values or norms, which was normally acquired by growing up in a good home, going to school and other forms of socialization that were not open to just anyone. But the other criterion, property, was more absolute and concrete. The rationale for this was the idea that those who were to take part in debates and decisions should be financially independent so that they were harder to bribe into taking this or that position on the issues debated. In a number of countries the right to vote was for a long time restricted to people who had an income above a certain level, who owned land etc. Only through the introduction of universal suffrage for men and women of all social classes, in most cases way into the twentieth century, were all adults officially recognized as fully *autonomous subjects*, worthy of full participation in the public sphere.

The idea of the democratic public sphere rests on the idea of the autonomous subject. The idea was, and is, that every citizen is to take part in the *formation of a public opinion* in a free, autonomous way, i.e. be able, independently, to form an opinion on the various issues by judging the information and arguments presented. The goal of public discourse was to identify the general will or the common good, and all participants were in principle to disregard their own private interests as business executives etc. The power of arguments was to decide, not, as mentioned above, the social status or financial strength of individual participants in the public discourse. One was supposed to be willing to give in and change one's position if better arguments for a different position were put forward. How often do we now see, for instance on TV, that a leading politician slaps his forehead and exclaims, 'You are actually quite right. I have been totally wrong here!' Such things were hardly common in nineteenth-century debates either, but this is what the ideal was like. Discussions in the public sphere were to aim for a *consensus*. The principles of the public sphere were primarily *the bourgeoisie's understanding of itself*, and the degree to which this was actually realized in practice obviously varied, to say the least. This is, importantly, not to say that there was anything wrong with the ideal. The idea or theory of the 'classical' public sphere is, first and foremost, a *normative* one; it is quite problematic, to say the least, as a description of real historical circumstances.

The task of the media in the public sphere was to mediate argumentation, information and general food for thought in books, magazines and newspapers, i.e. function as forums for public discourse. Newspapers, which in many cases were started as outlets for advertising and directly useful economic information were, however, in the classical public sphere most often also vehicles for individuals or groups with particular political and cultural views. They were, in other words, both *arenas* and *actors* – just like today's newspapers and other media.

The *normative ideas* underlying Habermas's notion of the classical public sphere live on. They remain a standard for how the public sphere and the media should function in a democracy. Basic values, such as freedom of expression and freedom of information, have their origins here, and the same goes for the related fundamental idea that democracy rests on autonomous, well-informed and actively participating citizens. It is a problem with Habermas's book that it is unclear whether he is describing a once-existing historical reality or a set of ideas that have never been fully or perfectly realized. But this lack of clarity may in fact belong to the matter itself: the ideas have been partially realized at some times in some places, but never fully anywhere at any time. Habermas does, however, quite obviously argue (1962) that the public sphere was, in certain fundamental ways, closer to its own ideals in the late seventeenth and early nineteenth centuries than in the post-Second World War years. At the time of writing, he thought that the ideas of a truth- and common good-seeking public discourse had changed from an ideal to an *ideology*: they covered up the fact that a fundamental change had taken place in the public sphere, one that was not beneficial to democracy. In later years Habermas significantly modified this view, seeing today's western democracies in a much more positive light.

The public sphere and conceptions of democracy

Especially in Germany and the Scandinavian countries, Habermas's study of the public sphere became a central source of inspiration for scholarly work in the 1970s, not least for work that eventually became today's humanistic media and communication studies. A main reason for this was its holistic, critical and historical approach to culture, politics and social life in general. This made it possible, for instance, to place and study factual and fictional literature, theatre and other arts in a meaningful, overarching social-historical context. At the same time, it was also regarded as a historically argued critique of serious shortcomings in western democracy, confronting today's realities with the officially still-cherished eighteenth-century ideals. But the strong interest in the book among radical students and younger scholars also reflected the fact that the book's understanding of democracy in many ways coincided with the (somewhat naive and unclear) ideas of a 'real' democracy, which were widespread on the more or less academic left in the 1970s. As a former student activist, now a colleague of mine, once put it: 'we imagined a democratic society as one giant teach-in or student meeting'. Habermas in a way provided a theoretical and historical basis for such ideas, ideas that already existed in a spontaneous, everyday form among students at the time.

Habermas's book presents a very clearly *deliberative* understanding of democracy (from the Latin *deliberare*). The public sphere is a space in which anyone, in principle, has an equal right to speak, where arguments rather than social positions and material resources are decisive, where untenable arguments and positions are given up through rational debate. Political lines and concrete measures would ideally be based in a *consensus* achieved through the exchange of arguments – they would not come about as compromises resulting from a tug of war between fixed, non-publicly based social interests. The radical student culture of the 1960s and 1970s could represent something like this, partly because the students might believe in such ideals, but also because they, to a high degree, shared a certain social position and thus had a number of interests in common. In this regard they might well resemble an idealized gathering of bourgeois men somewhere between 1750 and 1850.

The deliberative understanding of democracy stands in opposition to other, in some ways more 'realistic' and even cynical, conceptions of what characterizes political processes in western democracies. The US-based Norwegian political philosopher Jon Elster has provided a synthesized characterization of some of these (Elster [1986] 1997). He points out the following main features of what are called *social choice* theories of democracy:

- they regard the political process as purely instrumental (i.e. as an instrument to achieve certain things)
- the decisive political act is private (individual, secret voting)
- the goal of politics is the optimal compromise between opposed and actually antagonistic private interests.

In line with this it is also supposed that:

- both the preferences of the actors and the alternatives they are faced with are *given*, not dynamic and changeable entities.

Politics is, in this way, understood as analogous with market mechanisms and the choices of consumers on the basis of their private interests and desires. This has consequences for how the role of mass media is conceived. In a deliberative understanding of democracy, not least that of Habermas, they have a central role as arenas for the formation of public opinion, for real debates resulting in revised views among participants. In light of a 'social choice' type of understanding, on the other hand, the mass media primarily become manipulative instruments for the production of certain preferences among members of the audience. Such a view was, for instance, expressed directly by the economist and political scientist Schumpeter, who once said that the will of the people is the outcome of the political process, not its

234   **Understanding Media Culture**

'motive power' (quoted in Elster [1986] 1997: 27). As Elster points out, this view is fully in line with how Schumpeter regards the market: to him also the preferences of consumers were largely open to manipulation.

One could say that the market-analogous 'social choice' understanding of democracy makes virtues out of the tendencies Habermas deplores and condemns in his study of the public sphere. A more pragmatic, and in a sense more realistic, view might be that the deliberative and the 'social choice' versions point to two different, co-existing dimensions of political processes in western democracies. It is evidently correct that political decisions and measures will most often take the form of compromise between different social interests. It is also correct that voters ultimately make their choice between alternatives in the privacy of the voting booth, and that these choices are often made on the basis of private interests rather than concerns for the well-being of society as a whole; but at the same time the 'social choice' perspective appears inadequate in relation to very central aspects of real political processes, not least in a longer historical perspective. It is, for instance, possible to point out a number of obvious, more or less consensual, changes over time in political preferences and priorities. The role of ecological questions and the views on women's roles in society are two examples; the perception of the apartheid regime in South Africa and the understanding of the situation for Palestinians are two more. Over two or three decades we have seen major shifts in the dominant views on these issues in most western countries.

The 'social choice' perspective cannot really grasp the *dynamics* of democratic processes that must be ascribed to the existence of a public discourse and a complex public life, including a number of struggles for various 'causes', in which the mass media also play other roles than purely manipulative ones. The mass media are, as we pointed out above, both actors and arenas in these processes. They do, of course, influence the formation of opinion in both capacities, but this influence is hardly adequately described by the term 'manipulation'. The influence is moreover not exercised on the behalf of political parties (any more), the entities voters choose between in elections. Schumpeter's view of media audiences as being quite easily manipulated is also contradicted by modern media theory and empirical research. This is not to say that the media are without power to influence people in various ways and on various planes, but ideas about simple stimulus-response relations were discarded long ago (see Chapter 2 of the present volume, on influence). However cynical-realistic one wishes to be in an analysis of modern liberal democracy, there is no getting around the crucial element of deliberation, of public debate and opinion formation.

Whether one regards the individual member of society as analogous to the consumer in the market-place or as an actively participating citizen, it should be possible to agree that both views *normatively* come together in the idea that the *well-informed* individual, one who has a solid basis of knowledge and information for her or his opinions and actions, is of key importance in democracies. The *freedom of information*, understood as the right to a varied, truly pluralistic menu of cultural products, and substantial information and knowledge, is thus absolutely fundamental to any conception of democracy. ('Knowledge' can here be briefly defined as information integrated in broader contexts and thus understood in a more comprehensive way.) One could similarly argue that *freedom of expression* must also be regarded as fundamental to democracy in any understanding of the term. These two fundamental rights are each others' preconditions. There are still reasons to argue that the former is, in a sense, primary: it is the prerequisite for *well-informed* participation of any kind, be it public utterances or voting.

The strength of a deliberative, normative conception of democracy, like the one Habermas represents, is not least that it invites evaluations of the *quality* of the information offered in the public sphere, while it also focuses on the economic and organizational basis of public communication. It does not reduce democracy to majority votes and 'market share' for political parties.

The structural transformation of the public sphere, and 'tabloidization'

According to Habermas, two processes had, by 1960, effectively squeezed the air out of the public sphere. On the one hand, the state in western countries had become a very active one, constantly 'interfering' in the private areas, both the sphere of work and commerce, and the sphere of intimacy. In modern welfare states economic policies and measures in areas such as social and family policies deprived these areas of their autonomy. All of this came about after the criteria for admission to the public sphere had been changed so that (gradually) anyone was allowed to participate. The parliamentary and other representatives of the labour movement in the public sphere did not primarily see themselves as truth-seeking individuals but as representatives of a social class and its interests, based in the (private) economic sphere. The organization of political parties and the representation of non-bourgeois social groups changed the character of the political public sphere forever. To a great extent it became an arena for struggle and compromise between privately (non-publicly) defined interests. These tended to demand that the state engaged itself in areas where, according to classical liberal political theory, it was not supposed to be interfering.

In this perspective, the expansion of the right to vote and the introduction of organized, conflicting social interests in the public sphere becomes one of the explanations for the structural transformation of the public sphere referred to in the title of Habermas's book. Many of us will have problems accepting that anyone should deplore the expansion of democracy, but the point is still that it contributed to a change in the character of public discourse. Ideas such as 'the general will' and 'the common good' immediately became more problematic when real and deep social cleavages and conflicts were directly represented. Debates in the public sphere, then, appeared more like a tug of war between social interests where the goal was more or less acceptable compromises, rather than consensus.

It is perhaps easier to understand that the transformation of the public sphere has been perceived as a process of deterioration or even 'descent' if we look at the other 'process' that 'squeezed the air out of' it: the media – the arenas and actors of the public sphere – had become commercial enterprises. In the 'classical' public sphere, making money used to be secondary to contributing to enlightenment and the formation of public opinion. Logics that had previously been dominant only in the economic sphere had now moved to dominate the public sphere and transformed its very way of functioning, according to Habermas. The media's new desire for ever larger profits led them to give priority to what is commonly seen as entertaining material rather than socially relevant information and debate (and, indeed, material of the latter sort is presented in as entertaining a form as possible). The first of these tendencies means giving priority to material that is dramatic or spectacular in itself (such as various accidents, natural disasters, fires, violent crimes), or possibly sweet, cosy or just odd (the chimp in the zoo has got a new girlfriend etc.).

In France such stories are called *faits divers*, i.e. 'various facts'. They are mostly from outside the directly political field and are not necessarily generally relevant other than as a bit of drama that provides diversion, an emotional kick, or whatever, in our everyday lives. The second tendency is about making the directly politically relevant material appear as stories about personal conflicts, moral backbone, courage, grief or whatever moral and psychological *topoi* (see Chapter 6) that are chosen in what may be termed *melodramatic* journalism. This is a form of journalism that interprets or translates more or less abstract social and political matters as issues of everyday psychology or morality (cf. below and Gripsrud, 1992). These are the two tendencies referred to in the term *tabloidization*, along with the emphasis on brief stories, visualization and (in the press) screaming headlines.

The word 'tabloid' is related to the word 'tablet' (i.e. something small) and originally referred to a newspaper format half the size of a traditional broadsheet; but it is now also a name for a type of material and perspective that is not, in fact, found in all tabloid-sized newspapers but that, on the other hand, seems to be spreading in broadcast media. Tabloid media in this sense address audiences less as citizens than as *consumers of experiences* (see Chapter 9). It is, however, well worth remembering that both tabloid media and critiques of them are much older phenomena than current debates about the media seem to acknowledge. The British *Daily Mirror* was supposedly the first tabloid newspaper, in both form and content, from 1903, and in a Danish encyclopaedia from 1915 I once came across the following entry under 'newspapers'.

> The press is, with the exception of most of the German press and a few fine and restrained representatives in other civilized countries that are strong due to age and tradition, in a process of democratisation, i.e. the newspaper is written for the mass and not for those really educated. It follows the taste and not always delicate inclinations of common people. It is written more for those who simply can read than for those who are able to read intelligently and critically. Accordingly, its material and style becomes very different: the emphasis is on news, on having as much news as possible, and so telephone and telegraph are more valuable members of staff than the instructive journalist. The editorial disappears, and any coherent article becomes *tit-bits*, is chopped up and paragraph by paragraph equipped with more or less exciting and sensational titles. Such a medium no longer has room for real criticism; it becomes popular and not literary. There are of course still newspapers whose journalism meets with proper literary standards; but on the whole modern journalism as it has developed over the last couple of decades is of a totally different kind and most of today's leaders of the press in the various countries form their newspapers according to the taste of the mass and place them on an intellectually limited plane of culture.
>
> (*Salmonsens Konversationsleksikon* [a major Danish encyclopaedia],
> Copenhagen, 1915)

The fact that tabloidization and the critique of it is more than 100 years old is worth bearing in mind if one wishes to avoid an overdramatization of current developments and to try to approach a current critique of the media with a bit of healthy scepticism. On the other hand, the fact that a tendency is old does not mean that it should not still be met with critique and a defence of elementary ideals. An important problem here is, however, that so much of the critique of typically tabloid style and content is fraught with contempt for large parts of the public that is supposedly the basis of a functioning democracy. This should be well illustrated by the above quote. So-called tabloid media can, in a more optimistic and less elitist perspective, be regarded partly as devoted to the popularization of political and cultural issues, and partly as addressing existential aspects of people's lives that ordinary politics is more or less incapable of grasping. 'Tabloid' news items in an otherwise 'serious' newscast or newspaper could be seen as elements that allow the everyday concerns and interests of 'ordinary', non-intellectual and relatively powerless people to be represented in public discourse (cf. Langer, 1998). Such points in favour of tabloid media forms must be taken into account, but they do not, in my opinion, mean that we should stop critiquing many aspects of current tabloid media: other popular forms, with different political implications, are conceivable (cf. Gripsrud, 2000).

Public debate is often, in our day and age, arranged as a sort of stage entertainment where the audience is only supposed to applaud or boo. It is frequently presented as a form of duel where positions are clearly defined as opposites at the outset and where nobody expects an open, reasonable attitude, only verbal dog fights or, at least, competition. Debates on television in connection with election campaigns are commented on in the press as if they were sports events. The participants' rhetorical abilities are often evaluated with little consideration for the actual views argued and the substance of the arguments. In the cultural public sphere, similar things can be found; a public that used to be interested in rational reasoning about cultural matters is now (turned into?) a public or audience of entertainment-hungry consumers. The public sphere is as a result not so much a space where opinion is *formed*; it has rather become a space where opinions – and power – are *displayed* or demonstrated, having been developed behind closed doors. It has (again) become a *representative* or *refeudalized* public sphere, according to Habermas. The important political debates – those in which arguments really count and where the participants are reaching for a consensus of some sort – take place in the chambers of party leaders, in government meetings and at the top level of various organizations. Debates in parliamentary assemblies are not, in this respect, real debates. They are mostly about demonstrating that the political parties actually do have opinions on a number of issues and also have gifted speakers, especially when debates are televised. The same applies to party conventions. What goes on in the hall in front of delegates is the presentation of a series of pre-scripted speeches, often primarily written with media audiences in mind. All the really decisive discussions take place in committee meetings off-stage where only a highly select group of members are involved. When television and other media move in, the real formation of opinion moves out.

In accordance with this logic, the media are less engaged in the formation of opinion than in *publicity*, PR (i.e. a form of advertising, directed at producing support for already formulated political ideas and suggestions). It is now common to speak of the 'marketing' or 'selling' of political opinions, decisions and parties. An increasing part of public life is thought about and talked about in marketing terms. PR agencies, 'spin doctors' etc. have become ever more important elements in political life (cf., for example, Ewen, 1996).

The public at large is not normally aware of most of these well-paid activities. Most of us just watch the news or read the papers; we do not know how certain stories were fed to the media by, for instance, PR people hired by wealthy companies.

This principle of *publicity* also impacts areas or institutions that previously had no need for 'marketing'. Publicly owned universities in Europe offer but one example; the 'marketing' of their activities and employees has now become a necessary element in their struggle to maintain, or reduce the drop in, their level of funding. A policeman interviewed on local radio where I live was asked if he thought that the control of speeding and drunken driving he had just spent a whole night conducting would have any influence on the future frequency of such dangerous practices. 'No,' he said, 'but we do have to market ourselves'. Within the logic of publicity, bad rhetoric is good rhetoric in the sense that publicity breaks with the ethos of good rhetoric. Communication tends to become purely instrumental and manipulative. Good rhetoric's demands for truthfulness and solid, logical argumentation give way to an orientation towards *effect*. What works is good. The end justifies the means.

'The tyranny of intimacy'

In the 'refeudalized' public sphere it is not only the borders between the state and the private realm, and between the economy and the public sphere, that are weakened or erased. The same applies to the border between the sphere of intimacy and the public sphere. This is particularly evident if we look at those who are actors in the public light, e.g. politicians and various celebrities. Their private lives are defined as publicly relevant, in roughly the same way as was that of Louis XIV. But this is only one of many aspects of the process one could call the 'intimization' of the public sphere.

The American sociologist Richard Sennett has, in his book *The Fall of Public Man* ([1977] 1986), approached the changes in the public sphere from a slightly different angle than Habermas. He points out how 'intimate' and 'warm' relationships between people these days are regarded as unambiguously positive. According to Sennett, this is tied to the strong interest every individual now has in his or her own psyche. (Other theoreticians talk about *narcissism* as a characteristic of today's western world.) The most important thing in life is perceived as the quest to 'get to know oneself', so that one can then 'realize' or 'express' oneself. Within this way of thinking, one primarily learns about oneself through intimate, 'warm' personal relations. Intimacy and 'warmth' thus acquire a status as criteria for the evaluation of all social life. What is impersonal is cold and distanced, and consequently bad. Public life becomes less attractive to the extent that it appears separate from the sphere of intimacy and the sorts of human relations that dominate there. People prefer instead to devote themselves to warm and intimate relations.

Public life is thus evaluated on the basis of this principle of intimacy. Those who appear in public will be judged by the extent to which they appear warm and intimate *persons*, even if they talk about highly distant, cool and abstract matters. The fundamental values and truth are within us. This is the basis for the misunderstanding we mentioned in the chapter on rhetoric (Chapter 6), which is that those who are (or appear to be) *honest* are also perceived as speaking *truthfully*. Here is one example of how this may work, taken from Scandinavia in the late 1980s.

A leading leftist politician was very concerned about unemployment, and severely exaggerated the number of people who were actually unemployed. In a TV interview he was confronted with statistics, which showed clearly that unemployment figures were not very high at all. He then answered by telling the story of a profound emotional experience he had recently had. He had seen a man looking through the contents of a trash bin, seemingly driven by dire need. This had been such a shocking experience that it made him really care about the problem of unemployment. By thus speaking 'frankly' about his personal feelings, he avoided answering the question he had been asked. But the chances are that viewers did not experience this as problematic since he was such an honest and sensitive guy (Johansen, 1999).

A famous historical example of such a dubious exploitation of *ethos* in politics is Richard Nixon's so-called 'Checkers speech' of 1952. Nixon had received secret and illegal financial contributions to his campaign; this became a great scandal, particularly since Nixon had emphasized law and order so much. But Nixon saved the situation by going on TV and crying a little bit. Not too much; just enough to show he was a sensitive man, while he was talking about his honest intentions and subjective innocence … and his dog, Checkers. He loved dogs. Consequently he was a good man and people should forget about the money question. This worked according to the intention. Within the logic of intimacy, the motives and feelings of politicians are more important than their actions.

Politicians and others may make use of 'intimacy' as a rhetorical device. But intimacy is also something the media want and therefore seek. Newspapers, radio and television love to talk about the 'human' side of politicians and other influential people. The use of 'human' in expressions such as this, literally implies that their *public* functions, which in fact are the reason why they are interesting to us, are regarded as *in*human. A somewhat strange idea in a democracy, one might say. The point is, anyway, that there is now a historically new relationship between the private and personal on the one hand and the public on the other. Broadcast media have contributed to this situation by bringing the public sphere and public figures directly into people's homes. One result of this is that politicians have had to learn to address people in a different way to that they would have used had they been addressing large gatherings of people from a rostrum. In the 1930s, Adolf Hitler had not quite grasped this transition and continued to scream like a madman, even when he was speaking on the radio. Franklin D. Roosevelt was one of the first to understand how to adjust to the intimacy of the new medium. In his famous 'Fireside Talks', he addressed the American people in a warm, relaxed, intimate way, and this contributed significantly to their image of him as a 'human' president, and thus also to his popularity. Television makes such a subdued performance even more necessary. Anyone who waves his or her arms and speaks loudly, as if on a rostrum at a mass meeting, will appear a lunatic or fool, or both (cf. Johansen, 1999, where a number of other cultural-historical conditions are also invoked in an analysis of these matters.)

Television's particular contribution to the breakdown of the border between the public and the private is in part linked to the fact that it continuously shows politicians and other public figures in close-up. They are no longer the quite distant characters known only from newspapers and an occasional mass meeting. We now know very well their little tics, their tendency to sweat or blush etc. We judge them in close-up on the screen much as we judge other people we meet in everyday contexts: do they look sympathetic and trustworthy? The world of politics has, in many ways, moved closer to us, and this contributes to the increased importance of looks, behaviour or 'personal style'. Public figures have to take this into consideration when appearing in the media; Erving Goffman (1959) distinguished between a *frontstage* and a *backstage* sort of conduct. But in the new, TV-dominated public sphere, a *middle region behaviour* is the norm, according to Joshua Meyrowitz in his book *No Sense of Place* (1985). This middle region style is personal, and even intimate at times, but the continued existence of a *deep backstage* indicates that there are still some limits to intimacy and exhibitionism in public. Television's breaking down of boundaries applies to other fields too. Boys now know more about the world of girls than ever before and children who watch news, soaps and sitcoms know a lot more about the world of adults than children used to know (or perhaps should know). These processes evidently have a number of consequences, not least in relation to the formation of identities (cf. Chapter 1).

The influence that structures of the public sphere have on the formation of our identities is not, of course, something that came about with television. In the next section we will focus on types of public sphere other than the large and general one, and their importance as locations for the production of identities of considerable political and cultural importance.

For the marginalized and excluded: semi-alternative public spheres

The exclusion from the early European bourgeois public sphere of women, workers and peasants meant that these people felt a need to organize what one might call *semi-alternative* public spheres. This term, then, refers to the conglomerates of various associations and forms of communication that were, or are, tied to certain social groups and movements that are or were marginal to, or excluded from, the bourgeois or dominant public sphere. They partly serve as alternative public spheres, but generally also are, or become, more or less integrated elements in the overarching context of the dominant or general public sphere. Habermas did not discuss such semi-alternative public spheres in his study, but later contributions, both theoretical and historical, have done so in critical dialogue with Habermas's perspectives.

Clearly, the so-called 'classical' public sphere was conceived in terms that were not gender-neutral. The participants in the critical-rational public discourse were male, and women had basically to stay at home, in the sphere of intimacy. This was simply the way things were, according to the dominant ideology. However, as mentioned above, women were to a considerable extent allowed an active role in the early 'literary' or cultural public sphere, for instance as writers and as organizers of so-called salons, i.e. semi-public gatherings where literature and other art were presented and discussed. Throughout the nineteenth century, women also participated actively in a number of political movements, but they were not as a rule allowed to play a leading role or to advocate equal rights for women. Bourgeois and middle-class women formed charities and thus, to an extent, were publicly active there; but probably more important was the formation of various movements related to moral issues, particularly relating to sexuality. These were, both in the USA and in Europe, important in the early stages of a women's rights or feminist movement, such as that of the suffragettes in Britain, and similar movements elsewhere. To the extent that women were disenfranchised and also otherwise excluded from the dominant public sphere, one could regard the meetings, media and other forms of communication developed in these contexts as semi-separate or semi-alternative public spheres for women (cf., for instance, Fraser, 1989; Ryan, 1990)

But, at the same time, they clearly wanted to influence, and succeeded in influencing, the dominant (male) public sphere, and the aim of the early feminist movement was that women should have full civil rights, i.e. be accepted as autonomous subjects, fully capable of exercising their democratic rights. *The universalism of the principles of the public sphere was a source of inspiration and an arsenal of arguments for this and other social movements, and was played out against the prejudices of gender, class and race that were in breach of the universalistic ideas.* Those excluded from full participation on equal terms in the public sphere could, and can, rightly argue that their exclusion contradicts the very foundations of democracy. This is why the historically white, male, bourgeois ideas of democracy have also inspired and become powerful tools for all excluded and repressed non-white, non-bourgeois and non-male social groups, which have struggled for their emancipation and equal rights over the last 200 years. Their movements have in part been separate contexts of communication – where members supported each other in various ways and where their interests, strategies and tactics have been discussed and clarified – and in part elements of the overarching imperfect democratic context they were aiming to change. Directly and indirectly radical movements would also question the 'topography' of bourgeois society of which the classical public sphere was a part – in particular the division between the public and the private realms. Feminists would challenge the idea of the 'sphere of intimacy' as an area outside of politics where the state should in no way interfere, and might for instance also question the way in which 'rationality' was commonly understood in the public sphere. Other movements have had agendas with related and additional critiques.

The early organization of the working class, such as the English Chartist movement of the mid-nineteenth century, was to a large extent about being recognized as citizens, as members of society on equal terms. However, within this and similar movements elsewhere, there were more radical tendencies, raising a more fundamental critique of bourgeois society and its capitalist economic organization. So-called utopian socialist movements incorporated in their very forms as organizations a totally different relationship between the private and public realms of society, particularly the abolition of private ownership of the means of production. Such a de-privatization of the economy could be regarded as a democratization of it. The modern labour movement that appeared in the late nineteenth century was, however, mostly oriented towards integration in the existing society, and this was expressed in the way it was internally organized. It 'mimicked' bourgeois society's division between economy and politics by organizing a trades union movement separate from political parties (this is less true of the anarcho-syndicalists in certain countries). The labour movement was formed as a sort of 'campsite' where its members waited for entry into society at large. Not only did it have its own meeting places, cultural activities and media, it also developed various social institutions (unemployment support, health insurance) on a co-operative basis. This first sort of 'campsite' organization was in a sense forced on the movement by its exclusion from bourgeois society. Later, particularly after the First World War, when the working class had acquired the right to vote and in many ways was already integrated in a number of social institutions within the dominant public sphere, and labour parties even formed governments in some European countries, labour movements would often actively propagate and organize a '*campsite public sphere*' for different reasons. An extensive network of organizations and media was to offer alternatives to all the associative forms, cultural activities and media of bourgeois society. There was not only a labour press; there was also a workers' sports movement, a workers' theatre movement, workers' films, workers' literature, workers' scout movement, workers' chess clubs, and so on and so forth. The labour movement was to be a 'world of its own' where members would be ideologically prepared for the socialist society that lay ahead.

The German sociologist Oskar Negt and film-maker Alexander Kluge introduced the term 'campsite public sphere' (German = *Lageröffentlichkeit*) in their book *Public Sphere and Experience* ([1972] 1993). Negt and Kluge saw this type of organization and the ideology that went with it in the social democratic and communist European labour movements as repeating limits to radical democratization they thought inherent in the bourgeois model. They were much more enthusiastic about what they called a *proletarian public sphere*, a sort of communicative space which, they claimed, could appear in particular historical situations of social struggle where the boundaries between the public and the private, between the political and the cultural, between men and women etc. were more or less erased. Examples could be found in the history of working-class movements such as the above-mentioned Chartist movement or in certain so-called wildcat strikes that involved not only the workers but also their families and entire communities. These were occasions where the various areas of people's everyday lives in a sense came together, where it was possible to experience the ways in which personal life and work situation, the political and the economic, art and everyday practices are all closely related to each other and must be understood as a whole. The proletarian public sphere is, in other words, to be understood both as a unique opportunity for learning from experience and as a glimpse of a utopian social situation. But alas, these tend to be short-lived.

More enduring, and indeed a lot more important, in most people's lives from the early twentieth century onwards are what Negt and Kluge call *public spheres of production*. This is their term for the public space created by what others would call the cultural industries, the media and cultural forms that are openly and fully commercial. The public spheres of production are not (and do not claim to be) 'above' or beyond the (private) sphere of manufacturing and marketing, even if they also may try at times to portray themselves as linked to for instance the traditional institutions of art in the cultural public sphere. Negt and Kluge's point, however, is not that of the traditional Frankfurt School critique of the cultural industries, it is rather that these 'public spheres of production' somehow manage to relate more directly to the needs, desires and experiences of their audiences or customers than the traditional, bourgeois public sphere. They do this by exploiting these needs, desires and experiences as 'raw material' for their products. The raw material is thus, in a sense, deprived of specificity and substance (generalized, standardized, presented in preconceived formulas). But, according to Negt and Kluge, the industrially produced commodities (movies, TV shows or whatever) still represent and thus bring to light the desires and experiences of 'ordinary people', especially groups formally or informally excluded from the dominant public sphere, more than the products of the 'legitimate' public institutions and media.

There is obviously much to be said for this line of thought. It is basically a way of formulating the quite widespread view that the key to the success of the cultural industries or commercial mass media is that they, *via the market*, are in a sort of dialogue with their audiences and their life-worlds. People obviously find much of the output (but not the flops) from these industries *relevant* to their experiences and situations. Negt and Kluge also, importantly, maintain a critical edge related to that of the Frankfurt School when they talk about how the commodities of the public spheres of production also distort (standardize, put into formulas) the needs, desires and experiences they use and address. Also this public sphere, like the traditional, dominant one, is 'organized from above', and not 'from below', 'by the experiencing subjects themselves, on the basis of their context of living' (Hansen, 1991: 12), as in the so-called proletarian public sphere. A problem with the 'public spheres of production' is furthermore that the majority of their publics are not involved in a critical public discourse on the texts or products they are offered. The discourses about them are mostly quite hard to distinguish from the discourses of marketing and consumer advice. Interestingly, film-maker Alexander Kluge chose in the 1980s to produce a regular programme about film (old and new, documentary and fiction) with one of the most blatantly commercial TV channels in Germany (and, as far as I know, it's still running). His programme is very much one that represents rational-critical public discourse on film and other media, and thus it belongs in the 'proper' public sphere. But the channel in question (SAT1) would be categorized as a 'public sphere of production'. Kluge could thus be perceived as trying to carve out a space for functions typical of the 'proper' public sphere in the, by now, in many ways dominant commercial-industrial public sphere of production. This is, in a way, both commendable and heroic. The question is to what extent his weekly late-night intellectual programme really makes a difference, especially to the audiences he is, in principle, trying to address.

The project of enlightenment and state support for the public sphere

The public sphere was in principle, in both its cultural and its political sections, to be free from any state control or intervention; but the state has in modern societies always had a responsibility for certain types of infrastructure and services, from street lights and sewers to police and education, and so the public sphere is also a space where governments have been active to a varying degree, and in variable forms. This responsibility has been differently interpreted in different countries at different times. In the following paragraphs we will take a brief look at some of the ways in which the state is and has been involved in both infrastructure and services within the public sphere.

The National Theatre in Washington DC opened in 1835. This may be seen as an early example of government intervention in the US cultural public sphere. There may have been many reasons for this: a desire to emulate cultural institutions in certain European nations, a need for a place where elites could meet in style, a wish to create a cultural institution that would symbolize national unity or, simply, an interest in serious theatrical art. However, the main reason is simply that the establishment of such a theatre could not be left to the market. But the establishment of public cultural institutions in the US has not normally been a government priority. It has been left to individuals or associations to organize and fund museums, symphony orchestras, theatres and the like. The New Deal period in the 1930s was an exceptional political period in many ways, and its public support for the arts was one of the things that made it exceptional. The present main federal institution for public funding of the arts, the National Endowment for the Arts, was not established until 1964.

In the UK, the idea of a national theatre was first aired in 1848, but it did not materialize until 1951, when the Queen laid the first foundation stone for its building; or, rather, in 1963, when its first production was actually presented; or, in 1976, when the Queen officially opened the National Theatre, the building that had finally been constructed. The Arts Council, the UK's present main public funding body for the arts, was established in 1945 as a successor to the Council for the Encouragement of Music and the Arts (CEMA), which was at first funded privately by an American millionaire (!) in 1940 (McGuigan, 1996: 57).

Both in the USA and the UK, then, it seems that governments, for the most part, left the cultural sector (with the exception of the educational system) to itself, i.e. to private enterprise, until after the Second World War. Practices varied from country to country, of course, and the state took on more responsibility earlier in some places than in others. In western Europe, the establishment of state-owned public service broadcasting monopolies financed by licence fees in the years around 1930 was a significant turn (see Chapter 9 of the present volume, on broadcasting), but it remained an exception to the rule until after the war. A number of governments, not least in the northern and western parts of Europe, then established a number of institutions, programmes and laws that were intended to (i) produce and distribute art to the entire population and (ii) to support art, artists and media that would otherwise face serious financial problems or bankruptcy. The key rationale for these measures was basically that neither the market nor philanthropy could be relied upon to provide people everywhere with the quantity and quality (including diversity) of cultural experiences and knowledge that one regarded as a prerequisite for, or at least beneficial to, enlightened or well-informed social, cultural and political participation. But the measures were not only instrumentalist in this way, they also sprang from deeply held convictions that art and knowledge were simply useful for people, providing resources for self-understanding and a more varied and 'richer' everyday life.

Public support for the arts and for certain media is, in other words, in principle intended to secure *freedom of information* for citizens. Support for public radio and television, for certain types of film and other media and art production, reduced taxes and other measures to support newspapers and other print media, tax deductions for donations to fine arts institutions – these are just some examples of a wide variety of ways in which the governments of most countries intervene in the development and structure of the public sphere. In the USA, the Supreme Court decided in 1969 that the freedom of information, defined as a right to a varied menu of information and cultural experiences, was to be considered more important than editorial freedom (i.e. the freedom of expression) if the two fundamental rights conflicted in certain cases (FCC vs Red Lion Broadcasting).

All of this could be construed as a form of illegitimate *paternalism*, i.e. that the state, claiming some sort of fatherly wisdom and authority, is to decide what is recommendable cultural consumption for citizens. But it is also possible and highly reasonable to view it in the context of *relations of social power*: democratically decided government interventions of these kinds are ways of defending legitimate rights and interests that would otherwise be set aside or even trampled on by the immense financial power of the media and cultural industries.

Will unregulated media markets provide freedom in public communications?

The press and other media tend to be very sceptical about public interventions in their field. The reason for this is principled and in line with the fundamental ideas of the public sphere: the media should not in any way be dependent on the government they are supposed to monitor critically. This attitude may appear to be even more marked today than in the decades where a number of the measures we referred to in the previous section were introduced. Since about 1980, the general political trend in western countries has been to *deregulate* media, communication and culture markets, especially broadcasting. In 1989 the media tycoon Rupert Murdoch said in a much-quoted public address that a new age was dawning in the area of communication – an age of freedom and choice instead of regulation and scarcity (Murdoch, 1989). Market liberalists have always used a rhetoric of freedom related to the classical ideals of the public sphere when arguing against government regulation of media markets. They contrast an image of authoritarian, paternalist state control with an image of an open, free media market where a diverse multitude of actors have set up their own newspapers and broadcasting channels, thereby producing diversity and true freedom of choice for everyone. There are reasons to question this imagery.

As I have already suggested, the free play of market forces may weaken the democratic character of the public sphere, since the media's competition over sales and advertising revenues may lead to a focus on reaching and serving only the largest and most affluent parts of the public. Thus it will not only be the case that many social groups will be poorly served, a number of issues and perspectives that are not considered profitable may also be excluded.

Since the media are also businesses like any other, they are integrated in the ordinary business world and their stocks can be bought and sold like any others. The general tendency in capitalist economy towards ever greater concentration and centralization of capital – i.e. that ever greater amounts of capital are controlled by a diminishing number of capitalists – is also highly effective in the media industries. The concentration of *ownership* has, since the 1980s, been more rapid than before. Very tough competition, where some evidently will have to lose, goes hand in hand with mergers and takeovers. In the late 1980s, some 75 per cent of daily newspaper sales and some 80 per cent of the sales of Sunday papers in the UK were controlled by just three people – Murdoch, Maxwell and Stevens (Curran, 1988), and Maxwell is no longer around. Owners at this level also control companies in a variety of media industries, and frequently, as in the case of Murdoch, all over the globe – from the satellite TV company in Asia, Star TV, to the Hollywood film studio Fox. He also controls the Fox television network. An expensive Fox movie production can be promoted across a variety of journalistic print and broadcasting media, and end up on Murdoch-controlled TV channels after its cinema run, possibly also becoming the basis for a Murdoch-owned theme park (cf. also Chapter 10). In the USA, Disney has long been a colossal media conglomerate, stepping up to control distribution when buying Capitol Cities Communication, which included the TV network ABC, in 1995. Time Warner significantly strengthened its position in news journalism when buying CNN; it has a TV network, film studio, record company, cable company, magazines, publishing houses etc., and in merging with America Online it added a sizeable chunk of the Internet business that is still at an infant stage.

The enormous concentration of ownership across all sorts of media is the result of so-called free market competition. The present situation does not much resemble that of the early public sphere with its small printers' businesses, pamphlets distributed by hand and the plurality of generally small, not very capital-intensive media enterprises. In today's world, starting a new media business at a competitive, professional level is for the most part enormously capital-intensive, and it is becoming ever more expensive. Moreover, given the extremely tough competition, these are also very risky investments, something that further limits the number of possible participants.

If the owners' opinions and ideas can be assumed to influence the profile of, say, journalistic media, these strong tendencies towards what economists call *oligopoly* – the rule of a few – are highly problematic from a democratic point of view. Examples of quite heavy-handed editorial control by, for instance, Rupert Murdoch have been many, not least in connection with book publishing. He is alleged to have stopped the publication of a book by the last British governor of Hong Kong, Chris Patten, so as not to irritate the authorities in Beijing and thus risk losing (cf. e.g. the *Guardian* 6 September 2001) Star TV's right to broadcast in China. When his company HarperCollins took over the small but successful London publisher Fourth Estate in summer 2000, an author who had been contracted to write Mr Murdoch's biography was taken off the job (the *Guardian*, 12 July 2000). There are, of course, no legal limits to the influence or interference of owners on editorial policies or opinions. At best there is a sort of 'gentlemen's agreement' that owners should be 'professional' and not get directly involved in editorial decision-making; that is to say, this is a question of ethics, not of law. An ethical principle such as editorial independence will continuously be under various pressures. First, there is the tendency towards self-censorship in the editorial staff, i.e. that journalists and editors behave, perhaps only half consciously, as they expect the owners would like them to. They could let other papers or stations cover a particularly sensitive case, decide not to write that critical editorial comment, phrase a point differently, avoid mentioning certain names etc. Owners can then refrain from interfering, and editorial independence appears to be respected. Second, and even more important, however, there is the pressure on editorial decisions represented by what appear to be increasing demands for profit from media owners. Such demands may obviously influence editorial decisions in a multitude of ways and can hardly be said to be beneficial to freedom and pluralism in the public sphere, while they are, of course, perfectly in line with the freedom of the market.

State censorship in modern democracies

So far we have said quite a lot about the problematic role of strong commercial interests in relation to the ideals of the public sphere. Less has been said about how the state might operate in contradiction of these ideals. There are, for instance, certain governmental limitations to the free flow of information and the free formation of public opinion that may have received too little attention by critical media scholars than they deserve. They are of a different nature to those regulations that market liberalists have attacked most fervently. The British political scientist and media scholar John Keane (1991: 94–114) has viewed these limitations in light of a larger historical trend: the tendency for an increasing number of important decisions to be made in bureaucratic and top-level political circles, where ordinary citizens have little opportunity for insight and influence. Forms of extended international co-operation that may have far-reaching consequences but that are largely withdrawn from public scrutiny and critique further strengthen such a tendency. Keane more specifically lists the following five types of limitation – in effect, forms of political censorship – which, as he also demonstrates by way of examples, have been operative in western democracies.

1. *Emergency powers.* A variety of instructions and threats, bans and even arrests may be used to make journalistic media behave as those in political power prefer. Keane groups these methods into two categories. *Prior restraint* refers to a number of informal and formal limitations on what one is allowed to publish, from the friendly request via threatening telephone calls to formal guidelines. Laws regulating the public's (and thereby the media's) access to government documents etc. vary greatly from country to country, but even where such rights are formally quite far-reaching, governments and bureaucrats may bend the rules. The other category is *post-publication censorship*. Legal action may be instigated against media which publish material that the state would like to keep secret, and this may include the banning, confiscation and destruction of already published material. Both of these forms are employed in

particular at times of alleged 'national crisis'. The French government quite heavy-handedly censored the French press during the war against the liberation movement in Algeria, both through prior restraint and post-publication interventions. A more recent and much more sophisticated example is the US government's control of the coverage of the Gulf War. The British government for years upheld a ban on interviews with IRA members on British TV. Thus the claim that a 'national crisis' exists serves to limit the possibilities for a critical discussion of the government's policy.

2. *Armed secrecy*. This refers to the activities of secret services within the police or the military, such as secretly gathering information on politically 'suspect' individuals or organizations. Such secret services have a longer pre-history within western democracies, but it was not until the early twentieth century that permanent institutions were established. The Cold War boosted these organizations considerably and they were enabled to conduct extensive 'investigations' of suspected individuals and organizations, operations that might also include 'bugging' of homes, 'tapping' of phones, interception of mail, break-ins without judicial warrant etc. 'National security' has been used as a reason for keeping a large number of documents and extraordinary actions secret. The secret services have been allowed considerable freedom from democratic constraints and public insights, and they have also developed forms of transnational co-operation that escape the control of any single national government.

3. *Lying*. According to Keane, there is a long tradition of lying in western politics, going back to the period of state-formation in the early modern period. Various forms of lying have been regarded as legitimate means of attaining political goals. In more recent times, direct, coarse lying has become less important than the more slick practices of *information management* and public relations. Governments are always equipped with communication experts – sometimes referred to as *spin doctors* – who do their best to provide the public with positive-sounding versions of the government's activities, put a gloss on realities through carefully chosen formulations and evasions, and work hard to keep a lid on potential and emerging scandals. US administrations have historically been the leaders in this area. Press conferences become occasions where the government (and possibly the president) presents a message, and not occasions for critical questioning of the authorities. Not all journalists are admitted to such events. Carefully prepared opening statements set the agenda, questions may be planted and follow-up questions disallowed. 'Briefings are especially important occasions for gentle lying,' says Keane (1991: 102). They can be 'off the record', which means that the information

received cannot be used in the reporters' stories; they can be 'on the record', which means that remarks may be attributed to the speaker; 'on background', which means a specific source may not be named but reporters can, for instance, refer to a 'White House source'; or they may be 'deep background', meaning that no attribution is allowed. Those who dare break such rules may be efficiently punished in a number of informal ways. Such practices are not, of course, only found in the USA, and not only in central governments. They may also be found at a local level. To take one example from tiny Norway: in the city where I live, the local tabloid newspaper published articles that criticized police brutality. The police then denied the paper its everyday access to information about local crimes, information that was particularly important to this sort of paper.

4. *State advertising.* Modern states actively use advertising and related forms of communication to promote their policies and ideas. Around 1990, '[t]he self-promotion of state power absorb[ed] a budget of £200 million a year in Britain – where the state is the second largest advertiser, behind only Unilever – covering "campaigns" on every conceivable policy matter' (Keane, 1991: 104f.). In the months before the general election in 2001, the British government was the largest advertiser in the market-place. Such advertising works as positive PR for the state. In some countries it may also be used to support some media more than others; but Keane also includes certain types of journalism in the category 'state advertising': e.g. 'positively slanted coverage of political leaders through television and radio interviews' (1991: 105). Intimate links have developed between radio and television journalists and leading politicians and, supported by their expert advisers, the latter often negotiate the terms of their appearance. Says Keane: 'Political interviews tend to become vehicles for political persuasion and veiled party-political broadcasts' (1991: 106).

5. *Corporatism:* Throughout the twentieth century, private organizations of various kinds have become woven into a close co-operation with – and often financial dependency on – the state. The borderline between the state and civil society has become fleeting, a tendency also pointed out by Habermas (see above). A great many decisions of a political nature are taken in meetings between representatives of these organizations, and between them and representatives of the state. These meetings are closed to the public. Corporatism tends to favour the strongest organizations and the parts of the population they represent, possibly at the cost of those less resourceful. Large organizations tend to be bureaucratically driven, with a limited internal 'public sphere'. Bureaucrats strike deals with bureaucrats, behind closed doors. This is obviously a problem in light of the ideals of the public sphere.

Media ethics as defence of the public sphere

Journalistic practices in all media are supposed to adhere to certain ethical principles. These principles are explicitly formulated partly in laws and partly in professional codes of conduct. Some countries have quite detailed media laws that regulate practices of news-gathering and define the limits to what may be published etc. In other countries, special laws for the media do not exist. This increases the importance of rules formulated by press/media organizations or journalist's unions whereby the media themselves seek to define what constitutes ethically sound journalism. Some such codes of conduct are very detailed; others are more abstract, leaving the specifications to the individual journalist – and the judgement of the committees that handle complaints from the public.

Differences between countries are great in terms of the specificities in this area. The point in this section is, however, not to detail these differences. It is rather to demonstrate how the fundamental principles of media ethics are tied to the fundamental principles of the public sphere as outlined in this chapter. Media ethics are concerned with the ideal role of the media in a deliberative democracy; its dos and don'ts reveal how the ideals of the classical public sphere still live on also as a sort of professional yardstick for media practices.

The British Press Complaints Commission's Code of Conduct (the present version is from January 1998) says in one of its introductory paragraphs: 'All members of the press have a duty to maintain the highest professional and ethical standards. This code sets the benchmarks for those standards. *It both protects the rights of the individual and upholds the public's right to know*' (quoted in Frost, 2000: 246, my emphasis). The last sentence here in a sense says it all. Media ethics is, first and foremost, about providing the information needed in the formation of a public opinion, while also respecting the border between the public and the private spheres, i.e. the right to privacy, the right of the individual to be protected against unnecessary, unfair and possibly harmful public exposure. The implications of this may be differently perceived and practised, but all democratic countries will officially subscribe to the idea. It is about the freedom of expression, the freedom of information and the rights of the individual.

Let us now take a look at a concrete example of a professional code of conduct. I have chosen a relatively brief one, so as to illustrate the sort of principles on which these sets of ethical rules are based. This is the Code of Conduct for the British National Union of Journalists (NUJ) (quoted in Frost, 2000: 250).

1. A journalist has a duty to maintain the highest professional and ethical standards.

2. A journalist shall at all times defend the principle of the freedom of the press and other media in relation to the collection of information and the expression of comment and criticism. He/she shall strive to eliminate distortion, news suppression and censorship.

3. A journalist shall strive to ensure that the information he/she disseminates is fair and accurate, avoid the expression of comment and conjecture as established fact and falsification by distortion, selection or misrepresentation.

4. A journalist shall rectify promptly any harmful inaccuracies, ensure that correction and apologies receive due prominence and afford the right to reply to persons criticized when the issue is of sufficient importance.

5. A journalist shall obtain information, photographs and illustrations only by straightforward means. The use of other means can be justified only by overriding considerations of the public interest. The journalist is entitled to exercise a personal conscientious objection to the use of such means.

6. A journalist shall do nothing which entails intrusion into anybody's private life, grief or distress subject to justification by overriding considerations of the public interest.

7. A journalist shall protect confidential sources of information.

8. A journalist shall not accept bribes nor shall he/she allow other inducements to influence the performance of his/her professional duties.

9. A journalist shall not lend himself/herself to distortion or suppression of the truth because of advertising or other considerations.

10. A journalist shall mention a person's age, sex, race, colour, creed, illegitimacy, disability, marital status or sexual orientation only if this information is strictly relevant. A journalist shall neither originate nor process material which encourages discrimination, ridicule, prejudice or hatred on any of the above-mentioned grounds.

11. No journalist shall knowingly cause or allow the publication or broadcast of a photograph that has been manipulated unless that photograph is clearly labelled as such. Manipulation does not include normal dodging, burning, colour balancing, spotting, contrast adjustment, cropping and obvious masking for legal or safety reasons.

12. A journalist shall not take private advantage of information gained in the course of his/her duties before the information is public knowledge.

13. A journalist shall not by way of statement, voice or appearance endorse by advertisement any commercial product or service save for the promotion of his/her own work or of the medium by which he/she is employed.

Looking over these rules, one finds that they are about defending the possibilities for a free formation of a well-informed public opinion. The freedom of the press and other media in collecting information and expressing comment and criticism (see point 2) is essential here, and it must be defended both against state control (various forms of censorship) and the interference of private, commercial interests. This has to do with the integrity of each individual journalist (see, e.g., points 8, 9, 12 and 13), but point 9 also implicitly says that the media as organizations or institutions should not let financial considerations (the possibility of reduced revenues from advertising) influence their reporting. If this still happens, any journalist should oppose such an editorial policy. A principle of fairness underlies points 4 and 5, and the same goes for point 10, which warns not only against the spreading of prejudice and hatred, but also against the distortion of argumentation that lies in so-called *ad hominem* argumentation: talking about *who* presents an argument instead of the argument itself. Points 5 and, especially, 6 are about the protection of the 'sphere of intimacy' from unnecessary intrusion and exposure. The emphasis on separating facts from 'comment and conjecture', on accuracy and, for example, the concern over unlabelled manipulation of photographs, are examples of how one imagines public discussion is to be based on a set of inter-subjectively agreed, solid facts. This both presupposes a degree of consensus among the participants in public deliberation and suggests a possibility for consensus also on the implications of these facts for political principles, decisions and practices. All of this is well in line with the ideals of the classical public sphere, as outlined in Habermas's study.

Ideals are one thing, practice is something else. Any journalist will face difficult dilemmas all the time in his or her work. There are almost constant examples of quite obvious breaches of the above principles, but the fact that certain situations are experienced as dilemmas and that news items etc. are perceived as breaches of ethical rules testifies to the normative power of the ideas spelt out in codes of conduct such as that quoted here.

The genre system of the public sphere

As we have seen, the topology, or map, of society that is suggested by the classical ideals of the public sphere sets quite strict boundaries between various social areas, and implies a change of roles as one moves from work to leisure, from the private sphere of intimacy to public cultural and political life. *There's a time and place for everything* is an old expression that applies here. This may also be said to fit well with a rhetorical way of thinking, which prescribed (cf. Chapter 6 of the present volume, on rhetoric) different kinds of speech in different kinds of situation, about different things. The division of society into separate spheres also, of course, resulted in norms to do with which genres are fit for which sphere.

This topological set of genre-norms is part of our everyday consciousness, most clearly perhaps in widespread ideas concerning the 'place' for politics. Various forms or subgenres of political speech belong in the political public sphere. They do not belong in the workplace, at least not if they may lead to serious and divisive discussions. Traditionally, 'politics' does not belong in the arts and in entertainment; any markedly 'political' art risks condemnation for being non-artistic or of low aesthetic value. Valuable art can be, or even should be, marked by a particular personality, but it should be of a 'generalizable' kind, not too explicitly 'private', i.e. directly biographical. The political public sphere is not the place for either art or the intimately personal. A classic type of 'scandal' is precisely the public exposure of debatable intimate details about public figures, not least their sexual escapades.

Such limits and borders are more unclear now than they were, say, 100 years ago, but they are still in existence. The same goes for borders of a somewhat different sort. Editorials are never written in verse. News anchors do not declaim or recite the news while gesticulating to underline its contents. Politicians do not put in a dance sequence in order to highlight certain points when they speak from a stage to a large audience. The legitimate genres in the political public sphere are, in rhetorical terms, those that are marked by *logos* rather than *pathos*. In the cultural public sphere, the spectrum of possibilities is far wider, since all forms of artistic expression are included here. But a strict division exists between art and criticism or other discourse *about* art. Reviews of poetry are rarely themselves very poetic, theatrical reviews are rarely written as dramas or even dialogues. Within poststructuralist criticism, however, there have been attempts to reduce the distance between the genres of art and the genres of criticism – primarily in theory, less so in practice.

For all of these mostly unwritten rules, it applies that they only become clear to us when they are breached. Transgressions can cause considerable uproar, since they not only challenge norms for public discourse but also question a whole set of values and ideas, a whole worldview.

The public sphere, the nation and processes of internationalization

In most of what has been said so far about the public sphere as a system of ideas and as practical reality, it has been an implicit premise that we have been talking about conditions within a single nation-state. Even if the early bourgeoisie were preoccupied with ideas of universal human rights and universal truths, they were also in favour of ideas about the nation, about the community created by a shared language within a certain geographical area. The public spheres of the western world arose in close connection with the rise of the modern nation-state.

The sort of education or socialization that was a precondition for participation in the public sphere was, to begin with, primarily a responsibility of the family, but schools soon became an important addition. Learning to read and write the mother tongue was central among the elements of education, not only because reading and writing skills were important but also because the teaching of the mother tongue included the teaching of the national literary history. The nation was the large family that united all the small ones. Poets, novelists and playwrights were often presented as in some way representatives of the nation, the national spirit. To get to know them and learn to respect them was to get to know and learn to respect oneself. As economic, social and technological developments made society more complex, this sort of literary-national education lost some of its importance. Education had to be more economically, technologically and sociologically relevant, and it was thus in a sense, and to some degree, internationalized. Thorough knowledge of the specifically national cultural heritage, national myths and traditions is of minimal importance to today's elites beyond certain festive occasions.

This should be seen in the light of fundamental economical conditions. The development of a world market has been going on for centuries. But there was a decisive shift in terms of speed and scope in the colonialism of the nineteenth century and the radical expansion of world trade in the twentieth. Gigantic corporations, each with a turnover far exceeding the GNPs of a number of countries, have had worldwide interests for more than a century. Most of these corporations have been based in the USA, and a number of wars fought by that country may well be understood in light of the interests of big business. But European corporations have also, of course, been active globally since the days of colonialism and, particularly after the Second World War, so too have corporations from other parts of the world, notably Japan. In the last couple of decades something else has happened that is of decisive importance for what is now termed the *globalization* of the economy: the digital revolution means that gigantic amounts of capital can be moved instantly from one corner of the world to another at the touch of a button. This has made the links between economic trends in different countries more direct than they used to be; if there is a crisis in Asia, this will soon have an impact in various ways in Europe and the USA.

The role of computer technology here illustrates the role of technological developments more generally. Technologies develop in part as a result of 'internal' dynamics, tied, for instance, to progress in research conducted purely for scholarly reasons. But technological developments primarily go on in areas where there is a strong economic and/or military interest in innovations. The interplay between economic and military interests is, both historically and currently, of great importance. The development of satellite communications, computer technology etc. is a case in point. Research and development in these fields were conducted with a military motivation, but their economic importance soon became obvious; and then these technologies changed the world's communicative and cultural conditions forever in the course of a few decades. The first intercontinental television broadcast took place in 1962, when President Kennedy spoke 'live' to European viewers via the Telstar satellite; 20 years later this technology made some people worry over the mental and cultural health of children. But satellite television would soon become a widespread ingredient in everyday life – thereby doing away with total national control over broadcast media.

The term globalization could also cover the migratory movements or diasporas that have been changing the ethnic composition of North American and, perhaps particularly striking, European populations over the last four decades. Large contingents of people have been on the move, fleeing poverty or oppression, or just seeking a better life for themselves and their families, much as Europeans previously migrated to the USA and elsewhere. The globalized economy, air traffic and global media both enhance such migration and make staying in touch with the 'old country' far easier than it used to be for transcontinental migrants. Millions of Turkish immigrants in western Europe are, for example, tuned in to Turkish television, and thereby keep up to date with political and cultural developments in Turkey, much as they would have done had they still been living in Turkey. The Turkish public sphere and Turkish culture is, in this and other ways, *deterritorialized* – they are no longer exclusively tied to the geographical space of Turkey (cf. Aksoy and Robins, 2000).

All of this means that the processes of internationalization or globalization challenge traditional conceptions of the public sphere. It is not only that the public sphere is now more diversified than ever, and that for instance diasporic communities form their own semi-alternative public spheres, which will also have to communicate with each other and with the dominant, general public sphere of each country. Perhaps more important is the fact that governments are losing power since the economy is internationalized to such a degree. Also, it is becoming obvious to most of us that a number of problems cannot be solved if addressed only by individual countries – serious ecological problems, for instance, require international, co-ordinated action. It thus seems that there is a need for super- or transnational political entities to handle super- or transnational issues. If such entities are to have a democratic foundation, it seems that the establishment of international public spheres (at various levels) might be a good idea; spaces in which citizens take part in public discourse on common or shared problems across the borders that separate countries.

There is already talk of a 'global community', and a number of institutions, not least the bundle of organizations connected to the United Nations, operate globally. There are international fora of many kinds in a vast number of fields (professional, economic, academic, sports-related etc). Certain television channels, newspapers, magazines, journals, books and other cultural products reach an enormous, diverse, near-global audience. One might argue that all of these form some sort of (at least embryonic) 'global' public sphere where a phenomenon we could call the international public opinion is formed. Such an opinion was struggled over and formed, for instance, during the war in Vietnam, during the apartheid regime in South Africa, in relation to the conflicts in the Middle East etc. The question is, however, 'What is the executive power at which this international public opinion is directed?' So far, this has largely been the executive powers of specific countries. The United Nations is very far from becoming a world government; the USA is probably closer.

The European Union is an ambitious attempt at creating a super- or transnational political entity. Its main democratic problem is the creation of a functioning supranational public sphere with broad participation by citizens (cf. Schlesinger, 1995, especially pp. 20ff.). There is an EU parliament, which is politically weak even if it showed some teeth when forcing the whole EU commission to abdicate in the winter of 1999. Various efforts are made in the cultural field, including the academic, that point in the direction of a pan-European public sphere, and well-educated people may read newspapers and magazines from other European countries. Still a major obstacle to the establishment of a shared European public sphere remains: linguistic diversity. One of the reasons why the enormous geographical space and extremely heterogeneous population of the USA could be welded into a single market and one nation-state was precisely the position of English as the undisputed common language. In Europe something like that is a cultural and political impossibility. It thus seems that a pan-European public sphere, to the extent that it can be said to exist, will be reserved for the linguistically resourceful elites for a very long time.

9 Broadcasting: technology, society and policy

The centre of the public sphere

You may have noticed it in the news: in revolutionary situations, or situations of grave social and political import around the world, a great deal of attention tends to be devoted to radio and television stations, and transmission towers. Television, and before that radio, is the media of choice if one wants to address a whole nation or at least as large a portion of the populous as possible. The cameras and microphones of television are seen as extremely powerful and hence extremely important in terms of control; when speaking in front of them, one speaks from the centre of the public sphere.

Radio was dethroned when television became widespread from around 1950 onwards. Newspapers' coverage of radio programmes, for instance, shrunk rapidly (Andersen, 1986); television received just about all the attention. This can be tied to television's position as a primary medium, something the whole household would gather around – in principle, at least – following attentively what was on the screen. Radio relinquished this role and became largely a secondary medium, something to accompany various other activities, such as driving and housework. This is not to say that people stopped listening attentively to radio programmes, but the medium lost its ability to gather together the household, or groups of friends and neighbours.

There are several reasons for television's position as the most important medium in today's society. I list some of them below.

1. Television has, like radio, an *enormous reach* – the most important channels are available to the whole population.
2. Television is the medium *people spend the most time on* – even if it varies greatly from country to country how much time people on

average watch television every day, television is always the dominant medium in this sense.

3. Television is *centrally located in society*. Radio now appears more decentralized because of the large number and popularity of regional and local radio stations. Even if there is also local television, the medium appears more centralized since it is dominated by national networks with their headquarters either in the capital or in major metropolitan areas, as is the case in the USA. Television also appears 'centrally located' because it seems so close to the centres of social power: central political and, for instance, financial institutions are represented on television every night.

4. Television *dominates the agenda of the public sphere*. Newspapers, magazines and even book publishing are oriented towards television, and the people and issues presented there. If a cause, an opinion or some person is really to get attention, they have to get on television. The medium is thus the most central of all to politicians and all kinds of special interest groups. It is the central arena for election campaigns. Its debates and its journalism are followed up by newspapers and magazines. The radio may be faster with brief news, and it may offer more in-depth coverage on certain channels for smaller audiences; television's background material for the news will tend to be tailored to a broader audience, more dramatically appealing – but most often also more brief, less detailed, less in-depth.

5. Television is *the most important medium for culture*: 'culture' both in the sense of a 'way of life' (in the words of Raymond Williams) and in the sense of art. Television disseminates, or presents, values, attitudes, fashions, thoughts and lifestyles both in its programmes and in its commercials. But it is also a major (re)distributor of feature films, and it is filled with enormous amounts of other sorts of drama (series, serials and the occasional one-off drama). It presents us with various sorts of popular theatrical entertainment and it is the only socially significant channel of distribution for documentary films. On certain channels one can still find opera, serious theatre and classical concerts, and such forms of art have reached many more people through television than have ever visited opera houses, theatres and concert halls. Television is also of course, commercially, the most important medium for the presentation of popular music. The print media and radio have a much more differentiated output of art. Television is most important because it determines the more or less universally shared menu.

Both radio and television are *broadcast media*. Their socially and culturally central function is actually implicit in the term 'broadcasting'. Originally it meant, as mentioned previously in this book, to sow by hand, in semi-circles, as wide as possible. This agricultural metaphor expresses a very *modernist* optimism on behalf of the media in question. Radio programmes (later also TV) should be distributed in the widest possible circles and lead to growth everywhere. The metaphor presupposes that there is a bucket of seeds at the centre of the activity – i.e. centralized resources suitable for distribution – and a periphery where such resources are, in principle, lacking. The very notion of 'broadcasting' thus presupposes a *centralized social structure* and carries a belief in a general *project of enlightenment* which is to make the world progress, i.e. become a better place. Social and political movements such as the labour movement had great faith in the role of broadcast radio in breaking down social barriers and geographical distance.

Broadcasting was, and is, a particular way of organizing the social use of the technology in question. As we shall see, there were also other possibilities. The reasons why and the ways in which broadcasting triumphed over these other options are illustrative of more general relations between (media) technologies and society. We will, therefore, now take a closer look at this area, which has important implications for our understanding of today's rapid technological developments, some of which are said to be leading us into a *post-broadcasting age* (i.e. an age where broadcasting as such has all but disappeared, and only 'narrowcasting' to small groups and individually specific media use will supposedly remain).

The history of technology is part of social and cultural history

In school history books and other popular historical writing, one will often find formulations such as 'the steam engine created industrial society'. The underlying idea seems to be that a particular technical device or, possibly, a wider 'family' of such devices (i.e. a technology) is the *cause* of social developments. One may also sense similar ideas underlying journalistic terms such as 'the age of the computer' and the like. Thinking about technology in this way is problematic since it suggests isolating technology from its social and cultural contexts so that it – as a purely technical and non-social factor – can have decisive social effects. This way of understanding the relationship between technology and society is called *technological determinism*.

Another possibility is to regard social development as the *cause* of technological development. Various technical devices and the technologies of which they are parts will then be regarded as *effects*, as resulting from a need to satisfy certain social needs and demands. The history of technology becomes an effect of general social history: the distance between people's houses and their places of work grew, so there was a need for the car, and therefore this new means of transportation arrived. Technology becomes a sort of toolbox to which society turns whenever a need for some new invention arises, otherwise there is no link between the two; and so technology also becomes something non-social in this view.

What these two perspectives share is a relatively simple *cause–effect model* for historical development or change. With regard to broader social and cultural circumstances, such a model is dubious for a number of reasons. First, there are always *people* involved in historical processes, people who *interpret* a situation on the basis of complex preconditions and who also make *conscious choices* on this basis. There are no absolute natural laws in social life. Second, because of this element of human interpretation and agency, causes and effects are intertwined in highly complex ways. What was a reason or a point of departure for certain interpretations and acts is again influenced by these interpretations and acts, and their results. One may speak of *dialectics* in historical developments and say that the outcomes are *over-determined*, i.e. determined by a number of different circumstances and forces.

Transferred to the technological history of broadcasting media and its relations with general social history, all of this means that radio and television technologies were, at the outset, deeply marked (permeated) by social conditions, and that these technologies then influenced the social conditions that produced them. It is true that technological developments also have a degree of internal dynamics. Certain discoveries and inventions provide a basis for others. The realization of a certain technology is not, however, only the result of such technological conditions. Power relations and economic interests are also of central importance. Who defines what is needed, and who decides which resources are to be allocated for its production? Such definitions and decisions are, again, conditioned by more abstract social circumstances, i.e. at a macro level – such as 'industrial society', 'market economy' and the like.

All of this may appear somewhat abstract and hence difficult to grasp (if not totally incomprehensible). Hopefully, the following brief – but more concrete – presentation of the history of radio and television will provide a bit of substance.

The emergence of radio and television technology

Put simply, in technical terms, radio and television are ways of transmitting sound and pictures by way of electric impulses. Consequently, they have the nineteenth century's intense explorations of the many mysteries and applications of electricity as a precondition.

More specifically, it is of course the use of electricity for communication purposes that is important. *Telegraphy* was the first modern form of communication (after smoke signals and semaphore) that was not based on the physical transportation of the message in the form of letters, newspapers, books etc. Contrary to smoke signals and semaphore, however, telegraphy was not dependent on direct visibility between sender and receiver. This *transformation of linguistic signs into electric impulses* revolutionized communications within fields such as the economic, the military and general news-gathering from the 1840s onwards. Already by the 1850s a cable had been laid across the Atlantic. In conjunction with the progress in knowledge of physics, the international market economy and rapidly expanding industrial capitalism had produced the preconditions for, the need for and the realization of, a technology for the rapid exchange of information over great distances; and developments of tele*phone* systems started in the 1870s.

The scientific and technical basis for *radio*, i.e. the communication of verbal signs with the aid of *electromagnetic waves* instead of copper wire was created between 1885 and 1911. The German Heinrich Hertz demonstrated the existence of electromagnetic waves in the 1880s and, in 1901, the Italian Guglielmo Marconi managed, contrary to what physicists at the time believed possible, to transmit wireless signals from one side of the Atlantic to the other. This started a whole industry, primarily focusing on wireless telegraphic communication with and between ships. Around 1905 wireless telegraphs were installed in many countries' navy ships and, on transatlantic passenger ships, the same technology was used to produce 'fresh newspapers' during the crossings. The public on both sides of the ocean were, for example, quickly informed of the *Titanic* disaster due to the wireless telegraph it had on board (Dahl, 1991: 10).

Before the First World War, then, those who could steer the development of technology in certain directions, were primarily interested in two-way, person-to-person communication, for transmitting particular messages to particular people. But at the same time experiments were going on with other ways of using radio technology. It was demonstrated as early as 1902 that radio waves could also carry the human voice and music. When the radio tube, or the electronic tube, was invented, such use of radio waves could radically increase its reach: music and speech were successfully transmitted across the Atlantic. Radio-*telegraphy* had become radio-*telephony*.

Let's now take a brief look at the history of television technology. The further development of photographic technology, based on increased knowledge of chemistry, occurred in parallel with the progress in research on electricity in the nineteenth century. Various attempts at producing 'moving images' had been going on, at least since the eighteenth century (based on the *laterna magica*, magic lantern, a sort of slide projector with origins in the seventeenth century), but speed and direction in these developments did not really occur until the improvement of photographic techniques in the second half of the nineteenth century. The idea of 'television' was, at first, all about the transmission of pictures by telegraph (and, as late as in 1943, a Norwegian dictionary translated 'television' as 'picture telegraph'). A suggestion for such a device was first put forward by a Mr Bain in 1842. The 'copying telegraph' – obviously some sort of fax machine – was demonstrated in 1847 and, in 1862, there was a demonstration of the transmission of pictures through telegraph wires over considerable distance (Williams, 1975).

Discoveries and inventions that later would prove decisive for the realization of television technology were made over a long period of time. Two German inventions were more important than others: Nipkow's mechanical scanning system from 1884 and Braun's cathode ray tube from 1897. The point of departure for Nipkow's invention was that a picture that was to be transmitted by way of electricity would first have to be divided into a large number of separate units, as in some sort of mosaic, and that these units could then be transformed into some sort of 'electrical code'. Nipkow's idea was to use a rotating metal disc with holes in a spiral pattern through which a strong light would shine on an object. The parts of the object lit up by these minuscule light rays would reflect the light with uneven strength, and these reflections could be transformed into electric impulses of varying strength by way of light-sensitive selenium cells, discovered in 1873. Such impulses could then be sent by way of, say, telegraph lines to a receiver, who in theory had an apparatus that could reverse the process, i.e. transform the electric impulses into light that, with the aid of another *scanner*, could be projected on to some sort of screen.

This is in fact still the fundamental principle of television's transmission of images, but there is no rotating disc either in television cameras or in television sets. Karl Braun created the first cathode ray tube in 1897, and other people (a Russian and an Englishman) discovered that this could be used for television purposes. Independently of each other, they had the idea, more or less simultaneously in 1907, that an image could be formed on a thin plate covered by a light-sensitive material at one end of the sort of tube Braun had invented. This image could be bombarded with electrons from an 'electron cannon' at the other end of the tube. This would produce electronic impulses corresponding to the image, and these could then be transmitted to a receiver where the process was reversed so that the image was reproduced on an electric screen. With many sorts of improvements and complications (such as colour TV), this is still basically the way in which TV pictures are made and received. The television image we now see in European countries consists of

625 horizontal lines. These are electronically irradiated 25 times per second so that about 400 points along each of these lines are made to light up with varying intensity. The picture we feel we see so clearly consists, in other words, of 250,000 shining dots that are switched on and off 25 times per second. US TV viewers have to make do with about 210,000 dots since their screens only have 525 lines. Although their dots are switched on and off 30 times per second, US TV pictures are still, however, technically poorer than European ones – the standard was simply set earlier.

Looking back at this version of the early phase of the development of radio and television technology, we can see how people made discoveries and inventions of this and that, here and there, for different purposes, often without being aware of the efforts of others. Major investment and organized development work was not something that happened until the turn of the century, and in particular after Marconi's successful demonstration of radio-telegraphy. Struggles over patents then also slowed down the process. Industrial interests became still stronger after it was discovered that radio-telephony could be transformed from a point-to-point communication to a generally available spreading of music and speech: radio as a medium for *broadcasting*.

The establishment of broadcasting as the technology's social form

It is an interesting fact that decades went by between the first publication of ideas about broadcasting and the conscious organization of technological work in the direction of the realization of such ideas on an industrial scale. The very first ideas about television were ideas of a medium for two-way communication with pictures, a form of extension of the telephone. In 1879 the British magazine *Punch* published a drawing of a mother and father at home in their English sitting room, talking to their daughter, who was playing tennis in Ceylon (i.e. Sri Lanka), by telephone while also being able to see her and the tennis court on a screen hanging on the wall. But, and this is really remarkable, the idea of broadcast television was introduced more or less at the same time. In 1882, the French artist Robida published a series of pictures of moving images projected on people's living room walls. On one screen a teacher was busy teaching mathematics, on another a salesman was showing off a dress, on a third there was a ballet performance and on a fourth the shocked viewers could follow scenes from a desert war (Wheen, 1985: 11). Robida, in other words, envisaged a distribution of sound and pictures directly into people's homes, in four genres – education, advertising, art/entertainment and news/documentary – the main genres in television right up until the present. It is an indication of just how widespread such ideas were that the Norwegian writer Arne Garborg in 1891 published a novel in which a character who represents positivist optimism about the future insists that people in the future will have screens in their homes which will allow them to see and hear opera, ballet, circus, religious services, parliamentary debates or concerts. That same year, Thomas Alva Edison proclaimed that it was just a matter of months before he would have ready a device for the direct transmission of sound and pictures from real events to homes far away (Sklar, 1976: 11). Stories of the coming of television were circulated widely in magazines and books throughout the 1890s.

These historical examples show that the *idea* of broadcasting, *the idea of the transmission of sound and pictures to private homes from some central source*, was widespread long before the phenomenon became a reality. Broadcasting as a social form was, as I will later argue more thoroughly, *simply in line with the way in which modern society was structured*. The above examples indicate that there was a latent demand for radio and television sets, provided they delivered 'content' in which people were interested and were sold at a price they could afford. But the visions of artists are one thing, even if they do have a social basis; industrial planning and development is something very different. It is, as a rule, more short-sighted and organized in accordance with more or less impatient demands for profit.

The transition from idea to reality was therefore long and complicated. Edison's proclamation in 1891 was just business-strategic big talk. Early in the twentieth century a number of experiments with far-reaching transmissions of music and speech took place both in Europe and the USA. In an industrial context the idea of radio as a broadcasting medium is said to have been formulated for the first time in 1916 by an employee in Marconi's American company, David Sarnoff (Dahl, 1991: 11f.). But for several years after that the only radio listeners were still just enthusiastic radio amateurs – who also communicated with each other. The breakthrough for radio as a broadcasting medium came in the autumn of 1920, in Pittsburgh. An employee of the company Westinghouse was given extra money from the company to expand his amateur transmissions so that they would serve as advertising for the company's radio receivers. Within a year, the radio *receiver* was the new gadget that everyone just had to have. The speed with which this happened indicates precisely how the demand had been latent, a socially produced need.

The development of television technology also largely took place without broadcasting as a defined goal, even if central actors in the field probably also had this in mind, especially after radio's rapid breakthrough as a mass medium in the early 1920s. In that decade, however, work on the development of television was markedly different from what it had been before the First World War. It was conducted in a co-ordinated way, with lots of capital invested and a complex combination of international exchanges of patents on the one hand and fierce competition on the other. The state also intervened in several countries, realizing the industrial benefits of getting ahead in this race. But all of this activity, all of these resources, were not simply directed at producing the sort of broadcast TV with which we are now so well acquainted. Other ways of using the technology were still open.

In the 1930s there was, for instance, an amateur television movement in the USA. Like radio amateurs before them, these enthusiasts built their own transmitters and receivers and then sent TV to each other (Allen, 1983). But the pictures only had a maximum of 120 lines and these activities were mostly like those of a very impractical (picture) phone with a limited range. This sort of decentralized, grass-roots television was not primarily killed off by the heavy corporate interests that in the course of the decade gathered around the new medium and made sure that technical standards were set that, in practice, made continued amateur activity impossible. The real reason for the demise of TV amateurs was the fact that they simply could not offer an alternative to professional, broadcast television services.

Another alternative had better chances of survival: professional transmissions to *public television theatres*. The BBC started its experimental television broadcasts as early as 1931, but the first fully public transmission took place on 2 November 1936. A TV set then cost about £100 – more or less the average yearly income of an ordinary worker. In 1939 there were about 20,000 sets in Britain. Most of these were in very well-off people's homes, but many were also found in public places such as restaurants, department stores and, for example, Waterloo Station in London. It was primarily in these public contexts that ordinary people could watch television in the UK before the Second World War (Corrigan, 1990). When television was first introduced in the USA, movie theatres regarded it as a potential competitor.

It was, however, only in Nazi Germany that public TV theatres were really built on a large scale during the 1930s. There were hundreds of them, seating between 40 and 400 people each. The Germans began regular TV transmissions in 1935 (i.e. a year before the BBC) and the 1936 Olympics at Berlin were used to demonstrate to the world how far German TV technology had come – in part through co-operation with large American electronics companies. While the BBC stopped its TV broadcasts when the war began in September 1939, the Germans continued and kept on transmitting, for instance via the Eiffel Tower in Paris, until their military defeat. When their radio and TV towers were bombed, they switched to an extensive cable system, which had been established since 1936. For the Nazi regime, public TV theatres were the natural choice since the propaganda theory they relied upon claimed that people were more easily influenced when gathered in large groups (cf. mass society theory in Chapter 2 of the present volume, on influence). But the German electronics industry soon realized the profit potential of television as a household medium and pressed to get this market opened up. Production of household sets was just about to start when the war broke out and postponed these plans until six years later (Uricchio, 1989).

Clearly, the electronics industry's interest in a mass market for TV sets was one reason why the domestic form of TV viewing triumphed over the collective, public form; but a more fundamental reason is that a strong, latent desire for something like that existed among most ordinary people. Broadcast radio had spread incredibly fast all over the western world and equipped any household with a theatre stage, a concert hall and, for instance, direct transmissions from sports events etc. It made the home self-sufficient, while at the same time also opening it up to the world in a new way. Television could obviously do the same things only better (cf. Chapter 1). In order to understand the enormous success of the broadcasting media we need to regard them in light of certain fundamental historical processes.

Broadcasting and processes of modernization

As we saw in the previous chapter, modern capitalist society is based on both imagined and real divisions between the public and the private, and within the private realm between an economic sphere and the sphere of intimacy. The home and family life was, and is, centrally located within the sphere of intimacy. This is where we are 'simply human beings', deciding for ourselves what to do and how to do it. To many, domesticity appears as a sphere of freedom, in opposition to the sphere of work and many public arenas.

Some would hold that this way of thinking is *ideology*, in a more or less Marxist sense of the word: widespread ideas that conceal the real conditions, the real relations of power. Life in the home and the sphere of intimacy in general is, of course, socially conditioned in many ways – notions of gender and 'sex roles', salaries or wages, work conditions, ecology, and so on. But, as Marx had already pointed out, viable ideologies are never *entirely* false (if so, they would easily be revealed as such and fall apart); they are in fact, and to a considerable extent, in line with real conditions. Many people do indeed find that their home is a place of freedom compared to the workplace and its pressures, and the constant demands for decent, controlled behaviour 'out there'. They may notice that in the household they may be regarded and accepted as more 'whole' human beings, with strong and weak sides, not just as employees with a certain competence, as a football talent, a sexual object or whatever aspect of us may interest people in other parts of social life. The ties between members of a family (of some sort) tend to be much stronger and more complex than they are in most businesses, organizations, or pub or café 'communities'. (This is also why they may be experienced as *too* strong, even suffocating.) In short, since society in general is characterized by competition, partial and impersonal relations, and submission to all sorts of rules and power regimes, the home may to most people be extremely important as a place of (relative) freedom. It is a place where one can create one's own world, so to speak, and being able to equip this world with modern media of all kinds increases the sense of completeness and control. Not least to the working class and other social groups – who, historically, have lived in poor and cramped conditions – a spacious, well-equipped and in some sense self-sufficient home has become an important dream.

This centrality of the home in ideology and reality is an important precondition for broadcasting as a social form. Raymond Williams (1975) was the first to demonstrate the ways in which broadcasting and modern society are linked to each other. He used the term *mobile privatization* to characterize certain central aspects of social and economic modernization. Traditional social life, where relatively little was changed from one generation to another was disrupted by the development and expansion of a capitalist economy. Individuals and families could – or had to – move, geographically or socially; sociologists speak of geographic and social *mobility*. This implied that households consisting of extended families were dissolved, and that communities, both in the country and in rapidly growing cities, became less stable. The modern *nuclear family* – mum, dad and child(ren) – consequently became more important to its members. It became in a sense more closed around itself ('privatization') and was also, as we have just noted, increasingly 'on the move'.

Williams pointed out that the new mobility at grass-roots level was developed while increasing centralization marked other planes in society. The modern state apparatus was a lot bigger and more powerful than the state had been before and, in the economic field, enormous amounts of capital were concentrated in the hands of a small minority. In this situation broadcasting was a highly functional social form for central authorities. First, one could, through radio and later television, quickly reach the mobile, privatized subjects with important information, and more general knowledge and cultural material of many kinds. Second, broadcasting provided a common focus in a mobile, less stable and less locally centred society, thus producing a sense of *identity* in the population, especially a *national* identity that did not exist in locally oriented, traditional society. Besides the educational system and similar social institutions, the media in general were highly important in the creation of the nation as an 'imagined community' (Anderson, 1983; cf. Chapter 1 of this book). Newspapers certainly contributed here (as Benedict Anderson points out), but while their content varied from area to area, the contents of radio and television in many countries were the same all over the country for decades.

Broadcasting and democracy

So far, we have pointed to the interests of the electronics industry, an ideological focus on the home, and a social need for the dissemination of information and the production of (national) identity as reasons for the establishment of broadcasting as the social form of radio and television technology. These factors also indirectly point to some of the fundamental social functions of broadcasting. But one very important factor and function is missing here: *the links between broadcasting and democracy.*

Only in the twentieth century was *universal suffrage for men and women* established in all modern societies (except Switzerland). All adults were now formally regarded as fully autonomous human beings who, in principle, should take part in democratic processes on an independent, well-informed basis. Broadcasting was not only about informing and controlling populations from above, which Williams' critical perspective (1975) emphasizes. It was also, and perhaps much more, about connecting the entire population with the national public sphere and improving most people's ability to form their own opinions and make their own choices of actions on the basis of knowledge about culture and society. This has particularly been the case in most western European countries, where private radio broadcasting companies tended to be replaced by state-owned monopolies in the period between the two world wars. The BBC was established as a public corporation in 1927, and many others followed.

The ideal for these monopolies were what is called *public service broadcasting.* Radio, and later television, was to be available for the entire population at a low cost, just like roads, water, electricity and other so-called *public goods.* Funding was organized in the form of a *licence fee,* i.e. a special tax that anyone with a radio or TV set would have to pay. Radio and television was, of course, to communicate elementary social information to the public and also contribute to the formation and reproduction of a national identity, but at least as important was a reliable news service, and the communication of education, discussions, art and entertainment of the highest possible quality. Such a broad, generally accessible spectrum of programmes was to contribute to the reduction of systematic differences in social and cultural resources. Everyone was to be secured access to the 'central bucket of seeds' through the sowing activities of the broadcasting institution.

One can still find these elements in the authoritative nine-point definition of public service broadcasting that was unanimously supported by the Council of Europe's Fourth European Ministerial Conference on Mass Media Policy in Prague in December 1994. In summary, the nine points state that public service broadcasting should provide the following services (as quoted in Raboy, n.d.):

1. a common reference point for all members of the public
2. a forum for broad public discussion
3. impartial news coverage
4. pluralistic, innovative and varied programming
5. programming that is both of wide public interest and attentive to the needs of minorities
6. reflection of the different ideas and beliefs in multi-ethnic and multicultural societies
7. a diversity of national and European cultural heritage
8. original productions by independent producers, and
9. extended viewer and listener choice by offering programmes not provided by the commercial sector.

In practice, public service broadcasting institutions have somewhat different profiles in different countries. These differences may be linked to their financial situation, but also to the more general political, social and cultural conditions in the countries in question. It has, for instance, been argued that the BBC has been marked by a more elitist top-down attitude in its programming than its Norwegian counterpart, the NRK (Syvertsen, 1992: 95). This might be explained by the sharper class divisions in the UK and the traditionally strong position of broad, popular movements in Norway. Still, public service broadcasting in Europe has had many features in common that have made it different from broadcasting in other parts of the world, where it has been organized on a commercial basis. This is evident if we compare it to the American system.

Commercial broadcasting: the US television system

In the USA, television was also organized along the lines of radio; but radio was never a monopoly financed by a licence fee there. Instead, advertising financed programmes, originally so that sponsors financed whole programmes, and so that these suited the interests and needs of sponsors in terms of form and content. Some advertisers, such as the producer of detergents Procter & Gamble, actually owned and organized the production of their own series of programmes, and drama series in particular. As we have seen in a previous chapter, this was the origin of the generic term *soap opera*, which was coined in the 1930s; these were highly emotional daytime drama series, paid for, and sometimes produced by, makers of soap (cf. Chapters 7 and 10 of the present volume).

This system was transferred to television when that medium became widespread from the late 1940s onwards. In the 1950s one might find night-time drama programmes with titles such as *Philco Television Playhouse, Goodyear Television Playhouse* and *Kraft Television Theatre*, i.e. named after producers of car tyres, electrical appliances and foods (Barnouw, 1982: 156). These programme series consisted of one-off television dramas, transmitted live, written and produced in New York, and with artistic links to the theatre and film milieus in that city. Around 1955, however, two important changes occurred: first, there was a shift to *spot advertising*; and, second, there was a shift to *filmed series*, mostly made in Hollywood. The sponsors of the drama anthology series had often been worried about the somewhat critical tone of the New York-produced plays and, with one-off dramas, it was difficult to predict the size of the audience from one play to another. Spot advertising made it possible for companies to place advertisements in a number of different programmes, and the series format made predictions of audience size easier. Moreover, Hollywood was more reliable in terms of the tone of the shows, i.e. a more consumption-friendly, positive and optimistic one. New York productions had too often suggested that the solution to all problems was *not* necessarily to be found at the nearest supermarket. The television networks were also happy with these changes since they acquired more control with the programming they offered, and the transmission of filmed series could, in contrast to live shows, be adjusted to the different time zones present throughout the country.

This did not alter the basic logic of American broadcast TV, however. It was still about making money by delivering audiences to advertisers. The audience was primarily conceived as *consumers*, not *citizens* (cf. below). Advertising is, of course, always addressed to us as consumers, but here this would logically also go for the programmes themselves. In a system like this, programmes should not, as a rule, be demanding or disturbing, but should give rise to confidence, harmonize conflicts and generally recommend consumption as a cure for most maladies. The latter is of course the general message of advertising, and programmes should not openly contradict it. Democratic ideals of the sort we have presented above are, in principle, of secondary importance; they may still have some importance in the journalistic *ethos* of the newsroom, even if under pressure, but they do not mark the production of programmes and the construction of schedules in general.

The three major US networks (ABC, CBS, NBC) established early on oligopolistic control of the television medium. A fourth network, Fox, owned by Rupert Murdoch, came in the late 1980s and, in the 1990s, a fifth was added: WB (Warner Brothers, part of the mega corporate conglomerate Time Warner). The networks only own a handful of TV stations themselves, but decide the programming of hundreds of local stations where they rent air time. The 'free market' has, in other words, resulted in an oligopoly where all agents want to offer programmes that can draw a maximum of viewers, particularly certain kinds of viewers (relatively affluent and consumption-oriented ones). Americans are used to having lots of programmes to choose from, but the networks mostly offer programming of the same few sorts. The system can thus be said to produce volume rather than pluralism.

Pluralism arrived only through the rapid expansion of cable TV in the 1980s, especially in the larger cities, where it is quite usual to have up to about 100 cable channels. Many of these are subscription channels, though, so they will not be available to the poorer sections of the public. But the USA also had legislation which demanded that all cable companies should have at least one channel that would be open to all interested producers of video in the local community; these channels are called *public access* channels. In principle, anyone can get their video tape distributed on cable via these channels, with no editorial interference from the cable company. Religious, cultural, ethnic, sexual and political minorities have made use of this opportunity, but their programmes rarely attract others than those who already belong to the groups in question.

The term *public* is also tied to another alternative to the commercial channels: so-called *public television*. Already in the early days of radio certain frequencies had been reserved for educational radio stations, and the same was attempted when television was introduced. But since the funding of such stations was sparse and insecure, little happened in this field until 1967 when a law on *public television* was passed and a system of federal funding introduced. In 1997 there were as many as 348 local TV stations run by non-profit agencies such as universities and various organizations. These are to a considerable extent nationally co-ordinated through the Corporation for Public Broadcasting, which receives and distributes federal support for programme production, and Public Broadcasting System, which buys and distributes programmes to the local stations, all of which are members of this association. Correspondingly, there is also a National Public Radio, a system of non-commercial radio stations, which has a mix of national and local programming. The government thus to a certain extent supports both public television and public radio. But the support is so little that these forms of broadcasting are totally dependent on donations from viewers and listeners, and the support of sponsors. In more recent years sponsorship has become more and more important, and the brief announcements of which company sponsors a certain programme have begun to look much like ordinary TV commercials. These sponsors are particularly interested in reaching the types of people who make up most of public television's audience: they are better educated and tend to make more money than the average TV viewer (Hoynes, 1994).

This part of the population has also, since about 1980, been better served by the commercial networks, who suddenly realized that there were lots of well educated and relatively affluent, socially active people who hardly watched any television at all beyond a few newscasts and the news magazine *60 Minutes*; most television programmes simply did not appeal to them. This realization led to the production of a number of television series in the 1980s that were more unconventional and sophisticated than US series used to be, both formally and thematically. *Moonlighting*, *Max Headroom*, *Dynasty* (a show that working-class US audiences did not very much like), *LA Law* and *Twin Peaks* were all examples of this tendency, albeit also very different from one another. Later shows such as, say, *NYPD Blue* or for that matter *Ally McBeal*, would probably never have been made if networks and advertisers had not started to pay more attention to 'demographics' (i.e. the social differentiation of the market). Mercedes Benz and BMW will gladly pay for advertising in a programme that has the right audience *composition* even if the audience *size (rating)* is not so great.

The traditional oligopoly in US television has resulted in the networks having some of the fundamental functions of broadcast TV, as outlined by Raymond Williams (1975): they have been central distributors of elementary information and producers of a shared identity for a population characterized by 'mobile privatization' to an extreme degree. This role has also been their strength when facing tough competition from a large number of cable and satellite channels. They may appear, to most Americans, to represent community and solidity in a rapidly changing world. There are, however, reasons to doubt that the American television system sustains a democracy and a public sphere as good as the European ones, where the principles of public service television are still quite strong.

American commercialism and European public service: a comparison

One might say that it is totally unimportant how broadcasting is financed as long as the programming offered serves the interests of the public. But the question is, then, what these interests are. The Federal Communications Commission's chair in the 1980s, Mark Fowler, who was appointed by President Ronald Reagan, once said that *the public interest is what interests the public*. He then evidently played with the double meaning of the word 'public': i.e. (i) 'audience' and (ii) 'the general, the community, the 'not private'. Fowler's definition of the 'public interest' basically says that the general interests of society as a sort of community are the same as our interests as consumers in a broadcasting market. In line with this, Fowler also said that television is 'a toaster with pictures' (cf. Keane, 1991: 52ff.; Fowler and

Brenner, 1982, for a more thorough presentation of Fowler's argument). There are good reasons why this way of thinking is problematic.

In all sorts of cultural experiences we would like to be *engaged* in some sense, taken somewhere beyond immediate everyday life and at least partially into something else. The anthropologist Victor Turner has claimed that the English word *entertainment* stems from the French *entre tenir*, i.e. 'to hold between'. To be entertained is to be 'held between' the immediate (physical, factual) reality and some different sphere of experience (Turner, 1982). Entertainment is, according to this, a condition in which we are so engaged in/by something that we mentally leave our immediate surroundings to some extent. This is something that can be offered by serious reportage, essays, feature films, poetry and great music alike. When zapping or grazing between TV channels or radio stations, we may well be looking for this sort of experience. As zappers, our interests may be compared to those of shoppers in a supermarket or mall. We are consumers, with different tastes, lifestyles and so on, but we also have other types of interest. We are students or professionals, fathers or mothers, immigrants, sports fans or whatever – and we are people with an interest in social justice, we care about economic conditions and (other) social issues. In all of these capacities we are interested in how society works, how resources are allocated, who decides what etc. This is our interest as *citizens*. It is not identical to our interest as consumers. As citizens, we are interested in broad knowledge of the world and our place in it; we care about perspectives on, and debates about, our conditions and the larger contexts of our everyday lives. Television and radio (and, of course, other media) may well offer programmes that address us as citizens in entertaining ways, 'entertaining' in the sense outlined above. But the demands for a variety of genres and for in-depth treatment of various issues are greater in relation to our interests as citizens than they are in relation to the satisfaction of our 'needs' as consumers (cf. Murdock, 1992). Moreover, the public sphere has a central role in democracy, and so it is important that it functions well in relation to goals or tasks we do not necessarily consider in our capacity as individual zappers. Broadcasting 'in the public interest' is broadcasting that sustains a well-functioning public sphere, a functioning democracy. The extent to which this is realized cannot simply be measured by way of ratings, in the same way as sales figures may indicate whether a toaster works as it should.

European public service broadcasting has generally been characterized by greater variety in terms of programme formats and types of content than purely commercial broadcasting, like public service broadcasting in the USA. Raymond Williams documented this early on: between 3 and 9 March 1973, he carried out a very simple comparison between the programming on five TV channels, three British (BBC1, BBC2 and the commercially financed public service broadcaster Anglia), and two American (KQED, a public television channel in San Francisco, and Channel 7, i.e. ABC's channel in the same area). Williams placed programmes in one of two categories, which he called 'type A' and 'type B'. Type A programmes consisted of news and current affairs, documentaries, educational programmes, serious art and music programmes, children's programmes and one-off dramas. Type B consisted of drama series, feature films and general entertainment. He was then able to demonstrate in a simple table the systematic differences in programming between the five channels (see Table 9.1).

Table 9.1 The distribution of programme types in five selected channels (%)

Programme type	BBC 1	BBC2	Anglia	KQED	Channel 7
Type A	71	75	42.9	86	20.5
Type B	21	22.5	38.1	10.5	59.5

(Williams, 1975: 84)

As Williams pointed out, there are two interesting comparisons to be made here. The first is between the commercial (Anglia, Channel 7) and the public channels in each country. It is obvious that type B programming has much more room in commercial channels; but a second comparison can also be made between the situations in the two countries. The American system clearly differs from the British in being much more polarized. This is related to the fact that certain types of programme are simply missing in each of the two American channels, while all British channels offer a broader spectrum of genres. In the week Williams studied, ABC's Channel 7 had only 0.6 hours of documentary and reportage, no educational programmes, no one-off dramas and only 5.2 hours of children's programming. This means that most of the type A programming was news: 11.6 hours out of 19 were news and current affairs. On the other hand KQED had only 4.7 hours of drama (BBC1 had 11.5 hours, Anglia 20.3 and Channel 7 22.4) and no 'general entertainment' (BBC1 had 7.4 hours, Anglia 9.8 and Channel 7 32.4).

The problem with the 1973 US system as it is represented here is not so much that the total available programming menu is so much more meagre than the British or European one, but what it leads to is a situation where, for the most part, only a quite small, well-educated minority watches the public channels – where they are available – in addition to the commercial ones. Even after dozens of more specialized cable channels (movies, sports, religion, documentary, news, weather, and so on) have become widely available, especially in metropolitan areas, the networks may reach as much as two-thirds of the audience on a given evening, and their mix of programming is much as it has been for a quarter of a century. The reason for this is, not least, deep sociocultural differences in taste, i.e. preferences related to social and cultural resources (cf. Chapter 3). In this way the majority of the audience will miss the greater variation in information, knowledge and perspectives that comes with a broader selection of genres. They will simply never encounter certain serious genres. Such a television system contributes to the maintenance and possible widening of so-called *information gaps* among people. The resources needed to acquire new knowledge, to form a reasoned opinion on public issues, and participate in various democratic processes, are also very unequally distributed – for example, through the educational system – and the structure of the media further these differences. Those so inclined may also link this to the fact that, for decades, only about 50 per cent of those qualified to vote actually took part in the election of the US president. Some might regard this as a serious problem for a democratic society.

Much has changed in television since 1973, with the advent of satellite and cable TV and the introduction of many more, competing channels in Europe too. Still, one might argue that the fundamental principles detected by Williams in his elegantly simple study (1975) still apply. Commercialism (also as an ideology of competition in public broadcasting institutions) tends to reduce the diversity of programming in a certain way: anything regarded as 'demanding' or 'boring' (according to the prejudices of broadcasting executives) tends to be marginalized or removed altogether from the schedules of channels aiming for a maximum audience, and may only appear (if at all) on 'ghetto' channels directed at smaller, 'elite' audiences. The British and European situation has thus become more akin to that of the USA. There have, of course, always been considerable information gaps or differences in cultural resources in western Europe too, and there is now also a clear tendency towards political passivity; but the continued existence of relatively broadly programmed public service broadcasting channels may here serve to counter such tendencies. These channels are obliged, through their contracts with government, to ensure a broad mix of programmes, serious and reliable information, and the best possible programme quality in general. In countries such as the UK and France, more or less independent public agencies have been set up to control the adherence to such principles, including that of commercially financed channels. Some public channels are commercially funded while others are funded by licence fees. In some countries, such as Denmark and Germany, there are public service channels funded by a mixture of advertising and licence fee. (Purely commercial channels complain that such a mixed system leads to unfair competition and so it is under pressure in the European Union.) Raymond Williams' figures for Anglia vs the BBC's channels are still quite representative of the differences between commercial and non-commercial channels, and due to the British system of regulation, the distance to the polarized American system is also still quite clear.

Public regulation of broadcasting

In principle, anyone can at any time launch the publication of journals, magazines, newspapers or books in democratic societies. So why can't just anyone start transmitting radio and television programmes? The reason is not only that it takes such a lot of capital to do so. Television is especially expensive. One also needs permission from public authorities before one goes ahead with a broadcasting project. Does this not contradict basic democratic principles? If not, what sort of regulation is then acceptable? These are the sorts of questions we will examine in this section.

In the early to mid-1920s the airwaves were chaotic: amateurs and the new professional broadcasters constantly interfered with each others' transmissions. It therefore became clear that some public agency had to organize a sensible distribution of frequencies. The spectrum of radio waves was a scarce resource, and so the government had to intervene in order to organize its use in accordance with certain principles. This is the main reason why broadcasting has held such a special position in relation to other media in terms of regulation. Since the supply of paper and printer's ink is practically unlimited under normal circumstances, similar regulation of print media has not been an issue since the seventeenth century. Radio waves have been regarded as the property of the people, a publicly owned common resource. This idea has been fundamental to the way in which laws and regulations pertaining to broadcast media have developed. This is also the case in the USA; the then Secretary of Commerce, and later Republican President, Herbert Hoover, maintained in 1925 that radio communication could not be regarded as an activity performed solely for private profit; it had to be seen primarily from the standpoint of 'the public interest' (Hoynes, 1994: 38).

The first American Radio Act was passed in 1927; it said that all broadcasters had to operate in accordance with 'the public interest, convenience and necessity'. The semi-official Federal Radio Commission – a few years later re-baptized as the Federal Communications Commission (FCC) – was to award licences and ensure that rules and regulations were respected. The Commission had already stated in 1928 that 'broadcasters are not given these great privileges by the United States Government for the primary benefit of advertisers. Such benefit as is derived by advertisers must be incidental and entirely secondary to the interest of the public.' Towards the end of the statement it was again said that 'the emphasis must be on the interest, the convenience, and the necessity of the listening public, and not on the interest, convenience or necessity of the individual broadcaster or advertiser'. Ever since the 1930s, however, some people have criticized the way in which commercial broadcasters have made use of their privileges. In the USA, there have always been very strong political forces arguing that the freest possible play of market mechanisms is the best way to ensure the realization of the 'public interest'. Still, even the most ardent of market liberalists (such as Mark Fowler and his assistant David Brenner) have agreed that there are certain types of programming that are positive from a social point of view, but that commercial agents cannot be expected to offer. These include certain in-depth current affairs programmes, certain types of cultural and informational programming, and experiments with the media's forms of expression. This is one of the reasons why, since the 1930s, the authorities have tried to reserve parts of the spectrum for non-commercial operators both in radio and television; but, on the other hand, a licence fee or other secure and sufficient form of funding for non-commercial broadcasting has never been introduced (Hoynes, 1994).

The FCC is also responsible for the regulation of commercial broadcasting's programme content. Traditionally, this has, first and foremost, meant prohibition of 'indecent' programming – i.e. anything from four-letter words to female breasts, not to mention the genitalia of either sex. But, on the basis of a 1990 law on children's television, the FCC in 1996 presented stricter rules concerning when and how much 'educational' children's television each commercial TV station must air. This example demonstrates that, even in the USA, the regulation of television content may be considered legitimate when a vital interest such as the 'cultural health' of children is at stake.

In western Europe, the tradition is that public service broadcasters are granted editorial freedom within the framework provided by their statutes, broadcasting laws and the like. Each broadcaster will normally have some agency attached in which 'ordinary' listeners and viewers are represented by people with backgrounds from various areas of social life and who are supposed to evaluate the broadcaster's programmes (Robillard, 1995; Raboy, n.d.). Many of these agencies are, in reality, quite ineffectual, but in some countries, notably Germany, the 'council' of ZDF is involved even in decisions regarding budgets (ZDF = *Zweites Deutsches Fernsehen*). In the UK, the *BBC Governors* is a 'council' with 12 members from various social backgrounds and professions, appointed by the Department of Culture, Media and Sports, which is actually the corporation's board. It therefore appoints the BBC's Director General and other high-ranking executives and reports on the BBC's activities both to parliament and to ordinary licence fee payers, i.e. the public at large.

Two other UK regulatory bodies are formally independent and of a different nature altogether. The *Broadcasting Standards Council* is primarily concerned with sex and violence, and oversees the programming of all British broadcasters, while the *Broadcasting Complaints Commission* receives and handles complaints about unfair or unjust presentations of issues and unwarranted breaches of people's privacy. The *Radio Authority* is clearly more powerful than the latter two. It decides about licences for radio stations, and regulates their programming and advertising. The largest and most powerful of these bodies is the *Independent Television Commission* (ITC), which is led by a council with 10 members and funded by fees paid by the commercial licensees. The ITC employs almost 200 people, who grant licences and oversee all commercial TV channels in the UK, regardless of their form of distribution – including those whose broadcasts are directed at foreign countries, such as the Scandinavian TV3. All commercial television companies that distribute their programmes terrestrially pay handsomely for this privilege and furthermore have to adhere to quite detailed agreements about the mix and quality of programming. The ITC can administer fines and even retract their licences if they don't (Collins and Murroni, 1996).

France does not have the British division between regulators for commercial and non-commercial channels. Everything is taken care of by the *Conseil Superieure de l'Audiovisuel* (CSA), a semi-independent agency with about 300 employees. The CSA's tasks and authorities are otherwise parallel to those of the British Radio Authority and the ITC, that is to say rather far-reaching opportunities for regulation and sanctions.

A major general aim of the CSA and other regulatory bodies is to ensure that radio and television provide a plurality of programme genres and contents with a high professional standard, thus contributing to a rich cultural and informational menu for these media's audiences. The public regulation of programme content, even if guided by such aims, may still appear problematic in view of the principle of free expression. A central idea related to the freedom of expression is the notion of *editorial independence*, i.e. that all decisions concerning what is to be published by any medium are the responsibility of the editorial staff and, ultimately, the responsible editor-in-chief. Neither the government nor the owners or advertisers should in principle interfere with editorial decision-making; this is commonly regarded as a precondition for the fulfilment of journalism's critical functions in the public sphere. The argument for the special position of broadcasting media in relation to the principle of editorial freedom or independence has historically been the scarcity of frequencies, as we have seen. But one could also argue that the broadcast media are of such great importance to society that unrestricted market freedom is simply not desirable. A sentence passed by the US Supreme Court in 1969 (FCC vs Red Lion Broadcasting) is extremely interesting in this context, since it weighs the importance of editorial independence against the importance of another central democratic principle: the freedom of information. It stated that *'the right of viewers and listeners and not the right of broadcasters is paramount'* and that, consequently, the rights of viewers and listeners *'to receive suitable access to social, political, aesthetic, moral and other ideas and experiences'* was to have priority over the First Amendment rights of broadcasters if and when the two conflicted (cf. Porter, 1989). The efforts to regulate and evaluate the performance of broadcasters can thus be seen as a legitimate defence of the *freedom of information of audiences*, in the sense of 'the right to a varied menu of information, knowledge and cultural experiences', and this right is superior to the freedom of broadcasters if and when the two should conflict.

Cables, satellites and digitalization: is the Broadcasting Age over?

In 1962, as mentioned in the previous chapter, people in Europe could already watch and listen to President Kennedy speaking 'live' on television via the Telstar satellite; but it took about another 20 years until television transmitted via satellite became an alternative, or addition, to terrestrially distributed television. In the course of these two decades satellite technology had been radically improved, not least through research conducted for military reasons. At the same time many more households in several western countries had been hooked up to cable networks that were also technically improved, and so satellite television could easily be distributed to a lot more people than those who bought their own satellite dishes. Such dishes also soon became smaller, lighter and less expensive. In some countries, such as the Scandinavian ones, a majority of viewers now receive their television programmes by cable or satellite dishes.

These developments contributed to the dissolution of national broadcasting monopolies in western Europe during the 1980s. It was no longer possible to uphold the national television borders. Public service broadcasters of all sorts now had to compete for the attention of audiences with purely commercial channels, broadcasting either in the national language or in the widely known *lingua franca*, English. In countries like the Scandinavian ones, where advertising had been prohibited in broadcasting for decades, companies serving the national markets started to advertise on channels beamed into these countries from abroad, and so there was one more reason to abolish the prohibition of broadcast advertising. There seemed to be a need to support a national identity through the establishment of more channels in the national language, and these could only be funded commercially. The result was that previous one- and two-channel countries, in the course of just a few years, experienced the advent of multichannel radio and television, a quite far-reaching cultural change.

Multichannel broadcasting systems do, of course, divide audiences between channels and stations. People will move between channels according to what seems attractive at any given time, but at the same time they will tend to have their favourite channels to which they return more often. Both radio and television channels will tend to be profiled so as to address audiences with certain sociocultural characteristics more than others. No channel is an indisputable shared forum for all viewers or listeners at the same time, with the possible exception of certain (sports) events or very special situations. This may well be seen as a positive development compared to a situation where, say, a single public broadcaster defines the menu for everyone, such as was the case in Norway. The multichannel system is simply more pluralistic, and may thus appear as a more adequate system for an increasingly complex cultural situation. There are, however, some problems here too.

Since audiences in a multichannel system can always choose to watch or listen to something they already know, and know they like, it is rare for them to discover that they actually like something they thought they didn't like. If one looks at the profiles of commercial channels, one may also find that they are actually all directed at more or less the same sorts of audiences and tastes – and that this orientation also marks the profiles of the largest non-commercial channels, since they too have to aim for the largest possible audience in order to retain the political legitimacy of their licence fee funding. This means that all sorts of minority audiences are marginalized and, even on the public· channels, must seek out their particular preferences at uncomfortable hours, if they appear at all. Some will claim that a process of cultural *mainstreaming* is taking place. In some sense we all belong to some minority or other: we are wheelchair users, film buffs, stamp collectors, hard of hearing, rugby fans, jazz fans, poetry lovers, science fiction fans, immigrants, keen on philosophy, tango dancers, interested in local history, Buddhists, computer freaks, snowboard enthusiasts, coal miners' daughters, or whatever. Some minorities are larger than others, such as gays and lesbians, racial or ethnic minorities, people with disabilities, people who are interested in so-called high art, etc. If these larger minorities, in particular, are also marginalized (i.e. their special interests are not represented on channels that reach large audiences) this could be seen as a democratic problem. Such representation could well be regarded as an important contribution to the creation of a complex, enlightened, tolerant and inclusive public sphere and social community.

A related problem with a very mainstream-oriented multichannel system is one we have already mentioned: that it tends to classify any kind of serious, somewhat demanding or challenging programmes – whether these are about current affairs, international politics, art or whatever – as 'special interest' programmes, to be scheduled exclusively on special interest channels or at 'special interest hours'. This will in practice, given the well-known sociocultural patterns of taste, mean that most people will not encounter such programmes at all and will hence miss the particularly solid information, knowledge or food for thought they offer. Information gaps are in this way increased, not bridged.

This is a thought well worth keeping at the back of our minds as we enter the era of *digital broadcasting*. This is a technological shift that may have considerable cultural and social consequences. Digitalization means, briefly put, that auditory and visual information is coded as in computers, i.e. represented as series of zeros and ones. The difference between old-fashioned, vinyl long-playing records and CDs may illustrate some of the differences between analogue and digital storage and distribution of information. In the old vinyl records, the characteristics of the sound were, so to speak, directly mirrored in the microscopic patterns of the grooves, and these were then registered directly, mechanically, by the sensitive stylus which converted them to electric impulses that reached the amplifier and the speakers. On a CD it is not the physical shape of grooves that represents the qualities of the sound, it is a series of zeros and ones. These are 'read' by a laser beam and then 'translated' into electric impulses and thus sound waves by the CD player. Digital recording and reproduction is much more precise than the old analogue or mechanical system, so precise that some sound enthusiasts claim it is cold and lifeless compared to the sound experienced at live concerts.

Digitalization of radio and TV, where programmes are recorded and distributed as series of zeros and ones, rather than analogue electronic waves, may thus in principle mean *better sound and picture*. This is not, however, the most important consequence of the technological transition. Two other dimensions of the shift represent more exciting possibilities. First, digitalization means that the capacity for distribution is tremendously expanded in comparison with the old analogue spectrum, and so there is room for an enormous *increase in the number of channels*. With terrestrial distribution the increase is not very significant if today's technical standard is to be maintained, but with satellite distribution more than 1500 channels are possible. Second, digitalization opens the door to a *convergence* of hitherto separate media and distributional forms, i.e. that broadcasting, telecommunications and the Internet will overlap and merge. The distinctions between TV sets, computers and mobile phones will be fleeting. One may watch TV on one's computer or mobile phone, and surf the Internet with any of these appliances. This also illustrates how convergence opens new possibilities for *interactivity* between media and their users – 'receivers' can communicate with 'senders' in new, direct ways via computers, phones or digital TV sets. Digitalization will also facilitate the establishment of various types of pay-TV, either based on subscriptions or pay-per-view. Movies, gardening programmes, sports events or whatever can be ordered as easily as we now look up pages on the Internet. Consequently, one may envisage a situation where watching television becomes a much more *individualized* activity than it used to be.

However, much is still quite unclear about developments in this area. Nobody knows how long it will take until a major proportion of the population has invested in the equipment necessary to receive digital television. As long as the most important analogue channels are available, it seems that many (or most) people will tend to postpone such an investment. Transmitting programmes both in an analogue and a digital mode at the same time is costly; it is therefore considered necessary to set a date when analogue distribution will simply be stopped, so people are forced to buy digital equipment if they still want to have television in their homes. Some countries have decided such a date while others have not. Switching off analogue television, if millions of people are still sticking to it, is clearly a drastic action, which could be problematic for both social and commercial reasons.

A fully digitalized television system obviously implies a radical change from traditional broadcasting. The latter involves, as stated above, the distribution of programmes from some centre to the whole or major parts of the population. But with 500 or 1000 channels available, it is hard to maintain the idea that the senders are 'sowing' from a centre. It seems as if the notion of a 'centre' dissolves or becomes transformed into an enormous number of 'centres'. If so, the basic functions of broadcasting, as described by Raymond Williams (1975), especially the production of identity, of some feeling of commonality, must necessarily change quite drastically. The grand cultural community from the glory days of monopoly or duopoly broadcasting will be replaced by a far more differentiated pattern of groups with special interests or values.

This is at least how things appear if one only considers them with a view to the technological possibilities. The widespread fascination with technology often leaves social and cultural aspects of developments in the shade. The social functions of broadcasting are not something that only interests society's social and cultural 'centre' or top. Most people seem to appreciate broadcasting's offering of a *common forum and shared experience*. It is not probable that all TV viewing in the future will take place in front of computers or mobile phones. In countries with years of experience with dozens of channels, such as the USA, a small handful of national, terrestrially distributed channels have actually had an astonishing ability to withstand tough competition from a highly differentiated set of cable channels. Even if the networks' average audience share has been reduced, because a growing part of the population spends more and more time on various niche channels, people keep returning to the central channels *whenever they offer something of interest.* It is harder to attain the high audience numbers of the old days, but most people spend some time on the networks every week. In summer 2000, CBS managed to attract over 40 million viewers to a single episode of the docu-soap/game show *Survivor.* No other medium can assemble such a colossal audience, just waiting to be exposed to advertising. This sort of potential is precisely why Time Warner found it financially interesting to establish a fifth network as late as the 1990s. *The survival of traditional broadcasting is tied to people's socially motivated wish and/or need for what broadcasting can offer on the one hand, and the ability of broadcasters to provide generally relevant and attractive programmes on the other.* Broadcasting's fate is not decided by technological developments alone.

Traditional public regulation of broadcasting will, however, become problematic when digital distribution via satellite allows the number of available channels to explode and most people get their programmes via satellite. The traditional rationale that the spectrum is limited so one can demand certain services in return for the use of a communal scarce resource will appear not to be applicable any more. Terrestrial digital distribution is different since its capacity will be so limited that the traditional legitimation of regulation still holds. It is also worth remembering that there are already common European rules for satellite broadcasting. The European Union has already officially decided that public service broadcasting is worth protecting, and the European Council has unanimously reached the same conclusion. Satellites are positioned in outer space, but they may still be within reach of politically motivated regulations. The struggles over which regulations should be imposed will just have to take place in an international political arena. And they are already going on.

10 Production: creativity, contexts and power

From writing to reading matter

The simplest form of media production is perhaps what I am doing here. I sit here writing. My tool is quite different from goose-feather quills and ballpoint pens, but what I do does not really differ all that much from the work at the typing machines used by authors throughout most of the twentieth century. The practice of writing may have changed with changing technologies, but it is still a fundamentally individual practice. What I write will not, however, become reading matter for people like you until it has passed through a pretty complicated process at a publisher's, a printer's and a bookstore. My writing is the first stage in the production of a book, and the book is a mass medium. All media production is to some extent a collective process organized in a more or less industrial manner. The latter means that a rational division of labour and an emphasis on efficiency marks the process. To the extent that media production is a form of business, which it is, as a rule, in our type of society, the aim of producing a profit will regulate what gets produced and how.

This chapter is, first, to be about the relationship between the individual and the collective or industrial in all media production. Second, it is to be about how economic considerations influence production. And, third, it will, on the most general plane, be about the *power* that lies in production or 'the sender', to use a term associated with the elementary, linear communication model (see Chapter 4). This power is about deciding what we are offered as media users and thus about deciding our opportunities to receive meaning, pleasure, or the opposite, from our encounters with media. I have touched on this in all the previous chapters. Thus, fourth, this final chapter will also offer an opportunity to repeat, condense and provide additional perspectives on, some of what this whole book is about.

'Production' and 'consumption' are terms taken from the language of economics. They are abstract categories for a large number of very different practices or functions, and so they are perhaps best suited to talking about highly generalized features of all these different phenomena. Such a bird's eye view is necessary if we want to get an overview of some fundamental patterns. If we want to find out what is actually, concretely, going on, we will have to get down on the ground and have a closer look. First, we will deal with the very abstract, general links between production and consumption, i.e. between 'senders' and 'recipients' in the processes of media communication.

The power and responsibility of production

The power of production, or 'the senders', in media communication has been a central issue in debates within media and communication studies for decades. It concerns, first, to what extent that which is produced, 'texts', can determine our understanding, experience and evaluation of them. The power of production is evidently greater if the products can effectively, by and of themselves, control our perception of them than if we as recipients are more or less completely free to determine what the products are about and how we are to respond to them. The issue of the power of production is, in other words, directly related to how we conceive of the role of audiences – whether they are to be seen as helpless objects of influence or autonomous, critical subjects – or something in between these two extremes (cf. Chapter 2 of the present volume, on influence). But the question of the power of production is also about the composition of the total media output. It is thus also closely tied to more general economic and political debates about the functions of the *market*. I have written about this both in the chapter on the public sphere (Chapter 8) and in the chapter on broadcasting (Chapter 9), but it is so important that it deserves to be taken up again. Is it the power that lies in the aggregate of individual consumers' choices that decides what will be produced, or is it in the last instance the executives of various industries that are in control? This question is not only relevant when we wonder who has decided that there should be 89 different deodorants available in the stores, it is also the question underlying our attitude to the claims of commercial media that they only deliver what people want and that it is 'the market' that decides how, say, newspapers and TV channels develop. Some people say we 'get the media we deserve'. In previous chapters I have argued that this is a debatable view in quite concrete ways. In the following paragraphs, I will argue the same, albeit in a more abstract way.

In the mid-nineteenth century, the German philosopher, sociologist, historian and economist Karl Marx presented sharp analyses of capitalist society and its economy, where a main point in fact was that 'economy' is basically about social relations, i.e. relations between people, not some purely technical mechanism. In a famous text, the Introduction to the book known as *Grundrisse*, he also reflects on, among other things, the general relationship between production and consumption. The two are closely interconnected, he thought, not least because production always also implies that something is consumed and, correspondingly, that all consumption implies that something is produced (say, clean teeth). He moreover pointed out that consumption in a way completes production, realizes the product: a railway is not really a railway until trains run on it, as he put it. One might say that this is a point analogous to the idea of literary reception theory, that a literary text is not realized as a text until it is read ('consumed') by someone. But even if production and consumption thus can be seen as moments of one and the same circular process, production is, according to Marx, the *predominant* moment – it is 'the act through which the whole process again runs its course' (Marx [1857] 1973: 94). Production, among other things, decides consumption's 'specificity, its character, its *finish*', it decides 'the way in which it is consumed' ([1857] 1973: 92).

This latter point can in our context be illustrated by how the first soap opera shown on Norwegian television, *Dynasty*, actually demanded a new way of watching and relating to television fiction (see Chapter 7). The story of the first-ever soap in Norway can also illustrate the power of production in other ways. Many Norwegian television viewers in the early 1980s wanted more narrative, entertaining fiction on TV, but that this wish was to be satisfied by an American prime-time soap and, even more specifically by *Dynasty*, was not something that was decided by the general desire of Norwegian audiences. Even if this show was very popular, and thus evidently worked as some sort of answer to the wish of many viewers, it was the international power of the US television industry and the executives at the Norwegian public service broadcaster which decided that the wish would be satisfied in this particular way. Norwegian TV viewers could not have expressed a wish for US prime-time soaps, since they had never encountered the genre before. The general point is, then, that *the audience can never choose something it has not been offered, and any specific programme or product offered is always one of several imaginable 'answers' to a more general demand.* It is always producers or senders that decide what is offered, and how these offers are shaped; and these decisions are always made with a view to other factors than the demand of the audience – not least the desire for maximum profit.

It is thus correct that we as consumers – all together – may have an influence on what we are offered in terms of products and services, and also in the media field. It is not the case that whatever the media industries offers is shoved down our throats. A simple and good illustration of this is the colossal volume of the cultural industries' production compared to the number of profit-making successes. There are about 10 flops to a hit, both in the movie and music industries. Most people are not uncritical, that is to say without the ability to discern (to critique, etymologically, means to discern, or distinguish); but they can only choose between that which is offered, and the success of a product does not mean that it could not have been *better*. Neither does it mean that a very different product could not have been even *more* popular.

There are two points here. The first is that media producers have the power to decide what we are in fact offered, even if they do this after market research and experiences of what people have bought before. The characteristics of products set certain conditions for our experience of them, i.e. the meanings, significations and (dis)pleasure we can get out of the movie, the book, the music, the newspaper or the TV programme. The second point is that *those who produce have an unavoidable responsibility for their product.* This *ethical* responsibility cannot be disclaimed by saying that 'people want what we're making' because people might also (and perhaps *rather*) want a different and better product ('better' as judged by a number of relevant parameters of a non-economic sort). That people buy very polluting cars is not a good reason to stop trying to produce less polluting vehicles. That people spend money on semi-good media products is not a good reason to stop striving to produce all-good ones. It is not unthinkable that live executions on TV would attract quite a large, shock-hungry audience. When even the most hard-boiled of commercial TV executives still would not broadcast such stuff, it indicates that they accept at least *some* ethical limitations to what sorts of wishes from audiences they are happy to satisfy. They thereby also demonstrate how the legitimation of editorial choices *solely* by pointing to 'what the audience want' is to shirk the editorial responsibility for one's product.

Creativity and its constraints

Journalists now 'sign' their texts in newspapers and their broadcasts; this shows their willingness to accept the responsibility, and possible accolades, for the product they deliver. After any TV programme or movie we are furnished with the names of everyone involved in the production process, and the specific functions of each of them. All of this demonstrates that media institutions tend to emphasize that real, living human beings work there and in various ways 'express themselves' through the work they do. This may be a problematic issue, as we shall soon see, but the point here is that the notion of the productive, or *creative*, individual is central to the ways in which the media and their employees think about and present themselves.

The word *creative* is currently extremely popular. It refers to an ability many people would like to have. This, it seems, is particularly true of people in the advertising business, but it is also true of lots of people in a number of other media industry branches. The meaning of the word is, nowadays, often difficult to distinguish from 'inventive' or 'imaginative', but originally it was a term for the free production of something out of nothing, i.e. something *completely new* – an ability that actually would be restricted to God. Historically, the term is tied to the image of the artist that was characteristic of Romanticism. Here the artist was precisely understood as someone who was tied to something divine, as the term *inspiration* also indicates. As a Danish literary scholar once pointed out, Romanticist pictures of authors often portray them as people sitting with their faces lifted in the direction of heaven rather than looking down at the paper, their work, on the table in front of them (Thing, 1973). The term *creativity* thus carries echoes of this sort of close connection between God and the unique artist-individual – the *genius* (cf. Battersby, 1989).

The critique of traditional historical-biographical literary history in the 1960s and 1970s was directed at this religiously inflated or mythically flavoured image of the artist and the correlated reading of all 'proper' literature as the expression of a unique, and possibly divinely inspired, artist's soul. It was correctly argued that all literature is written on the basis of a shared language – some codes, forms and traditions that are always already present as a common human heritage and raw material. The same goes for all other media and forms of expression, both within and outside of the field of art. In many ways this is what semiotics, hermeneutics and rhetoric are all about. Similar critiques were directed at the traditional writing of art history and the interpretation of pictures, the writing of film history and the interpretation of films, and so on.

The struggle of the group tied to the French cinema journal *Cahiers du cinéma* to have the film director recognized as an *auteur* on a par with the authors of literature, took place (as mentioned in Chapter 7) in the 1950s and early 1960s. But just as they had succeeded, from the mid-1960s onwards, structuralist semiotics did its best to demystify and symbolically, so to speak, kill the author (cf. the title of the famous piece by Roland Barthes, 'The death of the author' ([1968] 1977c). The structuralists used to say that we are all locked up in 'the prison house of language', i.e. that we cannot escape the limitations inherent in the language we have available in our attempts to express something freely and uniquely. But as Graham Murdock once put it, it is rather strange that Roland Barthes, for example, enjoyed saying such things so much, since he more than most had a style that is immediately recognizable as his own: 'If Barthes served a life sentence in the prison house of language, his works strive remarkably hard to give the impression that he is out on parole' (Murdock, 1993: 131). The point is that, even if language represents a set of limitations, it is also an arsenal of possibilities. Language 'imprisons', but it also provides freedom. This is the case with any expressive material, such as images and sound, possibly in combination. Nobody who produces anything in these materials can free themselves completely from various limitations in terms of cultural, institutional and material conditions, but they also have a huge variety of possibilities within these strictures.

The question of the possibilities for individual expression in various media is a variety of what I, in Chapter 3, termed the structure-actor problem in the social sciences. All that was said there about so-called cultural fields is relevant for an understanding of the frameworks within which media production takes place. The problem is also relevant to the notion of *cultural industry* as developed by Theodor W. Adorno and Max Horkheimer in the book *The Dialectic of Enlightenment* (cf. Chapter 2 of the present volume, on influence). With this metaphorical term they compared the production of movies with the industrial production of, for example, locks, bicycles, electric appliances or whatever. They thought that so-called Yale locks offered an illuminating parallel to the products of the cultural industry. Thousands of locks are basically identical, only having minimal differences in the shape of the lock mechanism and keys to distinguish them from one another. Adorno and Horkheimer thought that this was also the case with thousands of Hollywood movies and pop tunes. The individual products could at best be said to contain some minimal inventive element that could give them what might be termed *pseudo-individuality*.

Even if we accept that there is a high degree of sameness or similarity between many films and pop tunes within the same genre, and that their production takes place in a way that resembles industrial production, there is, as pointed out by Bernard Gendron (1986), something important that gets lost in the industry-metaphor's claim that ordinary industrial production and production within the cultural industry are identical. For, while the production of *identical copies* of CDs, films, bicycles and electric appliances is clearly of an industrial, factory-like sort, *texts* – that is, words, music, images – have originally been produced in a different way and as *unique* objects. A pop tune is at the outset put together by a single person or a few people with either a computer or other electronic devices, or a piano, a guitar, and possibly pen and paper. It is later recorded at a studio where technicians and producers also contribute to its final form. Even if all these artists, or craftspeople, stick to certain genre rules, the final result will still be a pop tune that is different from all other pop tunes.

While Adorno and Horkheimer granted an element of individual variation to their lock parallel, they also clearly underestimated it: we accept any internal individual variation on a Yale lock as long as it works, but we do not accept just any pop tune as long as it lasts about 3 minutes and sticks to a four-four beat. The industry metaphor, in other words, misses the fundamental element of craftsmanship and individuality in the culture industry's production of *texts*, the element of real, unique individuals' imaginative work on the *original prototype* for the mass production of saleable copies, whether these are CDs, newspapers or films. It therefore also misses an important difference between the ordinary industrial standardization of products such as electrical ovens and the culture industry's standardization of it products in line with genre conventions. Ovens are standardized for purely rational technical and economic reasons while the standardization of culture industry products is closely related to *the 'standardization' of all sorts of cultural artefacts in traditional, pre-industrial folk culture.* You often need an educated ear to discern one piece of folk music played on the bagpipes or the Norwegian Hardanger fiddle from another, and folktales are to a high degree built on a limited number of formulas (cf. Vladimir Propp's classic analysis of Russian folktales, to which I referred in Chapter 7). Most people have at some time *appreciated* the interplay between sameness and difference in recognizable genre forms. Genre conventions are part of a *common cultural heritage* for both producers and audiences (cf. Chapter 4 of the present volume, on semiotics), and are further developed in the interaction between these two groups. Popular music is a particularly good example of the dynamism of popular culture production and of how much more varied this production is now than it was 50 to 60 years ago, when Adorno and Horkheimer were writing.

If we want to understand what media production is about, we will thus have to acknowledge the ways in which it differs from ordinary industrial production. Our point of departure must be that living human beings working within specific institutional or organizational ramifications constantly produce new 'originals' in a continuous dialogue with culturally established codes such as genres. We may try to understand this dialogue in hermeneutic terms (cf. Chapter 5). Interpretation not only takes place on the reception side of the communicative process, though. Media producers have acquired the same cultural competence as everyone else through socialization, before they entered their professional lives, where one of their main tasks is to conduct interpretations and evaluations of both former and prospective published texts.

In the chapter on social differences/distinctions (Chapter 3), I wrote about this as a continuously ongoing process of evaluation of the quality of texts. Journalists read lots of newspapers and watch a lot of news and current affairs programmes on TV. They interpret and evaluate these texts both on their own and in group meetings at various levels in a professional context, and compare them with their own products. They have their horizons of expectation, which are also dynamic, and these contain not least certain conceptions of the genres in which they work: what characterizes a news story, a talk show, a documentary? Interpretation is thus something that both 'senders' and 'receivers' do, and both groups normally do it on the basis of quite similar fundamental cultural conditions. The difference is not only that media producers know so much more about the intricacies of their medium, more important is the fact that they can *change* the products they interpret. Ordinary members of the audience cannot do this (cf. Ytreberg, 1999: 14ff.).

The dialectic relations between freedom and constraints, the individual and the collective, tradition and renewal, can be found in all media and arts. Concrete studies of specific conditions are needed if one wants to say anything about which of the two terms in these oppositions is dominant in various types of media production. I will, however, without going into too much detail, now try to say a bit about some specific areas.

Literary production

A lot of research has been carried out into the life histories of authors and other artists. Normally these biographies emphasize the childhood, adolescence and private life of these artists much more than the artistic process as such. The idea often seems to be that any experience in the life of the artist will somehow be represented in their work. If someone in a novel gets sea-sick, it is because the author some time in 1894 fed the fishes all the way between Plymouth and Bourdeaux, and this is actually the deeper meaning of the sequence in question. The artist's biography as a genre is more tied to a cult of the Artist as Genius than to a serious interest in what goes on when literary texts are written, and how they end up as books in bookstores and libraries.

A more sociological approach to the study of literary production and distribution does exist, but there is still a great deal to be done here. The French scholar Robert Escarpit's little book *Sociology of Literature* (1971), originally published in 1958, could be seen as something of a classic. It has chapters on authors as a professional group and about the publishing business; but its possible status as a classic has more to do with its description of what Escarpit called the two circuits in the distribution of literature, the educated and the popular circuit (i.e. basically bookstore vs kiosk or news-stand distribution). Another, better-known French sociologist, Pierre Bourdieu, has as part of his more general sociology of culture, provided theoretical tools for an understanding of how the literary field works (see, again, Chapter 3). In his book *The Rules of Art* (English edition, 1996) he has, among other things, analysed the emergence of this area as a relatively autonomous social field.

Bourdieu is also a central source of inspiration for a very solid and interesting study of the American Book of the Month Club, Janice Radway's *A Feeling for Books* (1998). Radway pays particular attention to the literary consultants of this club, and demonstrates and analyses how they form the club's selections of books for its members, whose 'middlebrow' tastes they knew, to a considerable extent shared, and contributed to the shaping of. Radway had previously published a landmark so-called ethnographic study of readers of popular literature for women, *Reading the Romance* (1984).The authors of fiction are, just as visual artists, most often considered very free from constraints in their work. Equipped with pen and paper, or a laptop computer, they can supposedly write whenever and wherever about whatever. This has some truth to it, but it is still for the most part wrong. Few authors, for instance, can make a living out of their writing. Most of them will have to do something else other than writing in order to survive, and so most authors simply have limited *time* for writing.

When an author starts writing, it is normally with an idea that she or he has conceived her/himself. But both this idea, and particularly its elaboration in the literary text, are of course thoroughly marked by literary traditions and the demands on craftsmanship that go with these traditions. In times past, the acquisition of the necessary knowledge and know-how was, beyond what anyone could pick up in school, to a great extent left to the individual's own efforts, trial and error. Admission to the realms of serious literature would be especially demanding for those with backgrounds that did not provide them with much cultural capital, and so they would have to spend a lot of time acquiring the necessary basis for qualified literary writing. On the other hand, much of the renewal of literature at any time was due to authors who were free from the orthodoxies of the literary establishment because they had other social backgrounds. Much of this is different these days. University courses in 'creative writing' and the fact that many authors have been through university courses in literary history and criticism have contributed to a more thorough institutional control of serious literary writing, i.e. stricter norms for anything from narrative techniques to more comprehensive aesthetic and thematic priorities. Importantly, this has not necessarily reduced the occurrence of bitter struggles between various tendencies and milieus in the literary field. But the sum total is still that a sort of streamlining of literary production has taken place.

Getting what one has written published at all may also be a problem. Only a minuscule part of all the manuscripts received unsolicited by publishers will ever end up in bookstores. Most will be returned or just forgotten after a quick check. Those selected for possible publication may be sent out to consultants, often already established authors or, in some cases, people who teach literature at universities. The consultants write a report where they either recommend publication with major or minor alterations, or deem the text unpublishable. Especially in the case of 'debutantes', a manuscript will go back and forth between the author, consultants and the editor at the publisher's several times. The author will also, of course, receive responses from unofficial consultants in his/her own family or circle of friends. When one finally arrives at an acceptable manuscript, there will be proofreading, decisions concerning graphic design, and so on. The book that eventually arrives in bookstores is, in other words, to a much higher degree than is normally acknowledged, a *collective* product, even if it, officially and legally, has a single person marked out on its cover as solely responsible.

There may still be reasons to maintain a distinction between the production of literarily ambitious, serious, or legitimate literature on the one hand, and the more industry-like production of trivial or popular literature on the other. In the latter type of literature, genre definitions are stricter and thus more binding, and books are most often written as parts of certain long series. The authors are contracted to deliver several manuscripts per year (cf. the discussion of quality in Chapter 3) and the publisher may well make use of market research in various forms in order to find out what its books should be about or how they should be written in order to sell. This is then a system that, much more clearly, turns authors into (often well-paid) *literary proletarians*, thus illustrating how much more free from constraints authors in the higher literary echelons actually are, in spite of the regime just described above.

As a whole, then, the production of literary fiction has features that also characterize other types of media production.

- Production is, to a greater or lesser extent, regulated by historically established traditions, conventions and genre rules that the individual producer is supposed to know and respect.
- The degree of regulation (constraints) varies with the degree of industry-like organization of production, and there exists a distinction between an industrially and commercially oriented sector on the one hand and, on the other, a sector that, at least officially, is based on as much individual freedom in the creative process as possible, i.e. a commitment to what, historically speaking, could be termed a romantic understanding of art and artists. It is this distinction that Pierre Bourdieu (1996) writes about as the tension between *an intellectual and a commercial pole* in any artistic field of production (see, again, Chapter 3). The other important axis in such fields cuts across the first, somewhere not too far from the intellectual pole, and goes between the *established*, somewhat older 'masters' and the younger, often somewhat rebellious members of the *avant-garde*. The tension between these two groups results in an ongoing renewal of the standards of the serious, more 'highbrow' section of the field.

The search for the artist in film

It's been a while since Hollywood was first referred to as a 'dream factory'. This term is interesting because it is an *oxymoron* (the two words seem to contradict one another). A dream is normally thought of as something individual, intimate, irrational and ephemeral, while a factory is a materially solid context for work that is collective, rationally organized, and produces concrete, immediately useful objects. The term thus points to a possible contradiction between the function of movies as more or less irrational dream-worlds for large audiences and their rational, industrially organized, blatantly commercial production. The latter characteristics have often, and especially in Europe, been attributed to Hollywood and, where this is the case, Hollywood films have been denied any status as 'art'. Art means that individual artists have been able to express their individuality, and there is much evidence to suggest that this isn't really possible in Hollywood. A classic study of the Hollywood system in its heyday, which demonstrates this idea is the anthropologist Hortense Powdermaker's *Hollywood: The Dream Factory* (1950), based on fieldwork in the industry carried out from 1946 to 1947. Another highly recommended study that may be less scholarly, but is still both solid and engagingly written, is the journalist Lillian Ross's novel-esque report *Picture*, published in 1953, about the conflict-ridden production of John Huston's film *The Red Badge of Courage* (1950). More recent scholarly literature about film production and its larger economic contexts is a huge field, and the authors are economists, sociologists, anthropologists, film scholars and the like. But the historical study by David Bordwell, Kristin Thompson and Janet Staiger, *The Classical Hollywood Cinema: Film Style and Mode of Production to 1960* (1988), holds a special position in this area. Here one finds very detailed descriptions of the system of production in the period covered, and attempts to understand the consequences of the system for the shape of the films produced. There is more emphasis on economic matters and more recent conditions in Tino Balio's books *The American Film Industry* (second edition, 1985) and *Hollywood in the Age of Television* (1990).

As mentioned in Chapter 7, on narratology, the naming of a central creative person behind a film has been important to the efforts towards elevating film to the status of 'art'. As early as 1920 there had already been talk of the director as the 'author' of films (some were greater authors than others). The silent movie star Mary Pickford regarded D.W. Griffith as the only director who really dared realize his own ideas and try out something new in Hollywood – and film classics such as *Birth of a Nation* and *Intolerance* may be said to support such a view. In the 1940s there were those, not least in France, who wanted to make the scriptwriter the main creative person behind a film, especially after the introduction of sound. Among those who held such a view, arguing against awarding this position to the director, was André Bazin, the well-known critic and theorist. Bazin was, interestingly, from the start involved in the legendary journal *Cahiers du cinéma*, the first issue of which appeared in 1951. *Cahiers* has become famous because of its emphasis on the director's role. A number of directors that became famous during the so-called New Wave of French film around 1960 were tied to the journal in the 1950s (people such as Jean-Luc Godard, Francois Truffaut, Claude Chabrol and Eric Rohmer). As indicated by the references to the 1920s above, the *Cahiers* group's view that the director was the author, or *auteur*, of a film was nothing new; and their idea was especially pertinent when dealing with directors who wrote their own scripts or had decisive control over scriptwriting (as had been, and then still was, the case with Jean Renoir, Jean Cocteau and Jacques Tati, and one of the many Germans who fled the Nazis via France to Hollywood, Max Ophüls). In the 1950s and 1960s there emerged a number of such writer-directors. Ingmar Bergman, Luis Buñuel, Michelangelo Antonioni and Federico Fellini are some of the best known – and *they are all Europeans*.

However, the most original and provocative view held by the younger members of the *Cahiers* group, and which was later to be picked up by British and US critics, was that they claimed to be able to see the individuality of the best directors expressed even in the most 'industrial', genre-confined and widely popular of Hollywood movies, i.e. where the division of labour was such that directors did not write their own scripts. John Ford, Howard Hawks, William Wyler and Alfred Hitchcock – but also directors like the musicals specialist Vincente Minnelli and the master of melodrama Douglas Sirk – were awarded status as *auteurs* with a unique artistic profile, especially when taking into consideration their total *oeuvre*. Around 1970 a theoretically more sophisticated and politicized version of this way of thinking was developed, again first and foremost in *Cahiers du cinéma*. It was now claimed that contradictions in the films between the ideologically bourgeois narrative and the *auteur*-director's personal favourite themes and motifs could be found, so that these industrially produced films could actually be seen as complex expressions (symptoms) of ideological contradictions in capitalist society. Otherwise the cult of the Artist as Creative Genius was very much in doubt in the 1970s, not least in France; as noted above, these were times when a death certificate was issued there for any *auteur* figure in any art form.

But it is not so simple to kill off the idea of the Artist with a capital A. It is simply too closely tied to our more general ideas of, and also our less conscious, spontaneous attitudes to, *the individual* and *personality* in modern societies. These days, the idea that the director is the central creative source of a film has become an integral part of journalistic film criticism and many 'ordinary' cinema-goers' ways of thinking about and categorizing films, especially the better educated among them. But classification according to star actors is also widespread, and is probably pretty unclear to most people who have directed, say, Arnold Schwarzenegger or Julia Roberts films. The ultimate *auteur* movies will thus be those where the same individual is scriptwriter, director and star actor. Woody Allen would be one of the few that make films in this way. Some Hollywood stars might also, once they had become extremely rich from acting, try to demonstrate that they are actually quite deep and creative people too. A good way to do this, it seems, is to direct a film, even if directors are normally paid much less than star actors. One might thus suspect that there is a tension between commercial and intellectual poles, even in the US film industry, as there is in other cultural fields. The intellectual pole is where cultural capital is located, the other is the place for money.

European film art and Hollywood's cultural industry

The sophisticated *Cahiers* argumentation for the greatness of much Hollywood film has not led to a completely different general perception of Hollywood in Europe. Everyone knows that, in most Hollywood productions, the director will be subordinate to the business executives. This is most clearly and simply revealed in what is called the *right to final cut*, i.e. control of the final editing of a film. In Europe, there is a long tradition for awarding the director the right to decide a film's final shape. In Hollywood it is the producer, i.e. the company or studio's top executives, who have this right. They may intervene in what Europeans would regard as the domain of the director at any stage of the production process, and after a first version has been screened for a test audience. The response of such a preview audience is registered in great detail and may lead to demands for re-editing or re-shooting of certain scenes, changes the director is obliged by contract to carry out. Exceptions to this rule may occur when a director has had a few successes that instil others with financial confidence in him or her. Michael Cimino won the right to the final cut after his success with *The Deer Hunter* (1978), but the financial disaster he went on to cause with his *Heaven's Gate* (1980) made it harder then ever for directors to be granted this right. Anyone working in Hollywood knows, and must accept, these conditions of power, but the business executives' often arbitrary fiddling with artistic products can still upset many.

The industrial character of US film production is also clearly revealed by its integration into large corporations that also have a hand in very different branches of business. Until about 1950, what is known as the *studio system* in

Hollywood was marked by so-called vertical integration. This implies that the five largest studios (MGM, Paramount, Twentieth Century Fox, Warner Brothers and RKO) were not only factories for movie production, they also to a great extent controlled distribution and cinemas (i.e. they controlled the market). In a decisive 1948 court case focusing on Paramount, the studios were denied such control of the whole chain from production to local cinema screens on the basis of general anti-monopolistic legislation. This and the introduction of television severely weakened the big studios in the course of the 1950s. In the early 1960s, then, financially strong companies in other branches of business started to buy their way into the movie-making industry. This process accelerated after a number of box office successes in the late 1970s had demonstrated the profit potential of film production. The 1980s was thus a decade where much happened in terms of the ownership of Hollywood studios. They were being bought and sold by various large corporations all the time, it seemed. For instance, Columbia Pictures was bought by Coca-Cola in 1982 and then sold to the Japanese company Sony in 1989. Transactions such as these made Hollywood studios parts of conglomerates that were otherwise involved in just about any line of business.

The main trend in the 1990s was different. Studios mostly became integrated into huge corporations with a focus on media, communications and leisure, such as Disney, Time Warner (now also merged with America Online) and Rupert Murdoch's News Corp. These mega-corporations control TV networks, cable companies and channels, various print media and often, say, theme parks in addition to their film studios. *In such constellations the film studios become key elements.* The movies they make are heavily promoted in the media controlled by the same corporations. Such campaigns facilitate the creation of successes that can then be the source of a great variety of extremely profitable spin-offs and tie-ins. The income from theatrical exhibition is now most often a minor part of the total profit generated by movies. There is not only the distribution of videos for sale and to rent, there are also soundtrack CDs, computer games, TV series and, not least, a host of products such as toys, baseball caps, T-shirts, crockery, towels, pens, or whatever. Then there are the theme parks. (For more on all of this, cf. Schatz, 1997). The term 'culture industry' has in this way become more fitting than ever before, and the market is practically global. Much of the cultural consumption around the world, not least among young people, is in practice decided in Hollywood and eagerly promoted for free by national and local media.

Europe does not have anything like the US film industry … yet. The British music industry is possibly the nearest thing to it. In this part of the world, film production is still regarded as an artistic activity of great importance to regional, national and European cultural identities, and it is therefore publicly supported in a number of different ways at various levels, including by the

European Union. The selection of projects for such support has traditionally been made on the basis of criteria that have to do with artistic or cultural values, even if potential profits are also (increasingly) considered. This is not to say that there is no purely commercial film production in Europe. That has been going on throughout the twentieth century. But the only period in which it was going on at a scale comparable with that of Hollywood was in Germany in the late 1920s, at the UFA studios outside Berlin. The only film-related theme park of any significance is Euro-Disney, just outside Paris. And one may wonder what sort of theme parks, towels, crockery and baseball caps could be made on the basis of, say, Bergman's or Lars von Trier's films.

The production of TV fiction

In the chapter on narratology (Chapter 7), I said that television is now the dominant story-telling medium; and television's narratives are, with the exception of re-runs of feature films, mainly in serial form. The USA is clearly the main provider of television fiction to screens all over the world, and so the conditions of production there will be particularly considered here. But it is worth underlining that British, Australian, Brazilian and Mexican producers are also major exporters. This, among other things, was emphasized in a very useful little book by Armand and Michelle Mattelart, *International Image Markets* (1984), where the authors argued for a more nuanced view than the previously strong perceptions of the USA as totally dominating (see also, for example, Allen, 1995; Martín-Barbero, 1993).

The literature on the US television industry is voluminous, even if one just concentrates on the scholarly part of it and looks only at those parts that are primarily concerned with the production of fiction. One example is Todd Gitlin's *Inside Prime Time* (1985), which has become a classic. It is a thorough, very well-written study of processes and power relations in the business, based not least on interviews with central figures. Another example is Robert Allen's *Speaking of Soap Operas* (1983), which concentrates on daytime soaps and their history. These days almost all US TV series are effectively soap operas, since storylines stretch across several episodes and there is a sense of a long story being slowly unfolded as seasons go by. This is one of the reasons why most of my examples in the following paragraphs are related to soap opera production. Another, and very simple, reason for this is that I have made a study of the production of soap opera (cf. Gripsrud, 1995, Chapter 1).

In the previous chapter, I described the change from sponsored drama anthologies produced in New York to spot advertising, and series and serials produced in Hollywood. This had consequences not only for the power relations between networks, production companies and advertisers, it also affected the distribution of power within drama production itself. The scriptwriters had their power significantly reduced. From having been *auteurs*, as 'playwrights' for one-off dramas, they became more or less anonymous proletarians producing variations on a theme decided by others. The production of filmed series was from then on taken care of by formally independent production companies that co-operated closely with the networks. The new *auteur* figure in US television became the (executive) producer, i.e. the leader of the production company (see Cantor, 1971; Newcomb and Alley, 1983). It is he (few are women) who controls the main lines of a show; directors and scriptwriters often change while the producer remains the same. In soap formats the executive producer will participate in, or be responsible for, the show's *bible*, i.e. an overview of the chain of events during one or two seasons, and every script for an episode needs to be controlled and approved by him: hardly a comma may be changed on set without his approval.

The 'bible' consists of episodes chopped up by a script editor who is also the boss of a team of subordinate writers who 'flesh out' the episodes with dialogue and movements on the basis of the section of the 'bible' in question. The script editor is responsible for checking that every detail is in line with what has been going on in previous episodes and what is due to happen later. Directors are called in to work for relatively short periods at a time. In a show with weekly episodes shot on film, they may for instance have 15 working days to complete one episode; this might consist of 7 days for preparation, 7 days of shooting and an extra day in case something goes wrong or the producer is not happy. (The example here is taken from *Dynasty* but the system is more or less the same for other weekly shows, including those made outside the USA.) When episodes are broadcast daily, the production of the script is organized in roughly the same way, while the director of these three-camera video productions will have to complete the shooting of an episode in a single day. The greater the time pressure, the less is the influence of the professional categories below the level of producer. One must constantly go for the simplest, most direct solutions, whether one is a scriptwriter, actor or director; these might be well-worn, clichéd solutions or devices. In light of all this, it is not hard to understand that television serials have largely had a low cultural status, and that the producer has been seen as the creative control centre.

Muriel Cantor (1971) found, in a classic study, that US television producers could be divided into three categories. *Old line producers* are people with little formal education but, as a rule, long and varied experience in the business. They tend to stick to standard procedures and do not believe that the audience would accept any sort of deviation from these, either thematically or formally. *Film-makers* are often educated as such and tend to regard their work in television as temporary. They are 'actually' film people, and regard television as a sort of waiting room, in which they have little interest and for which they have little respect. They do not have much confidence in television's audiences either, and tend to deliver standard goods. The third category, however, is that of *writer-producers*. As the term indicates, these are also scriptwriters. They often have some relevant education. They are sincerely interested in television as a medium, do not have a condescending attitude to its audiences, and often have certain social or cultural 'messages' and formal ideas they want to present to viewers.

It is this latter category that has brought about the most interesting changes in US television over the last couple of decades. The show I have studied most closely, *Dynasty*, was in many ways the work of Esther Shapiro, and she is a typical writer-producer. Working closely with her, however, was her husband, who is more of a film-maker type, and Aaron Spelling, who is an old line producer with a bit of a special style. This mix probably contributed to the show's broad appeal. Those who, since then, have acquired status as television *auteurs*, are all writer-producers; these include Stephen Bochco (*Hill Street Blues, LA Law, NYPD Blue*) and, not least, David E. Kelley (*Picket Fences, Chicago Hope, Ally McBeal, The Practice*). As mentioned in the previous chapter, the creative freedom granted to these *auteurs* is closely linked to the television industry's discovery around 1980 that a large part of the population – those best educated and most affluent – hardly watched any television at all. This made the networks open up to a number of experiments and new twists in an attempt to reach these financially interesting groups. One of the most memorable of these shows was *Twin Peaks*, the strange 'mystery soap' produced by film director David Lynch. So, when US television fiction did gain a little cultural respectability, this was financially motivated.

Here we may note a possible theoretical problem with Pierre Bourdieu's theory of cultural fields (cf. above and Chapter 3 of the present volume). If one regards the production of fiction for US television (that is to say, then, also for most of the world) as a cultural field in Bourdieu's sense, one might say that the 'centre of gravity' has been moved in the direction of some sort of intellectual pole. But this is clearly problematic since the reason for the observed change is purely business motivated. US television production is probably not a cultural field in Bourdieu's sense, since it is wholly and fully commercially driven. It lacks the autonomy required for cultural fields. This suggests that Bourdieu's concept is not adequate, either for US television or other dyed-in-the-wool commercial forms of cultural production.

But *film* production in Hollywood does, however, have similarities with Bourdieu's cultural fields. For instance, there are directors without huge commercial successes that still have very high status among colleagues for professional reasons (an example of this type is Robert Altman). The point is that commercial and artistic criteria have not necessarily been identical; there is a degree of tension between a commercial and an 'intellectual' pole. Hollywood has also long had a tendency towards the formation of generational groups (younger directors, for instance, have thought of themselves as being in some way in opposition to those older and more established, in ways that resemble the relation between the young avant-garde and established 'masters' in fields such as literature and the visual arts). It is possible that the developments in US television may lead to similar conditions there. Substantial production opportunities have opened up with the major pay channels (Discovery, HBO and the like). Here something like *The Sopranos* can be made beyond the networks and can garner awards and recognition without having the mass appeal that a Bochco production for Fox would have to achieve before it was regarded as a success.

In a European context, both film and television production have more clearly been structured around Bourdieu's oppositional pairs: commercial vs intellectual and avant-garde vs establishment. The British television *auteur* Dennis Potter was located at the intellectual pole of the field of television drama. The existence of such a pole is also demonstrated in the fact that, say, Ingmar Bergman has retained his good name and reputation even if he has delivered a number of television mini-series. The *feuilleton*, or what in US television is known as a mini-series is, with the exception of one-off plays, a preferred format for such 'legitimate' television drama (a genre that is now almost non-existent). The commercialization of European television over the last two decades or so has strengthened tremendously the commercial pole in this field. There are those who think, for instance, that the BBC's mini-series are more and more marked by generic stereotypes and other signs of the commercial principles of production. Daring experiments are extremely rare, while crime shows are seemingly innumerable.

Collective products, polyphony and images of the audience

In the chapter on narratology we talked about 'the narrator' and 'the narrator's voice' in narrative texts, and it was briefly mentioned that we might find several 'voices', and not just different fictional narrators telling parts of the story. Thinking of the work of the Russian theorist Mikhail Bakhtin one might also speak of *polyphony* in texts, i.e. what appear to be several implicit authors, several and possibly contradictory underlying norms. These notions are developed with a view to literature, which is, in principle, created by individuals, even if there may be traces both of editors and various informal consultants. So what about media products that originate in collective processes?

Long before anyone in the West had heard as much as a rumour about Mikhail Bakhtin, an idea about a multiplicity of voices in film – albeit very different from Bakhtin's theory – was introduced on the basis of a sociological analysis of a production process that involved many 'empirical authors'. I am thinking of an empirical study conducted in the 1950s by the media sociologist Herbert Gans (1957). He was particularly interested in how the *images of the audience* in the heads of those involved in the production of a film influenced how it turned out. Starting from the point that any production must, logically, be a production *for* somebody, Gans thought that all those involved in the process would, more or less consciously, be working with a view to a more or less clearly defined audience for the specific film on which they were working. The images of the audience functioned as what Gans called 'external judges' in relation to the innumerable decisions that had to be made by everyone involved in the production. They might well vary and be partly contradictory, but the decisions were made within a hierarchically ordered structure where those at the top (i.e. the director and, ultimately, the studio's executives) would determine the appearance of the final 'compromise'. The finished film might thus look quite coherent but still have traces of many images of the audience. Gans thought this degree of 'polyphony' (a term he never used) might help explain the broad appeal of so many films

In Hollywood the central question at all stages of production, both in film and television, is precisely 'How will the audience react to this?' This is because potential market success is the first, and fundamental, consideration. This may appear in sharp contrast to the serious production of art where, in principle, all that matters is how the artist reacts to this or that feature of a work in progress. But the artist will, of course, to a considerable degree regard his or her work on the basis of norms that apply in the field of art; the artist's 'image of the audience' thus consists of people quite similar to her/himself, colleagues and connoisseurs, whether they are to be caressed or provoked. In the old public service broadcasting institutions it was a widespread practice to concentrate fully on the (anticipated) responses of oneself and the similarly minded (see, for example, the study of a British documentary production in Elliott, 1972). It is not certain that there are *only* negative aspects to the fact that commercialization and competition have made the people working in these institutions more aware that they, in fact, address and are paid by a broadly composed audience. This should not, of course, lead to the conclusion that all programmes should be made for everyone. It might just as well lead to a better rhetorical understanding, i.e. increased attention to the speech situation in which these people work and the need to address different audiences differently (cf. Chapter 6 of the present volume, on rhetoric).

Structures and actors in research on journalism

The productive journalistic collectives called editorial staffs are interesting objects of research. They have central social functions, but what is most interesting in our context is the question of how one should understand the relations between the individual journalists, the hierarchically organized collectives of which they are a part, these collectives' relations with the rest of the world, and the consequences of all this for the editorial product. One might say that this is the main theme of research on journalism. Such research has, in particular, looked at news journalism, and we will do the same here. The field is large and complex, so I have chosen to concentrate on a few relatively simple points.

David Manning White (1950) was interested in how newspapers' news coverage actually came about, and he thought he could find out something about this by studying how a single news editor somewhere in the USA did his work. He borrowed a term from social psychological research on the distribution of commodities and regarded the news editor as a *gatekeeper*. His job was about making *selections* from a steady stream of possible news items from news agencies and other sources. Taking this perspective one might think that the individual gatekeeper's personality, values and opinions will decide which news the public will be served with by the newspapers and broadcast media; but there are other perspectives too. Another classic study of news research is Warren Breed's examination of the editorial staff at a newspaper; this has the interesting title 'Social control in the newsroom' (1955). This article was not least about how newcomers in the editorial collective fast apprehended and interiorized the collective's norms on, for instance, how to define what news is. Such norms were effectively part of the air they were breathing in the newsroom, so socialization was quick and smooth. According to this perspective, then, the selection of news would be carried out on the basis of collective professional norms rather than the independent or autonomous judgement of individuals.

A more developed *organizational perspective* on news journalism did not really achieve a breakthrough until later, with books such as J. Tunstall's *Journalists at Work* (1971), E.J. Epstein's *News from Nowhere* (1973) and Herbert Gans' *Deciding What's News* (1980). All of these studies emphasized that journalists' work is regulated by a common set of professional norms that were linked to the news organization's external relations to factors such as economy, technological conditions and legal questions. With this perspective, there was a tendency to see the organization as almighty while the individual journalist disappeared. *Structure* got all the attention while the *actor* was all but forgotten.

In light of all this, one might well say that 1978 was a very good year for research on news journalism. That year a handful of books were published that marked a new understanding of the field (which, of course, had at that time been around for a while): the anthropologist Gaye Tuchman published her *Making News: A Study in the Construction of Reality*; Philip Schlesinger, once a film scholar, published *Putting Reality Together: BBC News*; and some of the same insights were included in Michael Schudson's historical study, *Discovering the News: A Social History of American Newspapers*. The key word is in the title of Schlesinger's and Tuchman's books: news journalism is not only about gathering and selecting news to be published, either on the basis of individual or collective criteria, it is about a textual *construction*, or 'putting together', of 'reality' at a certain time (i.e. the construction of a certain representation or image of reality). It is a form of textual *production*, not just a reflection of how things actually are. This allowed for a renewed interest in the individual journalist without abolishing the organizational perspective. In this *constructivist perspective* organizational structures would be understood as interacting with wider cultural and social contexts in the establishment of preconditions for the work of journalists, which is about the *textual production of interpretations* of events and social conditions.

This development in the main perspective of scholarly work – from a focus on selection, via a focus on organizations to the emphasis on textual production or construction – is of course simplified here. But it also reflects a very important, more general scholarly trend: the tendency towards a merger between social-scientist and humanistic approaches in media studies. Some time in the 1970s there was a breakthrough for a general critique of language and ideology, inspired by structuralism and semiotics, i.e. humanistic theories, in the social scientific research on mass media. 'Reality' became a more problematic concept, not something that simply was positively given, because it was now seen as something mediated to a great extent through language and images, by specific sorts of people in specific social positions with a certain range of expressive means at their disposal. Working on the basis of this insight, a number of scholars in many countries have contributed greatly to a better understanding of how the *interaction* between structures and actors decides the shape of both journalistic texts and processes of change in media history.

Media production and social power

This book started out with us, media users, as individuals placed in various social contexts. This starting point seemed reasonable since most of us primarily relate to the media as readers, listeners and viewers. We are, in multiple ways, dependent on these media's representations of the world when we form our conscious and unconscious ideas about ourselves and the world we inhabit. But the media do not only concern us as media users in a narrow sense. My hope is that these 10 chapters have demonstrated, from various angles, how massive the media's presence is in our everyday lives, in politics, the economy and social life in general. It is the ubiquity of the media and their formative influence on culture and society that is referred to in the terms 'media society' and 'media culture'. Still, one should not forget that the media operate in a dialectic relationship with other cultural and social conditions. It is, contrary to what seems to be a widespread belief, rarely correct to nominate one or several media as a simple *cause* of broader social changes. My colleague Anders Johansen (1999: 168) put this point well when writing that the media are 'culturally determinant – *to the extent that they also are culturally symptomatic*'. Broader processes of change, with a number of causes, take place over time, and the media contribute to the forming of these processes through the particular expressions they have there.

The media are decisively important to how our type of democracy functions. 'The world' is a highly complex, diverse phenomenon, so it is clearly a good thing if the media we rely on when forming our perceptions and opinions about it are also diverse rather than uniform in all sorts of ways. This will increase the space for our individual autonomy, and it also increases the space for both critical thinking and action-orientated conversations with other people. It facilitates our being and acting as, in principle, *autonomous subjects*. Fundamental rights in democratic societies, such as the freedom of information and the freedom of expression, are fundamental precisely because they both produce and presuppose individuals who are autonomous in both politically relevant and personal, existential areas of life (cf. the previous chapter).

Media policy is basically about how one can best maintain and strengthen people's freedom of information and expression in a wide sense, and the same can be said of all cultural policy. There will be struggles over ways and means here, but much less over the general aims. Disagreements will concern to what extent and in what ways political authorities should – and can – intervene in the internal affairs of the media and the economic freedom of action for their owners. This is a difficult question. The editorial independence of media is of decisive importance for their ability to fulfil their social mission and, in a capitalist economy, the principle of freedom of action for owners of capital is commonly seen as a fundamental right. But the alternatives in our type of society are not unlimited freedom on the one hand and authoritarian violations of fundamental rights by the (democratically elected) government on the other. Today's capitalist economy cannot function without various extensive public interventions: from anti-monopolistic regulation of competition to the establishment and maintenance of the necessary infrastructure. A totally 'free' market is a liberalist phantasm, it has never existed in reality. The same may be said of total editorial independence. It is precisely the economic pressures on most media that will limit their freedom of action all the way into the daily editorial staff meetings. These pressures have also intensified as competition has hardened, and owners now demand more profits than they used to. Many good journalistic ideas may be set aside with reference to what market research has said about prioritized audience segments and their presumed preferences. In many media milieus this tends to be perceived as a *natural* type of limitation on editorial freedom. Politically decided requirements are much more easily regarded as 'unnatural' and dictatorial.

Since it undoubtedly *is* very important to be cautious about political intervention in the editorial freedom of media, there are obviously limitations to what can be achieved by media policies with such intents. Therefore, media policies directed at the media as economic entities are probably more important. Precisely because economic conditions so efficiently influence what the media actually offer audiences, political efforts concerning monopolistic tendencies and other structural matters are highly important for the contents and qualities of the media. Increasingly, though, measures in this area must be on a par with the international and even global character of today's media. Interesting things are going on in the European Union, but California is not a member …

Regardless of national and international media policies, the situation in the foreseeable future will be that we are faced with media over whose contents we have limited influence, both as consumers and citizens. Two strategies are particularly relevant to those who are interested in the best possible media output from a democratic point of view. One is a continuous dialogue with those media producers one *can* reach, in which one may attempt to contribute to a strengthening of the professional *ethos* that should characterize their work. (This does, of course, presuppose that such a dialogue also goes on within the media themselves.) The other strategy is to contribute to the critical awareness of media audiences. (This does not mean attempting to prevent people from enjoying what enjoyable material may be available.) This can be done via institutions such as schools and various community organizations. People who have studied the media can also act as critics in private, professional and public contexts, each thus functioning as what Umberto Eco once called a *semiotic guerrilla*, opposing the seemingly overwhelming power of Big Media in local, small – but possibly important – battles.

Bibliography

Adorno, Theodor W. and Max Horkheimer ([1947]1981) *Upplysningens dialektik* ('The dialectic of enlightenment'), Gothenburg: Röda Bokförlaget

Aksoy, Asu and Robins, Kevin (2000) 'Thinking across spaces: transnational television from Turkey', pp. 343–365 in: *European Journal of Cultural Studies,* vol. 3, no. 3, September

Allen, Jeanne (1983) 'The Social Matrix of Television: Invention in the United States', pp. 109–19 in E. A. Kaplan (ed.) *Regarding Television: Critical Approaches – An Anthology.* American Film Institute, Los Angeles: University Publications of America

Allen, Robert C. (1985) *Speaking of Soap Operas.* Chapel Hill and London: The University of North Carolina Press

Allen, Robert C. (ed.) (1995) *To be Continued...Soap Operas Around the World.* New York and London: Routledge

Altenloh, Emilie (1914) *Zur Soziologie des Kino: Die Kino-Unternehmung und die sozialen Schichten ihrer Besucher,* ('On the sociology of the cinema: The cinema business and the social composition of its customers'), Leipzig: Spamerschen Buchdruckerei

Althusser, Louis (1971) 'Ideology and Ideological State Apparatuses (notes towards an investigation'), in his *Lenin and Philosophy and Other Essays*, trans. Ben Brewster, New York: Monthly Review Press

Anderson, Benedict (1983) *Imagined Communities: Reflections on the Origin and Spread of Nationalism.* London and New York: Verso

Andersen, Lis Karin (1986) *TV på papiret ('Television on paper')* Master's thesis, Dept. of Nordic Languages and Literatures, University of Bergen

Andersen, Øyvind (1995) *I retorikkens hage* ('In the garden of rhetoric') Oslo: Universitetsforlaget

Ang, Ien (1985) *Watching* Dallas: *Soap Opera and the Melodramatic Imagination.* London and New York: Methuen

Ariès, Philippe (1965) *Centuries of Childhood: A Social History of Family Life* New York: Random House

Bakhtin, Mikhail (1981) *The Dialogical Imagination.* Austin: University of Texas Press

Bakhtin, Mikhail (1984) *Problems of Dostoevsky's Poetics.* Minneapolis: University of Minnesota Press

Balio, Tino (ed.) (1985) *The American Film Industry.* Revised edition. Madison, London: The University of Wisconsin Press

Balio, Tino (ed.) (1990) *Hollywood in the age of television*. Boston: Unwin Hyman

Barnouw, Eric (1982) *Tube of Plenty: The Evolution of American Television*. Oxford, New York Toronto, Melbourne: Oxford University Press

Barthes, Roland ([1957]1975) *Mytologier* ('Mythologies') Oslo: Gyldendal

Barthes, Roland ([1964]1977) 'Rhetoric of the Image', pp. 32–51 in R. Barthes *Image, Music, Text*. London: Fontana

Barthes, Roland ([1966]1977) 'Introduction to the Structural Analysis of Narratives', pp. 79–124 in R. Barthes *Image, Music, Text*. London: Fontana

Barthes, Roland ([1968]1977) 'The Death of the Author', pp. 142–148 in R. Barthes *Image, Music, Text*. London: Fontana

Battersby, Christine (1989) *Gender and Genius: Towards a Feminist Aesthetics*. London: The Women's Press

Benjamin, Walter ([1936]1969) 'The storyteller. Reflections on the Works of Nikolai Leskov', pp. 83–110 in W. Benjamin *Illuminations*. New York: Schocken Books

Benveniste, Emile (1966) *Problèmes de linguistique générale*. Paris: Gallimard

Berger, John (1972) *Ways of seeing*. London: BBC/Penguin

Bjurström, Erling (2000) "The Taste Games of High and Low Culture", pp. 13–40, in J. Gripsrud (ed.) *Sociology and Aesthetics*, Kristiansand: Norwegian Academic Press

Blumer, Herbert (1933) *Movies and Conduct*. New York: Macmillan

Blumer, Herbert and P.M. Hauser (1933) *Movies, Delinquency, and Crime*. New York: Macmillan

Booth, Wayne C. (1983) *The Rhetoric of Fiction*. 2nd edn., Chicago: University of Chicago Press

Bordwell David and Kristin Thompson (1986) *Film Art. An Introduction*. 2nd edn., New York: Alfred A. Knopf

Bordwell, David (1985) *Narration in the Fiction Film*. London: Methuen

Bordwell, David, Kristin Thompson and Janet Staiger (1988) *The Classical Hollywood Cinema: Film Style and Mode of Production to 1960*. London: Routledge

Bourdieu, Pierre (1989 [1979]) *Distinction: A social critique of the judgement of taste*. London: Routledge

Bourdieu, Pierre (1990) *Homo Academicus*. Cambridge: Polity Press

Bourdieu, Pierre (1992) *The Logic of Practice*. Cambridge: Polity Press

Bourdieu, Pierre (1996): *The Rules of Art: Genesis and Structure of the Literary Field*. Stanford, CA: Stanford University Press/Cambridge: Polity Press

Bourdieu, Pierre (1997 [1969]) *The Love of Art: European Art Museums and their Public*. Cambridge: Polity Press

Bourdieu, Pierre (1998) *On Television*. New York: New Press

Brandt, Per Aage and Jørgen Dines Johansen (1971) 'Om tekstanalyser' ('On textual analyses') in J. Dines Johansen (ed.) *Analyser af dansk kortprosa* ('Analyses of Danish short prose') Copenhagen: Borgen

Brecht, Bertolt ([1948]1973) 'Lille organon for teatret' ('A short organum for the theatre'), in B. Brecht *Om tidens teater* ('On today's theatre'), Copenhagen: Gyldendal. English language version in B. Brecht ([1964]1994) *Brecht on Theatre: The Development of an Aesthetic*, New York: Hill & Wang

Breed, Warren (1955) 'Social Control in the Newsroom: A Functional Analysis', in *Social Forces*, pp. 326–335

Bremond, Claude (1966) 'La logique des possibles narratif', in *Communications* 8

Broady, Donald (1990) *Sociologi och epistemologi. Om Pierre Bourdieus författarskap och den historiska epitemologin.* ('Sociology and epistomology. On the works of Pierre Bourdieu and the historical epistemology') Stockholm: HLS Förlag

Brooks, Peter ([1976]1984) *The Melodramatic Imagination.* New York: Columbia University Press

Browne, Nick (1982) 'The Spectator-in-the-Text: The Rhetoric of Stagecoach', pp. 1–24 in N. Browne *The Rhetoric of Filmic Narration.* Ann Arbor: University of Michigan Research Press

Brunsdon, Charlotte and D. Morley (1978) *Everyday Television: 'Nationwide'.* London: British Film Institute

Burke, Peter (1978) *Popular Culture in Early Modern Europe.* London: Temple Smith

Cantor, Muriel (1971) *The Hollywood TV Producer: His Work and His Audience.* New York: Basic Books

Chatman, Seymour (1983) *Story and Discourse: Narrative Structure in Fiction and Film.* Ithaca and London: Cornell University Press

Cohen, Stanley (1972) *Folk Devils and Moral Panics: The Creation of Mods and Rockers.* London: MacGibbon & Kee

Collins, Richard and Cristina Murroni (1996) *New Media, New Policies: Media and Communications Strategies for the Future.* Cambridge: Polity Press

Cooley, Charles Horton (1902) *Human Nature and the Social Order.* New York: Charles Scribner's Sons

Corrigan, Philip (1990) 'On the difficulty of being sociological (historical materialist) in the study of television: The 'moment' of English television, 1936–1939', pp. 130–160 in T. Syvertsen (ed.) *1992 and After: Nordic Television in Transition.* Bergen: Department of Media Studies, University of Bergen (Report no. 10)

Cressey, Paul (1938) 'The Motion Picture Experience as Modified by Social Background and Personality', in: *American Sociological Review* 3/4, pp. 516–25

Curran, James (1988) 'The Press in the Age of Conglomerates', ch. 7 in J. Curran and J. Seaton (eds.) *Power Without Responsibility. The Press and Broadcasting in Britain.* London and New York: Routledge

Dahl, Hans Fredrik (1991) *NRK i fred og krig. Kringkastingen i Norge 1920–1945* ('The NRK in war and peace: Broadcasting in Norway 1925–1945') Oslo: Universitetsforlaget

Dahl, Hans Fredrik, J. Gripsrud, G. Iversen, K. Skretting and B. Sørenssen (1996) *Kinoens mørke og fjernsynets lys. Levende bilder i Norge gjennom hundre år.* ('The darkness of cinemas, the light of television. Moving images in Norway through one hundred years') Oslo: Gyldendal

Dahl, Henrik (1997) *Hvis din nabo var en bil* ('If your neighbour were a car') Copenhagen: Akademisk Forlag

Dayan, Daniel and Elihu Katz (1992) *Media Events: The Live Broadcasting of History.* Cambridge, Mass. and London: Harvard University Press

DiMaggio, Paul (1986) 'Cultural entrepreneurship in nineteenth-century Boston: the creation of an organizational base for high culture in America', pp. 194–211 in: R. Collins et al. (eds.) *Media, Culture and Society: A Critical Reader.* London, Beverly Hills, Newbury Park, New Dehli: Sage Publications

Eagleton, Terry (1983) *Literary Theory: An Introduction* Oxford: Blackwell (2nd edn., 1996, University of Minnesota Press)

Eco, Umberto (1981) *The Role of the Reader. Explorations in the semiotics of texts.* London, Melbourne, Sydney, Auckland, Johannesburg: Hutchinson

Eco, Umberto (1984) *Apokalyptiker und Integrierte: Zur kritischen Kritik der Massenkultur.* Frankfurt am Main.: S. Fischer Verlag

Eco, Umberto (1985) 'Innovation and Repetition: Between Modern and Post-Modern Aesthetics', in *Daedalus*, vol. 114, no. 4, pp. 161–185

Eide, Martin and Gudmund Hernes (1987) *Død og pine! Om massemedia og helsepolitikk* ('On mass media and the politics of health') Oslo: FAFO

Eisenstein, Sergei (1949) *Film Form.* New York: Harcourt, Brace and World

Elliott, Philip (1974) 'Uses and Gratifications Research: A Critique and A Sociological Alternative', pp. 249–268 in J. Blumler and E. Katz (eds.) *The Uses of Mass Communications: Current Perspectives on Gratifications Research.* Beverly Hills and London: Sage Publications

Elliott, Philip (1972) *The Making of a Television Series.* London: Constable

Ellis, John (1982) *Visible Fictions. Cinema, Television, Video.* London: Routledge & Kegan Paul

Ellis, John (1999): 'Television as Working Through', pp. 55–70 in: J. Gripsrud (ed.): *Television and Common Knowledge.* London and New York: Routledge

Elsaesser, Thomas ([1972]1986) 'Tales of Sound and Fury: Observations on the Family Melodrama', pp. 278–308 in B.K. Grant (ed.) *Film Genre Reader*, Austin: University of Texas Press

Elster, Jon ([1986]1997) 'The Market and the Forum: Three Varieties of Political Theory', pp. 3–34 in J. Bohman and W. Rehg (eds.): *Deliberative Democracy. Essays on Reason and Politics.* Cambridge, Mass. and London: The MIT Press

Epstein, Edward Jay (1973) *News from Nowhere: Television and the News.* New York: Vintage Books

Escarpit, Robert (1971) *Sociology of Literature.* London: Frank Cass & Co

Ewen, Stuart (1996) *PR! A Social History of Spin,* New York: Basic Books

Fafner, Jørgen (1992) *Tanke og tale. Den retoriske tradition i Vesteuropa.* ('Thought and speech. The rhetorical tradition in Western Europe') Copenhagen: C.A. Reitzels forlag

von Feilitzen, Cecilia, M. Forsman, K. Roe (eds.) (1993) *Våld från alla håll. Forskningsperspektiv på våld i rörliga bilder.* ('Research perspectives on violence in moving pictures') Stockholm/Stehag: Brutus Östlings Bokförlag Symposion

Ferment in the field (1983) *Journal of Communication* special issue, vol. 33, no. 3, summer

Feschbach, S. and Singer, R.D. (1971) *Television and aggression: An experimental field study.* San Francisco: Jossey-Bass

Fish, Stanley (1980) *Is There a Text in this Class? The Authority of Interpretive Communities,* Cambridge, Mass. and London: Harvard University Press

Fiske, John (1989) *Reading the Popular*. Boston: Unwin Hyman

Fiske, John (1996) *Media Matters: Everyday Culture and Political Change*. Minneapolis: University of Minnesota Press

Foucault, Michel (1970) *The Order of Things: An Archaeology of the Human Sciences*. London: Tavistock Publications

Foucault, Michel (1972) *The Archaeology of Knowledge*, London: Tavistock Publications

Foucault, Michel (1979) 'Samtal med Michel Foucault' ('A conversation with Michel Foucault') (by S. Larsson and Å. Sandgren), in *Kris* no. 11–12, pp. 6–9

Foucault, Michel (1979a) 'What Is an Author?', pp. 141–160 in J. V. Harari (ed.) *Textual Strategies. Perspectives in Post-Structuralist Criticism*. Ithaca and New York: Cornell University Press

Fowler, Mark and Daniel L. Brenner (1982) 'A Marketplace Approach to Broadcast Regulation', in *Texas Law Review*, vol. 60, no. 207

Fraser, Nancy (1989) 'What's Critical about Critical Theory? The Case of Habermas and Gender', in N. Fraser: *Unruly Practices: Power, Discourse, and Gender in Contemporary Social Theory*. Minneapolis: University of Minnesota Press

Fraser, Nancy (1992) 'Rethinking the Public Sphere: A Contribution to the Critique of Actually Existing Democracy', in C. Calhoun (ed.) *Habermas and the Public Sphere* Cambridge, Mass. and London: The MIT Press

Freud, Sigmund ([1909]1977) 'Der Dichter und das Phantasieren', [The creative writer and daydreaming']. Danish edition in J. Dines Johansen (ed.): *Psykoanalyse, Litteratur, Tekstteori*, Copenhagen: Borgen

Frost, Chris (2000) *Media Ethics and Self-Regulation*. Harlow, England etc: Longman/Pearson Education Ltd

Gadamer, Hans-Georg ([1960]1975 *Truth and Method*. London: Sheed & Ward

Gans, Herbert J. (1957) 'The Creator-Audience Relationship in The Mass Media: An Analysis of Movie Making', pp. 315–324 in B. Rosenberg and D. White (eds.) *Mass Culture: The Popular Arts in America*. New York: Free Press

Gans, Herbert J. (1980) *Deciding What's News: A Study of CBS Evening News, NBC Nightly News, Newsweek and Time*. New York: Vintage Books

Geertz, Clifford (1973) *The Interpretation of Cultures*. New York: Basic Books

Gendron, Bernard (1986) 'Adorno meets the Cadillacs', pp. 18–38 in T. Modleski (ed.) *Studies in Enterntainment: Critical Approaches to Mass Culture*. Bloomington and Indianapoli: Indiana University Press

Genette, Gérard ([1972] 1980) *Narrative Discourse*. Ithaca and London: Cornell University Press

Gerbner, George (1973): 'Cultural Indicators – The Third Voice', pp. 553–573 in: G. Gerbner, L. Gross and W. Melody (eds.): *Communicaions Technology and Social Policy*. New York: Wiley

Gitlin, Todd (1978) 'Media Sociology: The Dominant Paradigm', in: *Theory and Society* 6, pp. 205–253

Gitlin, Todd ([1983] 1985) *Inside Prime Time*. New York: Pantheon Books

Goffman, Erving (1959) *The Presentation of Self in Everyday Life*. New York: Anchor

Graciàn, Baltasar ([1647]1993) *The Art of Worldly Wisdom*. Shambhala Publications

Gripsrud, Jostein (1981) *La denne vår scene bli flammen...Perspektiv og praksis i og omkring sosialdemokratiets arbeiderteater ca 1890–1940.* ['Let our stage be the flame... Perspectives and practices in and around the social-democratic worker's theatre 1890–1940'] Oslo: Universitetsforlaget

Gripsrud, Jostein (1989) 'Autoritet og virkelighetsframstilling', ('Authority and the representation of reality'), conference paper, Dept of Media Studies, University of Bergen

Gripsrud, Jostein (1992) 'The Aesthetics and Politics of Melodrama' in P. Dahlgren and C. Sparks (eds.) *Journalism and Popular Culture.* London, Newbury Park and New Delhi: Sage Publications

Gripsrud, Jostein (1995) *The Dynasty Years: Hollywood Television and Critical Media Studies*, London and New York: Routledge

Gripsrud, Jostein (1998) 'Film Audiences', pp. 202–211 in: J.Hill and P. Church Gibson (eds.): *The Oxford Guide to Film Studies.* Oxford and New York: Oxford University Press

Gripsrud, Jostein (1998a) 'Television, Broadcasting, Flow: Key Metaphors in TV Theory', pp. 17–32 in C. Geraghty and D. Lusted (eds.) *The Television Studies Book.* London, New York, Sidney, Auckland: Arnold

Gripsrud, Jostein (2000) 'Tabloidisation, Popular Journalism, and Democracy", pp. 285–300, in C. Sparks and John Tulloch (eds.): *Tabloid Tales: Global Debates over Media Standards.* Lanham, Boulder, New York, Oxford: Rowman & Littlefield Publishers Inc

Habermas, Jürgen (1989, originally published 1962) *The Structural Transformatuion of the Public Sphere: An Inquiry into a Category of Bourgeois Society.* Cambridge: Polity Press

Habermas, Jürgen ([1981] 1984, 1989) *Theory of Communicative Action.* 2 vols. Boston: Beacon Press

Hagen, Ingunn (1994) 'The Ambivalences of TV News Viewing: Between Ideals and Everyday Practices', in: *European Journal of Communication*, vol. 9, pp. 193–220.

Hall, Stuart (1973): *Encoding and Decoding in the Television Discourse*, Stencilled Occasional Paper no. 7, CCCS, Birmingham

Hall, Stuart (1980) 'Encoding/Decoding', pp. 128–138 in: S. Hall, D. Hobson, A. Lowe, P.Willis (eds.) *Culture, Media, Language.* London: Hutchinson [Abbreviated version of Hall, Stuart (1973): *Encoding and Decoding in the Television Discourse*, Stencilled Occasional Paper no. 7, CCCS, Birmingham

Hall, Stuart and T. Jefferson (eds.) (1976) *Resistance Through Rituals: Youth Subcultures in Post-War Britain.* London: Hutchinson

Hansen, Miriam (1991) *Babel and Babylon: Spectatorship in American Silent Film.* Cambridge, Mass, and London: Harvard University Press

Hebdige, Dick (1978) *Subculture: The Meaning of Style.* London: Methuen

Herzog, Herta (1941) 'On Borrowed Experience. An Analysis of Listening to Daytime Sketches', in: *Zeitschrift fôr Sozialforschung / Studies in Philosophy and Social Science*, vol. IX, no. 1, pp. 65–95

Hoggart, Richard (1957) *The Uses of Literacy: Aspects of working-class life with special reference to publications and entertainment* London: Chatto & Windus

Horton, Donald and Richard Wohl (1956) 'Mass Communication and Para-Social Interaction. Observations on Intimacy at a Distance', in: *Psychiatry* 19:3, pp. 215–29

Hoynes, William (1994) *Public Television for Sale: Media, the Market and the Public Sphere*. Boulder, San Francisco, Oxford: Westview Press

Hume, David (1994) 'Of the Standard of Taste', pp. 78–92 in: S.D. Ross (ed.) *Art and Its Significance: An Anthology of Aesthetic Theory*. Albany: State University of New York Press

Jakobson, Roman (1988) 'The metaphoric and metonymic poles', pp. 57–61 in D. Lodge (ed.) *Modern Criticism and Theory* London and New York: Longman

Jakobson, Roman ([1956]1971) 'Two Aspects of Language and Two Types of Aphasic Disturbances', pp. 45–96 in R. Jakobson *Fundamentals of Language*. Gravenhage: Mouton (2nd rev. edn. 1971, The Hague: Mouton) (For an excerpt, see Jakobson 1988)

Jakobson, Roman and Lévi-Strauss ([1962]1971) 'Les Chats av Charles Baudelaire', pp.158–178 i K. Aspelin and B.A. Lundberg (eds.) *Form och struktur*. Stockholm: PAN/Norstedts

Jauss, Hans Robert (1977) *Ästhetische Erfahrung und literarische Hermeneutik I*, Mönchen: W.S. Fink Verlag

Jauss, Hans Robert ([1970]1974) *Literaturgeschichte als Provokation*. Frankfurt: Suhrkamp

Jensen, Klaus Bruhn (1995) *The Social Semiotics of Mass Communication*. London, Thousand Oaks, New Delhi: Sage, p 21

Johansen, Anders (1997) "Fellowmen, compatriots, contemporaries: on the formation of identity within the expanding 'now' of communication", pp. 169–209 in: Burgess, J. Peter (ed.): *Cultural politics and political culture in postmodern Europe*. Amsterdam: Editions Rodopi

Johansen, Anders (1999) 'Credibility and Media Development', pp. 159–172 in J. Gripsrud (ed.) *Television and Common Knowledge*. London and New York: Routledge

Kant, Immanuel ([1790]1987) *Critique of Judgment*, Hackett Publishing

Katz, Elihu and P. F. Lazarsfeld (1955) *Personal Influence: The part played by people in the flow of mass communication*. New York: Free Press

Keane, John (1991) *The Media and Democracy*. Cambridge: Polity Press

Kennedy, George A. (1994) *A New History of Classical Rhetoric*. Princeton, N.J.: Princeton University Press

Kermode, Frank (1967) *The Sense of an Ending: Studies in the Theory of Fiction*. London, Oxford and New York: Oxford University Press

Kittang, Atle (1977) 'Hermeneutikk og litteraturvitskap', ('Hermeneutics and literary studies') pp.15–55 in H. Engdahl et al. (eds.) *Hermeneutik*. Stockholm: Rabén & Sjögren

Kjørup, Søren (1993) 'Billedmanipulation – og den indeksikalske teori om fotografiet' ('Image manipulation and the indexical theory of photography'), pp. 161–174 in J. Gripsrud (ed.) *Mediegleder* ('Media Pleasures') Oslo: Ad Notam Gyldendal

Kristeva, Julia ([1974]1988) 'The ethics of linguistics', pp. 230–293 in: D. Lodge (ed.): *Modern Criticism and Theory*. London and New York: Longman

Kuhn, Thomas S. (1971) *The Structure of Scientific Revolutions*. Chicago: University of Chicago Press

Lacan, Jacques ([1957]1988) 'The insistence of the letter in the unconscious', pp. 79–106 in D. Lodge (ed.) *Modern Criticism and Theory. A Reader*. London and New York: Longman

Lakoff George (1991) 'Metaphor & War', in: *Express* vol.13, no 20

Lakoff, George and Mark Johnson (1980) *Metaphors We Live By*. Chicago: University of Chicago Press

Larsen, Peter (1974) 'En analyse af TV-avisen', ('An analysis of TV news') in M.Bruun Andersen and J. Poulsen (eds.) *Mediesociologi. Introduktion til massekommunikationsforskning* ('Media Sociology: Introduction to mass communication research'). Copenhagen: Rhodos

Larsen, Peter (1993) 'TV-nyheiter og representasjon', ('TV news and representation') pp. 104–119 in I. Hagen and K. Helland (eds.): *Verda på skjermen – om nyheiter og fjernsyn*.('The world on a screen: On news and television) Oslo: Det norske Samlaget

Larsen, Peter (1995) *Tv-analyse for mediestuderende. Tre kapitler om betydning og fortalleanalyse*. ('TV analysis for media students. Three chapters on signification and narrative analysis') Bergen: Department of Media Studies

Lazarsfeld, Paul F. (1941) 'Remarks on Administrative and Critical Communications Research', in: *Zeitschrift fôr Sozialforschung / Studies in Philosophy and Social Science* vol. 9, pp. 2–16

Lazarsfeld, Paul F., B. Berelson, H. Gaudet ([1944]1968) *The People's Choice: How the Voter Makes Up His Mind in a Presidential Election Campaign*. New York: Columbia University Press

LeBon, Gustave ([1895]1981) *The Crowd*. Harmondsworth: Penguin

Lévi-Strauss, Claude (1966): *The Savage Mind*. London: Weidenfeld & Nicolson

Lindhardt, Jan (1975) *Retorik* ('Rhetoric'). Copenhagen: Berlingske Forlag

Lippman, Walter ([1922]1997) *Public Opinion*. New York: Free Press Paperbacks/Simon & Schuster

Lyotard, Jean Francois ([1979]1984) *The Postmodern Condition: A Report on Knowledge*. Manchester: Manchester University Press

McCombs, Maxwell E. and D.L. Shaw (1972) 'The Agenda-Setting Function of the Mass Media', in: *Public Opinion Quarterly*, vol. 36, no. 2, pp. 176–187

McGuigan, Jim (1996) *Culture and the Public Sphere*. London and New York: Routledge

Madsen, Peter (1975) 'Litteraturvidenskab og socialvidenskab', ('Literary studies and social science')i: R. Pittelkow., C. Thau, P. Madsen *Samfundsteori og teksttteori* ('Social theory and textual theory'). Roskilde: Roskilde Universitetscenter

Martín-Barbero, Jesús (1993) *Communication, Culture and Hegemony: From the Media to Mediations*. London, Newbury Park, New Delhi: Sage Publications

Marx, Karl ([1857]1973) *Grundrisse*. Harmondsworth: Penguin Books

Mattelart, Armand, Xavier Delcourt ànd Michelle Mattelart (1984) *International Image Markets: In Search of an Alternative Perspective*. London and New York: Comedia Publishing Group

Metz, Christian (1982) *The Imaginary Signifier: Psychoanalysis and the Cinema.* Bloomington: Indiana University Press

Meyrowitz, Joshua (1985) *No Sense of Place: The Impact of Electronic Media on Social Behavior.* New York and Oxford: Oxford University Press

Mølster, Ragnhild (1996) *'I kveldens reportasje viser vi virkeligheten...' Journalistisk retorikk i fjernsyn: Dokument 2 i et retorisk perspektiv.* ('"In tonight's report we show you reality...." Journalistic rhetoric in television: "Document 2" in a rhetorical perspective') Bergen: Department of media studies (Report no. 27)

Morley, David (1980) *The 'Nationwide' Audience: Structure and Decoding.* London: British Film Institute

Morley, David (1992) *Television, Audiences, and Cultural Studies.* London and New York: Routledge

Morse, Margaret (1990) 'An ontology of everyday distraction: the freeway, the mall, and television', in: P. Mellencamp (ed.) *Logics of Television.* Bloomington, Indianapolis, London: Indiana University Press and BFI Publishing

Mukarovsky, Jan ([1931]1970) *Aesthetic Function, Norm and Value as Social Facts.* Ann Arbor: University of Michigan Press

Mulvey, Laura (1975) 'Visual Pleasure and Narrative Cinema', in: *Screen* vol. 16, no. 3, pp. 6–18

Murdoch, Rupert (1989) 'Freedom in Broadcasting'. MacTaggart Lecture delivered at the Edinburgh International Television Festival, 25 August

Murdock, Graham (1992) 'Citizens, Consumers, and Public Culture', pp. 17–41 in M. Skovmand and K.C. Schrøder (eds.) *Media Cultures: Reappraising Transnational Media.* London and New York: Routledge

Murdock, Graham ([1980]1993) 'Authorship and Organisation', pp. 123–43 in M. Alvarado, E. Buscombe, R. Collins (eds.) *The Screen Education Reader: Cinema, Television, Culture.* London: Macmillan

Negt, Oskar and Alexander Kluge (1993 [1972]) *Public Sphere and Experience: Toward an Analysis of the Bourgeois and Proletarian Public Sphere.* Minneapolis: University of Minnesota Press

Newcomb, Horace and Robert S. Alley (1983) *The Producer's Medium.* New York and Oxford: Oxford University Press

Nielsen, Niels Fredrik (1984) *Ekte sekstiåttere spiser ikke seipanetter. Portretter fra 68–generasjonens indre og ytre liv.* ('Real 68'ers don't eat fish fingers. Portraits from the internal and external life of the ('68 generation') Oslo: Gyldendal

Noble, Grant (1973) 'Effects of different forms of filmed aggression on children's constructive and destructive play', in: *Journal of personality and social psychology,* 26, pp. 54–59

Noble, Grant (1975) *Children in front of the small screen.* London: Constable

Østerberg, Dag (1995) 'Kunsten som sosial institusjon og sosial konstruksjon – en begrepsavklaring', ('Art as social institution and social construction: A clarification of terms') pp. 143–160 in: D. Sveen (ed.) *Om kunst, kunstinstitusjon og kunstforståelse* ('On art, the institution of art and the understanding of art'). Oslo: Pax

Parkin, Frank (1972) *Class Inequality and Political Order* London: Routledge

Peterson, R.A. and Kern, R.M. (1996): 'Changing Highbrow Taste: From Snob to Omnivore', in: *American Sociological Review*, vol. 61, no. 5

Popper, Karl (1979 [1972]): *Objective Knowledge. An Evolutionary Approach*, rev. edn., Oxford etc: Oxford University Press

Porter, Dennis (1982) 'Soap Time: Thoughts on a Commodity Art Form', in H. Newcomb (ed.) *Television: The Critical View*. 3rd edn., New York and Oxford: Oxford University Press

Porter, Vincent (1989) The re-regulation of television: pluralism, constitutionality and the free market in the USA, West Germany, France and the UK. *Media Culture and Society* 11(1), 5–27

Porter, Vincent (1995) 'The New European Order for Public Service Broadcasting', pp. 81–100 in E. Barendt et al. (eds.) *The Yearbook of Media and Entertainment Law 1995*. Oxford: Clarendon Press

Powdermaker, Hortense (1950) *Hollywood: The Dream Factory*. Boston: Little, Brown

Propp, Vladimir ([1928] 1968) *Morphology of the Folktale*. Austin: University of Texas Press Raboy, Marc ed., n.d. *Public Broadcasting for the 21st Century*. Acamedia Research Monograph 17. Luton: John Libbey Media

Radway, Janice (1984): *Reading the Romance. Feminism and the Representation of Women in Popular Culture*. Chapel Hill: The University of North Carolina Press

Radway, Janice (1998) *A Feeling for Books: The Book-of-the-Month Club, Literary Taste, and Middle-Class Desire*. Chapel Hill and London: University of North Carolina Press

Renov, Michael (1993) 'Introduction: The Truth About Non-Fiction', pp. 1–11 in M. Renov (ed.) *Theorizing Documentary*. New York and London: Routledge

Ricoeur, Paul (1981) *Hermeneutics and the Human Sciences* Cambridge, New York, Melbourne: Cambridge University Press

Robillard, Serge (1995) *Television in Europe: Regulatory Bodies. Status, Functions and Powers in 35 European Countries*. London, Paris, Rome: John Libbey (European Institute for the Media, Media Monograph no. 19)

Rosenlund, Lennart (2000) *Social structures and change: applying Pierre Bourdieu's approach and analytic framework*. Working Papers from Stavanger University College, no. 85

Ross, Lillian ([1953]1986) *Picture*. London: André Deutsch Ltd.

Ryan, Mary P. (1990) *Women in Public: Between Banners and Ballots, 1825–1880*. Baltimore: Johns Hopkins University Press

Peirce, Charles Saunders (1931–58) *Collected Papers*, vols. 1–8. Cambridge, Mass.: Harvard University Press

Scannell, Paddy (1996) *Radio, Television and Modern Life: A Phenomenological Approach*. Oxford: Blackwell Publishers

Schatz, Thomas (1997) 'The Return of the Hollywood Studio System', pp. 73–106 in E.Barnouw et al. *Conglomerates and the Media*. New York: The New Press

Schlesinger, Philip (1978) *Putting Reality Together: BBC News*. London: Constable

Schlesinger, Philip (1995) *Europeanisation and the Media: Naional Identity and the Public Sphere*. Oslo: ARENA/The Norwegian Research Council, Working Paper no. 7

Schrøder, Kim (1988) 'The Pleasure of *Dynasty*: The Weekly Reconstruction of Self-Confidence', in P.Drummond and R. Paterson (eds.) *Televison and its Audience. International Research Perspectives*. London: British Film Institute

Schudson, Michael (1978) *Discovering the News: A Social History of American Newspapers*. New York: Basic Books

Sennett, Richard ([1977]1986) *The Fall of Public Man*. London and Boston: Faber & Faber

Silverstone, Roger (1994) *Television and Everyday Life*. London and New York: Routledge

Shklovsky, Viktor B, ([1917]1988) 'Art as technique', pp. 16–30 in D. Lodge (ed.) *Modern Criticism and Theory*. London and New York: Longman

Skjervheim, Hans (1987) 'Den klassiske journalistikken og den nye medieideologien' ('Classical journalism and the new media ideology') in: *Nytt Norsk Tidsskrift*, no. 1, pp. 13–20.

Skjervheim, Hans ([1958]1974) *Objectivism and the Study of Man*, in *Inquiry* pp. 213 ff and 265 ff

Sklar, Robert (1976) *Movie-Made America: A Cultural History of American Movies*. New York: Vintage Books

Spigel, Lynn (1992) *Make Room for TV: Television and the Family Ideal in Post-War America*. Chicago: Chicago University Press

Stam, Robert (1989) *Subversive pleasures: Bakhtin, cultural criticism, and film*. Baltimore, Md.: Johns Hopkins University Press

Sveen, Dag (1995) 'Kunstforståelse og kunstinstitusjon – et historisk perspektiv', i ds. (red.) *Om kunst, kunstinstitusjon og kunstforståelse*. Oslo: Pax

Syvertsen, Trine (1992) *Public Television in Transition*. Ph.D. dissertation, University of Leicester, publisert som *Levende Bilder* no. 5/92, Oslo: KULT/NAVF

Thing, Morten (1973) *Ideologier og litteratur.*('Ideologies and literature') Copenhagen: Kurasje

Todorov, Tzvetan (1977) *The Poetics of Prose*. Ithaca: Cornell University Press

Todorov, Tzvetan ([1978]1990) *Genres in Discourse*. Cambridge, New York, Port Chester, Melbourne and Sydney: Cambridge University Press

Trenaman, J.S.M. and D. McQuail (1961) *Television and the Political Image*. London: Methuen

Tuchman, Gaye (1978) *Making News: A Study in the Construction of Reality*. New York: The Free Press

Tunstall, Jeremy (1971) *Journalists at work: Specialist correspondents, their news organizations, news sources, & competitor colleagues*. London: Constable

Turner, Victor (1982) 'Acting in everyday life and everyday life in acting', pp. 83–105 in *Humanities in Review* vol. 1, New York Institute for the Humanities. Cambridge, London, New York, New Rochelle, Melbourne, Sydney: Cambridge University Press

Turnock, Robert (2000) *The Death of Diana*. London: British Film Institute

Ulvær, Bjørn Petter (1984) 'Vold i fjernsynet. Konsekvenser for barns aggresjon, angst og virkelighetsoppfatning', ('Violence in television. Consequences for children's aggression, anxiety and perception of reality'), pp. 103–123 in: H. Andresen (ed.):

Hva skjer foran skjermen? Barn og elektroniske medier. ('What happens in front of the screen? Children and electronic media') Oslo: J.W. Cappelens forlag

Uricchio, William (1989) 'Rituals of reception, patterns of neglect: Nazi television and its postwar representation', in *Wide Angle* vol. 11, no. 1, pp. 48–66

Veblen, Thorstein ([1899]1953) *The Theory of the Leisure Class: an Economic Study of Institutions.* Rev. edn., New York: New American Library

Waldecranz, Rune (1976) *Så föddes filmen* ('How film was born') Stockholm: Prisma

Weber, Max (1968) *Economy and Society: An Outline of Interpretive Sociology.* Berkeley, Los Angeles and London: University of California Press

Weber, Max ([1904–5]1992) *The Protestant Ethic and the Spirit of Capitalism.* London and New York. Routledge

Weber, Max ([1922]1949) 'Objectivity in Social Science and Social Policy', pp. 49–112 in M. Weber *The Methodology of the Social Sciences.* New York: The Free Press

Wheen, Francis (1985) *Television.* London: Century Publishing

White, David Manning (1950) 'The Gatekeeper: A Case Study in the Selection of News', in *Journalism Quarterly*, vol. 27, Fall, pp. 383–390

Whorf, Benjamin Lee (1956) *Language, Thought, and Reality.* New York: Wiley

Williams, Raymond (1958) *Culture and Society.* London: Chatto & Windus / New York: Columbia University Press

Williams, Raymond (1961) *The Long Revolution.* London: Chatto & Windus

Williams, Raymond (1975) *Television: Technology and Cultural Form.* New York: Schocken Books

Willis, Paul (1977) *Learning to Labour.* Farnborough, Hants: Saxon House

Wolfe, Tom (1975) *The New Journalism* London: Picador

Ytreberg, Espen (1999) *Allmennkringkastingens autoritet. Endringer i NRK Fjernsynets tekstproduksjon 1987–1994.* ('The authority of public service broadcasting. Changes in the textual production of NRK Television 1987–1994') Oslo: Department of Media and Communication, University of Oslo. Report no. 35

Ziehe, Thomas and Herbert Stubenrauch (1983): *Ny ungdom og usædvanlige læreprocesser.* ('New youth and unconventional processes of learning'). Viborg: Politisk revy

Index